ENVIRONMENT:
North and South

ENVIRONMENT: North and South

An Economic Interpretation

Charles Pearson
School of Advanced International Studies
The Johns Hopkins University

Anthony Pryor
Resources for the Future

A Wiley-Interscience Publication
JOHN WILEY & SONS
New York • Chichester • Brisbane • Toronto

Library of Congress Cataloging in Publication Data:

Pearson, Charles S
Environment, North and South.

"A Wiley-Interscience publication."
Bibliography: p.
Includes index.
1. Underdeveloped areas—Environmental policy.
2. Environmental policy. 3. Economic development.
4. International economic relations. I. Pryor, Anthony, 1951– joint author. II. Title.

HC59.7.P394 301.31'09172'4 77-11143
ISBN 0-471-02741-3

Printed in the United States of America

10 9 8 7 6 5 4 3 2 1

To
Ethan, Noelle, and Morgan

and to
Elizabeth

PREFACE AND ACKNOWLEDGMENTS

The importance of environmental concerns to developing countries has been a confused and somewhat contentious issue. Are pollution and environmental degradation only associated with affluence? Can poor countries afford rigorous environmental protection programs? Are rapid economic growth and preservation of the environment compatible or incompatible? This study represents the first comprehensive analysis of the relations between economic development and environment, and the environmental relations between the industrial countries of the North and the developing countries of the South. The issues addressed are of fundamental importance for the economic development of the poor regions of the world and for conservation of our environmental heritage.

Economic analysis is the major approach used in the study. The intended audience, however, is much broader than the economics profession, and the book will fail in its purpose if its use is restricted to economists. We have attempted to make the material useful to anyone seriously interested in the development of the Third World, in the protection of environmental resources, and in international relations generally. We hope most of all that the study will be widely read and of some assistance to government officials, development planners, economists, and environmentalists in developing countries.

In researching and writing the study we were assisted by a large number of people, and we wish to thank them all for the help they provided. We wish especially to thank Lincoln Gordon, Patricia Rosenfield, Wendy Takacs, and Ingo Walter, who have read through the entire manuscript and have offered countless suggestions for improvement. A number of experts have read sections of the manuscript, and their comments have also greatly improved the coverage, accuracy, and style of the book. In this connection we sincerely thank Carroll Leslie Bastian, Pierre Crosson, Erik Eckholm, Isaiah Frank, Price Gittinger, Kirby Hansen, William Knowland, Molly Kux, Edwin Martin, Elizabeth Pryor, Lyle Schertz, and Gordon Wolman.

In addition we wish to thank Stephen Baumiduro and Tawhid Nawaz for research assistance, Linda Carlson for exceptional library help, and James O'Brian for his craftsmanship with the maps and diagrams. Typing and retyping the many drafts has been a long and arduous task, and we wish to thank Andrea Catapano, Jean Fujinaga, Woljie Lee, and Mary Nolz, who have worked on portions of the manuscript. Linda Solomon carried the major typing responsibility, and we thank her for the superior job she has done.

Finally, a portion of the initial research was supported by a grant from the Mellon Foundation through The Johns Hopkins School of Advanced International Studies, and we wish to express our appreciation for this support. All these people have improved the study, and the responsibility for any remaining errors rests entirely with the authors.

CHARLES PEARSON
ANTHONY PRYOR

Washington, D.C.
March 1977

GUIDE TO THE READER

Because we wish this study to be fully accessible to a broad audience, we have avoided where possible technical economic analysis and jargon. In most cases verbal presentation of the argument and conclusions is sufficient. In several cases the exposition is facilitated through the use of diagrams. These are found in the third section of Chapter 3 (concerned with international trade), the second section of Chapter 4 (concerned with modifying cost benefit analysis), and the first section of Chapter 5 (concerned with the theory of transnational pollution control). In addition, the Appendix to Chapter 4 contains a mathematical model of optimal fallow period in agriculture. While the diagrammatic material could have been placed in appendices, there are two compelling reasons for keeping it in the text. First, the concepts and theory underlying the diagrams are central to the analysis of the chapter in which they are found. Second, diagrams are a particularly useful method of presenting theory and conclusions to serious readers who are not accustomed to mathematical formulations of economic problems.

We also wish to draw attention to a transparency overlay of our population density map. This map can be used to overlay maps throughout the text to indicate relationships between population clusters and the other relevant variables.

Whenever possible, we have tried to describe and document the text material through the use of tables. Indeed, Chapter 2 is mainly a quantitative description of the environmental landscape in developed and developing countries, and much of this description is fully original. The Appendix to Chapter 2 contains the complete set of 54 variables for 122 countries and should be consulted together with the Chapter text. Also, the Appendix to Chapter 3 summarizes all the major disaggregated trade/environment studies that have been done to date. Chapter 6, which focuses on grain production, also uses tables extensively to describe environmental constraints and consequences.

The theory of environmental externalities is used throughout the study, and it is worthwhile stating the main elements for those to whom it is unfamiliar. More technical definitions are given in the literature cited. Briefly, waste disposal from either production or consumption activities enters environmental media and impairs beneficial use of the resources (ambient air pollutants, acid runoff from mine tailing, downstream siltation of irrigation channels from upstream erosion, etc.). The costs of the environmental deterioration are external to the firms or individuals engaged in the economic activity and are borne elsewhere in society. The costs can be considered incidental, since waste disposal is not the purpose of the activity, but they are not necessarily inadvertent in the sense of being unanticipated. Because external costs are lodged elsewhere in society, there is no incentive for polluters (consumers or producers) to consider them and to undertake abatement measures. Thus there is a split between the private costs of an activity and the full social costs, including external environmental costs. The result is a misallocation of resources, with social welfare less than its potential. In market systems that rely on prices to indicate economic scarcity and to guide allocation and consumption decisions, market prices are distorted, and both production and consumption decisions are inefficient. Uncorrected externalities represent a failure of the price/market system. Forcing polluters to include the full social costs of their activities will encourage pollution abatement, reduce environmental damages, and improve social welfare.

CONTENTS

TABLES

Appendix Tables

DIAGRAMS

MAPS

ENVIRONMENT:
North and South

INTRODUCTION

This book has two central themes. The first is the relationship between economic growth and environmental quality in the poor countries of the world. What are the environmental consequences of growth in developing countries, and how should they be managed? Are the environmental problems of developing countries essentially different from those of industrial countries? Do environmental constraints place limits on growth and development?

The second theme concerns environmental issues that are outstanding between rich and poor countries. Is there a global harmony of environmental interests, or are there substantive conflicts? Are the issues important or trivial? Do North–South issues arise directly, through the shared use of international environmental resources, or are they experienced indirectly, through international trade, investment, and development assistance flows? Is there evidence of environmental exploitation or environmental imperialism in North–South relations?

These are not easy questions to answer. To date, much of the discussion has been unsatisfactory or inconclusive. Arguments have been speculative and not based on empirical observation; comprehensive studies have not been done. The definitional scope of environmental concerns has been vague and confusing. North–South environmental relations have not escaped the political rhetoric that characterizes economic discussions between the two groups. This study attempts to construct a systematic and comprehensive framework for analyzing these questions and to assemble empirical evidence bearing on the major issues.

The Founex Symposium is a useful starting point for understanding the relationship between environment and economic development, and environmental relations between rich and poor countries. In 1971, at Founex, Switzerland, an uneasy compromise was struck that successfully brought the developing countries into the international environmental movement. The occasion was a meeting of intellectuals from the industrialized North and the developing South, brought together in preparation for the then forthcoming U.N. Conference on the Human Environment (Stockholm Conference). The broad purpose was to convince developing countries that environmental issues were indeed global and that concern for environmental quality was not exclusively the domain of the rich, but was of direct and immediate importance to developing countries as well. The narrower purpose was to seek the involvement of developing countries in the Stockholm Conference. Measured against the fate of most symposia, the meeting was spectacularly successful. The Founex Report became the basis for active debate in a series of regional Third World seminars preceding the Stockholm Conference. Developing countries were articulate participants in the U.N. Conference and exerted great influence on the final Declaration and Action Plan. Equally important, the conference preparations stimulated serious inquiry into the relationship between environmental quality and economic development. The subsequent location of the U.N. Environment Programme (UNEP) in Nairobi, the first United Nations specialized agency in the Third World, is testimony to the involvement of developing countries and the success of Founex.

The essence of the compromise engineered at Founex is a redefinition of environmental degradation. Not only is the environment subject to the abuses of affluence—high and growing levels of waste disposal, the introduction of new, exotic, and often toxic substances, the disamenities from urban sprawl, the loss of wilderness areas and wildlife—but also, the condition of poverty itself is a dominant and controlling feature of the human environment. The attributes of poverty—unsanitary water supplies, endemic diseases, grossly inadequate housing—became legitimate environmental problems under the new definition. Pollution and deprivation became co-equal. Accordingly, poor countries also endure a situation of environmental degradation and aspire to a state of environmental quality.

The Founex compromise reflects the indifference, ambivalence, and hostility that characterized developing countries' attitude towards environmental matters at the time. It was politically necessary to expand the definition of environmental problems if developing countries were to be included in the environmental movement. However, despite the clarity of the Report and its initial success, the true importance of environmental concerns to poor countries is not known, and the environment continues to be a contentious issue between North and South. Part of the confusion arises from the expanded definition of environmental concerns. These concerns now embrace traditional pollution problems, conservation of wildlife and wilderness areas, the attributes of poverty, and such topics as soil erosion, urban blight, and cultural contamination from imported Western consumption patterns. With these vague and diverse meanings, it is not surprising that the relationship between environment and economic development remains unclear.

Part of the confusion reflects the limited and inadequate data on the nature and causes of environmental deterioration. In many industrial countries environmental data collection is barely past its infancy. The contributions to environmental stress of population growth, affluence, technology, and structural economic and demographic shifts are still contested. In the narrower area of pollution, there are insufficient data on the sources and amounts of pollutants, their physical dispersal and concentration in ambient environmental media, their chemical and biological effects, and the consequent economic damages. In developing countries even less is known.

Perhaps most important, confusion surrounding environmental quality and economic development in the Third World arises from the apparent simplicity of the Founex redefinition. If the environmental problem of developing countries were, at its core, one of poverty, the resolution would be economic growth. Environmental concerns in developing countries would then be incidental to the great task of development. In fact, some observers have been more sophisticated. They acknowledge that the features of poverty can be described as a debased environment, but they suggest that the deterioration in the quality of environmental resources can itself contribute to poverty. They see that developing countries also exhibit some environmental abuses traditionally associated with industrial countries, largely questions of waste disposal. They recognize that there are complex interactions between environmental quality and economic growth. Not only might the environment deteriorate from rapid growth, but growth itself can encounter environmental constraints. This deterioration is particularly visible in the agricultural sector, and poor countries are still mainly agricultural. Finally, these observers note the high environmental price paid by the industrial countries for their affluence, and they ask if this is a necessary burden or if a more environmentally harmonious development strategy could be found at a reasonable economic cost.

Thus fundamental questions remain. Is there another "vicious circle" in which poverty degrades the environment and the deteriorated environment strengthens the grip of poverty? Are economic growth needs so compelling in low income countries that these countries can afford to pay some price in a degraded environment for material improvement? Is there a Hobbesian choice between accepting the dirty industries and jobs from the North or conserving environmental patrimony? Or, on the contrary, is there a basic compatibility between sound development and sound environmental policies? Put more strongly, does sustained economic growth demand the conservation of environmental resources as the ultimate base for productive activity?

The issue of environment and development has emerged during a period of increasing tension between North and South over a wide range of economic issues—from commodity prices to international monetary reform and from the conduct of multinational firms to negotiating a new regime for access to ocean wealth. It is perhaps inevitable that the environment also finds a place in the set of issues dividing North and South. The discussions have not become fully polarized, nor is the perception in the South uniformly one of environmental imperialism. On the contrary, environmental concerns, more than most issues, transcend national borders and can evoke an internationalist perspective. Still, the environment has been deliberately linked with North-South economic issues and has not escaped some rhetorical fallout from the debate over the so-called "New International Economic Order."[1]

More important, there are valid substantive issues between industrial and developing countries regarding the use of environmental resources. It is all well and good to assert a global ecological unity and a common interest of mankind in preserving environmental resources. But in fact neither North nor South fully respects this unity, nor are their immediate environmental interests always harmonious. To paper over these real differences by exclusive attention to a global community of interests would be unwise. In short, developing countries are attempting to redress the distribution of economic power between North and South. Environmental relations between the two reflect this attempt. There is a deepseated suspicion in developing countries that in one way or another the environmental movement is foreign to their true interests. Some of this suspicion merely reflects the larger economic tensions, but some is grounded in legitimate differences.

The structure of the book reflects the two themes of the relationship between development and environment, and the environmental issues between industrial and developing countries. Chapter 1 examines some concepts and issues that underlie the two themes. Its purpose is to clarify the distinction between environmental problems of poverty and problems of affluence. One suggestion is to view environmental resources as both a consumers' good and a producers' good. Within this framework, environmental quality objectives can be sought by different income level countries for different reasons. In addition, the chapter introduces the issues of uniform versus dual environmental standards for rich and poor countries, the links between natural resource exploitation and the environment, and temporal aspects of environmental management.

Chapter 2 is somewhat experimental. Its objective is to systematically describe the environmental landscape of developing countries and to highlight differences in the environmental characteristics of developed and developing countries. To accomplish this we construct a descriptive environmental geography. Unfortunately, there is no single index of physical environments nor a single index of environmental stress. Indeed, there is no single index of air or water quality. Therefore, the chapter assembles international data on a number of variables related to the environment. These variables are grouped into three broad classes: climate, geography, and demography; economic structure and activity as an indirect measure of environmental stress; more direct aspects of the human environment. Although the data are incomplete, some interesting features of the environmental landscape emerge.

Chapter 3 considers the ways in which environmental controls in industrial countries can affect trade and investment flows between North and South. This subject has been widely speculated on, with little empirical research. It is also a potentially sensitive issue between North and South. A special effort has been made to present the material systematically and to evaluate the impacts quantitatively when possible.

Chapter 4 takes up the question of incorporating environmental consequences in development project analysis and comments on the experience of The United States Agency for International Development and the World Bank in this connection. Although past failures to incorporate environmental considerations in development projects have received considerable publicity, the focus of this chapter is on the methods and techniques for modifying project analysis.

Environmental resources jointly shared by industrial and developing countries present exceptionally interesting theoretical and policy questions. The problem is one of transfrontier pollution of international common property resources. Chapter 5 first examines some conceptual issues and difficulties in negotiating rational management controls over international environmental resources. It then considers evidence that industrial countries have made disproportionate use of international commons for waste disposal. Because the ocean environment provides the most direct physical link between North and South and because the current U.N. Law of the Sea Conference provides factual material, the chapter also analyzes North–South relations concerning the environment within the Law of the Sea negotiations.

Chapter 6 examines environment and agriculture in developing countries.

Agriculture was chosen as a case study because of its enormous importance in developing countries. Also, if deterioration of environmental quality does become a limiting factor on economic growth, it should appear first in agriculture, where the productivity of resources themselves is directly eroded. One purpose of the chapter is to set forth the types of environmental damages that are likely from increased agricultural output, to qualitatively evaluate their relative seriousness, and to reach a preliminary conclusion as to whether environmental deterioration will be a constraint on growth. To accomplish this, materials on projected population increases and consequent food needs are assembled with special reference to grain production. Also, information on the major types of agricultural systems is presented.[2]

Chapter 7 presents general observations and conclusions that emerge from the study. The two themes of North–South environmental relations and environment–development interactions are intertwined throughout the book. However, the chapters on trade and investment, and global common property resources stress the former, whereas the project analysis and the agriculture chapters emphasize the latter.

This study will be useful in part because it collects material from a wide variety of sources, some rather obscure, and presents it in a systematic and comprehensive manner. Moreover, much of the analysis is fully original. Still, the scope of the study is very broad, and conclusions are often preliminary. Also, important areas have not been included. In particular, we have not analyzed environmental policies as they currently exist within developing countries—how they and UNEP have responded to the environmental crisis. Nor do we discuss the political, institutional, and organizational requirements for establishing an effective set of environmental controls within developing countries. These areas are critical to a full understanding of environment and development, but they are better approached through detailed study of individual countries.

A word should be said about the terms environment, environmental quality, and environmental deterioration as they are used in this book. No single definition of environment captures the multiplicity of meanings associated with the word. Indeed, the diversity of meanings has itself become an issue. Still, to be useful, the terms need some comment. The concept of pollution is too narrow for our purposes, although it furnishes many examples of environmental deterioration. Also, restricting environmental deterioration to situations involving external diseconomies is too confining, although these situations account for a large proportion of such deterioration. At the other extreme, we do not wish to include all modifications of nature and ecological systems, whether or not they effect human well-being. Nor do we wish to include all aspects of "the human environment"—cultural heritage, extent of political freedom, social mobility, and so forth. Accordingly, we use the term environmental deterioration to describe a process that has four essential characteristics:

- The quality of air, water, soil, or biological resources is affected.
- The initial cause of the deterioration is economic in nature—extraction, processing, transport, or consumption.

- External diseconomies involving environmental media are commonly but not invariably present.
- There is an adverse effect, direct or indirect, on human well-being.

Finally, the terms "North" and "South" are deliberately used to represent the developed and developing countries. Not only are these terms widely used, but they are suggestive of a tropical-temperate division that we believe is environmentally significant. Naturally, there is great variation among countries of the North and the South, including variation in environmental policies.

NOTES

1. Contrast the sober, often brilliant language of the Founex Report with the more impassioned language of the Cocoyoc Declaration. The Cocoyoc Declaration itself is more strident than the (Cocoyoc) Symposium Draft Report prepared by Chairman Lady Jackson. *Founex Report: Development and Environment, Report and Working Papers of a Panel of Experts Convened by the Secretary General of the United Nations Conference on the Human Environment* (Paris: Mouton, 1972); *The Cocoyoc Declaration*, adopted by the Participants in the UNEP/UNCTAD Symposium on "Patterns of Resource Use, Environment and Development Strategies", Cocoyoc, Mexico, October 8–12, 1974; United Nations Environment Programme, *Draft Report on the UNEP/UNCTAD Symposium on Patterns of Resource Use, Environment and Development Strategies* (UNEP/GC (III)/Inf. 4, 16 April 1975).
2. Agriculture provides a good example of "problems" that have been long studied but only recently rediscovered as "environmental." For a dramatic description of global soil erosion written late in the Great Depression see G. V. Jacks and R. O. Whyte, *Vanishing Lands: A World Survey of Soil Erosion* (New York: Doubleday, Doran, 1939) reprinted by Arno Press (New York, 1972).

Chapter 1

CONCEPTS AND ISSUES

POVERTY AND AFFLUENCE

It is now commonplace to observe that environmental problems in industrial and developing countries are dissimilar, indeed, opposites. Distinguishing between problems of poverty and problems of affluence was instrumental in persuading the South to enter international environmental discussions. The distinction captures some of the differences between industrial and developing countries and has certain descriptive value. However, to characterize environmental problems as those of affluence or poverty requires qualification. There are other approaches that perhaps contribute more to understanding the importance of environmental concerns in economic development.

According to the traditional view, rich countries have waste disposal loads that exceed their assimilative capacity—the ability of environmental media to accept wastes and render them harmless. Environmental deterioration in industrial countries is seen as the result of two factors. First, environmental resources historically have existed as common property. The legal and institutional regime has encouraged their use and abuse for waste disposal because the costs of pollution are not brought home to the polluter but are borne elsewhere in society. Second, wasteloads in excess of assimilative capacity are seen as the result of prodigious levels of materials consumption, a trend toward the spatial concentration of economic activity, and technological advances that have been biased toward environmentally damaging techniques and products.[1] These two factors are considered to be associated with affluence.

The traditional view asserts that the environmental problems of developing countries are of a quite different character. The condition of poverty generally does not result in waste loads exceeding assimilative capacity. Environmentally damaging technological advances are not a pervasive problem. Rather, this view contends that the attributes of poverty itself are direct evidence of an unsatisfactory and unwholesome environment, or pollution by poverty. The attributes of poverty are identified as unsanitary water supplies and inadequate sewage treatment and disposal facilities, a high incidence of environmentally related diseases, and grossly inferior housing. In addition, agriculture and land-use problems are mentioned—soil erosion and nutrient exhaustion, rapid deforestation, siltation, salination, water-logging, and so forth.

However, this distinction between poverty and affluence requires qualification. The first qualification concerns wasteloads. There is no necessarily proportional relation between per capita GNP and total wasteloads. Whether a strong functional relation exists is an empirical question that has not been answered. More important, it is the composition of wastes and the points at which they enter environmental media that determine whether damage is done. Waste heat discharged in the open ocean is not a problem; heat discharged in small shallow lakes may be. Carbon monoxide can be damaging in congested urban areas but harmless in rural areas. If, by the severity of environmental problems we mean the relative damage associated with waste disposal, it is necessary to move beyond assertions comparing gross waste volume between North and South and look directly at the nature of the wastes generated in both regions, together with information on the disposal sites and media.

In addition, attention should be given to the vulnerability of receptors to environmental insult and hence the extent of physical damages. For example, it may be that equivalent ambient air pollution levels are more injurious to health in developing than in developed countries because of lower resistance and tolerance of a generally less healthy population.[2] Also, as discussed in Chapters 2 and 6, tropical soils may be more fragile than temperate zone soils. A focus on relative waste loads or ambient pollution levels may fail to properly assess damages. Finally, the spatial allocation of wastes and not their total quantity often is most important. Urban centers in developing countries experience wastes from production and consumption activities in much the same fashion as urban areas in industrial countries, even if the volumes are smaller.

A second qualification to the distinction between problems of poverty and problems of affluence is that the focus on waste loads in industrial countries is an unnecessarily narrow view of environmental disruption. There is a wide variety of activities ranging from fisheries effect of stream channelization to threats to wildlife from increased use of off-road vehicles, such as trail bikes, snow mobiles, and dune buggies, that cause environmental damage quite apart from any waste disposal. Conservation of natural resources, including wilderness areas, has been a powerful motivating force in the environmental movement in the United States. These aspects of environmental disruption are in some cases related to increased affluence. However, direct intervention into environmental and ecological systems is common to both industrial and developing countries. A broader view of environmental disruption weakens the distinction between problems of poverty and problems of affluence.

These qualifications do not invalidate a presumption that rich countries have greater waste disposal problems than poor countries. They do suggest that a distinction between the environmental problems of countries on the basis of income levels needs careful and detailed analysis. Chapter 2 assembles some data and observations concerning environmental differences between industrial and developing countries. At this point we simply wish to remark on some of the conclusions that have been drawn from this formulation. Correct or not, the distinction between environmental problems of affluence and poverty has been very persuasive.

The grouping of environmental problems as those of affluence or those of poverty has suggested certain policy conclusions. For industrial countries at high levels of development, the quick and simplistic response of a few is that rich countries are economically overdeveloped, and that the solution to environmental problems arising from affluence is sharply limited or zero economic growth.[3] We disagree. Although some arguments can be mustered against sustained economic growth on the basis of increasing resource scarcity and perhaps on the basis of a degenerate culture of materialism (and these seem weak), the environmental constraint argument of increasing waste loads has little force. First and most obvious, economic growth provides the material resources that can be used for pollution abatement and for augmenting the assimilative capacity of environmental resources. Rising levels of economic production are consistent with improvements in environmental quality if a sufficient portion of incremental output is allocated to environmental protection. A stagnant economy is less likely to exhibit a collective willingness to pay for environmental protection and may even accelerate the destruction of environmental resources. At the extreme, a stagnant, low-income country with population pressures is almost forced to draw down its environmental capital.

Second, environmental quality objectives can be attained by modifying the nature and composition of economic growth. Illustrations are legion—pollution emissions per ton mile for rail transport are a small fraction of those for truck transport; miniaturization of consumer goods and increased durability are resource saving and minimize extractive and waste disposal problems; biodegradable or reusable packaging can substitute for persistent and throw-away materials. Economic structure has evolved without due concern for environmental disruption, but modifying that structure is quite different from limiting growth in order to limit waste loads.

More fundamentally, an attempt to limit economic growth to secure environmental objectives confounds the problem and obscures more important issues. There is a legitimate question for both industrial and developing countries as to whether reallocating resources away from traditional production toward environmental protection will reduce economic growth as conventionally measured. This question is examined in some detail at a later point. However, it should be recognized that the central justification for environmental protection policy rests on the divergence between social welfare, including that component derived directly from the consumption of environmental services, and the inadequate index of welfare from traditionally measured economic output. Even if environmental protection does lead to some decrease in conventionally measured GNP, the decrease is not evidence of reduced welfare. On the contrary, if the protection measures are economically rational, welfare will increase despite a possible reduction in GNP growth rates.[4] In any event, the order of the argument is important. Growth should not be limited to protect the environment. Rather, there may be some limit placed on conventional growth as a result of environmental protection.

The distinction between problems of poverty and affluence has been attractive because it also suggests policy conclusions for developing countries. Economic growth and development supply the material resources for mitigating environmental problems. Environmental quality merges with the overarching task of development. The concern for environment in developing countries is then a concern for development. Yet within this widely accepted conclusion, one can identify different points of emphasis. Developmentalists who have had a strong commitment to the quality of growth—increasing welfare for the broad masses through improved nutrition, health care, and so on—and who have been disillusioned with earlier concentration on economic growth without regard for income distribution, have seized on concern for the environment as yet another argument for shifting the pattern of development away from economic growth per se. To them the human environment is the touchstone, and development without sustained improvement in the human condition of the very poor is contradictory.[5]

Another group has emphasized that the identification of the environmental problem as one of poverty and the solution to be development supplies a new argument for resource transfers from rich to poor countries. This view is more sophisticated than it first sounds. On one level there has been a deep concern that environmental protection measures in industrial countries will divert resources away from development assistance. Thus requests for increased aid are made in part simply to forestall a possible reduction. At another level, developing countries recognize that industrial countries have felt free to use up much of their own environmental "capital" and also the capital embodied in international common property resources. Accordingly, if the North is serious in desiring environmental restraint on the part of developing countries, it would be equitable for them to pay some form of compensation. This contention is examined in more detail in Chapters 4 and 5. Also, more optimistic observers have noted that environmental concerns do arouse globalist feelings, and a link between environment and poverty might be used to repair the deteriorating constituency for development assistance in industrial countries.[6]

A third group is suspicious that the environmental issue is being used inadvertantly or covertly by industrial countries as a pretext for maintaining the economic status quo. For example, the former Brazilian Ambassador to the United States, Joao Augusto de Araujo Castro, wrote, "The working hypothesis [of his study] is that the implementation of any world-wide environmental policy based on the realities of the developed countries tends to perpetuate the existing gap in socio-economic development between developed and developing countries and to promote the freezing of the present international order."[7] The developing countries would then continue their role as "hewers of wood and drawers of water" or suppliers of cheap raw materials.

For those who hold this view, the extension of environmental problems to those of poverty was welcomed as a further justification for rapid economic growth without particular regard for income distribution. Countries already sensitive about their income distribution policies were also sensitive to outside meddling in their environmental policies (or lack thereof) and were quick to assert sovereign rights. By sharply distinguishing between environmental problems of poverty and affluence, they rejected any need for industrial countries to become involved in their internal environmental programs. The more extreme argued that poverty was so compelling that almost any damage arising from economic growth should be tolerated. They were willing to trade off one set of problems, those associated with poverty, for another set, those resulting from rapid economic growth.[8]

A fourth position has emerged with a more balanced perspective. This view supports development as the major method for overcoming environmental problems of poverty but recognizes that the environmental damages resulting from economic growth should be minimized. However, hard choices cannot be avoided. In some instances protection of the environment will be at the expense of resources available for productive activity. One highly visible issue is the extent to which developing countries wish to attract polluting industries from the developed countries.

ENVIRONMENT AS A PRODUCERS' AND A CONSUMERS' GOOD

Framing environmental issues by distinguishing between problems of poverty and affluence has been the dominant view. Another approach that may be more useful is to emphasize that the services of environmental resources are simultaneously producers' goods and consumers' goods.[9] That is, environmental resources provide services that enter both production functions and directly into utility functions. Environmental deterioration then is either a reduction in the capacity to produce conventional output or a reduction in welfare derived from the direct consumption of environmental services. In both cases the services of environmental resources generally do not pass through markets. Therefore, they are conveniently ignored or underpriced in allocation decisions. The first step in rational environmental policy is to explicitly recognize and value these services. Moreover, an appreciation of the dual role of environmental resource services as producers' and consumers' goods greatly assists in understanding the true importance of environmental quality in developing countries. It also helps distinguish the environmental concerns of rich and poor countries.

The proposition is simple enough. Poor countries may be less willing than rich countries to protect environmental resources when the resources provide directly consumed services. However, poor countries must be concerned with environmental quality when it involves the productivity of resources. This is not a novel contention, yet the literature on environment and development is curiously unintegrated on this point. On one hand, there is a large body of material concerned with the relationship of agricultural productivity and environmental stresses on soils such as erosion and nutrient leaching. In these studies the role of soil quality in maintaining productivity is so basic that it is treated as axiomatic. The deterioration of these resources necessarily affects production functions within agriculture. At the same time, less technical discussions of environment and development often fail to see environmental protection as an attempt to conserve the productivity of resources, even when they touch on the most clear-cut case, environmental problems in agriculture. Rather, these discussions assume that protection of the environment diverts resources from productive activity and reduces conventional production. For example, Streeten writes, "Applied to the environment in underdeveloped countries, the problem is how to strike a balance between the benefits of raising the level of living of the mass of people in poor countries, and its cost in terms of the deterioration of the environment."[10] The converse proposition, that preservation of the environment is fundamental to improved levels of living, is not entertained.

	To	
	Producers	Consumers
From		
Producers	a_{11}	a_{12}
Consumers	a_{21}	a_{22}

Diagram 1.1. Environmental damage flows.

This point can be illustrated. Consider this schematic representation of environmental-type externalities or direct (nonmarket) damage flows. The a_{11} cell represents environmental damages arising from and adversely affecting production activity. An example is upstream chemical wastes harming a downstream commercial fishery. The a_{12} cell represents the flow of environmental damages from producers to consumers and a_{21} the less common reverse flow of damages from consumers to producers. The a_{22} cell represents reciprocal damages among consumers arising from consumption activities. The a_{12} and a_{22} type damages are the most frequently cited—industrial emmissions and effluents damaging health and aesthetic values and reciprocal external costs from uncontrolled auto emmissions are illustrations. The relative importance of each type of damage is an empirical question that has not been conclusively answered.

Environmental control measures that reduce any of the damage flows will require real resources and, by diverting productive factors away from conventional goods and services, will initially tend to reduce conventional output.[11] However, measures to control a_{11} and a_{21} type externalities will also preserve or *augment* the productive capacity for conventional goods. For example, upstream waste treatment will preserve the productivity of downstream fisheries or reduce downstream expenditures on industrial water purification. Indeed, if the externality is exclusively of the a_{11} type, the test for economic efficiency of the control measure is that total output increases.

a_{12} and a_{22} type damages can impair the productivity of factor inputs, although less visibly. Uncontrolled environmental externalities of these two types can reduce the capacity for producing conventional goods and services, in addition to their acknowledged direct loss to consumer welfare. The most important channel is probably the adverse effects on health and the physical quality of labor as a factor input into production. Output falls below its potential when workers lose time or efficiency through environmentally related illness. Environmental controls should increase the health and productivity of workers. Unfortunately, it is becoming conventional wisdom that the opportunity cost of resources employed in pollution control is also a measure of product that must be foregone. This is simply not so.

Diagram 1.2 attempts to combine the distinction between problems of poverty and affluence and between environmental services as a producers' good and a consumers' good to provide a typology of environmental problems. Environmental damages are listed along a spectrum of initial receptors: natural resources, physical capital, and direct impact on humans. The damages are further divided by those which are typically associated with poverty and those which are typically associated with high income levels. Of course, the eco-

Initial Damage Receptors	Problems Associated with Affluence	Problems Associated with Poverty
A Natural resources used for production soil water vegetation	Examples: excessive use of fertilizer, vegetation damage from air pollution	Examples: erosion, nutrient leaching, siltation of river channels
B Physical capital	Examples: corrosion, fouling of machinery	Example: deterioration of transport infrastructure from increased flooding
C Direct human impact C.1. Health	Examples: chronic diseases from air pollution	Examples: environmental diseases from unsanitary water supplies
C.2. Recreation and amenities	congestion, loss of wilderness areas, scenic losses	urban slum conditions, congestion

Diagram 1.2. Typology of environmental problems.

nomic measure of damages in each case is the direct or indirect effect on human welfare. However, this schema is useful in determining whether production is affected. For example, the first row contains damages to natural resources adversely affecting production. Generally these damages arise from activities within the extractive sector,—mining, agriculture, forestry. The distinction between affluence and poverty damages should not be pushed too far. Industrial countries also confront soil erosion and salinization problems. The important point to keep in mind is that environmental control measures in this area will preserve or increase productive capacity. The same conclusion holds for row B—damages to physical capital such as fouling of machinery, excessive wear, and corrosion. Reducing environmental damages will also reduce the costs of preventative measures—painting, cleaning, intake water filtration, and so on—and will also free resources for conventional production.

The direct impact on humans is more complicated. The population plays a dual role—as direct consumers of environmental services and as providers of a productive resource, labor. It seems sensible to subdivide direct human impacts into health damages and recreation and other amenity losses. Health damages may or may not reduce productive capacity, depending on circumstances. In any event, there is always a direct loss of welfare. A rough division of environmental health problems between those related to poverty and those related to affluence is possible, but again the division should not be pushed too far. Air pollution damages to health dominate in rich countries; water pollution damages to health appear to dominate in poor countries. It is only when we reach row C.2, losses of recreational opportunity and other amenity services directly provided by the environment, that the productivity effect is trivial. Here environmental protection measures will indeed divert real resources away from conventional production and, while presumably increasing welfare from amenity services directly consumed, will reduce the output of conventional goods and services available for consumption.

The schema presented in Diagram 1.2 is imperfect. It does not illustrate that damages to, say, the productivity of natural resources may also cause amenity losses. For example, deterioration of water quality may reduce commercial fish yields and also reduce recreational value of the water. Still, the classification serves a useful illustrative purpose and leads to interesting propositions. If environmental damages of type A, B and C.1 are widespread in developing countries, environmental protection is in no sense a luxury of the rich. Protection is absolutely essential to maintain productive capacity and to lay the foundation for sustained economic growth. The question is no longer one of ability to afford environmental measures. A call for environmental awareness in developing countries is not merely evangelism by industrial countries recently converted to an environmental ethic. The prevention of soil deterioration is perhaps the least controvertible activity, but environmental health expenditures can also be justified. For example, a study of the costs of air pollution in the United Kingdom concluded that direct production losses from bronchitis incidental to air pollution was £16 million per annum. An earlier study by Lave and Seskin estimated that a 50% reduction in urban air pollution in the United States might yield an annual saving of \$250–\$500 million from reducing bronchitis.[12]

The extent to which air pollution affects the productivity of workers in developing countries is simply unknown. Casual observation suggests that air quality is poor in many urban centers. There are, however, numerous studies that document the adverse impact of river basin development on public health. The list of diseases that are spread by water projects is somber: schistosomiasis, malaria, onchocerciasis (river blindness), sleeping sickness, and others.[13] These diseases reduce productivity through time lost from work, decreased physical effort, and removal of infested land from cultivation. Expenditure on medical care also diverts resources away from other productive activities. The production effect must be large, apart from the direct suffering.

Another proposition emerging from the distinction between environmental services as producers and consumers goods is that attributing a high income elasticity of demand for environmental quality is, at best, only relevant for damages of the C.2 and perhaps C.1 type. It is frequently asserted that the demand for environmental quality is income elastic, implying that at higher income levels a larger proportion of income is spent on the purchase of environmental quality (or would be if adequate markets were available) than at lower income levels. Given stronger preferences for environmental quality in rich countries than poor countries and given certain assumptions about the supply distribution of environmental services among countries, the international extension of this argument is that it is economically rational to reallocate polluting industries from North to South.[14] This is an extension of traditional comparative advantage theory to accommodate international differences in the supply of and demand for environmental quality. The argument is examined in some detail in Chapter 3. Here we simply note that the analytical use of an assumed high income elasticity of demand for environmental quality should be restricted to only those services which directly enter utility functions. When environmental damages are to productive resources, the appropriate perspective is no longer consumer demand elasticities but those branches of capital and investment theory concerned with the development of natural resources and investment in human capital. Divergent objectives between North and South are no longer as apparent.

Why has the simultaneous role of environmental resources providing producers' and consumers' goods been neglected in most discussions of environment and development? One reason is that deterioration of natural resources has long been recognized but has traditionally been examined within specific resource management fields such as agronomy, forestry, and fisheries. Only recently have the problems been rediscovered as environmental problems. Moreover, some problems such as soil deterioration do not fit neatly into the theory of externalities and common property resources, on which economists have constructed an elaborate explanation for deterioration in environmental quality.[15] Soil erosion can involve externalities when, for example, upstream erosion causes downstream siltation. It also can exhibit the classic abuses of common property resources, as, for example, overgrazing the commons. Often, however, the damage is not external to the individual farmer but reduces productivity of the land under his ownership. In these circumstances the paradigm of common property resources and externalities loses its force, and economists tend to overlook this type of environmental problem.

Another reason has been the tendency to analyze the demand for environmental quality within the theory of public goods. In this formulation, environment services are consumed much like other public goods. The analytically interesting features of a public good are that consumption by one individual does not lead to any reduction in supply available for others and that it is difficult to exclude users. Clean air and water and recreation areas before the level of congestion are examples. Given these characteristics, private markets fail to provide sufficient amounts of public goods, and there is an invitation for government provision. Much effort is spent on estimating demand without the guidance of private markets.

Because public goods are generally directly consumed and do not enter into production functions, viewing environmental quality as a public good emphasizes the consumers' good aspect and plays down its producers' good role. The stress in industrial countries on pollution-related health and amenity losses reinforces the biased view. If environmental quality is seen as a "good" to be consumed, its obverse is pollution, a "bad," which enters utility functions with a negative sign. Pollution abatement becomes the activity of supplying environmental quality services, or suppressing the bad—pollution. Abatement has a cost measured in terms of the real resources necessary to reach environmental quality objectives. Its benefit is the amount of environmental quality provided, or pollution suppressed. From this perspective, given reasonable assumptions about the supply of resources available for abatement and the demand for the "good" environmental quality, it is not difficult to conclude that industrial countries have a greater interest in environmental quality than do poor countries. Baumol reflects this view of environmental protection providing a public good when he asserts, "It is generally recognized that rich and poor countries do not have the same stake in measures to protect the environment."[16]

This view is not totally incorrect, but it is excessively narrow. It shifts attention away from the task of preserving the supply of environmental capital for productive purposes. When this function is introduced in the developing country context, the need for environmental protection measures becomes apparent.

DUAL VERSUS UNIFORM STANDARDS

Developing countries have strongly asserted that environmental standards chosen by industrial countries are inappropriate to the circumstances of poor countries. They maintain that there should be dual or multiple standards, more lenient for developing countries, to properly reflect their lower levels of income and economic capabilities. Set against their position is an untidy group of arguments supporting internationally uniform environmental standards. These supporting arguments range from a desire to avoid disturbances to international trade that might arise if there were international differences in abatement costs to declarations of a global ecological unity and the consequent need for uniform stringent standards. The issue of dual versus internationally uniform standards has been controversial and confused. The issue has been most evident in international discussions of shared resources (mainly the oceans) and with regard to trade.

Is the dual standard position taken by developing countries economically rational? To answer, we first observe that there has been some confusion between internationally uniform standards and internationally formulated standards. A moment's reflection makes clear that internationally uniform standards need not be formulated by an international body and that an international agency with environmental jurisdiction is under no compulsion to establish uniform standards. Most standards are decided on the national level, although sometimes an international body such as the International Maritime Consultative Organization (IMCO) will take the lead in negotiating conventions, as was the case with marine vessel pollution.[17] In either event standards may be uniform or may differ among countries and regions. Both industrial and developing countries have exhibited extreme unwillingness to yield standard-setting authority to international organizations.

Moreover, the term "environmental standards" is too vague to be used without further explanation. Standards can be of several types: product standards, standards on effluents and emissions from productive activity, ambient standards, and biological standards. Product standards are regulations covering operating and disposal characteristics of consumer goods. Examples are auto emission standards, radiation emission levels for microwave ovens, and consumer packaging requirements. Production standards are quantitative restrictions on wastes generated from production activities. These wastes include the traditional air and water pollutants in addition to noise and heat residuals. The standards are generally expressed in terms of quantities emitted per unit time or per unit production, with specified dilution characteristics. Regulations governing production activities themselves are closely related, and these are found mainly in the extractive industries. Limits on clear cutting and the required use of high-lead, balloon, or helicopter for log removal from fragile or steep terrain are two examples of regulations on production drawn from forestry. Ambient environmental standards are designated objectives for specific pollution levels in environmental media, such as parts per million of asbestos fibers in the air or pathogens in recreational waters. Finally, biological standards prescribe maximum permissible exposure to, or levels of concentration of pollutants in living organisms. One example is limits on the heavy metal content of seafood offered for sale. Environmentally related occupational health standards are generally combinations of ambient workplace standards and biological exposure standards.

The relations between these types of standards are clear. Product and production standards in conjunction with levels of economic activity, physical dispersal characteristics, assimilative capacity, and so on, determine ambient air and water quality. In turn, ambient quality levels together with a complicated set of variables relating to intake, concentration, and chemical alteration determine the biological impact of pollutants on living organisms, including man. If the regulatory approach is to establish ambient standards, it is necessary to devise methods to reach back to control product and production pollution. For example, the establishment of ambient air quality objectives in the United States makes it necessary to establish controls on stationary air pollution sources such as utilities, as well as to place limits on auto emissions and use patterns. If product and production standards are set, an implicit ambient quality objective is present.

Internationally uniform product or production standards (for example, auto emissions or sulfur oxide discharge from electric power production) will result in neither identical ambient quality nor comparable biological impact among countries. Differences in the level and structure of economic activity and in physical dispersion will ensure that the ambient levels will differ. Conversely, identical ambient standards will require different product and production controls in different countries, depending on their spatial concentration of economic activity, environmental media characteristics, and so on. At a minimum, discussions of uniform versus dual environmental standards should explicitly state which type of standards are under consideration.

Having said this, we wish to stress that the question of selecting appropriate environmental standards is central to the rational and efficient use of environmental resources. If standards are set too low (or, if the price system is used, pollution taxes are set too low), the environment is given insufficient protection, and welfare suffers. If standards are too high, real resources are wasted. In addition, there is a distributional consequence of establishing pollution standards. The imposition of standards will revoke previous entitlements to common property resources for waste disposal purposes and award rights to beneficial users of the resource, either for production or for direct consumption. Welfare will shift from polluters to beneficial consumers of environmental services.[18] In the North–South context developing countries do have a strong interest in whether there will be a multiplicity of standards. If inappropriate uniform standards are imposed on them, they risk the waste of real resources. With respect to resources shared between North and South, the choice of environmental standards will effect the international distribution of welfare.

More generally, the issue of dual standards—lower for developing countries—is a persistent theme running through North–South environmental discussions. The theme has been present in the Law of the Sea negotiations for the establishment of an environmental regime for the oceans. It enters into the selection of environmental controls in project analysis and accordingly is part of the development assistance relationship between industrial and developing countries. It is also central to the trade and investment implications for developing countries of environmental control. The theme is examined in each of these contexts. At this point we wish to establish some general principles regarding the economic desirability of dual versus uniform standards.

There is no economic case for internationally uniform standards for production when the damages are purely local and do not involve transnational pollution. When the damages are to productive resources, the problem is close to typical investment decisions—how much money should be devoted to maintaining the productive capacity of the resource in question? If, for example, the environmental protection measure involves windbreaks to reduce soil erosion, the appropriate analytical tools are those of project analysis. The discounted flow of benefits (soil erosion prevented) is compared to the investment costs; if a favorable net present discounted value results, the project is justified.[19] Capital investment in pollution abatement equipment to protect a commercial fishery presents similar analytical characteristics. Alternatively, if the problem is one of maintaining soil fertility under intensified cultivation, the analysis requires determining maximum sustainable economic yield (not biological), and principles from fisheries and forestry management can be applied. In any event, the appropriate level of conservation effort is determined by the particular features of the environmental problem. The application of internationally uniform standards would be inappropriate. It does not follow, however, that developing countries should choose lower standards. In fact, the scarcity of productive resources in developing countries may result in a greater need for conservation and in some instances higher standards than those set in industrial countries.

In addition, in situations in which a direct effect on productive resources cannot be identified—for example, atmospheric pollution from industrial emissions—and if the effects are assumed to be local, there is still no strong case for internationally uniform ambient or production emission and effluent standards. The theoretically correct level of pollution abatement is that level at which the marginal costs of abatement are equal to the marginal benefits, or damages avoided. International differences in demand for environmental quality, particularly for recreational and aesthetic enjoyment, that arise from differences in income levels and social and cultural values should be considered. The cost–benefit calculus for establishing quality objectives should reflect local conditions.

In general, the calculations will support diversity rather than uniformity of standards. Again, this does not mean that developing countries will invariably select lower standards. On the contrary, under unfavorable atmospheric conditions and where considerable industry is already present, as, for example, the

Valley of Mexico, more stringent standards than are found in some industrial countries may be needed. The superficial argument for uniform standards—that they would reduce differential production costs and hence disturbances to international trade—completely misses the point that some spatial rearrangement of economic activity to accord more closely with the supply of and demand for environmental quality is precisely what should be sought and encouraged. This point is explored in more detail in Chapter 3.

The case for internationally uniform environmental standards on products is somewhat stronger. Here the developing countries have an interest in avoiding the use of environmental product standards as barriers to their exports. One way this may be accomplished is to harmonize product design and operating specifications imposed by industrial countries. Harmonization of product standards has been a long-standing issue in international trade, and environmental standards are, in principle, no different from other types of standards, including traditional health and safety requirements. The advantage of uniform product standards is that they lower compliance costs by eliminating differing design requirements for specific markets and thus permit longer production runs. They also minimize arbitrary and capricious behavior by importing countries. Set against this advantage is the recognized right of countries to establish nondiscriminatory standards on products that accord with their individual circumstances. Something of the same dilemma arises for auto emission standards in the United States—urban areas and especially those with unfavorable atmospheric conditions and heavy automobile use, such as Los Angeles, will properly seek stricter auto emission controls, but differentiating the product to meet nonuniform standards adds to production costs. There is a tradeoff between product differentiation to meet local market needs and the additional costs of differentiation.

Transfrontier pollution, particularly the use of international common property resources by North and South, is examined in Chapter 5. Here we make two assertions that are subsequently developed more fully. First, assume an international body of water with several riparian states jointly contributing pollutants through, say, dirty river discharge. The Mediterranean would be a good example. Assume also that it is possible to select an ambient water quality level such that, on the margin, the incremental costs of abatement are equal to the incremental benefits from damages avoided. Then, for efficient abatement, the marginal abatement costs for all polluters must be equal; if, as is likely, their abatement cost functions differ (perhaps because of different disposal alternatives), identical effluent standards measured either in terms of parts per million of discharge or total volume of pollutants discharged will be inefficient. In this instance uniform effluent standards applied to all sources would be uneconomic and would not respect differences in abatement cost functions. However, it does not follow that developing countries would necessarily enjoy less restrictive standards unless they had generally higher abatement costs.

The second point is that, with respect to vessel source pollution of the marine environment, there is little justification for supporting dual design standards for commercial fleets, with less stringent standards for developing countries. Ship design standards are a rather inflexible instrument for securing environmental objectives, but if they are chosen by virtue of their low inspection and enforcement costs, uniform design standards applied to industrial and developing country fleets are preferred. The alternative of dual standards would tend to enter a distortion into relative transport costs, shifting cargo to developing country bottoms and ultimately perhaps defeating the intent of the environmental standards themselves.

In summary, there is a presumption that environmental standards should be tailored to a local calculus of costs and benefits to be efficient. This may, but need not always, imply lower standards for developing countries. With respect to product standards, developing countries will generally wish to see some uniform standards to minimize their export trade problems. With regard to transnational pollution, there are some situations in which multiple standards are justified. The most serious issue for transnational pollution, however, is how to avoid having multiple standards degenerate into purely national regulations set on the basis of a parochial calculus of costs and benefits.

ENVIRONMENT AND RESOURCE EXPLOITATION

The exploitation of renewable and nonrenewable resources and the quality of the environment are closely linked.[20] We wish to emphasize two aspects of this linkage—the usefulness of the materials balance approach and the North–South issues that have arisen.[21]

The central features of the materials balance approach are that the flow of materials through an economy can be described in quantitative terms, and the materials flow is a closed system. An accounting balance is established so that inflows into a sector equal outflows plus stock changes. It follows from the accounting identities that in a closed economy the amount of residuals entering environmental media is roughly equal in weight to the total weight of basic food, fuel, and other raw materials entering production.[22] As Ayres and Kneese point out, this is not always obvious because the residuals are in large part gaseous and liquid and therefore do not require handling.

This approach provides several useful insights. First, as a closed system, it is apparent that the rate at which materials are extracted from the natural environment is the major determinent of the rate at which residuals are disposed of in environmental media. The rate of extraction is linked to the level of economic activity, and the rate of residuals disposal is related to pollution loads. Therefore, a link is established between the level and growth of production and the gross pollution load. Although at first glance it might appear that the extreme differences between rich and poor countries in per capita consumption of materials might provide an index of the relative magnitude of environmental problems, on reflection it is clear that gross materials flows are an inadequate measure. Environmental damage is also a function of the composition of wastes, the spatial disposal pattern, assimilative capacity, and the demand for environmental services. Still, when restricted to narrower groups of resources such as fossil fuels or heavy metals, comparisons of materials use levels may give some information about the intensity of pollution problems.

Second, the materials balance approach makes clear that the economists' term "final consumption" is misleading. Goods are not used up but provide services. In their use and disposal they add to waste loads unless they can be recycled. Although they may change form or state in the process of consumption, they do not disappear. The role of resource recovery in minimizing damages is highlighted. Not only will the recovery of wastes from processing, "consumption," and disposal reduce the damages from the wastes themselves, but the availability of recovered material will reduce demand for virgin materials and the environmental damages from primary exploitation.

Finally, the materials balance approach provides a method for classifying environmental problems according to the type of economic activity in which they occur. Raw materials exploitation both produces wastes (e.g., mine tailings) and other environmental disturbances (e.g., loss of wildlife habitat and soil erosion). Materials processing and manufacturing, including the production of energy from fossil fuels, releases wastes to the environment. Consumption and final disposal produce wastes (e.g., auto emissions and junked autos) but also cause other types of environmental problems, for example, erosion and infringement on wildlife from recreational use of trail bikes and dune buggies. Because materials must be physically transported, residuals from the transport of raw and processed materials must also be noted. To take but one example, these environmental damages may arise from the production and use of coal for energy: in production, coal miners' pneumoniosis (black lung disease), acid mine drainage, erosion, temporary or permanent loss of land surface through stripping, emissions from truck and rail transport; in use, sulfur emissions hazardous to health and sulfuric acid rains damaging to vegetation, fish and soils. The extraction of natural resources and their ultimate use shape the extent of environmental damages. Natural resource policy is in part environmental policy.

The materials balance approach is equally useful for developed and developing countries as an accounting system for keeping track of waste generation and disposal. It also is similar to two other techniques. The first is pathways analysis of toxic substances, for example, pesticides. Production sources, transport and transport losses, and end uses are identified both quantitatively and spatially. Dispersion models to ultimate sinks may be added. The second technique is water budget analysis, which identifies quantities of water entering a production process, either in the raw materials themselves, as process make-up water, or as wash water. The budget then identifies the quantities and form of water discharges and estimates the water quality characteristics (BOD, suspended solids, turbidity, odor, etc.) of the waste water flows. Both these techniques rely on quantitative accounting and are important tools in the formulation of pollution abatement policy.[23]

The North–South aspects of the link between resource exploitation and environmental quality are complicated. Developing countries are major suppliers of raw materials to industrial countries. If left unregulated, environmental damages associated with the extraction and initial processing of raw materials are borne by the South. A claim *could* be made that rich countries are practicing environmental exploitation of the developing world through an insatiable demand for raw materials. One example might be the rapid increase in the harvesting of tropical hardwood in Indonesia, Malaysia, and the Philippines to satisfy hardwood plywood and wood panel demand in Japan and the United States that has resulted in the erosion and destruction of fragile soil cover in supplying countries.[24]

However, the problem is not entirely one sided. Developing countries are currently net importers of foodstuffs from the United States of about $4 billion per annum, and this has placed additional environmental stress on United States agricultural resources.[25] However, calculations of net disadvantage of this sort are of little use. The appropriate policy principle for any country that exports raw materials is to institute whatever environmental safeguards are justified on the basis of its local cost–benefit calculus and to price its exports to cover full social costs, including environmental protection measures. This principle may be hard to apply. As explained later, local cost–benefit analysis is inadequate when damages are regional or global. Also, it is unlikely that long-term damages are properly accounted for in countries with imperfect markets and high immediate consumption needs. In practice it may be difficult to avoid marginal adjustments among suppliers as they place environmental constraints on production, and the problems of inspection and enforcement in developing countries may be severe.[26] However, it remains true that raping the landscape for export is neither more nor less reprehensible than rape for domestic consumption. Primary responsibility for curbing environmental abuses rests with the producing country. When resource exploitation involves international common property resources such as the oceans or when waste disposal involves transfrontier pollution—the physical movement of pollutants from the territory of one country to another—assigning responsibility for controls is more complex. Countries that are the recipients of damage flows do not have extraterritorial authority to impose controls on polluting countries.

There has been a deliberate attempt to place resource/environment issues within the broader set of demands for restructuring the international economic system or, as it has come to be known, The New International Economic Order. A good example of this was the symposium in Cocoyoc, Mexico, in 1974, sponsored by the U.N. Conference on Trade and Development (UNCTAD) and the U.N. Environmental Programme (UNEP).[27] Three separate arguments are used in the conference Declaration. The first is the charge of environmental exploitation of the South by the North through excessive use of international commons for waste disposal. Without evaluating the quantitative significance, the charge appears to have merit. It would carry much more weight, however, if the dimensions of the damage done to developing countries could be estimated. A more controversial assertion is that unequal economic relations between North and South, of which a major aspect is depressed terms of trade for raw materials exports, has led to a failure of efforts to eliminate poverty and has "compelled the people to cultivate marginal lands at great risk of soil erosion." That is, the existing economic order, by sustaining poverty in the Third World, has contributed to environmental despoilation in those countries.

In the third argument the focus switches to resource use patterns, and the assertion is made that "preemption by the rich of a disproportionate share of key resources conflicts strictly with the longer term interests of the poor by impairing their ultimate access to resources necessary to their development and by increasing their costs." Although the point is only indirectly related to environmental quality in developing countries, it has been repeated in many contexts and, because of a surface plausibility, deserves comment. Dramatic comparisons between rich and poor in terms of per capita resource use are easy to come by but can be seriously misleading. Differential rates of resource consumption, no matter how striking, are not the cause of poverty but a reflection of the vast differences in income between rich and poor. To argue that differential rates are responsible for poverty confounds cause and effect. Indeed, substantial reduction in resource use in industrial countries, either through conservation or economic recession, reduces the export earnings of developing countries and impairs their growth prospects. The recession of 1974–1975 provides clear evidence of this. More generally, the disproportionate use argument neglects the critical role of price. The proper question to ask is, are markets operating well, or is monopsony power being exercised by industrial country purchasers, driving prices down? Also, do export prices include full environmental costs of production? Is future resource scarcity correctly anticipated in present price? The extraction rate for nonrenewable resources is governed by current prices and costs, anticipated increases in asset prices (ores in the ground), and the interest rate. In turn, current materials price depends on extraction rates and current level of demand.[28]

Although the optimum rate of resource extraction and use can be modeled, it is questionable if market structures operate sufficiently well to acheive this optimum. The disproportionate use argument does have some validity, but it is really an extension of the terms of trade issue (and hence prices) rather than rates of resource consumption alone. Also, if environmental externalities from extraction and waste disposal are left uncorrected, private market price understates social marginal costs, and the rate of materials consumption will be excessive. Environmental controls will increase cost and price, reduce demand, and slow the rate of resource use. In this sense there is a natural harmony between conservationists concerned with conserving nonrenewable resources and those concerned with maintaining or improving environmental quality. Neglecting environmental consequences can lead to excessive rates of resource use, but this is different from asserting that industrial countries are preempting the share of resources that should be left for developing countries.[29]

A final resource–environment question between North and South involves wildlife resources and wilderness areas located in developing countries.[30] Conservationists, mainly those in rich countries, derive considerable satisfaction from wildlife populations and wilderness areas located in developing areas. The value or benefit to them is not merely the result of direct experience through travel and viewing but exists independent of direct contact, as the awareness that such areas exist. At the same time there can be considerable opportunity costs for developing countries in preserving these resources, particularly in the face of strong population pressure. The costs may not only be the loss of agricultural land or potential industrial sites, but restrictions on pesticide use to protect food chains, soil erosion controls, effluent treatment, and so on to protect the ecological integrity of the resource.[31]

Even if the benefits and costs of conservation were fully internal to the developing country, the application of standard benefit cost analysis for protection would be difficult. Benefits are not generally priced through the market, and, treated as intangibles, they are less likely to be included in the calculus than are preservation costs, which can be more easily estimated. Set in the North–South framework, in which revenues from tourism capture only a part of the benefits for developing countries, conservation implies the provision of a "free good" from the poor to the rich. As long as international institutional mechanisms are not adequate to compel conservationists in developed countries to express their preferences in monetary form, the result will be either a transfer from the poor to the rich or inadequate protection of wildlife and wilderness areas in developing countries.

TIME

Questions of time are central to the analysis of environmental deterioration and control policies. In some instances incorporating time into the analysis is similar in developed and developing countries, but sometimes the special features of developing countries suggest different approaches.

Pollutants vary considerably with regard to persistence and hence the importance of time. If pollutants were arrayed along a spectrum according to persistence, radioactive wastes, with the ability to inflict damages over several thousand years, would be at one extreme. At the other would be noise pollution, for no matter how damaging, it ceases to be a problem after it occurs. Other pollutants would occupy intermediate positions—fluorocarbons in the atmosphere, DDT and related compounds, biological oxygen demand (BOD) from discharge of organic materials, waste heat discharges into local waters, and so on.

Pollutants that exhibit persistence require models that incorporate the time paths of the variables. Time rates will be needed for measuring emission levels, physical dispersion through environmental media, bioaccumulation in living organisms if present, rates of biodegradation and chemical alteration, and accumulation in ultimate "sinks." For some pollutants a simple dynamic stock flow relation is sufficient in which the stock value or concentration of a pollutant in a body of water is a function of the flow rate of discharge into the water, the degradation rate, and the flushing time for the body of water. In other cases in which the pollutant is most damaging during movement toward its ultimate state and sink, the time profile of the dispersion model is most important. This may be the case for pollution of the marine environment by oil.

If there is a substantial lag between the introduction of a pollutant and its ultimate damage, there can be a delayed perception of it as a harmful pollutant. For example, DDT was first manufactured in the 1930s and came into widespread use following World War II, but it was not until the publication of Rachel Carson's *Silent Spring* in 1962 that the dangers were widely noted. Similar delays in recognizing dangers have occurred with fluorocarbons, polychlorinated byphenols (PCBs), vinyl chloride, and others. Ironically, the dye used to stamp meat that conforms to U.S. Department of Agriculture regulations was found to be carcinogenic in 1973, thirteen years after its introduction. Added to the perception lag can be an additional delay while pollutants travel toward their ultimate sink. For some pollutants, ambient concentrations can continue to rise long after their emissions have been curbed. As discussed in Chapter 5, fluorocarbons are a good example. PCBs may be another.

Environmental uncertainty is asymmetric. There are few instances in which unanticipated effects turn out to be beneficial and not harmful. This suggests that great caution should be exercised in the introduction of new and exotic substances into the environment and that predictive analysis needs improvement.[32] Caution is appropriate for both industrial and developing countries, but the former are technological innovators and the first to use new substances or processes on a substantial scale and therefore have special responsibility. For developing countries the remedial argument that is sometimes heard—they can afford clean-up measures after they become richer—is not satisfactory when the pollutant involves delayed perception of damage and long lags in accumulation.

Another persuasive reason why developing countries should be immediately concerned with environmental controls instead of deferring action until they are more affluent is that preventive action is almost invariably less costly than remedial pollution control. Some environmental degradation involves irreversible changes. The loss of wilderness areas and the extinction of species are examples. Some environmental changes could perhaps technically be reversed, but they also should be considered irreversible because the time scale is so long or the economic costs so prohibitive.

For a large group of pollution problems, especially in the area of industrial production, remedial pollution abatement is feasible, either by process modification or "end of pipe" effluent and emission treatment. However, modification of existing plants to meet abatement standards is considerably more expensive than the cost of abatement in new plant construction.[33] For example, the recent convention concerning pollution from vessels requires segregated ballasting for newly constructed oil tankers above 70,000 DWT but did not seriously consider retrofitting the existing tanker fleet to segregated ballasting because of the large costs involved. Also, it has been shown that the sulphite process for paper pulp manufacture is up to ten times more polluting than the sulphate process. However, once the paper mill is constructed, conversion from sulphite to sulphate is not likely, and for this reason the pollution levels should be considered before an investment is undertaken.[34]

Developing countries just starting to industrialize have some advantage in minimizing environmental control costs and avoiding undue stress on environmental resources. There will be considerable savings by initially installing pollution abatement equipment or selecting production techniques that minimize waste loads, as compared to later conversion. The ability to site plants to minimize environmental damage and control costs is also important. The spatial dimension of environmental problems has not been emphasized by most observers, but it is apparent that damages can be minimized by avoiding environmentally sensitive areas (such as "fragile" water bodies or locations subject to thermal inversions). Even if full pollution abatement is not contemplated, siting industrial activity downwind or downstream from other users and population centers can greatly reduce damage. Moreover, countries starting their industrialization have greater flexibility with regard to the composition of industrial output, although this flexibility should not be exaggerated. These issues are discussed more thoroughly in Chapter 4. The point to stress here is that, although the current costs of undertaking pollution abatement in new investment may appear to be a diversion of resources away from productive use, the entire time profile of benefits should be considered. This should extend to the possible cumulative nature of ambient pollution levels as industrial investment increases and to the higher future costs of conversion.

One exceedingly difficult problem of time in environmental management arises from the delays in environmental damages and the consequent need to discount future benefits and costs of abatement. There is a large literature on the question of the "proper" rate of discount for project analysis in developing countries and the proper rate for discounting environmental damages. The different aspects of the question are examined in Chapter 4. Here we note that the choice of a high discount rate for environmental protection expenditures in developing countries, as compared to a lower discount rate for similar expenditures in industrial countries, can be supported on grounds that resources used for abatement are relatively scarce in developing countries and should command a high opportunity cost/price. But this is a limited argument and can be turned on its head. If the environmental problem in developing countries is one in which the productivity of resources is threatened, as suggested earlier, their relative scarcity requires greater, not less, conservation, and a low rather than a high rate of discount applied to environmental protection might be appropriate. It is only if the pollution abatement activity protects consumption items such as scenic amenities that the argument may have merit.

In a sense, economic growth in industrial countries has proceeded by building up an enormous stock of physical capital, including the means of production and the supporting infrastructure of transportation and communications. This has been accomplished in part by drawing down or depleting our environmental capital, including most visibly our mineral resources and by degrading or exhausting environmental media and in some instances the environmental and mineral resources of developing countries. Both physical capital and environmental "capital" are stocks that give rise to a flow of services. The increase in one at the expense of the other alters the composition of welfare toward material goods. One can formulate the question of whether the increased welfare arising from material goods production (high levels of GNP as traditionally measured) compensates for the loss of welfare associated with environmental deterioration. The extreme zero-economic-growth proponents have answered the question in the negative. But the question is poorly formulated. The more relevant question is whether, on the margin, some small diversion of resources away from material goods production and some small diversion of resources toward environmental preservation would have added to total welfare. Despite the poverty of the South in terms of material goods, development economists should seek to answer the latter question. In doing so, they will recognize that in many instances physical capital (including agricultural resources) becomes less productive over time if environmental quality is permitted to decline.

NOTES

1. The term consumption can be misleading. It is the services of final goods that are consumed. Materials can be recycled, treated, or dumped, but they do not disappear. See Allen V. Kneese, Robert U. Ayres, and Ralph C. d'Arge, *Economics and the Environment: A Materials Balance Approach* (Washington, D.C.: Resources for the Future, 1970). For a preliminary attempt to quantify the sources of waste loads, see Norman Lee and P.J.W. Saunders, "Pollution as a

Function of Affluence and Population Increase," in Peter R. Cox and John Peel, Eds. *Population and Pollution* (London: Academic Press, 1972).

2. We have found no studies relating air pollution levels and health in developing countries.
3. For a comprehensive discussion of the no-growth proposition see "The No-Growth Society," *Daedalus* **102,** No. 4 (Fall 1974) entire issue. See also Wilfred Beckerman, *Two Cheers for the Affluent Society: A Spirited Defense of Economic Growth* (New York: St. Martin's Press, 1975).
4. The effects of abatement expenditure on measured GNP are not self-evident. With unemployed resources GNP may rise from increased aggregate demand. At full employment a diversion of resources to abatement will directly reduce conventional output but, as discussed elsewhere, may augment productive capacity. Abatement measures built into consumer products (such as auto emission controls) can be treated as quality improvements at the discretion of GNP statisticians. See Organization for Economic Cooperation and Development, *Economic Implications of Pollution Control: A General Assessment* (Paris, 1974) and Maurice Weinrobe, "Accounting for Pollution: Pollution Abatement and the National Product," *Land Economics*, **49,** No. 2 (May 1973) p. 115.
5. Mahbub Ul-Haq has been an eloquent spokesman for this group.
6. Concerning resource transfers for environmental protection in developing countries see Scott MacLeod, *Financing Environmental Measures in Developing Countries: The Principle of Additionality*, International Union for the Conservation of Nature and Natural Resources, Environmental Policy and Law Paper no. 6 (Morges, Switzerland, 1974).
7. Jouo Augusto de Araujo Castro, "Environment and Development: The Case of the Less Developed Countries," *International Organization*, **26,** No. 2 (Spring 1972) p. 401.
8. Brazil has been an extreme example of this in international discussions. In part this can be traced to its sensitivity to outside criticism of its Amazon development program and its treatment of native Indians.
9. We are indebted to Dr. Lincoln Gordon for first suggesting this approach to us.
10. Paul Streeten, "Cost-Benefit and Other Problems of Method," in *Political Economy of Environment* (Paris: Mouton, 1972), p. 47.
11. Some adjustments, particularly among consumers, need not require real resources. For example, separate smoking sections on aircraft restrict consumer sovereignty but have no resource cost.
12. *An Economic and Technical Appraisal of Air Pollution in the United Kingdom* (Programmes Analysis Unit, Chilton, Didcot, Berks, 1971) and Lave and Seskin, "Air Pollution and Human Health" *Science*, **169,** 723, cited by R.E. Wyzga, "A Survey of Environmental Damage Functions," in Organization for Economic Cooperation and Development, *Environmental Damage Costs* (Paris, 1974), p. 51.
13. For a brief review see Raymond F. Dasman, John P. Milton, and Peter H. Freeman, *Ecological Principles for Economic Development* (London: Wiley, 1973). For an empirical investigation of the relation between irrigation projects and the spread of schistosomiasis see Patricia Rosenfield, *Development and Verification of a Schistosomiasis Transmission Model*, USAID (Washington, D.C.: GPO, 1975).
14. For example, see William F. Baxter, "International Implications of an Effluent Tax System: Some Preliminary Observations," *Stanford Journal of International Studies*, 8 (Spring 1973) p. 1.
15. Dales states that soil problems result from "inappropriate property rights" in contrast to air and water problems resulting from the absence of property rights. J.H. Dales, "The Property Interface," in Robert Dorfman and Nancy Dorfman, Eds., *Economics of the Environment* (New York: Norton, 1972) p. 320.
16. William Baumol, "Environmental Protection and the Distribution of Incomes," in Organization for Economic Cooperation and Development, *Problems of Environmental Economics* (Paris, 1972) p. 67.
17. *International Convention for the Prevention of Pollution from Ships*, (1973).
18. This is oversimplified because the welfare effect will also depend on the manner in which pollution abatement is financed.

19. See Chapter 4 for environmental protection and project appraisal.
20. Environmental exploitation is a pejorative term, but natural resource exploitation can mean orderly development.
21. Kneese, Ayres, and d'Arge, *Economics and the Environment*.
22. Adjustments should be made for changes in the stock of goods and for oxygen used in combustion.
23. Water budget analysis has been used by the EPA in the development of water effluent guidelines under the 1972 water pollution control legislation.
24. For a discussion of erosion and silvaculture, see U.S. Environmental Protection Agency, *Processes, Procedures, and Methods to Control Pollution Resulting from Silvacultural Activities*, EPA 430/9-73-010 (Washington, D.C., 1973).
25. Pierre R. Crosson and Kenneth D. Frederick, *The World Food Situation: Resource and Environmental Issues in the Developing Countries and the United States*, in preparation.
26. For example, the most recent forestry code for the Philippines is a model of concern for environment and conservation, but few observers expect good compliance.
27. *The Cocoyoc Declaration*, adopted by the participants in the UNEP/UNCTAD Symposium on "Patterns of Resource Use, Environment and Development Strategies" (Cocoyoc, Mexico, Oct. 8–12, 1974).
28. Robert M. Solow, "The Economics of Resources or the Resources of Economics," *American Economic Review Papers and Proceedings* **64**, No. 2 (May 1974) p. 1.
29. See William D. Schulze, "The Optimal Use of Non-Renewable Resources: The Theory of Extraction," *Journal of Environmental Economics and Management* **1**, No. 1 (May 1974) p. 53.
30. For an excellent case study see Norman Meyers, "The Ecological/Socio-economic Interface of Wildlife Conservation in Emergent Africa: Lakes Nakuru and Naivasha in Kenya," *Journal of Environmental Economics and Management*, **1**, No. 4 (December 1974) p. 319.
31. *Ibid*.
32. For predictive methods see National Academy of Sciences, *Assessing Potential Ocean Pollutants* (Washington, D.C., 1975).
33. Cost differences are confirmed in the Environmental Protection Agency's series of Development Documents establishing water pollution discharge limits. We are not aware of any comprehensive estimate of remedial versus new construction abatement costs.
34. Organization for Economic Cooperation and Development, *Pollution by the Pulp and Paper Industry* (Paris, 1973).

Chapter 2

THE ENVIRONMENTAL LANDSCAPE

This chapter describes the environmental conditions of developing countries and compares the resulting picture with the rest of the world. The chapter helps to group countries by environmental characteristics. Such a grouping is the first step toward answering fundamental questions: Do similar-income-level countries share similar environmental problems? Is the concept of environmental assimilative capacity sufficiently rigorous to use in empirical studies of international trade? How valid is the assertion that developing countries suffer from environmental problems of poverty, whereas rich countries confront problems arising from affluence?

Environmental stress, as the term is used in this study, refers to a *discordance* between man's economic activities and his natural surroundings. The result of the discordance is a deterioration in the quality of the natural surroundings that leads directly or indirectly to a reduction in human welfare. It follows that a description of environmental stress must be concerned with both the natural environment and the economic activities that cause the stress. The need to describe the physical environment is not merely to note the degree of degradation, if any. The physical environment and its characteristics—temperature and rainfall patterns, water systems, soil types, and topography—have a profound influence on the economic and demographic structure of a region. Agricultural practices, industrial structure, population density patterns, and so on are all shaped by the physical environment. And it is precisely the economic and demographic characteristics of a region that determine the types and extent of environmental stresses placed on the physical resources of the region. Indeed, in some cases economic activity can alter major features of the physical environment.

But the point goes further. The biological and chemical consequences of pollution-generating activity and ultimately the economic damages from that activity will be dependent in part on the physical characteristics of the region. For example, soils newly exposed by deforestation will erode more quickly in heavy tropical rains. Organic materials decompose more rapidly in higher temperature media. Air pollutants are more dangerous in regions subject to atmospheric temperature inversions. Therefore, to investigate the consequences of environmentally disruptive activities in different regions, some attention should be given to the physical character of the region itself. Environmental differences (or similarities) between North and South may be due as much to regional climatic and geologic characteristics as to regional economic and demographic structures.

The description, then, should include both the characteristics of the physical environment and the economic activities that place stress on that environment. Also, the material should facilitate a comparison among countries or regions. But how to do that? If the objective were to assemble a comparative picture of the extent of environmental stress in North and South, it might be sufficient to devise a number of indices of ambient environmental quality and present data on measured levels. For example, in the area of water pollution, water quality parameters, such as BOD level, odor, taste, suspended solids, dissolved solids, turbidity, and pH can be identified. Conceptually, these parameters could be measured, weighted, and aggregated to form an index of water quality, and cross-country comparisons could be made.[1] As a practical matter, this is not possible because an adequate data base is not available, especially for developing countries, but also for industrial countries. Nor is it necessarily desirable, for it would not reveal very much about the two factors that give rise to environmental stress: the physical environment and economic (as well as demographic) patterns.

The spatial aspects of environmental problems are central. What is needed is some form of environmental geography, related perhaps to economic geography. With these considerations in mind, international comparative data on three broad groups of variables are included in this chapter: climate, geography, and demography; levels and structures of economic activity; and more direct measures of environmental stress.

The first set of data concerns the climatic and physical character of the developing (mostly tropical) world and compares that with the more developed (mostly temperate) regions. Emphasis is placed on those elements of climate and geography, such as rainfall variability and soil type, which have some environmental significance, either in assisting pollution dispersion or in creating environments particularly sensitive to damage. Climate differences between North and South are striking, but the interpretation of the differences is ambiguous. Still, climate differences play a major role in distinguishing types of environmental problems among regions. At this point it is useful to introduce demographic material, including the distribution of the world's population among climate zones, data on comparative population densities among countries, and some indices of the spatial concentration of populations within countries.

Having set forth material on the physical, climatic and demographic "landscape" of developing countries, the next set of data describes the level and structure of economic activity. Again the choice of variables and the method of presentation is governed by a desire to illustrate how economic activity can threaten environmental quality. If good indices of environmental quality were available, variables concerning economic activity would still be useful in identifying the source of environmental problems. Without these indices, the economic activity variables are proxies for environmental stress.

The final set of variables consists of more direct measures or evidence of pollution and a degraded environment. Included are some elements of the "expanded" definition of environment, or the attributes of poverty.

All this is very ambitious, and some caveats are in order. Data for selected variables are often hard to come by, are open to criticism, and are difficult to present in a way that illuminates the environmental dimension. There are in fact several difficulties. The first concerns the availability and reliability of the data. By and large, data for the United States and some other industrial countries are the most accurate, but even in these countries weaknesses exist—for example, the severity of erosion. The development of UNEP's Global Environmental Monitoring Systems (GEMS) and the landsat satellite system promise to provide a better understanding of environmental features in the future.

The other difficulties are partly presentational—disaggregated data, by country, provide detail but must be consolidated for ready interpretation, whereas regional aggregations provide convenient summaries but conceal important intraregional differences. Also, variables are not spatially uniform within countries, and national averages can conceal important variations. This holds for all three classes of variables—physical environment, economic structure, and the more direct measures of environmental stress. Because the spatial aspect of environmental problems is central, these are serious presentational difficulties. Additionally, for certain variables such as precipitation and riverflows, there are major seasonal variations that have profound environmental impacts. The presentation of comparative data on seasonal variation is not always easy. Finally, the extent of environmental disruption or pollution depends on the pollution controls currently in place. For example, data on gasoline consumption per square kilometer should be adjusted for auto emission devices in use to arrive at a judgment about environmental stress. However, this has not been possible.

These difficulties have been met in a variety of ways. We have relied on the use of maps to summarize information visually, for rapid comparisons among regions, and to indicate densities within countries. Additionally, we have compiled extensive tables in the chapter appendix that present material by country, while summarizing the material in tables that are included in the text. We summarized this data by rather arbitrary geographical groupings, which also generally divide countries economically (except in the case of Japan, which is included in Asia). The reader can refer from regional consolidations to country details in the appendix. Finally, we have experimented with some seasonal and spatial distribution coefficients to capture in a crude fashion the degree of concentration or dispersion.[2]

We take a global approach to the collection and presentation of environmental data. This can conceal intraregional and intracountry variations. An alternative method of environmental geography would be to focus on national or subnational geographic areas. Finally, the numbers themselves should not be taken too seriously. This is particularly true for the regional summaries. However, the concepts that the numbers illustrate, such as seasonal variation in rainfall, remain important.

PHYSICAL AND DEMOGRAPHIC FEATURES

Climate

The inhabitable earth is often divided into two general regions: temperate and tropical.[3] The division is based on temperature, with subdivisions often based on vegetation, rainfall, and latitude. Temperate climates experience frost, and tropical regions are those with year-round temperatures above freezing. The frost line is important in demarking vegetation and crop patterns. It also can effect the life cycle of parasitic diseases such as hookworm, which affect human health and productive effort. To a remarkable extent, the frost line divides the industrial and developing world: no industrial country is wholly in the tropics; few developing coutries are predominantly temperate. The relation between temperature and level of economic development is not clear and has been the subject of considerable speculation.[4]

The tropics can be usefully subdivided by rainfall patterns: dry, wet-dry, humid seasonal, and rainy.[5] Appendix Table 2.1 provides estimates of the climate characteristics of 122 countries. Table 2.1 summarizes tropical climates by continent, and Map 2.2 provides a visual description of climate regions. Table 2.1 indicates that the majority of tropical Asia as well as Latin America, are rainy or humid. Africa has the full spectrum of tropical climates. The seasonal humid (monsoon) and rainy tropics contain the majority of the world's population.

Obviously, countries are not delineated by climate, and several of the larger developing countries, such as China and India, span two or more climate regions. Also, there are a few important departures from the general relation between temperature and level of per capita income, for instance, the subtropical (arid) countries of OPEC and the temperate regions of Argentina and Chile.

Map 2.2 and Table 2.1 use the climate zones devised by Troll. These are extensively used (by the 1967 White House Report on the World Food Problem and the International Crop Research Institute on the Semi-Arid Tropics (ICRISAT), among others), but other divisions are also possible. Grigg, for example, has devised his own divisions based in part on vegetative differences; although these are not directly comparable to Troll, they are useful because of population estimates.[6] Table 2.2 reports world area by Grigg's climate regions as well as population and population density. Although Grigg's monsoon and arid regions include some of what Troll has defined as the subtropics, the picture remains striking. With only one-tenth of the world's land area, monsoon regions contain over half the world's population, with a density of 127 persons/km^2. None of the other tropical regions approach the monsoon region in terms of population density, with savanna regions (13% of land area) having the lowest population (2%) and density (4 persons/km^2). Temperate regions comprise one-third of the world's land surface, contain one-quarter the world's population, and have a density of 17 people/km^2.

It may be useful to mention briefly some general attributes of the various climatic regions that have environmental significance. In general, the tropical zones are capable of year-round planting. However, there may be serious variations in rainfall. Both the desert and the wet and dry regions (as well as subtropical arid) have serious rainfall deficiencies, either in absolute or month-by-month terms. Soils are not usually as leached of nutrients in the desert and wet-dry regions as they are in the wetter parts of the tropics, but irrigation usually is necessary to exploit their fertility. Major environmental stresses in these regions are often salinization, water logging, erosion, and desertification. Arid regions support a low population density, although there

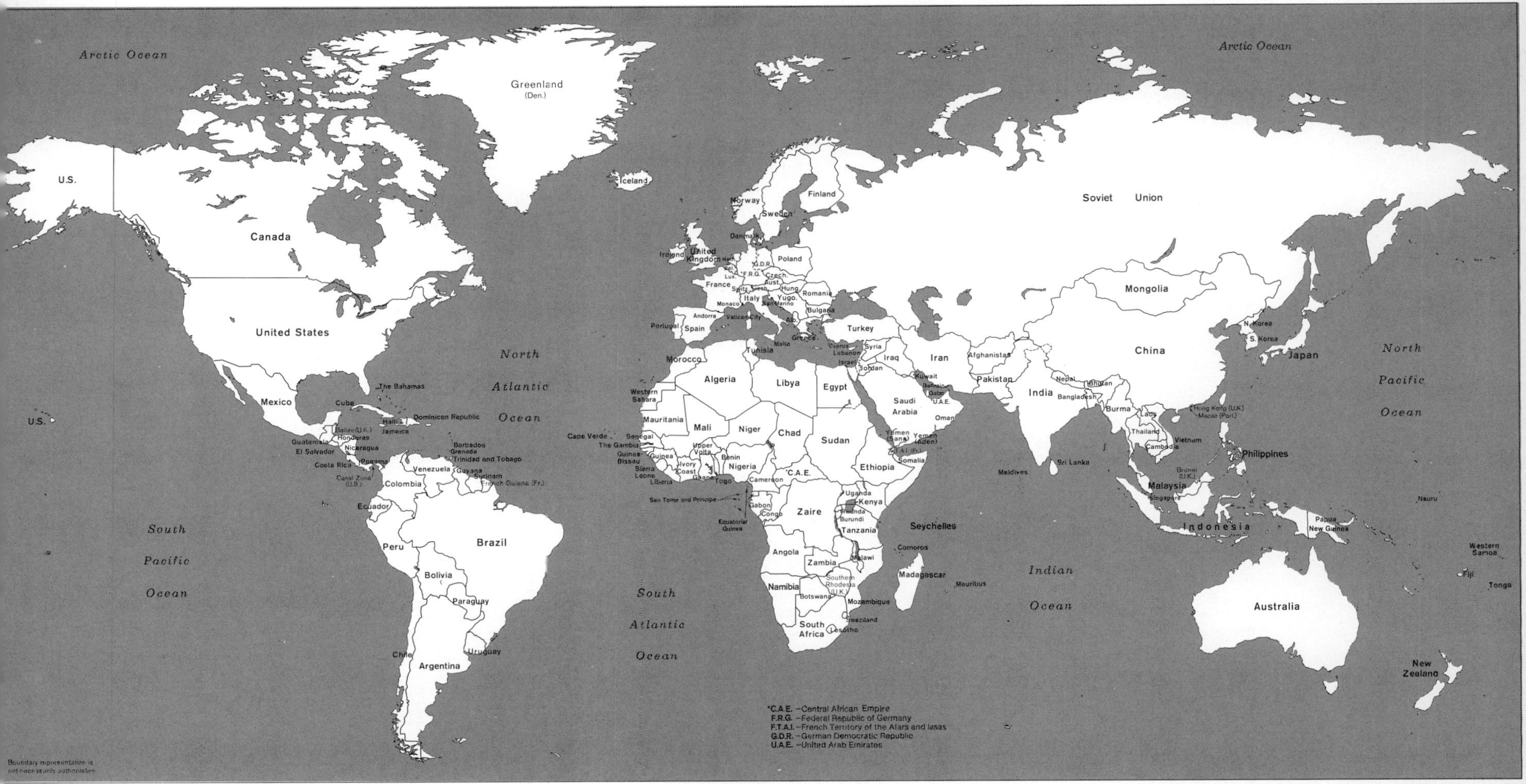

*C.A.E. –Central African Empire
F.R.G. –Federal Republic of Germany
F.T.A.I. –French Territory of the Afars and Issas
G.D.R. –German Democratic Republic
U.A.E. –United Arab Emirates

Boundary representation is not necessarily authoritative

518335 12-76

Map 2.1. World-political divisions.

Table 2.1 Percentage Distribution of Climatic Zones by Region

	Regions							
Climatic Zones	Africa	Latin America	Middle East	Asia	North America	Western Europe	Eastern Europe	Oceania
Tropical total	76	76	21	45	0	0	0	47
Desert	11	0	16	0	0	0	0	18
Dry, wet and dry	40	16	3	11	0	0	0	23
Humid	16	30	2	20	0	0	0	3
Rainy	9	30	0	14	0	0	0	3
Temperate subtropical total	24	23	68	20	10	22	0	51
Arid	22	8	58	2	2	1	0	43
Humid	2	15	10	18	8	21	0	8
Total tropical and temperate subtropical	100	99	89	65	10	22	0	98
Temperate cool and cold	0	1	11	35	90	78	100	2

Source. Based on Troll et al., "Climatic Zones," in *World Maps of Climatology* (Berlin: Springer-Verlag, 1966).

(Because of rounding, tropical desert zones in Latin America and temperate subtropical-humid zones in Eastern Europe are missing from the summary table. See Appendix Table A2.2).

Unless otherwise noted the summary tables are divided by regions as shown in the appendix tables. People's Republic of China is in "Asia," the Soviet Union is in "Eastern Europe." In some tables, these two countries will be included under Centrally Planned Economies. In others, where the division is between developed and developing countries, the USSR will be listed under developed and the CPC under developing. All countries with populations larger than 1 million in 1973 (except for the Republic of the Congo, Lesotho, Bhutan, and Trinidad and Tobago) are listed. Data are not necessarily complete for all tables.

CLIMATIC ZONES

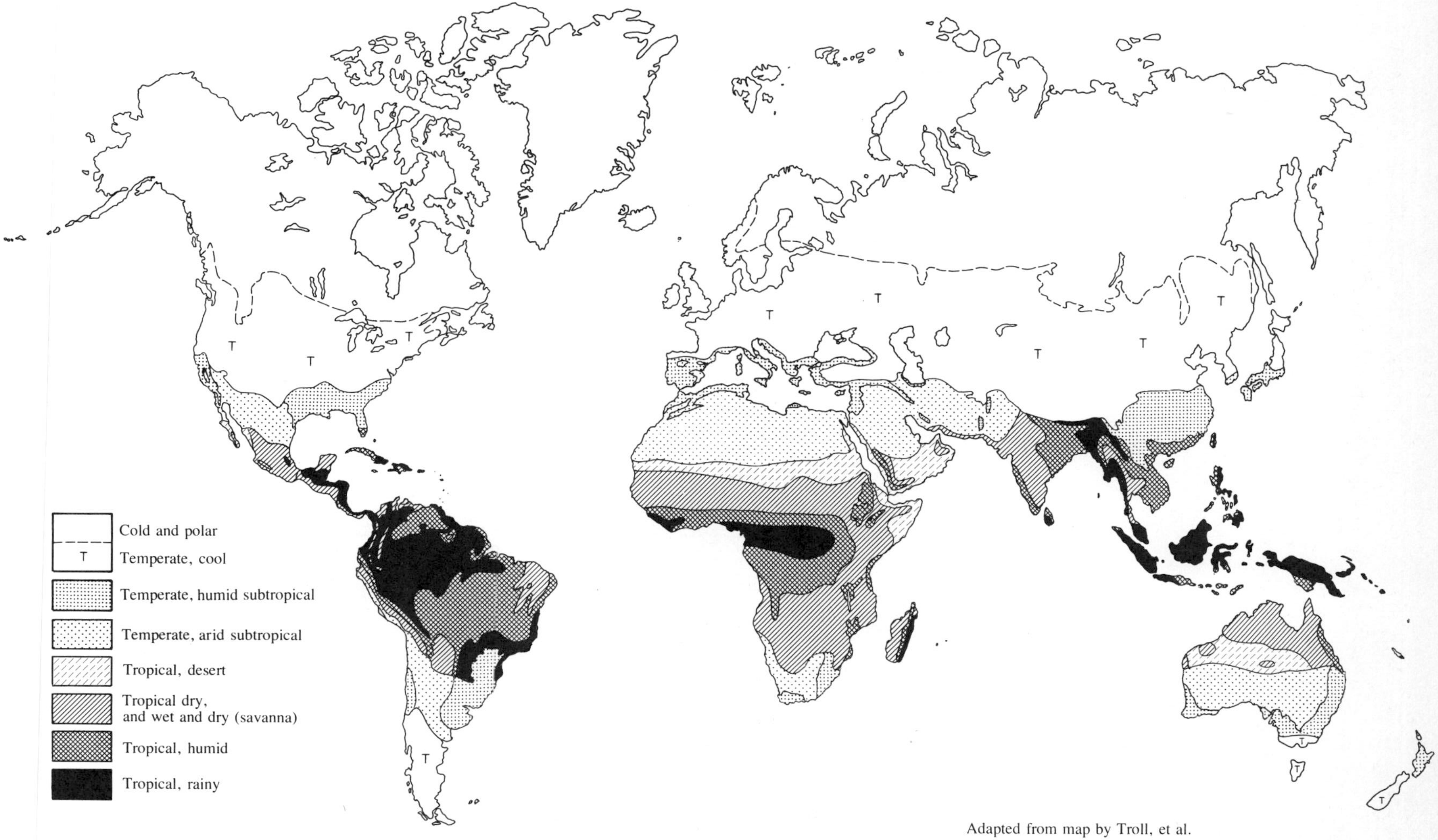

Adapted from map by Troll, et al.

Map 2.2. Climate zones.

Table 2.2 World Population by Climate Region

Climate Region	Year	Percentage World Area	Percentage World Population	Population Density (persons per km²)
Monsoon	1966	10	55	127.0
Humid tropics	1966	9	6	18.3
Arid, semi-arid	1960	36	13	7.9
Savanna	1960	13	2	4.0
Temperate	1960	32	24	17.0

Source. Derived from Grigg, *The Harsh Lands.*

Densities are only approximations. The climate region divisions are based on Grigg and do not correspond to those used in Map 2.2, Table 2.1 or Appendix Table 2.2.

are significant localized zones of concentration. In parts of the Middle East, human habitation has brought severe problems due to overgrazing of livestock and the continued gathering of firewood. As is obvious on the map, Troll's definition excludes much of the Middle East from the tropics, but it should be noted that many similar problems will be encountered in all of the world's arid regions, temperate through tropical.

The other two major regions in the tropics are distinctly separate from the drier regions. The rainy tropics receive an abundance of rain and generally do not have serious water constraints. There are some serious problems, however, arising from the large quantity of rainfall as well as the large amount of solar energy received. These include potentially severe leaching and erosion and other environmental consequences of economic activity. The rainy tropics, although lightly populated, are often characterized as particularly fragile.

Tropical humid regions in general have distinctive rainfall patterns of wet and dry seasons. However, tremendous variation exists within this region, which includes Bangladesh, Sri Lanka, Southeast Asia, parts of China, Pakistan, and India, as well as segments of Africa and Latin America. The Asian segment of the humid tropics supports the vast bulk of the South's population. This is due in large part to the ability of farmers to grow rice in these regions, which is made possible by an abundance of water and alluvial soils. Agriculturally, these regions, with a fair amount of fertile land and abundant (although seasonal) rainfall, are highly productive and are not severely limited by internal environmental problems. However, they also support a large and growing population, one which eventually may cause severe problems even in these fairly fertile areas.

We do not pretend that the world can be neatly divided into seven "climates," for even small countries have many distinct climate regions and ecosystems. We have used Troll's divisions solely for the sake of convenience in aggregation, fully aware that a range of climatic regimes exists between and within our generalized set. It is also obvious that our data tell nothing about population densities by climatic zones by country. Approximations have been attempted in the past, but we feel that such a task, based on a series of estimations, would be treacherous here. A brief comparison of Maps 2.2 and 2.5 will be helpful. Our main point in presenting the material is to graphically demonstrate the great variety between and within regions, both geographic and economic. Contrary to some popular views, most developing countries do not have the rain forest conditions of the rainy tropics.

One climatic region that we are unable to show on our map are mountainous regions. Not only do these have unique climatic features, but they are also extraordinarily important in terms of environmental problems. The consequences of population growth in these areas are often more serious than those in the lowland areas. Overpopulation in the mountain areas can cause severe erosion that will effect both the mountain areas and the lowland areas further downstream.

Detailed descriptions of climatic differences and their effect on agricultural potential and economic development, as well as possible environmental problems, can be found in other works.[7] In Chapter 6 we discuss in some detail the environmental consequences of agriculture in the various tropical climatic regions. It is beyond the scope of this chapter to analyze the differences between climatic regions for all our indices. However, climate differences are often ignored in work on environment and development and deserve concerted research.

Rainfall

Rainfall and temperature are the two major features of climate. Like temperature data, comparative data on rainfall are difficult to present and interpret because they vary within regions, from one season to another, and from one year to another. Map 2.3, based on average annual rainfall data, illustrates variations among countries and regions. Data on average annual precipitation for selected weather stations in various countries are presented in Appendix Table A2.3. Table 2.3 attempts to consolidate this information. Column one, which is the simple (unweighted) average of the annual rainfall of these stations in the countries within a region, shows that precipitation is almost consistently higher in the developing world than in the industrial world. The only exception is the arid Middle East. Computation of the standard deviation of these regional averages, reported in column two, indicates that deviations are more substantial in the developing areas. Accordingly, our limited data indicate that the industrial countries have more uniform and generally lower annual rainfall than developing countries. These conclusions, however, are dependent on the selection of weather stations and might be incorrect if the full distribution of rainfall within countries could be measured. Also, stations are mostly in urban centers and may not reflect weather patterns in agricultural areas.

Annual averages conceal the degree of irregularity in rainfall throughout the year. As noted below, the seasonal variation in rainfall has a profound impact on agriculture and environmental conditions. One way to present cross-country comparisons of seasonal variation in rainfall is to construct an index measuring the concentration of rainfall during the year and to compare the concentration coefficient among countries.[8] Monthly data on rainfall for 105 countries (and 132 individual stations) were obtained, and the seasonal concentration coefficient for each country (station) was computed. The results are reported in Appendix Table A2.3. The highest concentration is for Mauritania, .654, and

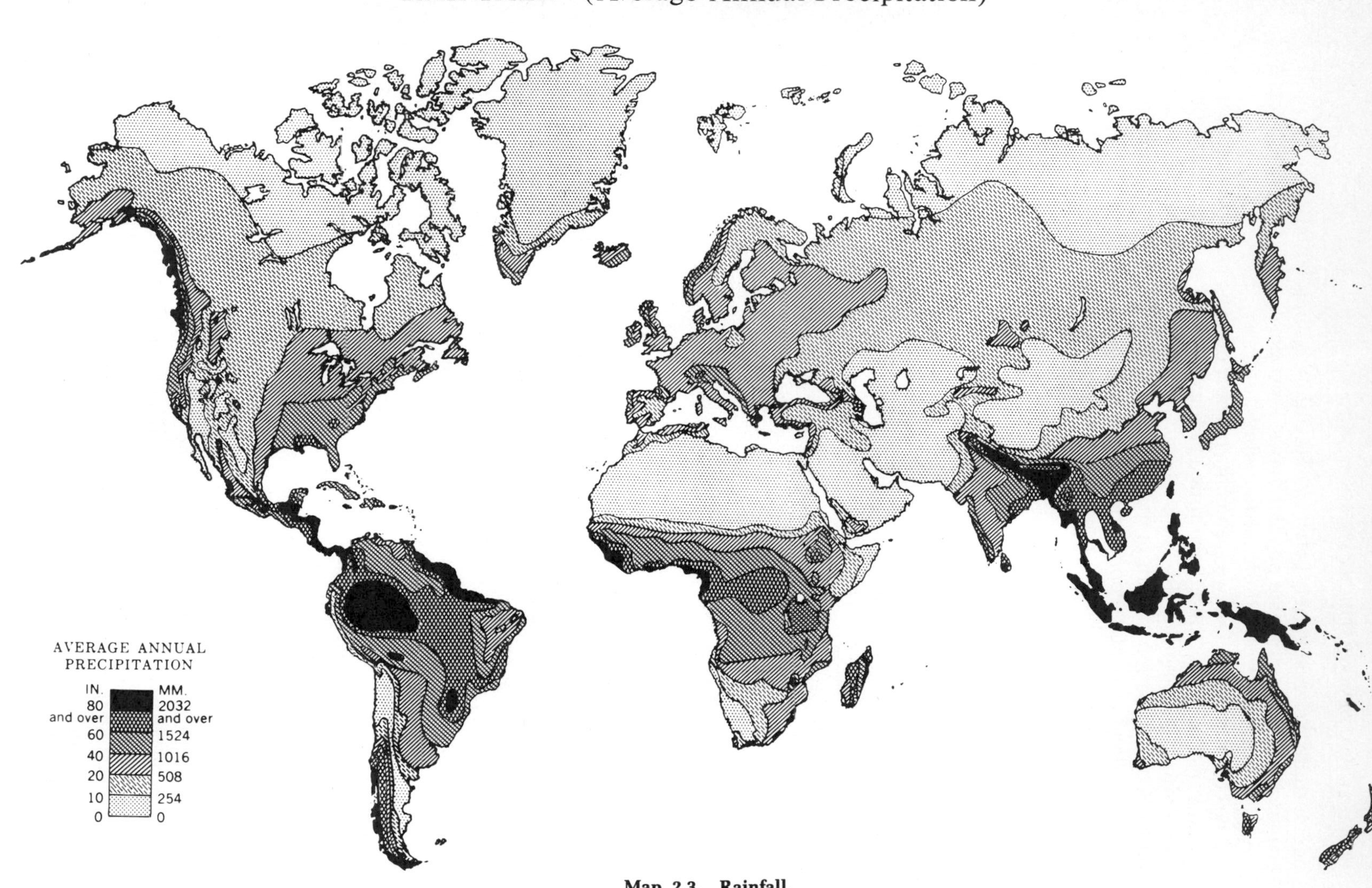

Map 2.3. Rainfall.

Table 2.3 Rainfall Data by Region, 1930–1960 (Selected Stations)

Region	Average Annual Rainfall[a] (mm)	Standard Deviation[b]	Seasonal Rainfall Concentration Coefficient[c]	Standard Deviation[d]
Africa	1070	972	.410	.077
Latin America	1119	912	.351	.044
Middle East	332	292	.393	.038
Asia	1368	685	.389	.055
North America	795	400	.326	.044
W. Europe	638	131	.305	.016
E. Europe[e]	578	235	.311	.017
Oceania	948	292	.322	.051

Source. Appendix Table A2.3.

[a] Simple average of national averages within region.

[b] Standard deviation of country averages from regional average.

[c] Coefficient measuring the concentration of rainfall within a year. See text footnote 8 for details.

[d] Standard deviation of country coefficients from region coefficient.

[e] Excludes Soviet Union.

the lowest concentration, or most seasonally evenly distributed rainfall, is for Australia (Melbourne) at .290, followed by Canada (Ottawa) at .291. Columns three and four of Table 2.3 attempt to consolidate this information for larger regions (excluding the Soviet Union). The highest concentration coefficients are for Africa (.410), Middle East (.393), Asia (.389), and Latin America (.351). On the basis of stations included, all industrial areas have lower concentration coefficients, indicating more uniform rainfall across seasons. Column four, which reports the standard deviation for the countries within a region, indicates that Africa exhibits the most diversity with respect to seasonal concentration of rainfall, and Eastern and Western Europe the least. It appears that industrial countries enjoy greater uniformity of rainfall throughout the year than developing countries, and they are more uniform among themselves with respect to seasonal rainfall distribution than developing countries. However, the strength of these conclusions is limited. Rainfall data collection is site specific, and we have not found a measure that adjusts for variations in rainfall within countries. Second, our data represent a small fraction of total available stations, although we did choose major population concentrations. Also, precipitation data do not display the seasonal storage and release of water through snow accumulation.

There is a third method for presenting precipitation information that is somewhat more complex than average annual data or seasonal concentration coefficients. It is more directly useful for water availability analysis of particular regions than for cross-country comparative purposes. The basic concept is to compare on a monthly basis the actual level of precipitation and the potential evapo-transpiration of water (evaporation plus transpiration from vegetation) that would take place if there were an adequate moisture supply. An adjustment is then made for changes in water storage in soils—upward with an excess of precipitation over evaporation or downward when evaporation exceeds rainfall. The result is a time profile measure of water surplus or deficit. A water deficit period involves a gap between actual precipitation and potential evaporation that is partly offset by drawing down water storage buildup in soils and impoundments.[9]

This approach is particularly interesting because it captures the impact of seasonal fluctuations in evaporation rates, as solar energy, temperature, and wind velocity wax and wane. It also must include soil structure in determining the distribution of excess water between soil retention and surface runoff and must look at the water release properties of soils. Appendix Table A2.4 reports a water balance study by Subrahmanyam for four locations in South Asia and comparative data for four cities in developed countries. A comparison of two cities, Calcutta and Rangoon, is instructive. Both exhibit water surplus during the summer months and water deficits from mid-fall to mid-spring, but the intensity of deficit and surplus in Rangoon (reaching 11.7 and 42.3 cm, respectively) is much more pronounced than in Calcutta (with a maximum surplus of 17.0 cm). This is not explained by differences in potential evaporation rates, since the range for Rangoon (10.8 cm in January to 17.6 cm in May) is less than the range for Calcutta (3.7 cm for December to 18.5 cm for May). The explanation is in the differences in precipitation range (0.3–58.0 cm for Rangoon, 0.5–33.8 cm for Calcutta) and the differences in the range of storage change (−6.8 − +13.6 cm for Rangoon, −5.4 − +11.8 cm for Calcutta).

The time profiles of water balances—surplus and deficits—and other measures of rainfall levels and variability have direct and indirect environmental consequences. It would appear that the extremes of annual rainfall, low or high, and extreme concentration of rainfall may produce the greatest environmental stress on land resources. Erosion may be most severe in situations of high-level, concentrated rainfall (and at the same time account for higher levels of nutrient leaching from soils) and in semi-arid climates where ground cover is light, surface water runoff levels are high, and water courses are highly seasonal.[10] Less directly, rainfall levels and seasonal patterns effect the type of agriculture, including the need for irrigation. Hence cropping patterns, nutrient requirements, water logging, and salination are indirectly related to rainfall levels and variability. Again, highly concentrated rainfall presumably increases the need for irrigation, although it is quite possible for crops to be grown during the dry season using ground water built up from the wet months.

Finally, the level and seasonal distribution of rainfall are a rough measure of the ability of the physical environment to dilute, disperse, and render pollutants harmless. The illustrations are most direct with air pollution, where rain can literally wash or flush the atmosphere. (However, atmospheric sulfur dioxide may wash out as sulfuric acid, with adverse effects on terrestrial biota.) In addition, the level and variability of river flows relative to rainfall patterns is a measure of flushing properties. The variability of river flow also affects the need for irrigation reservoirs. When considering the cleansing function of rainfall, an even distribution would seem most desirable and high concentration less desirable. Accordingly, the earlier conclusions from the data—that industrial countries tend to have midrange annual rainfall levels, that the rain tends toward even seasonal distribution, and that developing countries tend to have extremes of annual rainfall levels, with seasonal concentration—suggest that developing countries confront greater inherent environmental stress on land resources. They also may have a smaller endowment of assimilative capacity (in terms of water) to absorb pollutants than industrial countries. The latter point is examined in greater detail in Chapter 3.

Obviously, rainfall level and variability are only two aspects of assimilative capacity. In fact, the dispersal of air-borne pollutants is probably affected more by the lack of rain and by air flow patterns. Although some air pollution, notably sulfur dioxide, is removed by rainfall, a more complete analysis should include data on wind velocity and variability, topographical features, and the frequency of thermal inversions.[11]

River Flows

River flow data, like rainfall, should be included in a description of the physical environment of developing countries. Like rainfall, the seasonal variation of river flows is perhaps as important as the annual average. Great seasonal variations in flow levels are generally undesirable for two reasons. First, rivers are used to assimilate and disperse wastes from industrial and urban centers. Rivers that experience periods of extreme low flow may easily become overloaded with wastes. For example, the dissolved oxygen levels necessary to support certain fish species may be exhausted by organic discharges, or other desired water quality parameters, such as suspended solids, acidity, and so on, may be unattainable. If waste discharges show little seasonal variation, the cost of maintaining water quality standards will be less with uniform flow rates. If dimensions of assimilative capacity were being measured, one would be the volume of water flow per unit of land surface, with some adjustment for seasonal variation.

In addition, great variability in river flow would suggest that water erosion and flooding problems are more extreme, although the topography of river channels would also be important. Some of the richest soils are, of course, produced and replenished through regular flooding as alluvial deposits are built up. Still, uncontrolled flooding causes erosion, and damages crops and physical structures, including roadbeds and bridges. High water can carry much larger silt loads, affecting navigation channels and shortening the life span of hydroelectric reservoirs and irrigation impoundments. It can also contaminate water supplies.[12]

The obverse proposition is that environmentally unsound practices, especially careless deforestation and destruction of ground cover, leads to increased extremes of river flow. This has been asserted for the United States and a few developing countries, including Tanzania.[13] An ideal set of data on river flows might include the following:

- Annual flow volume, adjusted for seasonal variation, by country and expressed per unit of land surface. This would indicate assimilative and dispersive capacity for waste disposal.
- The amount of industrial effluents per unit river flow (adjusted for seasonal variation) to indicate the extent to which assimilative capacity is being used (or abused). Alternately, direct measures of water quality by area would be useful.
- Long-run data by country on flood levels and frequency to test the

hypothesis that deforestation and other damaging agricultural practices have increased downstream flooding.

- Long-run data by country and river on sediment loads to verify trends in soil erosion.

These data are not available in ideal form. However, we have assembled information on drainage areas, flow rates, and seasonal variation for 33 major rivers, 15 in developed and 18 in developing countries. The data on seasonal variation, measured by the ratio of average monthly high flow to low flow, recorded in Table 2.4, show an interesting pattern. The average high–low ratio for developed country rivers is 6.2; the average for developing countries is 26.2 excluding the Senegal and 50.4 including that river. Of the great rivers measured, the Mississippi, the Parana, the Ganges, and the Mekong, the ratios are 4, 3, 22, and 14, respectively. The United States and Western European rivers exhibit the most uniform flows. The table also calculates a concentration coefficient for regularity of river flow similar to the rainfall concentration index. The average coefficient for developed countries, .341, is less than for developing countries, .392, and is consistent with the variation between the two regions as measured by the ratio of high to low flow. On the basis of this imperfect information, it appears that the industrial countries enjoy greater uniformity of river flow, as they do seasonal rainfall.

Eckholm has discussed the role of shifting cultivation and loss of forest cover for firewood and charcoal in intensifying river variability. He concludes that seasonal variation and flooding is increasing in some regions for these reasons. We have examined UNESCO's river flow data, covering 50 years for some rivers, but have been unable to discern any major trends in gross annual flow, seasonal concentration, or in extreme highs and lows. The UNESCO long-term material covers a number of rivers listed in Table 2.4. Part of the reason for the absence of corroborative results may be that measuring stations are generally on the lower reaches of larger rivers accounting for a far larger drainage area, for changes in seasonal variability should be more pronounced closer to the headwaters and on smaller tributary streams.[14]

Having examining rainfall, river flows, and water balances, it is useful to briefly discuss the global location of runoff. Tables 2.5 and 2.6 show the distribution of total runoff in the world. Note in Table 2.5 the large amount of water relative to land area available in South America and the relatively small amount available in Africa. Also, compare the percentage of total land area for the various regions with the total amount of river runoff. South America has approximately 27% of total runoff compared to only 13% of land area. Asia has exactly the same percentage for both, 34%, whereas Africa is estimated to account for only 11% of total runoff while having 23% of the world's land area. It is also interesting to note that South America has a higher percentage of the total ground water runoff of the world than the total surface water runoff of the world, whereas Asia has precisely the reverse. The percentage of ground water runoff to total runoff in Asia is only 26%, for South America it is 36%. The only other region with a lower ratio is Oceania. The low percentage for Asia could be due to the fact that much of the rainfall goes into surface runoff rather than into ground water. The ratio of total runoff to total precipitation is larger in Asia than anywhere else except, surprisingly, Europe.

Table 2.6 shows average annual runoff figures for a sample of countries both

Table 2.4 Selected River Flows–Average Monthly High and Low Flows and Concentration
(Average 1965–1968[a])

River and Country[b]	Drainage Area (km^2)	Average Monthly Flow (m^3/sec)	Average Monthly High	Average Monthly Low	Ratio of High to Low	Concentration Coefficient[c]	Stations	UNESCO Coordinates
Sanaga, Cameroon	135,000	2,109	5,500	347	16	.373	Edea	BA 03
Tana, Kenya	32,890	256	622	66	9	.351	Garissa	Da 90
Niger, Niger	NA	1,109	2,072	75	28	.347	NA	NA
Senegal, Senegal	232,000	944	4,620	10	462	.518	Bakel	dB 24
Parana, Argentina	975,380	13,770	22,305	7527	3	.305	Posadas	fc 57
Paraiba, Brazil	55,800	1,000	2,519	348	7	.344	Campos	ec 11
Parana, Brazil	806,000	10,777	18,549	5432	3	.309	Guaira	fc 44
Pacuno, Mexico	58,000	444	1,294	109	12	.407	Las Adjuntas	jC 81
Santiago, Mexico	128,000	357	1,165	54	54	.447	El Campomal	kC 51
Uruguay, Uruguay	238,900	5.109	10,667	1740	6	.349	Salto	Fd 71
Euphrates, Turkey	63,800	798	2,566	252	10	.390	Keban	DD 88
Ganges, India	951,600	9,518	36,437	1673	22	.448	NA	NA
Godivari, India[d]	299,320	1,084	14,308	58	245	.512	Dowlaishwaram	IB 06
Tista, India	NA	581	1,602	109	15	.391	NA	NA
Yodo, Japan	7,280	493	1,299	165	8	.349	Hirakate	ND 54
Han, Korea	24,045	478	1,848	109	17	.428	Indogyo	MD 67
Perak, Malaysia	7,700	333	919	128	7	.359	Iskorder Bridge	IB 06
Cho-Shui, Taiwan	2,300	120	343	34	10	.376	Salto	Fd 71
Mekong Thailand	391,000	8,092	23,224	1646	14	.392	Mukdahan	KB 76
North Saskatchewan, Canada	119,500	295	850	56	15	.376	Prince Albert	kF 53
St. Lawrence, Canada	766,000	6,432	7,295	6000	1.2	.294	Cornwall	hE 45
Colorado, USA	NA	100	653	215	3	.326	NA	ID 16
Delaware, USA	17,600	209	456	83	5	.335	Trenton, New Jersey	hE 40

Table 2.4 (Continued)

River and Country[b]	Drainage Area (km^2)	Average Monthly Flow (m^3/sec)	Average Monthly High	Average Monthly Low	Ratio of High to Low	Concentration Coefficient[c]	Stations	UNESCO Coordinates
Missouri, USA	NA	153	943	343	2	.308	Yankton, South Dakota	jE 72
Mississippi, USA	NA	15,705	30,890	7473	4	.318	Talbot Landing, Louisiana	jD 11
Ohio, USA	236,000	6,808	15,770	2391	7	.345	Metropolis, Illinois	iD 8740
Red of the North, USA	NA	209	630	83	8	.455	Grand Forks, North Dakota	jE 77
Rio Grande, USA	NA	81	266	30	9	.362	Laredo, Texas	jC 97
Sacramento, USA	NA	742	1,606	338	5	.330	Sacramento, California	mD 18
Seine, France	44,320	321	890	80	11	.360	Paris	AE 28
Rhine, Germany	159,680	3,025	5,203	1707	3	.303	Rees	AF 61
Maas, Netherlands	28,900	517	1,422	159	9	.347	Lith	AF 51
Tevere, Italy	16,500	246	406	125	3	.308	Rome	BE 21

Source. UNESCO, *Discharge of Selected Rivers of the World*, Vol. I, II and III, 1971, 1973.

[a] 1965–1968 is preliminary. Like rainfall, river flow data should be an average of a much longer period to avoid cyclical precipitation changes.

[b] According to UNESCO, "Dams, water works diversions and similar works have been built on many rivers of the world and there will be still more of these works as time goes on. The discharges measured in gauging stations must therefore be adjusted to derive the 'natural discharges'. It is these natural discharges (calculated when necessary) which are shown in the present volume." (Vol. I, p. 15) Whether this is entirely true, of course, is impossible to estimate.

[c] The concentration coefficient for the ith river is

$$C_i = \sqrt{\sum\left(\frac{F_{ij}}{F_i}\right)^2}$$

where F_{ij} is the average flow of the ith river in the jth month, and F_i is the average annual flow rate for the ith river.

[d] Godivari data from 1905 to 1968.

Table 2.5 World Water Runoff

			Percent World Total					
	Units	World Total[a]	Africa	South America[b]	Asia[c]	North America[d]	Europe[e]	Oceania
Area	$km^2 \times 10^6$	132.3	23	13	34	16	7	7
Precipitation	km^3	110,303.0	19	27	30	13	6	6
Total river runoff[f]	km^3	38,830.0	11	27	34	15	8	5
Groundwater runoff	km^3	11,885.0	12	31	29	15	9	4
Surface water runoff	km^3	26,945.0	10	25	36	16	8	6
Total soil moisture[g]	km^3	83,360.0	22	27	27	12	6	6
Evaporation	km^3	71,475.0	23	27	27	11	6	6
Ratio of regional per capita runoff to world average per capital runoff[h]		1.00	1.12	5.13	.59	1.75	.44	1.00
Groundwater runoff as percentage total runoff	%	31	35	36	26	32	34	24
Coefficients of runoff[i]	%	36	23	35	40	31	43	31
Stable runoff as percentage total runoff[j]	%	36	45	38	30	40	43	23

Source. Adapted from Frits van der Leeden, *Water Resources of the World: Selected Statistics* (Water Information Center, 1975).

[a] Does not include Greenland, Canadian archipelago, and Antarctica.
[b] Excludes Central America.
[c] Includes Middle East.
[d] Includes Central America.
[e] Includes Eastern Europe and USSR.
[f] Equals total of groundwater and surface water runoff.
[g] Equals precipitation minus surface water runoff.
[h] World per capita in 1969 equals 1.00.
[i] Total runoff as percentage of total precipitation.
[j] Stable runoff, excluding flood flows, equals runoff "of underground origin, regulated by lakes, and regulated by water reservoirs."

Table 2.6 River Runoff in Selected Countries

	Billions of Cubic Meters	Thousands of Cubic Meters		
Country	Average Annual Runoff	Runoff Per Capita	Runoff Per Km^2	Runoff Per Dollar of GNP (US$)
Malagasy R.	337	42.13	574.1	234.03
Argentina	750	29.53	270.1	15.99
Brazil	5190	47.31	609.7	55.70
Mexico	390	6.59	197.8	6.71
Venezuela	700	57.38	765.0	35.30
Egypt	84	2.24	83.8	8.33
Burma	1069	34.26	1576.7	394.46
China (PR)	2620	3.18	273.0	10.66
India	1678	2.74	513.5	21.24
Thailand	220	5.23	428.0	18.12
Canada	2267	99.43	227.2	16.60
USA	1630	7.62	174.1	1.16
France	200	3.78	365.6	0.73
Italy	159	2.88	528.2	1.04
USSR	4340	17.02	193.7	7.45
Australia	345	25.00	44.9	5.44

Source. Adapted from Framji and Mahajan, *Irrigation and Drainage in the World* (New Delhi, 1969).

in the developing and developed world. These figures are then compared with population, area, and GNP data. Again, these figures, without some analysis of the spatial location of runoff as well as industry, are inadequate to describe the "assimilative capacity" of one area compared to another, yet the figures are instructive. There are countries in the developing world that have low levels of runoff per capita, runoff per unit area, as well as runoff per dollar of GNP; Egypt is the most interesting. Also, as one would assume, runoff per dollar of GNP is quite low for a number of developed countries (although note should be made of Canada). However, runoff per capita in some of these sample developing countries is fairly low. If one considers problems of "poverty," relating as much to the number of people as to the per capita levels of income, perhaps a per capita runoff figure is more instructive of relative available runoff in developing countries versus developed countries. Also, the developing countries have more variation in rainfall during the year; thus the average figures overestimate the amount available at particular times of the year.

Our evidence does not support any conclusions regarding trends in flow volume or variability. The conclusion from available information is that rivers in developing countries do not tend to have as great an assimilative capacity as those in industrial countries if seasonal variation of rainfall and river flows are accepted as measures of that capacity.

In addition to material on river flow volume and variability, some data are available on sediment loads. They should be considered together with the discussion of erosion found later in this chapter. It is estimated that 68% of the world's land surface, or about 40 million square miles, contributes to sediment runoff to the oceans. The balance of the land surface is either under permanent ice or lacks surface runoff ultimately contributing to the oceans because of evaporation. Various estimates of sediment loads reaching the oceans range from 14 to 64 billion short tons per year. According to Holeman, 20 billion short tons would cover France, Belgium, the Netherlands, Luxembourg, Switzerland, and Portugal with an inch of mud. The amount of sediment that finally reaches the ocean in any given year is only a fraction of the total amount of soil actually eroded. Holeman reports that one study in the Potomac River watershed estimated that "only about 5% of the products of erosion in this watershed reach tidewater."[15]

Sediment loads, measured either absolutely (by weight) as tons per km^2 of drainage area or as a fraction of the volume of water discharge, appear to vary considerably among continents. Holeman estimates that Asia contributes up to 80% of the global load reaching the oceans. The absolute tonnage and tonnage per square mile of drainage area, by continent, are shown in Table 2.7. Table 2.8 displays, for 24 major rivers on four continents:

- Sediment loads to the oceans in tons per square mile of drainage area.
- Discharge of water at the mouth in thousands of cubic feet per second.
- The percentage of discharged water consisting of suspended sediments.
- Measures of river variability, when available.

What causes the large disparity in sediment loads? More rain per year may produce greater erosion unless the rain permits heavy ground cover sufficient to limit erosion. Also, rivers that flow directly from mountainous regions, such as the Himalayan South Asian rivers, or through alluvial material, such as many of China's rivers, may cause heavy erosion. This is especially relevent

Table 2.7 Average Annual Sediment Loads to the Oceans by Continent

	Tons per Square Mile of Drainage Area	Extrapolated Total Sediment (10^9 tons)
North America	245	1.96
South America	160	1.20
Africa	70	0.54
Australia	115	0.23
Europe	90	0.32
Asia	1530	15.91
World total		20.16

Source: "The Sediment Yield of Major Rivers of the World," in J. N. Holeman, *Water Resources Research* (August 1968). Holeman's sample represents more than 30% of the sediment carried by rivers. His extrapolation should be considered as only an estimate of the general orders of magnitude differences between continents. As mentioned in the text, there have been many estimates of total sediment flows, with studies reviewed by Holeman ranging from 16 to 64 × 10^9 tons. See also J. Gilluly, "Geologic Contrasts Between Continents and Ocean Basins," *Geolog. Soc. Am. Spec.*, Paper 62, 1955 and F. Fournier, Climate et Erosion, Paris: Presses Universitaires de France, 1960).

Table 2.8 Sediment Loads and Water Discharges for Selected Rivers

River	Average Annual Suspended Load in Tons per Square Mile of Drainage Area[a]	Average Water Discharge at Mouth[b] (10^3 ft^3/sec)	Average Percentage of Water Discharge Consisting of Suspended Load[c]	Seasonal Concentration Coefficient[d]	High-low Ratio of River Flow[e]
Mississippi	277	630	0.058	.318	4
St. Lawrence	8	500	0.0008	.294	1.2
Colorado	1082	6	2.90	.326	3
Rio Grande	352	3	0.37	.362	9
Potomac	170	11	0.024	NA	NA
Delaware	147	20	0.0052	.335	5
Amazon	170	6400	0.0066	NA	NA
Parana	100	526	0.018	.309	3
Uruguay	100	140	0.011	.347	6
Congo	46	1400	0.0054	NA	NA
Nile	100	100	0.013	NA	NA
Niger	12	215	0.024	.347	28
Danube	40	218	0.010	NA	NA
Rhine (mouth)	9	78	0.0007	.303	3

Rhine (Lake Constance)	2094	NA	NA	NA	NA
Loire	10	30	0.016	NA	NA
Seine	71	NA	NA	.360	11
Tiber	1005	NA	NA	NA	NA
Ganges	4000	498	0.30	.448	22
Yantze	1400	770	0.076	NA	NA
Indus	1300	239	0.21	NA	NA
Yellow	7545	53	4.15	NA	NA
Bramaputra	3700	706	0.12	NA	NA
Mekong	1240	530	0.037	.392	14

Sources.

[a] John N. Holeman, "The Sediment Yield of Major Rivers of the World," in *Water Resources Research* (1968).

[b] *Ibid.*

[c] *Ibid.*, using the conversion factor of 1 ton of suspended sediment equaling 33.3 ft^3.

[d] From Table 2.4.

[e] From Table 2.4.

NA — not available.

when coupled with variable, heavy rainfall as occurs in monsoon Asia. Latin America has a number of large rivers, but sediment loads are modest. (This may not hold for the short, turbulent West Coast rivers fed by the Andes.) Although the Amazon contributes between 11 and 18% of the world's fresh water discharge to the oceans, it "transports only about 2% of the sediment reaching the oceans annually," and 82% of this is from the Andes mountains.[16] Sediment loads for the African rivers are estimated to be very low: measured in tons per square mile of drainage area, the figures are 46 for the Congo, 100 for the Nile, and 12 for the Niger.[17]

The European rivers are small on a world scale and carry low sediment loads to the oceans. This is partly due to sediment removal in upper reaches (for example, with the Rhine at Lake Constance) and in part because "erosion is not a big problem in Europe . . . rainfall is distributed well throughout the year, and low intensity, gentle rains are typical."[18] The Asian river systems, especially the Yellow River in China and the Ganges and Brahmaputra of India, carry vast amounts of sediment. Eleven of the 16 rivers examined that carry more than 10^8 tons are located in South Asia. These rivers have high loads in part because of the erosion rates inherent in the Himalayan highlands "because of the high relief and monsoon climate."[19] The Kosi, a tributary of the Ganges, carries the same average yearly load as the Nile and Congo rivers combined.

Considering that Asia, with one-quarter of the world's land surface, contributes 80% of sediment loads and considering its dominant position in world population, the importance of environmental stress on the Himalayan region from increased population densities, deforestation, and other factors should not be ignored. At the present time there is not enough information to determine if the naturally massive sediment flows in this region have increased or have become more variable because of human actions. In any event, rapid sedimentation of irrigation systems and hydroelectric reservoirs will continue to be a problem. Sediments catchment in irrigation projects or dam sites should be inherently greater in Asia than elsewhere. Even in North America, dams are often quite successful in diverting sediment movement. Holeman notes the case of the Missouri River at Yankton, South Dakota. Before dams were built 82 and 615 miles upstream, approximately 134.0 million tons per year passed Yankton. After the dams were in operation, the sediment load at Yankton dropped to 2.36 million tons, a decline of 98%.[20]

Finally, temperature, rainfall, and river flow rates are of course related to topographical features. Ecological zones are often delineated by surface elevation and land features; thus one speaks of semitropical coastal plains or the Altiplano in Peru or Bolivia. Map 2.4 is a visual guide to the principal classes of land forms. Data on the length of coast lines by country can be found in the Appendix Table A2.1.

Soil

Map 2.5 describes the global distribution of soil types. Table 2.9 presents information on the extent of various soil types, their percentage share of land surface, and the amount of potentially arable land for each soil type. A brief summary of the agricultural and environmental attributes of each soil type follows.[21]

MAP 2.4

PRINCIPAL CLASSES OF LANDFORMS

PLAINS
Surfaces less than 500 feet

PLATEAUS
Elevated masses with moderately flat upland surfaces often dissected by stream valleys

HILL LAND
Have a local relief of 500 to about 2,000 feet and are so dissected through stream erosion that few flat uplands occur

MOUNTAINS
More rugged than hills and their features are more complicated in pattern—usually exceed 2,000 feet

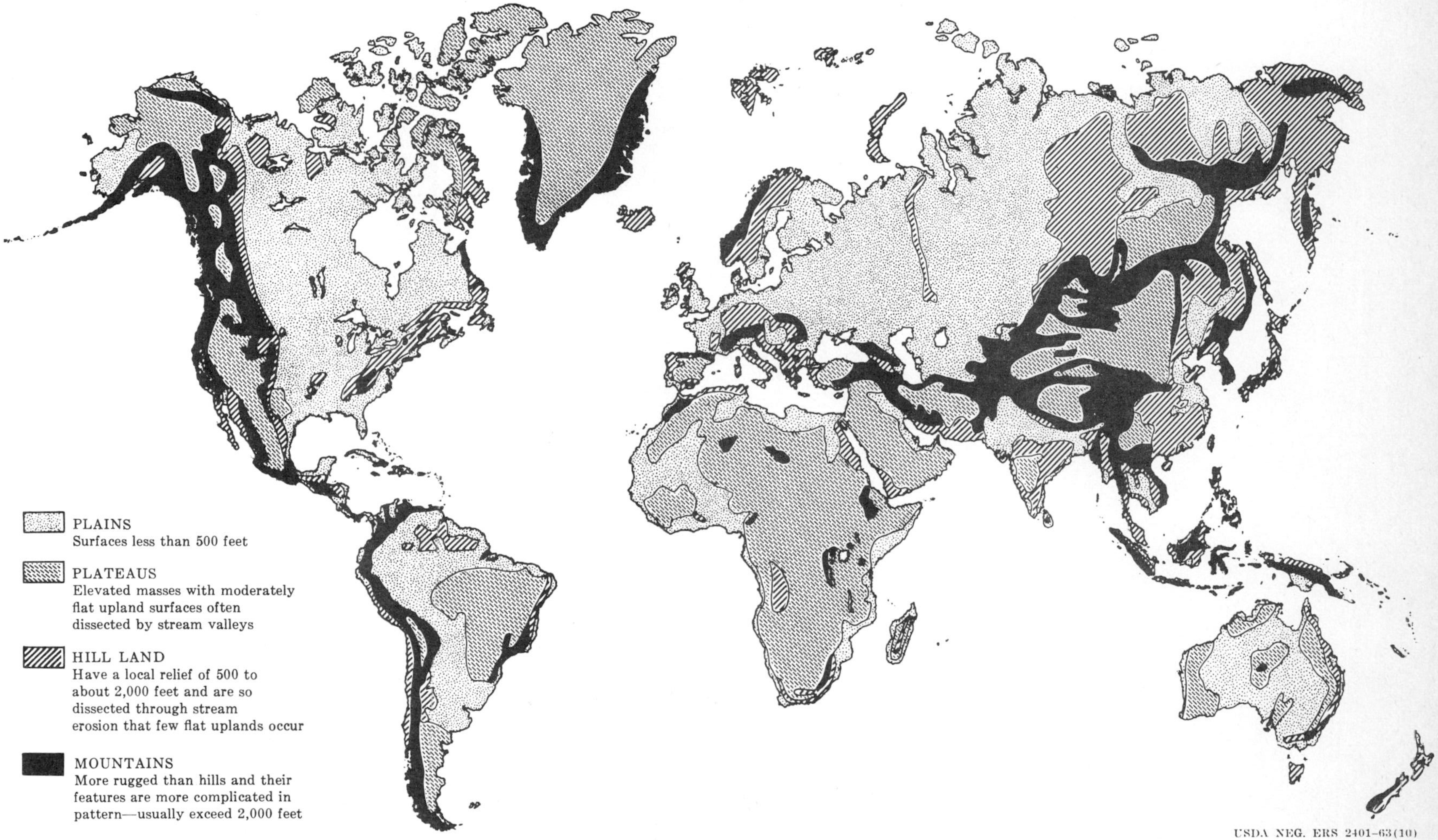

USDA NEG. ERS 2401-63(10)

Map 2.4. Principal classes of landforms.

MAP 2.5

PRIMARY GROUPS OF SOILS

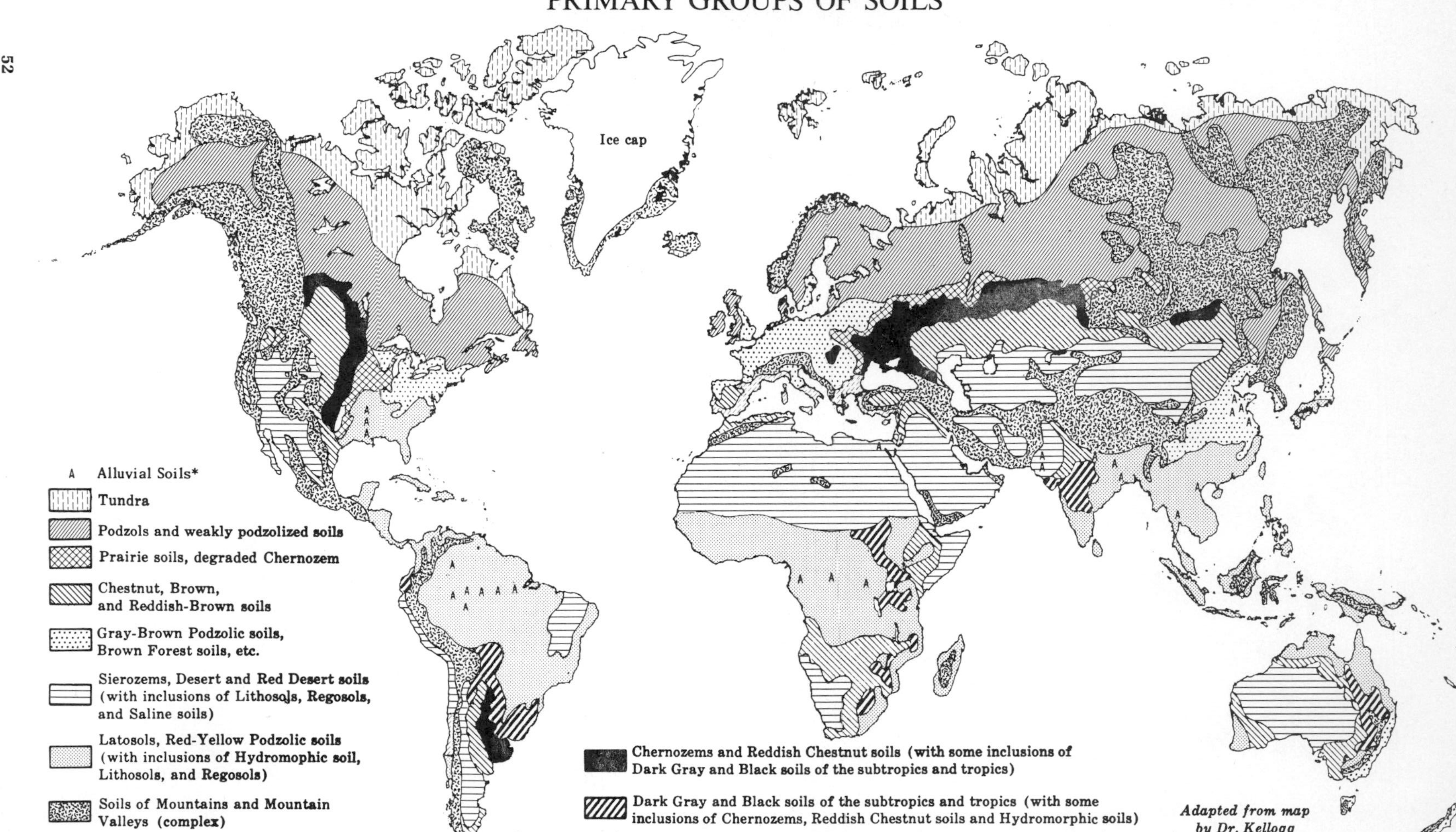

Map 2.5. Primary groups of soils.

Table 2.9 Soil Types

Soil Type[a]	Total Area Million Hectares	Percentage World Area	Potentially Arable Million Hectares	Percentage Potentially Arable
(1) Prairie and degraded chernozems	122.3	1	97.9	80
(2) Chernozems and reddish chestnut	381.5	3	282.3	74
(3) Dark gray and black	500.0	4	250.0	50
(4) Chestnut brown and reddish brown	1,203.8	9	601.9	50
(5) Sierozems, desert, and red desert	2,798.2	21	14.0	1
(6) Podzols	1,294.5	10	29.4	10
(7) Gray, brown podzols	605.2	5	393.3	65
(8) Latisols and red-yellow podzols	3,214.0	24	1352.0	43
(9) Red-yellow mediterranean	111.8	1	16.8	15
(10) Mountains-tundra	2,926.5	22	14.8	1
(11) Alluvial soils	590.0	[b]	NA	NA
World	13,155.8	100	3182.4	22

Source. Derived from Kellogg and Orvedahl, *Potentially Arable Soils of the World*, USDA, (Washington, DC: GPO, 1969).

[a] *Soils* (new terminology in parentheses).

(1) Prairie and degraded chernozems (alfisols and some mollisols).

(2) Chernozems and reddish chestnut (mollisols).

(3) Dark gray and black soils (vertisols).

(4) Chestnut, brown and reddish brown soils (aridisols, alfisols, mollisols).

(5) Sierozems, desert and red desert (aridisols).

(6) Podzols (spodosols).

(7) Gray-brown podzolic and brown forest (alfisols and inceptisols).

(8) Latisols and red-yellow podzols (oxisols, ultisols, and inceptisols).

(9) Red-yellow mediterranean (alfisols).

[b] Alluvial soils are included within most other soil types.

NA — not available.

1. Prairie and degraded chernozems make up only 1% of the world's land area, and although double cropping is not possible, they are generally fertile and receive enough rainfall to grow high-yield cereal crops such as maize. They are found mostly in the United States and the USSR.

2. Chernozems and reddish chestnut soils also are high in fertility, but they are somewhat more limited in moisture and require some fertilizer inputs. Wheat, sorghum, and other lower-yield cereal grains are often grown on these soils.

3. Dark gray and black soils of the subtropics and tropics account for 4% of the world's soils. Although they are reasonably fertile, they are hard to work. Moisture conservation is very important for these soils, as is protection from erosion. Cereal yields are low, but with proper management, yields could be increased. Environmental problems probably come more from erosion caused by traditional farming techniques than from nutrient losses. Note that much of the Indian subcontinent, although not the most populous regions, have this soil.

4. Chestnut, brown and reddish brown soils cover around 9% of the world's land area, with 50% of the soil being considered potentially arable. Although these soils are fertile, soil moisture problems normally limit the use of these soils to grazing unless irrigation is used. Note the existence of these soils in the northern area of the Indian peninsula, particularly in some of the regions growing the new HYV irrigated wheat. With traditional grain production (without irrigation) dryness may increase erosion problems. With irrigation and intensive agriculture, there may be serious salination and leaching problems. If population pressures are not too extreme, this soil is probably best adapted to grazing and some extensive, low-yield cereal production.

5. Sierozems, desert and red desert soils, cover over 21% of the world's land area, but less than 1% of that is considered potentially arable. These soils, including the world's desert and semidesert areas, have severe moisture limitations. Any agriculture beyond low-yield crops, such as millet, or some grazing is unlikely without irrigation.

6. Podzolic soils cover over 10% of the world's land area, yet only 10% of that is potentially arable. These soils occur mostly in the northernmost reaches of the northern hemisphere. Very little cereal production can be expected in these regions because of the short growing season, except in certain regions such as parts of Canada.

7. The gray-brown podzolic and brown forest soils, although accounting for only 5% of the world's land area, are extremely important agriculturally. Although they tend to be nutrient poor, these soils in general receive adequate rainfall, do not require irrigation except when demanded by moisture-sensitive crops, and, most important, are responsive to tilling and soil management. High yields can and have been achieved on these soils through the addition of fertilizers. They are found mainly in Europe.

8. The latosols and red-yellow podzols account for most of the soil in the tropics and subtropics. More so than any other group, the latosolic soils are far from uniform, and there are wide variations in natural fertility and soil characteristics. In general, latosols and related soils appear to be low in nutrients, are moderately easy to work, and possess good moisture-holding characteristics. However, all these characteristics have been recently questioned. We know far

too little about the complexities of these soils, their capacity for agricultural production, and their tendency to erode after deforestation.[22]

9. Red-yellow Mediterranean soils account for only 1% of the world's soils, and very little of that is arable. They possess more nutrients than the latisols but still require fertilizer.

10 and 11. Alluvial soils cover over 590 million hectares and include those regions where the soil is, or until recently has been, regularly flooded. A large proportion of the "mountain" soils are in fact alluvial, and alluvial soils are found as inclusions in all other soil groups. Because of their relatively high fertility, the ready availability of water, and, often, a recurring annual deposit of new soil, the arable alluvial soils feed over 25% of the world's population, mostly through the growing of lowland paddy rice. Although rich in nutrients, alluvial soils are often responsive to fertilizer inputs. The critical problem with alluvial soils is water control—in wet regions, flooding and waterlogging must be controlled and moderated. In dry climates salinization must be avoided by proper draining.

An important controversy regarding tropical soils has recently emerged. For many years, it was felt that these soils were dominated by the type of soil labeled latisols. Latisols in turn were thought to be extremely susceptible to being turned into "laterite." Excerpts from two recent works help to explain this somewhat mysterious process:

> Over a very large part of the tropics, the soil becomes lateritic. That is, through leaching the main plant foods, the assimilable bases and phosphorus are removed from the top horizons of the earth. What is left is reddish mottled clay, consisting almost entirely of hydroxides of iron and alumina, . . . whose most distinctive trait is its tendency to solidify on exposure to air.[23]

> The final laterite soil is infertile, since it lacks organic material and soluble minerals, and it is very hard in dry weather. It is found very widely in the tropics: in Southern India, in Malaysia and Indonesia, in North and West Australia, in West and East Africa and Madagascar, in the Amazon Basin and South and East Brazil, and in much of Central America . . . Exceptions in the tropics to the poor laterite soils are mainly the flood plains of the rivers . . . and areas fertilized by repeated volcanic eruptions.[24]

This view is significant because it implies that these soils are peculiarly susceptible to leaching and have always had low fertility and that under the harsh sun and wet-dry rain cycle, much of the tropics are made almost totally unproductive.

Some, however, disagree with this formulation. In 1970, Grigg observed that "some writers have questioned whether there is a distinctive soil process called laterisation, and argued that leaching in the tropics has consequences similar to leaching in cool, humid regions. The essential difference lies in the longer period during which tropical areas have been subject to the process."[25] It is also possible that the extremes of wet and dry found in many tropical regions facilitate this leaching process. In addition, Sanchez and Buol claim that the "total area of the tropics in which laterites may be found at or close to the soil surface is on the order of seven percent."[26]

Although the tropics may not be totally composed of pavement-like laterite, there are numerous problems inherent to the soil type that are correlated to the region's climate. To simplify discussion, as well as to point out an extremely important distinction, this section broadly follows Sanchez and Buol's (1975) distinction of high-base and low-base soils.[27]

High-base soils (altisols, vertisols, mollisols, and others) are considered to be those possessing "natural fertility." In these soils the main limiting factors are nitrogen, water, and other relatively abundant additives. Low-base soils (oxisols and ultisols) are deficient in a number of bases, particularly phosphorus. High- and low-base soils are not separated by our temperate—tropic division; North America has both for example. There are climatic factors that may differentially affect the same type soil in different climatic regions, however.

According to Sanchez and Buol, "Agriculture in the tropics first developed in areas of high base status soils . . . the centers of population in the tropics are in areas having these soils. The impact of the Green Revolution programs is very much limited to areas with high base status soils, particularly those that are irrigated."[28]

They conclude that intensive agriculture should be stressed in those regions possessing high-base soils, whereas those with low-base soils may be limited to animal husbandry of an extensive nature. They also note that the low-base soils in general,"especially the Oxisols, possess excellent physical properties which facilitate tillage and reduce erosion hazards."[29] It may therefore be incorrect to say that these soils are more prone to environmental degradation, given similar climatic regimes. It is also significant that much of the Southeastern United States and China (containing low-base level soils) support sizeable populations and have a strong agricultural base.

As an example of the importance of soil type, the great savannah regions of Africa and South America have similar climates but have different agriculture potentials and ecological stress limits, because the savanna soils in West and East Africa "are generally well supplied in bases, while those of South America are generally almost devoid of bases."[30]

The connection between soil type and environmental stress is complex. One link is the population density that the soil permits. A second is the fertilizer requirements of the soil. A third is the sensitivity of the soil to erosion and compactation, which in turn is related to the region's climate and agricultural practices. Also related are the permeability, friability, water capacity, and drainage characteristics of the soil. We wish to emphasize the interactive nature of soil types and environmental stress—soil type helps determine crop patterns, farming techniques, production inputs, and population densities, but the potential environmental stress created by these factors will vary depending on the soil characteristics.

Demographic Structure

Demographic patterns, together with characteristics of the physical environment and the structure and level of economic activity, are the broad determinants of environmental stress.[31] Appendix Tables A2.5 assembles basic data on population by country. Material is included on current population, current growth rates, projections to 2000, urbanization ratios, and trends in urbanization. This table should be consulted along with other country data contained in the Appendix to provide basic profiles for individual countries.

Simple listings of population by country, however, fail to convey the regional concentrations of population and the concentrations within countries. Map 2.6 helps clarify this by illustrating the three great population clusters—Europe, China/Japan, and the Indian subcontinent. The reader can compare map 2.5 with all other maps (except map 2.1), by using the overlay (in the back of the book attached). Another approach is to list the countries with large land areas, large populations, and high population densities, as is done in Table 2.10. Eight countries account for 60% of the world's population, and another eight bring the total to over 70%. The 20 most densely populated countries (excluding Hong Kong and Singapore) are about equally distributed between North and South.

Population densities by country are averages of areas within a country. It is clear that ambient environmental quality at particular locations is affected by the spatial concentration of population and economic activity, and a measure of concentration within countries may be more revealing than country averages. For example, the United States average of 22.8 persons/km^2 or the average for Kenya of 22.7 persons/km^2 does not indicate the high concentrations in the northeast of the United States or the southwest corner of Kenya. We do not have sufficient data to derive concentration coefficients in a uniform fashion, but we have included material on urbanization (see Tables 2.32–2.35) and on

Table 2.10 Countries Ranked by Size and Population

	Area (1000 km^2)		Population mid-1975 (millions)		Most Densely Populated (persons per km^2)	
(1)	USSR	22,402	China	822.8	Bangladesh	519.0
(2)	Canada	9,976	India	613.2	Taiwan	444.4
(3)	China	9,597	USSR	255.0	Republic of Korea	345.9
(4)	USA	9,363	USA	213.9	Netherlands	331.7
(5)	Brazil	8,512	Indonesia	136.0	Puerto Rico	322.2
(6)	Australia	7,687	Japan	111.1	Belgium	316.1
(7)	India	3,268	Brazil	109.7	Japan	300.3
(8)	Argentina	2,777	Bangladesh	73.7	Lebanon	290.0
(9)	Sudan	2,506	Pakistan	70.6	West Germany	249.6
(10)	Algeria	2,282	Nigeria	62.9	United Kingdom	231.1
(11)	Zaire	2,345	West Germany	61.9	Sri Lanka	215.4
(12)	Saudi Arabia	2,253	Mexico	59.2	El Salvador	195.2
(13)	Mexico	1,973	United Kingdom	56.4	India	187.6
(14)	Indonesia	1,904	Italy	55.0	Italy	182.7
(15)	Libya	1,769	France	52.9	Jamaica	181.8
(16)	Iran	1,648	Philippines	44.4	Haiti	164.3
(17)	Mongolia	1,565	Thailand	42.1	Israel	161.9
(18)	Peru	1,285	Turkey	39.9	Rwanda	161.5
(19)	Chad	1,284	Egypt	37.5	East Germany	159.2
(20)	Niger	1,267	Spain	35.4	Switzerland	158.5

Source. Appendix Tables A2.1 and A2.5.

MAP 2.6

WORLD POPULATION DISTRIBUTION, 1961

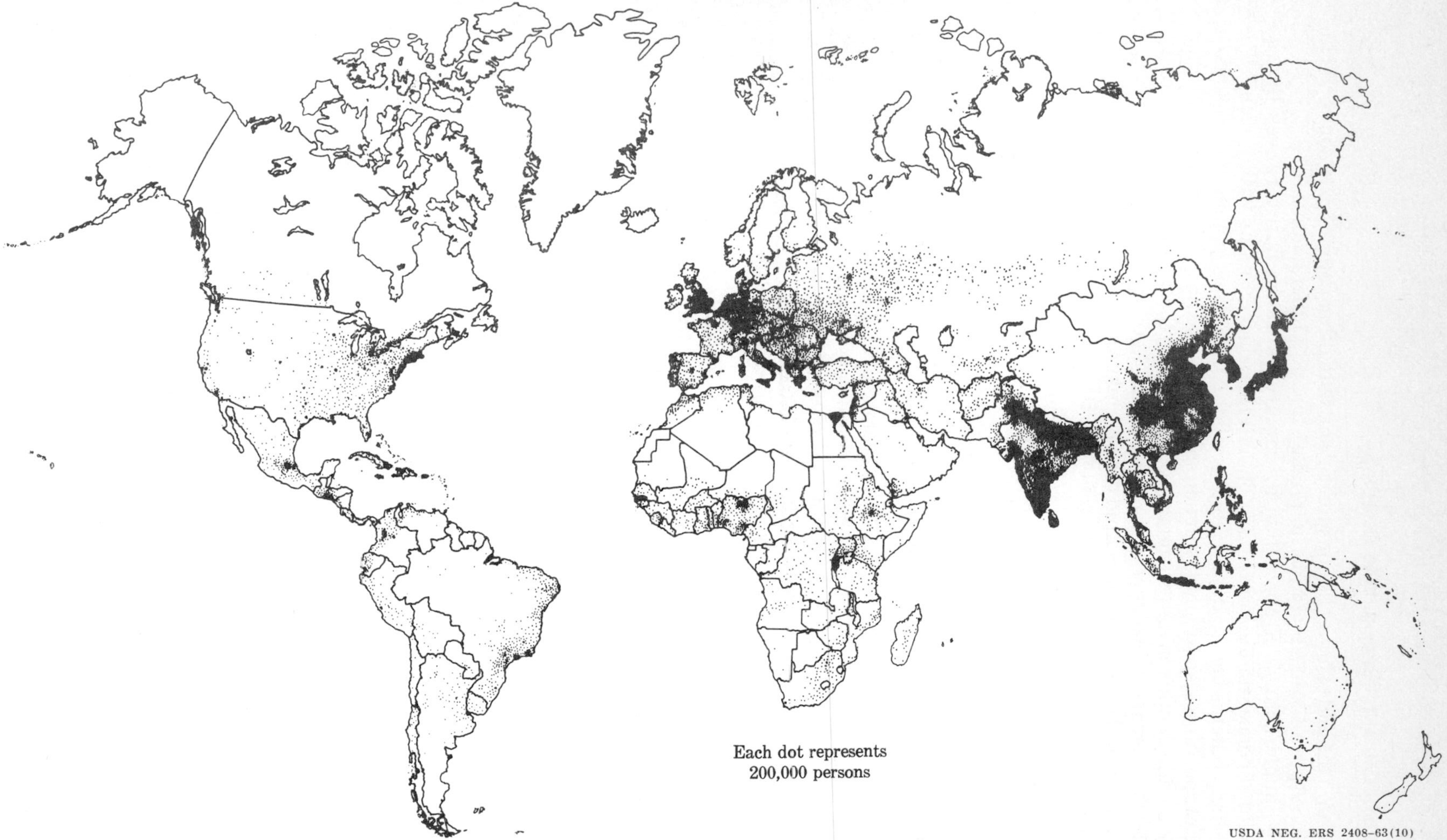

Each dot represents
200,000 persons

USDA NEG. ERS 2408-63(10)

Map 2.6 World population distribution, 1961.

agricultural workers per unit of arable land. These are suggestive of the concentration of population in urban centers and agricultural areas.

Further insight into demographic structure can be gained by looking at historical trends and projections. Note that it was not until the decade of 1930–1940 that the growth rate in developing countries outstripped the growth rate in developed countries, and that a sharp acceleration has occurred in the South since about 1950. Table 2.11 summarizes population and population density data by region for mid-1975. As Table 2.12 indicates, the abrupt increase in population in developing countries is attributable to a decline in death rates.

The United Nations has developed population projections by region to the year 2100 (see Table 2.13). Obviously, projections are subject to substantial error and should be treated with great caution.[32] According to these estimates, the share of world population accounted for by the currently developed countries is expected to decline from 30% in 1970 to 22% in 2000 and 15% in 2100. Developing countries, including China, will increase to 85% by 2100. Thus, in a period of 200 years, from 1900 to 2100, world population will have grown from about 1.6 to 12.3 billion, and within this total, developing countries will have gone from 1.1 to 10.5 billion. Diagram 2.1 charts the growth of world population from 1900 to 2100. Table 2.13 also provides a view of regional population growth. Africa and Latin America show the most rapid growth, but because of its greater base, South Asia has by far the largest absolute increase.

None of this is new. The outlines of the population explosion and the relation to food supplies have been the subject of urgent and extensive debate. From the point of view of environmental resources, the population explosion forces consideration of two questions—what will be the impact of population increase on pollution loads and environmental disruption, and, conversely, will environmental limits force down the projected population increase?

The implications for population densities, by region, of this growth are set forth in Table 2.14. Current world density is about 29 people/km^2 and will increase according to these estimates to 88/km^2 by 2075. For developed coun-

Table 2.11 Population and Population Density by Region, 1975

Region	Total Population (millions)	Population (per km^2 total land area)		
		For Region	Country High	Country Low
Africa	392.7	14.1	161.5	1.3
Latin America	319.5	15.9	322.2	4.9
Middle East	117.6	19.8	290.0	4.0
Asia	2131.6	99.9[a]	519.0	0.9
North America	236.7	12.2	22.8	2.3
Western Europe	341.8	100.8	331.7	12.3
Eastern Europe	385.1	16.3	159.2	11.4
Oceania	19.5	2.3	11.2	1.8
World	3944.5	30.3	519.0	0.9

Source. Appendix Table A2.5.

[a] Excluding Hong Kong (4200) and Singapore (3667).

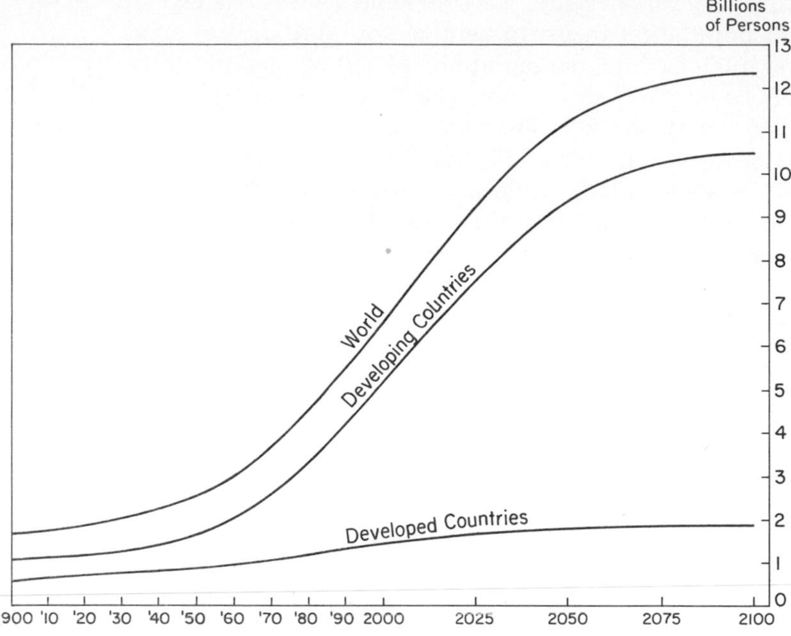

Diagram 2.1. World population trends.

tries as a group the increase will be fairly modest—from a current level of 33 to 51/km² in 2075. Developing countries as a group will increase from 26 to 116/km², and densities in South Asia will reach 268/km². This is almost 12 times the current United States density and three times the current European density.

Finally, further estimates of population growth, density, and urbanization for the period 1950–2000 are presented in Table 2.15. The urbanization trends again are strong—both developed and developing countries are becoming more highly urbanized and will continue to do so. The rate of growth of urbanization in developing countries over the period is higher than in industrial countries,

Table 2.12 Birth and Death Rates

	1935–1939	1950–1955	1965–1970
Birth rates (per 1000)			
Developed countries	24.9	22.9	18.6
Developing countries	40–45	43.9	40.6
World	34–38	36.7	33.8
Death rates (per 1000)			
Developed countries	14.7	10.2	9.1
Developing countries	29–34	24.0	16.1
World	24–27	19.3	14.0

Source. Historical population data from United Nations, *Population and Development Perspective: Demographic Trends in the World and Its Major Regions, 1950–1970,* E/CONF. 60/BP/1, May 3, 1973.

Table 2.13 Estimated Population in Millions, U.N. Medium Variant 1970–2100

	World	MDC[a]	Percentage (World)	LDC[b]	Percentage (World)	South Asia[c]	Percentage (World)	Latin America[c]	Percentage (World)	Africa[c]	Percentage (World)
1970	3,632	1090	30	2,542	70	1126	31	283	8	344	9
1980	4,457	1210	27	3,247	73	1486	33	377	8	457	10
1985	4,933	1275	26	3,658	74	1693	34	435	9	530	11
1990	5,438	1336	25	4,102	75	1912	35	500	9	616	11
1995	5,961	1396	23	4,565	77	2134	36	572	9	713	12
2000	6,515	1454	22	2,542	78	2354	36	652	10	818	13
2025	9,202	1700	18	7,502	82	3496	38	1072	12	1389	15
2050	11,228	1836	16	9,392	84	4353	39	1409	12	1926	17
2075	12,120	1875	16	10,245	84	4698	39	1575	13	2236	18
2100	12,333	1877	15	10,455	85	4780	39	1608	13	2323	19

Source. United Nations, *World and Regional Population Prospects*, E./CONF. 60/BP/3 and BP/3/Add. 1., 1973.

[a] Centrally planned countries (excluding China and Asian CPC's), are included in more developed countries (MDCs).
[b] Less developed countries.
[c] These regions exclude MDCs.

Table 2.14 Projected Increase in Population Density U.N. "Medium" Variant, 1925–2075, by Region

Region	Population/km²						
	1925	1950	1975	2000	2025	2050	2075
World	14	18	29	46	65	80	88
MDC[a]	20	23	33	42	48	51	51
North America	6	8	11	14	15	16	16
Europe	69	78	96	110	118	120	120
USSR	7	8	11	14	16	18	18
Japan	49	57	86	111	141	150	151
LDC	10	14	26	49	78	103	116
Latin America	5	8	16	30	47	59	63
Africa	5	7	13	28	49	70	83
South Asia	25	36	65	122	187	241	268

Source. United Nations, *The World Population Situation in 1970–75 and Its Long-Range Implications*, ST/ESA/SER. A/56, 1974.

[a] Includes European centrally planned economies.

but the low starting base leaves them at lower urbanization rates at the end of the period. However, the concentration of developing country population in urban centers suggests that urban environmental problems will become more acute, just as the increasing population will exacerbate environmental stress on agricultural resources.

ECONOMIC STRUCTURE

Physical and demographic features tell part of the story of environmental stress. It is also necessary to describe the type and intensity of economic activity that produces the stress. For expositional convenience it is useful to divide the discussion of economic structure into two broad areas—agricultural and industrial production. Before doing so, however, it is important to review comparative data on the overall level of economic activity and the distribution of activity between the agricultural and industrial sectors. Appendix Table A2.6 provides data by country on total and per capita GNP and the percentage of GDP accounted for by the agricultural sector. Appendix Table A2.6 also shows GNP/km², a crude measure of certain types of environmental stress. The tables confirm what is already well known—the range between North and South in terms of GNP and GNP per capita is extremely large—the total United States GNP was $1,407 billion (1974); 21 countries had GNPs less than 1 billion. Disregarding well-known objections to comparative data, the per capita range is also extreme—$6640 for the United States, $60 for Mali. With regard to the relative share of agriculture in GNP, the extremes are Yemen (71%) and West Germany (3%). Of course, much depends on definition and measurement.

Of more interest is the measure of GNP per unit of land area. Here again, the very lowest ratios are found among the poorest countries ($281/km² for

Table 2.15 Rates of Growth of Population, Population Density and Percentage Urban, 1950–2000, U.N. "Medium" Variant

	1950–1955	1955–1960	1960–1965	1965–1970	1970–1975	1975–1980	1980–1985	1985–1990	1990–1995	1995–2000	
Rates of Growth, Per Annum											
World	1.69	1.85	1.73	1.87	1.89	1.95	1.93	1.84	1.75	1.64	
MDC	1.30	1.29	1.21	0.90	0.86	0.85	0.83	0.75	0.00	0.00	
LDC	1.90	2.13	2.27	2.30	2.31	2.37	2.32	2.20	2.09	1.94	
	1950	1955	1960	1965	1970	1975	1980	1985	1990	1995	2000
Population density (per km²)											
World	18	20	22	24	27	29	32	35	39	42	46
MDC	14	15	16	17	18	19	19	20	21	22	22
LDC	22	24	27	30	34	38	43	48	53	59	65
Percentage urban											
World	28.6	31.1	33.7	35.5	37.4	39.3	41.1	43.1	45.2	47.3	49.6
MDC	53.3	56.7	60.1	63.0	66.2	69.2	71.9	74.6	77.0	79.3	81.4
LDC	15.7	18.2	20.9	22.9	25.0	27.3	29.8	32.3	35.0	37.9	40.8

Source. United Nations, *Selected World Demographic Indicators by Countries, 1950–2000*, ESA/P/WP.55, May 19, 1975.

Table 2.16 GNP and GNP Per Capita, 1974

			GNP Per Capita		
Region	Total GNP for Region (million US$)	Average GNP per Country (million US$)	For Region	High Country	Low Country
Africa	128,560	3,475	348	3360	70
Latin America	286,500	12,568	936	2400	140
Middle East	108,920	10,892	1066	3380	120
Asia[a]	452,020	20,546	242	2120	70
Japan	425,880	425,880	3880		
North America	1,543,180	771,590	6584	6640	6080
Western Europe	1,402,540	87,658	4108	6730	1540
Eastern Europe	833,830	104,228	1975	3430	530
Oceania	77,040	25,680	4050	4760	440

Source. The World Bank, *1975 World Bank Atlas,* 1976.
[a] Excluding Japan.

Mauritania and Chad), but the countries with the highest ratios, excluding the city states of Singapore and Hong Kong, are not entirely industrial countries. The United States is exceeded by Jamaica and Lebanon, for example. Still, the Western European countries and Japan display the highest ratios.

The information on GNP, GNP per capita, the share of GNP arising from industry and agriculture, and GNP/km² is consolidated in Tables 2.16 and 2.17 for the major regions. Per capita GNP is given for each region and for the high and low countries within the region. GNP per square kilometer is also given for each region and for the high and low countries within the region. According to these summary tables, excluding the city states of Hong Kong and Singapore, GNP/km² is the highest for Japan at $1,151,649 followed by Western Europe at $413,729. The lowest ranking is Africa with $4615. We believe that measures of economic activity per unit of land surface are of some use in comparing environmental conditions but should be used with great care. At higher levels of aggregation as are found in Table 2.16 and 2.17, the concentration of activity within regions is concealed. As is well known, neither production nor consumption is distributed uniformly across the landscape, either within regions or countries. Since the spatial concentration or dispersal of pollutants helps determine their biological damages, the more appropriate measure would illustrate the extent of concentration. The spatial dispersion of industrial activity is described in a subsequent section.[33]

Agriculture

A comparative description of agriculture as an economic activity with environmental constraints and consequences should present basic data by country on arable land, the intensity of its use, crop patterns and yields, the extent of irrigation, the use of fertilizers and pesticides, and the more direct measures of environmental deterioration—erosion, waterlogging, salination, and des-

Table 2.17 GNP Per Square Kilometer and Share of Agriculture by Region

	GNP per km²			Percentage Share of Agriculture			
Region	For Region	High Country	Low Country	For Region	High Country	Low Country	Percentage of Countries in Regions Covered
Africa	4,615	23,929	281	31	51	10	68
Latin America	13,802	815,730	1,265	20	51	3	95
Middle East	18,377	538,647	697	22	71	6	100
Asia[a]	21,029	160,406	549	23	69	6	64
Japan	1,151,649						
Hong Kong	655,000						
Singapore	7,833,333						
North America	79,795	150,229	13,690	4	4	3	100
W. Europe	413,729	1,619,118	57,418	8	16	3	100
E. Europe	35,217	544,178	25,924	18	23	11	89
Oceania	9,153	46,297	2,491	6	6	6	33

Source. Appendix Table A2.6.

[a] Excludes Japan, Hong Kong, and Singapore.

Table 2.18 Arable Land, by Region 1974

	Arable as Percentage of Total Land		
Region	For Region	High Country	Low Country
Africa	7.6	52.2	1.1
Latin America	7.5	33.7	2.2
Middle East	10.4	36.2	0.4
Asia	19.3	50.0	9.4
North America	13.6	22.7	4.7
Western Europe	26.0	62.7	2.6
Eastern Europe	12.2	59.2	10.4
Oceania	5.5	5.9	0.8

Source: Appendix Table A2.7.

ertification. Some of this material is presented in Chapter 6 where the environmental aspects of agriculture are considered in detail.

Appendix Table A2.7 presents by country total arable land and arable land as a percentage of the total land surface for those countries for which data are available. Map 2.7 displays arable land and should be studied along with the population map. Arable land is defined by the FAO to include land sown to annual crops.[34] The appendix table also shows agricultural land—arable land plus most grazing land and land used for perennial crops. Finally, as a crude measure of pressure on land, the population per square kilometer of arable land is shown. The range for arable as a percentage of the total ranges from 1.0% for Mauritania to 63% for Denmark. The most interesting measure is population per square kilometer of arable land, and here the range is from 1950 for Japan to 30 for Niger, Australia, and Central African Republic. The United States has a ratio of 102.

We summarize this information for major regions in Table 2.18. Again, we compute the ratios both for the regions as a whole and the high and low countries within each region. The table shows a contrast between Asia and Western Europe on one hand, and Africa, Latin America, North America, Oceania, and the Middle East on the other hand, when measuring arable land as a percentage of total land area in the region.

Table 2.19 computes population per square kilometer of arable land for the regions and the high and low countries within each region. Column one of Table 2.19 confirms that major differences exist among regions with respect to population pressures per unit of arable land. Oceania has a population density per unit arable land that is only about 8% of the density for Asia. The other major food surplus area, North America, also has a low ratio. As expected, Asia has by far the highest ratio of population to arable land. Of course, these are only crude measures of the population stress on land. Specifically, they do not adjust for net trade in foodstuffs, which can either increase or decrease the intensity of land use, the differences in yield per acre among regions, the use of land for agricultural raw materials, or the differences in the composition of food crops. This latter feature is particularly interesting because the high

MAP 2.7

APPROXIMATE CROPLAND AREA

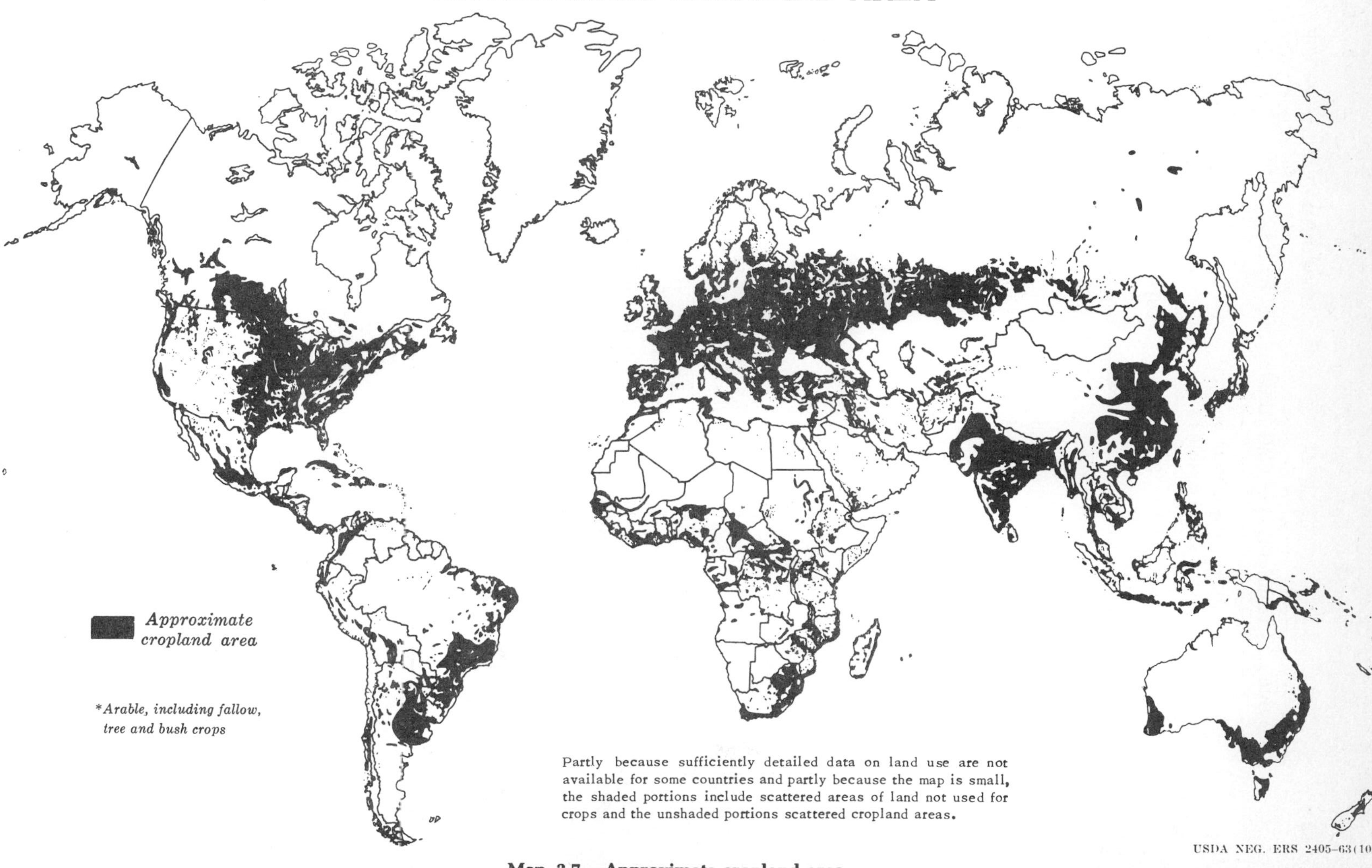

Partly because sufficiently detailed data on land use are not available for some countries and partly because the map is small, the shaded portions include scattered areas of land not used for crops and the unshaded portions scattered cropland areas.

Map 2.7. Approximate cropland area.

Table 2.19 Population Per Unit Arable Land, by Region, 1974

Region	Population Per km² of Arable Land: For Region	High Country	Low Country	Percentage of Countries in Region Covered
Africa	162.9	1282.3	29.8	100
Latin America	225.6	1434.0	165.4	100
Middle East	233.9	1115.6	116.7	80
Asia[a]	500.0	1951.0	175.6	100
North America	94.1	102.4	52.2	100
Western Europe	374.5	1707.6	167.2	100
Eastern Europe	129.1[b]	372.5	108.3	100
Oceania	41.2	757.4	29.7	67

Source. Appendix Table A2.7.
[a] Excludes Hong Kong and Singapore.
[b] 238.5 excluding Soviet Union.

population densities per unit of arable land in Asia are a result both of the ability to cultivate rice intensively and the necessity to do so to meet basic regional food needs. Population densities per unit of arable land help determine the intensity of land use and the composition of crops and therefore have a direct bearing on the types of environmental problems encountered.

Any definition and measurement of arable land is necessarily arbitrary. Even more arbitrary is an estimate of potentially arable land because sufficient investment in water supplies, plant nutrients, and physical constructions (e.g., terracing and drainage) can generally transform the productivity of soils. Still, the ratio of currently cultivated to potentially cultivatable land provides a rough measure of the population pressure on land and the scope for extensive expansion. Table 2.20 presents data on potential and current cultivated acreage by region and their ratio. The estimates are quite striking—both Western

Table 2.20 Currently Cultivated and Potentially Arable Land, by Region, 1965

Region	Potentially Arable (billions ha)	Currently Cultivated (billions ha)	Ratio of Currently Cultivated to Potentially Arable Land (%)
Africa	1.81	0.39	22
Asia	1.55	1.28	83
Oceania	0.38	0.04	10
Europe	0.43	0.38	88
North America	1.15	0.59	51
South America	1.68	0.19	11
USSR	0.88	0.56	64

Source. President's Science Advisory Council, *The World Food Problem*, Report of the Panel on the World Food Supply, Vol. II (Washington, DC:GPO, 1967) p. 434.

Europe and Asia, which have relatively high population densities per unit arable land, also have high ratios of current utilization (88% and 83%), whereas regions that have low population densities (Oceania and North America) have generally much lower ratios and therefore better expansion prospects. South America is the exception, with medium population densities per unit arable land (255.3) but a very low ratio of currently cultivated to potentially arable land (11%). Even taking into account the production for export in these regions, the regional imbalance in arable land relative to population is striking. In one sense, of course, these data are not surprising. Countries and regions with high population densities have already exploited opportunities for expanded acreage. Extensive expansion of agriculture will be centered in these regions with "idle" arable land.

Some data on the prospective expansion of arable land is available from the U.S. Department of Agriculture and is presented in Table 2.21. According to these estimates, world arable land will increase by 10.2% from 1970 to 1985 (much faster than the 3% increase from 1950 to 1970), with more rapid growth in the developed countries. Despite the absolute increase, per capita arable land is expected to decline from 0.4 to 0.33 ha in the 1970 to 1985 period, a decline of 17%. Oceania is expected to increase its per capita arable land from 3.0 to 3.5 ha, but Asia is expected to have a sharp decline of 26%, from its 1970 low of 0.23 to only 0.17 ha per capita.[35] Even if productivity increases manage to maintain per capita food supplies, these trends imply an intensification of agriculture and a pattern of environmental stress that is associated with high levels of inputs—water, fertilizers, insecticides, and others.

A more direct indication of the intensity of land use and the nature of environmental stress is the extent of irrigation. Data by country on land under irrigation and irrigated as a percentage of arable land are presented in Appendix Table A2.9. The appendix data have been aggregated for major regions in Table 2.22. Once again they are displayed in two ways: as regional averages (for those countries for which data are available) and as the high and low countries within regions.

The extent of irrigation is related to climate, available surface water, demographic pressures, and the sophistication of the agricultural system. Regions in

Table 2.21 Expansion of Arable Land: Estimates and Projections, 1950–1985

	Million Hectares				Percentage Increase	
Region	1950	1960	1970	1985	1950–1970	1970–1985
World	1418	1426	1461	1610	3.0	10.2
Developed countries	398	407	428	484	7.5	13.1
Developing countries[a]	795	798	800	874	0.6	9.2
USSR	225	221	233	252	3.6	8.2

Source. Derived from U.S. Department of Agriculture, *Perspectives on Prime Lands* (Washington: GPO, July 1975) p. 53.

[a] Includes Communist China.

Table 2.22 Irrigated as Percentage of Arable Land by Region, 1974

Region	Irrigated Land	Percentage of Countries in Region Covered	Irrigated as Percentage of Arable Land			Percentage of Countries in Region Covered
	(1000 km^2)		For Region	High Country	Low Country	
Africa	68.8	73	3.5	100.0	0.03	73
Latin America	116.7	100	8.3	39.6	1.6	100
Middle East	126.1	100	15.6	42.1	1.7	100
Asia	1495.4	78	37.8	73.8	8.0	78
North America	168.5	100	6.6	8.6	1.0	100
Western Europe	89.5	94	9.3	28.9	0.03	94
Eastern Europe	173.4	100	6.2	49.7	1.7	100
Oceania	18.8	66	3.8	—	—	66

Source. United Nations Food and Agriculture Organization, *1975 Production Yearbook* (New York: United Nations, 1976).

which variable or minimal rainfall limits rain-fed farming are dependent on irrigation for anything beyond grazing and land-extensive practices such as shifting cultivation. Much of the semi-arid region is forced to use irrigation to extend cropping, especially when soil per se is not a limiting factor.

In the monsoon regions of Asia, large populations have forced the development over centuries of a complex irrigation system to increase intensive agricultural production.[36] Water in the monsoon regions is not a limiting factor to agriculture per se, but intensive agriculture in the Asian tropics demands water control, not only because of the climatic variability but also because of the peculiar needs of the world's most important, and productive, cereal—rice. Irrigation in the tropics as a whole is therefore not devised for a single purpose. It may be designed to raise yields from subsistence wheat and maize production in semi-arid regions (by providing a steady water supply otherwise unavailable from rainfall) or to encourage cash-crop production. In other areas, however, irrigation is designed to more systematically intensify grain production.

Chapter 6 is concerned specifically with environmental constraints and consequences of agriculture, and this chapter is primarily descriptive. Still, it is useful to point out some of the ways in which irrigation impinges on environmental concerns. Obviously, irrigation systems relying on water impoundment can decrease flooding and reduce erosion damages. In a broader sense, irrigation reduces pressure for cultivating marginal lands and the destructive aspects of shifting cultivation and inappropriate cropping of grazing lands.

And yet irrigation itself may be environmentally damaging. Salts can build up in the soils as irrigation water evaporates, unless the soils are adequately flushed. Irrigation tends to compact the soil by decreasing air spaces. Without adequate drainage the land can become waterlogged. Irrigation water returned to river courses can be highly saline and unfit for downstream use.[37] Moreover, irrigation systems contribute to the spread of water-borne diseases, including schistosomiasis.[38] Irrigation can be a contributing factor to surface runoff of pesticides and fertilizers, contaminating surrounding water bodies. Extensive irrigation may divert water available for removing urban and industrial wastes. Conversely, the use of contaminated water for irrigation can pose a health problem.

It may be that these adverse consequences are more prevalent in the semi-arid regions than in monsoon region irrigation. Indeed, some observers feel that the soil quality, erosion, and pollution problems associated with irrigation may be more acute in temperate semi-arid regions than in tropical semi-arid irrigation. They point to the higher water usage per acre, the crop mix, and the concurrent use of larger amounts of fertilizers and pesticides.[39] In any event, the connection between irrigation and environmental stress is complicated, and the differences in type and purpose of irrigation—monsoon rice, semi-arid grain production, semi-arid specialty and cash crops—should be considered.

Moreover, it is arbitrary to focus on irrigation without acknowledging that, increasingly, intensive agriculture is accomplished through a package of inputs—controlled water, pesticides, fertilizers, perhaps herbicides, and high-yield varieties of rice, maize, and wheat. It is the environmental stress of this package that is at issue. Available information on commercial fertilizer production and consumption (defined as amount bought) is presented in Appendix Table A2.8. To provide an indication of the intensity of fertilizer use, consumption per unit of arable land is calculated. For those countries in which both fertilizer consumption and arable land data are available, the extremes are the Netherlands (66.4 metric tons/km^2) and Niger (less than 0.1 metric ton/km^2). The United States ratio is 9.16 metric tons/km^2. In addition, Appendix Table A2.8 provides data by country on insecticide and herbicide use in absolute amounts and per square kilometer of arable land, where available.

The material on fertilizer, insecticide, and herbicide consumption per unit of arable land is summarized for the major regions in Table 2.23. Again the data are presented as the regional average and as the high and low countries within each region (for those countries for which data are available). As expected, there are sharp differences between North and South in the use of these inputs per unit of land area. However, there are major differences within the industrial and developing regions. Because fertilizer and pesticide use are connected with the types of crops grown (with especially heavy usage for cotton and tobacco), a more complete discussion is deferred to Chapter 6. Here we simply note that consumption rates per unit of arable land at the country level have serious limitations. The spatial concentration of these potential pollutants within countries is generally not available, nor is information on their pathways and ultimate sinks. Moreover, consumption rates do not indicate the care and precautions with which they are used or the physical conditions at the time of use—runoff patterns, soil build up, and so on. The data in Table 2.23 do not differentiate between public health and agricultural use. Finally, although pesticides and herbicides play some role in grain production in the tropics, they are mainly used on nonfood crops where the economic return is more favorable. In the United States over 50% of pesticide purchases go on cotton.[40]

Another indicator of the intensity of production, agricultural workers per square kilometer of arable land, is presented in Appendix Table A2.9 and summarized in Table 2.24.

Erosion. Soil erosion is a classic example of land misuse, and illustrations from Biblical times to the present can be found. Yet a reasonably accurate and comprehensive description of the extent and trends of erosion is impossible to compile. Eckholm's valuable new study on land misuse in developing countries demonstrates several points—there is no single cause of erosion, but rather it is the result of a complex set of conditions including population pressure, increased cost of conventional fuels, and inappropriate policies; that land misuse is not only the handiwork of the poor but the rich as well. Perhaps most important, his work confirms the paucity of information on erosion and erosion potential among and within regions, either in the past, at present, or in the future.[41]

The proximate causes of erosion attributable to man can be identified as the cultivation of lands for crops when the land is better suited for extensive grazing or less intensive cropping; deforestation and loss of forest cover in upstream watershed areas for the purposes of lumbering, provision of firewood fuel, and extension of agriculture; and overgrazing. Moving one step backward from these causes, three explanations may be the squeeze on land resources from increasing population, the failure of economic and legal systems to compel consideration of the external costs of these activities, and, closely

Table 2.23 Fertilizer, Insecticide, and Herbicide Use Per Square Kilometer of Arable Land, by Region, 1972[a]

	Fertilizer Consumption per km² of Arable Land (metric tons)				Insecticide Consumption per km² of Arable Land (kg)				Herbicide Consumption per km² of Arable Land (kg)			
Region	For Region	High Country	Low Country	Percentage of Countries in Region Covered	For Region	High Country	Low Country	Percentage of Countries in Region Covered	For Region	High Country	Low Country	Percentage of Countries in Region Covered
Africa	1.3	16.4	0.03	62	70.0	924.3	0.3	24	0.7	0.7	0.5	5
Latin America	3.2	16.6	0.3	82	72.8	544.6	9.7	36	13.5	427.0	6.0	36
Middle East	2.0	23.0	0.2	80	3.9			10	50.2			10
Asia	3.1	43.9	1.4	44	18.7[b]	555.7	2.4	18	2.7	79.8	0.1	18
North America	7.8	9.2	2.7	100	70.3	84.5	7.0	100	74.6	85.6	26.2	100
Western Europe	20.6	66.4	6.2	100	19.7	25.9	2.2	25	128.2	344.4	48.7	44
Eastern Europe	7.9[c]	36.3	5.5	100	174.5	313.6	28.2	22	72.1	242.1	13.8	44
Oceania	3.3	NA	NA	33	NA	NA	NA	0	NA	NA	NA	NA

Source. Appendix Table A2.8.

[a] See Appendix source notes for specific fertilizers, insecticides and herbicides included.

[b] 3.6 excluding Japan.

[c] 18.2 excluding USSR.

Table 2.24 Agricultural Workers Per Square Kilometer of Arable Land, by Region, 1970

	Agricultural Workers Per km² of Arable Land			
Region	For Region	High Country	Low Country	Percentage of Countries in Region Covered
Africa	9.8	161.0	1.0	40
Latin America	7.1	42.0	1.0	59
Middle East	10.0	26.0	5.0	50
Asia	60.2	129.0	30.0	36
North America	1.0	1.0	1.0	100
Western Europe	7.7	17.0	3.0	94
Eastern Europe[a]	3.7	15.0	2.0	100
Oceania	1.0			33

Source. Appendix Table A2.9.

[a] Excludes USSR.

related, commercial markets that encourage short-run exploitation of land in response to price increases for marketable crops.

Although each of these explanations may have merit, they all fail to provide an adequate measure of the extent and severity of erosion. The best method would be direct observation and the compilation of regional statistics. Less directly, long-run data on the variability of river flows and sediment loads (especially for smaller streams and tributaries) could test various hypotheses of deforestation.[42] These indices were discussed above, but the results for our data were inconclusive.

One direct measure of erosion rates and, theoretically, of overcultivation and deforestation may be the siltation rate of reservoirs. There are considerable data to prove that many reservoirs in Asia, particularly in India, are filling up with sediment at a rate significantly higher than first predicted (see Table 2.25). Data

Table 2.25 Siltation of Indian Reservoirs[a]

Average loss of storage capacity per year (percent)	0.45
Highest loss of storage capacity	2.63
Lowest loss of storage capacity	0.01
Standard deviation of lost storage	0.67
Average ratio of actual siltation rate over assumed rate	7.68
Highest ratio	69.49
Lowest ratio	0.69
Standard deviation of ratios	16.04

Source: J. S. Bali, "Soil Degradation and Conservation Problems in India" (New Delhi: Soil Conservation Division, Ministry of Agriculture and Irrigation, Department of Agriculture, Government of India, 1974).

[a] Twenty-two reservoirs, built from 1933 to 1972, with catchment areas from 900 to 87,500 km².

from 22 reservoirs built from 1933 to 1972 show that the actual siltation rate was, on the average, around eight times higher than the assumed rate. The question, of course, is, why is the rate higher? The Indian government's study on irrigation in 1972[43] discusses the importance of erosion caused by deforestation in the upper reaches of the watershed, as well as cultivation techniques (particularly shifting cultivation) directly within the watershed area. They also mention that the Himalayan foothill area is particularly critical in the production of sediment. Yet they do not state explicitly that the difference between assumed and actual sediment rates is accounted for by man-induced erosion. It is probable that a major factor is the lack of knowledge. Data on sediment, particularly time series that would show changes in sediment losses, do not exist in sufficient numbers. Also, in some cases the assumed amount of sediment and the related lifetime of the particular reservoir was imperfectly estimated. With the data available, it is difficult to say whether the difference between assumed and actual reservoir siltation rates is due to an increase in erosion or a lack of knowledge at the time of the original estimates. There is some evidence that man-induced erosion may produce more flooding[44], but the evidence is still sketchy. It probably does occur, but data documenting this is not readily available for many developing countries.

Even more indirect measures, such as the extent of shifting cultivation and population densities per unit arable land, were suggested. It does not appear that a generalized measure of "carrying capacity" of agricultural land stating the agricultural output per unit of land that can be sustained without long-term soil deterioration can be constructed and used for interregional comparisons. Too much depends on the composition of crops, the climate and soil conditions, the techniques of production, and other variables.

Although there is a presumption that increasing population densities will result in agricultural practices that encourage erosion, conclusions remain conjectural.[45] One can assemble data on activities such as tropical forest logging and show striking increases in recent years. For example, exports of hardwood saw logs and veneer logs from the Ivory Coast increased by 330% in the decade 1963–1973, and Indonesian exports increased from $1 million to 574 million in the same period. Surely the direct disturbance to forest cover and soils from harvesting and transport and the indirect effect of opening areas to new cultivators through logging roads have had an impact on erosion in these areas. It is also possible to document the relative importance of firewood consumption in the tropics (see pp. 79–83, particularly.) We cannot provide estimates of the extent of erosion in the semi-arid and humid tropics but suggest that it is probably a serious problem.

Attempts have been made to distinguish among erosion processes on the basis of climate zones. Birot states that in temperate regions the erosion process is slow, but eroded material is quickly transported. Rivers are important erosion agents, cutting through the landscape.[46] In contrast, he states that in the humid tropics "the decomposition of rock (mainly the result of chemical weathering) is more rapid than the transport of material on the slopes, which in turn is more effective than fluvial erosion." He argues that the rapid decomposition of rock is caused by the greatly increased subsurface chemical transformation caused by higher heat input, and this often creates deeper mineral soils than exist in temperate regions. However, eroded material is not moved as rapidly in the tropics because of heavy ground cover and the relative absence of rock outcrops.

In semi-arid and arid regions, erosion generally takes place over a broad surface, and the soil-bearing water is a highly effective erosion tool, differentially eroding the area by the differing resistance of the soil. "The arid system of erosion is marked by the overwhelming importance of two agents of transport on slopes: wash and wind."[47]

Temperature and vegetation are key factors in predicting erosion rates. Warm climates (given equal slope, soil, and vegetation) tend to have less runoff than cool climates because of increased evaporation.[48] Jansen and Painter do not discuss the decomposition of material in the same manner as Birot; however, they do conclude that heavy vegetation tends to protect the humid tropical soil from erosion. Several writers have concluded that erosion varies inversely with temperature, with lower rates of erosion being found in the humid tropics. Jansen and Painter examined data from 79 catchments, including those in Table 2.8. They conclude that the humid tropics have the lowest erosion rates, the arid and semi-arid regions intermediate rates, and the Mediterranean climates very high rates, "with extreme values in areas of high altitudes and relief."[49] Their analysis supports the generalization that sediment increases with increasing runoff, altitude, relief, precipitation, temperature, and rock softness and decreases with increasing area and protective vegetation.[50] Those studies support our earlier discussion of river flows: low rates of sediment are found in humid tropic regions. Extremely high rates are found in the tropical monsoon regions and China, not because of temperature but because of the steep slopes found upstream coupled with variable, heavy rainfall.

Industrial Production and Energy Use

As was done for the other variables, basic data on industrial production and energy use by available country are presented in Appendix Tables A2.10, A2.11, and A2.12. The industrial production variables include total industry, manufacturing, mining and quarrying, a selection of highly polluting industries (pulp and paper, industrial chemicals, petroleum refining, iron and steel, and nonferrous metals), and manufacturing output per square kilometer. All are for value added, which seems preferable to value of shipments.[51] Excluding Singapore, manufacturing output per square kilometer ranges from $24 for Central African Republic to $425,452 for West Germany.

Table 2.26 consolidates the information on manufacturing output (value added) and manufacturing output per square kilometer for major regions. Again, the table presents the data for the region as a whole and for the high and low countries within the region. The percentage of countries covered is also shown. The resulting picture is not fully accurate because of the absence of certain important countries. The range is very considerable but not surprising. Value added per square kilometer is $449 in Africa, almost $20,000 in North America, and over $93,000 in Western Europe.

It appears reasonable that the level of industrial output per unit of land surface is at least indirectly related to certain types of pollution stress. However, a serious objection to international comparisons is that the spatial concentration or dispersion within countries is not adjusted for. Given sufficient data

Table 2.26 Value Added in Manufacturing, by Region

Region	Value Added (million $)	Value Added per km² For Region	High Country	Low Country	Percentage of Countries in Region Covered
Africa	8,379	449	3,465	24	54
Latin America[a]	14,741	1,195	15,882	688	45
Middle East	6,486	2,038	78,981	273	60
Asia excluding Japan[b]	10,741	1,474	22,999	259	39
Japan	90,521	244,651			
North America	377,859	19,538	37,564	2,621	100
Western Europe	311,535	93,023	425,452	10,648	94
Eastern Europe and USSR	216,604	9,467	147,234	8,001	44
Oceania	14,145	1,681	6,409	145	100

Source. Derived from Appendix Table A2.10.

[a] The major countries of Argentina, Mexico, and Venezuela are not included.

[b] Excludes Singapore and Hong Kong.

compiled by subnational units it is possible to construct an internal concentration measure that could be used for international comparisons together with national averages of industrial output per unit land surface. This could be done either graphically, by plotting percentage distribution of industry against percentage of land area (similar to the familiar Lorenz curve for income distribution), or by calculating a single number measuring the deviation of the existing distribution from a hypothetical "perfect" distribution.[52]

We have not attempted a full-scale construction of industrial concentration coefficients because of time and data constraints. We have, however, computed value added in manufacturing per square kilometer for various states in the United States, and the information is displayed in Diagram 2.2 and Table 2.27. The distribution curves show the percentage of total manufacturing accounted for by different percentages of United States land area—for example, the most densely industrialized 5% of United States land area accounts for 32% of United States manufacturing output, and the output per unit land area in this 5% is about $290,000/km². This is roughly equal to the industrial output per square kilometer of Connecticut.[53] The most densely industrialized 20% of the United States accounts for 68.2% of manufacturing, and the output per square kilometer for this 20% is about $154,000. This is equivalent to the industrial density of Michigan.

Some rough international comparisons can be made by looking at Appendix Table A2.10 in conjunction with Table 2.27. For example, less than 2% of United States land area is as densely industrialized as the average for West Germany; less than 5% of United States land surface is equal to the average manufacturing density of Belgium; about 60% of United States land area is more densely industrialized than is the average for Greece; South Korea, with an average of $22,999/km² is equal in density to the 49–50% range in the

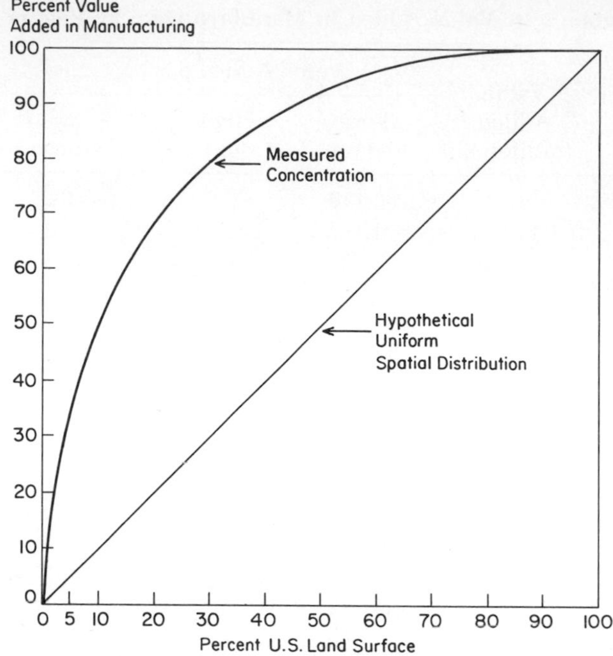

Diagram 2.2. Spatial concentration of Unites States manufacturing activity.

Table 2.27 Spatial Concentration of United States Manufacturing, 1972

Percentiles U.S. Land Surface: Decreasing Manufacturing Density	Percentage of Total Value Added in Manufacturing (Cumulative)	Valued Added per km² (Cumulative)	Total Value Added in Manufacturing (Cumulative) (Millions US$)	Value Added (per km² for Percentile Interval)
1	11.6	522,165	40,873	522,165
5	32.0	289,243	113,204	231,013
10	50.5	227,842	178,346	166,441
20	68.2	153,817	240,803	79,790
30	79.8	119,973	281,730	52,286
40	87.1	98,232	307,568	33,009
50	92.2	83,171	325,514	22,927
60	96.1	72,243	339,297	17,608
70	98.5	63,441	347,615	10,608
80	99.6	56,125	351,459	4,911
90	99.8	50,026	352,422	1,230
100	100.0	45,102	353,044	795

Source. Statistical Abstract of the U.S. 1975. Value added by manufacturing data for 1972. Excludes Alaska and Hawaii.

Method of computation: Value added and land area by state were obtained, and states were ranked by manufacturing concentration. Percentiles of land area were marked off and value of manufacturing by percentile intervals calculated.

United States (or equal to Mississippi); Jamaica has a manufacturing density equivalent to the 60–65% range in the United States (or about equal to Maine).

None of this is a satisfactory measure of environmental stress from industrial activity. Much will depend on the exact location of industry relative to population centers, the composition and techniques of production, climate (including air circulation patterns), the presence of pollutants from transportation and household activities, and other factors. The measures of industrial output do not consider the nature of the production techniques or the extent of pollution abatement controls, if any. However, they do dramatize the very striking differences between developed and developing countries, and they suggest that industrial pollution abatement is much more a prospective than remedial task in much of the developing world. As observed in Chapter 4, this reduces the cost of abatement.

Energy production and consumption is another measure of economic activity. Perhaps more important, energy is related to pollution and environmental stress both in extraction/production and in consumption.[54] Appendix Tables A2.11 and A2.12 assemble basic data on energy by country. Variables include total commercial energy use, per capita and per square kilometer use, the use of solid and liquid fuel energy sources, gasoline consumption, and gasoline consumption per capita. Some of the information is summarized in Table 2.28, which contains regional data on per capita energy use, energy use per unit of land, and gasoline consumption per capita. Once again, the material is presented on a regional basis with the high and low countries within regions. Again, national averages conceal concentrations within countries.

According to Table 2.28, per capita energy use in North America is 11,627 kg (coal equivalent) per year. This is more than double the next region (Oceania, 5189 kg) and 67 times greater than Africa. The per capita gasoline consumption is 468 gallons for North America, more than four times the level of Europe and 51 times the level of Africa.

When placed on a per square kilometer basis, which may be a better measure of environmental stress, the rankings change. Japan has the highest energy use per unit land surface, 934 metric tons/km^2, Western Europe is second at 413, North America is third at 137, and Africa is low at 2.3.

Table 2.29 provides further insight into historical patterns of energy use by major regions. All areas except Communist Asia show sharp decreases between 1925 and 1968 in the use of solid fuels (coal and lignite) and corresponding increases in the use of liquid fuel. For example, Western Europe decreased its use of solid fuel from 96 to 37% over the period and increased its use of liquid fuels from 3 to 54%. The share of total world energy consumption by Western Europe and North America declined from 86% to 42% for solid fuels and from 80 to 63% for liquid fuels.

Information on commercial energy use rather than total energy use is due in part to data deficiencies. However, noncommercial energy use (firewood, dung, etc.) is particularly interesting because it presents a different set of environmental problems and because it is more directly related to stress on land and agriculture than is commercial energy.

Darmstadter has discussed the importance of noncommercial fuel in developing countries:

Table 2.28 Energy Use by Major Region

Region	Commercial Energy Use 1972 (kg of coal equivalent/capita)				Commercial Energy Use 1972 (metric tons of coal equivalent/km²)				Gasoline Consumption Per Capita 1973 (gallons/yr/capita)			
	For Region	High Country	Low Country	Percentage of Countries in Region Covered	For Region	High Country	Low Country	Percentage of Countries in Region Covered	For Region	High Country	Low Country	Percentage of Countries in Region Covered
Africa	181.8	4708.6	9.4	92	2.3	1.5	0.1	92	9.0	61.2	1.2	46
Latin America	961.6	4468.7	29.5	86	13.3	1322.5	0.8	86	43.4	114.1	8.0	77
Middle East	697.2	1018.0	57.0	80	13.0	253.8	0.4	80	15.9	40.5	11.7	90
Asia, excluding Japan[a]	193.4	1101.0	15.8	81	54.9	4210.0	1.0	81	3.4	24.4	0.4	50
Japan	3101.0				933.7				63.4			
North America	11627.2	1239.8	1147.8	100	137.6	259.1	23.6	100	467.9	480.0	352.3	100
Western Europe	4650.0	7141.8	942.4	100	413.2	2131.1	67.6	100	101.2	145.4	27.2	100
Eastern Europe	4575.5	7301.9	712.8	100	71.9	946.1	52.7	100	29.2			10
Oceania	5189.4	6081.8	3086.6	67	10.3	31.3	9.6	67	231.1	240.4	191.2	67

Source. Appendix tables A2.11 and A2.12.

[a] Asia, including Japan — gasoline consumption per capita equals 9.1 gallons/yr. Energy consumption is 468 kg/capita.

Table 2.29 World Energy Consumption, 1925 and 1968

	Percentage of Region's Total Energy Consumption				Percentage of World Consumption of Each Type			
	Solid Fuels		Liquid Fuels		Solid Fuels		Liquid Fuels	
Region	1925	1968	1925	1968	1925	1968	1925	1968
Africa	92.0	55.0	8.0	41.0	1.0	2.0	0.6	2.0
Latin America	38.0	6.0	57.0	71.0	0.8	0.7	7.0	6.0
Asia[a]	83.0	30.0	14.0	62.0	4.1	7.0	4.0	12.0
North America	74.0	23.0	19.0	43.0	45.4	22.0	72.0	38.0
W. Europe	96.0	37.0	3.0	54.0	40.4	20.1	8.5	25.0
E. Europe	83.0	53.0	15.0	28.0	5.4	32.9	6.2	14.8
Oceania	93.0	49.0	7.0	49.0	1.2	1.5	0.5	1.3
Comm. Asia	94.0	92.0	6.0	7.0	1.8	13.2	0.7	0.9

Source. Joel Darmstadter et al., *Energy in the World Economy, Resources for the Future* (Baltimore: Johns Hopkins Press, 1971), p. 14.
[a] Asia includes the Middle East.

According to rough estimates by the U.N., as recently as the early 1950's non-commercial energy (in terms of heat content) was more important than commercial categories in Africa and Asia and nearly as important in South America:

Non-Commercial Energy as % of Total Energy

Consumption	%
Africa	51
Central America	35
South America	45
Asia	58
North America	3
Europe	7
Oceania	13
Non-Communist World	15

In a more recent (though geographically less specific) estimate of the relative importance of the role of noncommercial fuels, the United Nations Economic Commission for Europe finds that although the non-commercial sources of world energy are slowly declining in importance (representing in 1967 perhaps 4% of the worldwide total compared with the 15% indicated above for the non-Communist world total in the 1950's) in some countries as much as 30 or even 50% of the total supply of inanimate energy may still be derived from non-commercial fuels.[55]

The more recent book by Makhijani for the Ford Energy Policy Project summarizes a report by the Energy Survey of India Committee, 1965:

About 120 million tons of wood, 50 million tons of dry dung and 30 million tons of 'vegetable wastes' were burned each year, largely in the villages, but also in the towns . . . if the energy taken in by draft animals is included, the per capita consumption of non-commercial energy is about 12 million BTU per year (about ½ of which is burned directly as a fuel) compared to the commercial energy use of 6 million BTU per year (about ¼ of which is used to generate electricity). About 10% of the commercial fuels are consumed in the villages primarily for irrigation and farm machines. The other 90% is consumed in the towns and cities, most of it going to industry and transport.[56]

The World Bank estimates that firewood accounted for two-thirds of the total Indian noncommercial fuel consumption, vegetable wastes accounted for 20%, and cow dung for about 15%.[57] The IBRD's figures on the growth of energy use in India point out in general terms the potential arising from energy consumption in Third World countries (Table 2.30).

With increased industrialization and urban growth commercial fuel accounts for a larger percentage of total energy consumption, yet the significance of the absolute increase in noncommercial fuel use should not be ignored. The Bank estimates that over 130 million tons of firewood were consumed in 1974 in India. Most of that (over 90%) is officially unrecorded and probably came from local scavenging. Of the 22 million tons originating from state-controlled logging operations, over 13 million were used for firewood.

Table 2.31 shows FAO estimates for the amount of round wood produced and the amount produced for firewood. On the average, the world produces almost half its wood solely for fuel. Although the developed countries use only 8% of their wood production for this purpose, the developing world uses almost 81%. The regional differences are even more striking, between 4% for North America and 86% for Africa. Globally, total wood production is growing at a far greater rate than the production of wood for fuel, the latter growing at only 0.86% compared to 1.57%. It is also striking that the amount of wood used for fuel in the developed countries is diminishing very quickly, almost 6% per year. The developing countries, on the other hand, are increasing their fuel wood production at a rate of about 1.8% per year, slower than the rate of growth for round wood as a whole, 2.4% per year, but still quite substantial. In fact, it is this use of wood for fuel rather than other uses that probably is more critical in terms of potential erosion.

The absolute increase of firewood for fuel may cause serious problems for the environment, particularly if that increase is from unrecorded, uncontrolled home-use consumption. Increased deforestation may lead to erosion, flooding,

Table 2.30 Estimated Energy Consumption for India; Amounts Consumed Million Tons of Coal Replacement[a]

	1953 1954	1960 1961	1965 1966	1968 1969	1970 1971	Annual Growth
Commercial	60	101	147	177	197	7.2
Noncommercial	127	147	164	175	183	2.2
Total	187	248	311	352	380	4.3
Percentage share commercial	32	41	47	50	52	
Percentage share noncommercial	68	59	53	50	40	

Source. From World Bank, "Economic Situation and Prospects for India," vol. II, *The Energy Sector* (Washington, D.C., 1974) p. 20.

[a] For a description of this measure see the report noted in source.

Table 2.31 Round Wood and Fuel Wood Production, by Region, 1973

	Round Wood Production[a] 1973 (1000 m^2)	Percentage Round Wood Produced[b] for Fuel 1973	Per Annum Growth 1963–1973	
			Round Wood Production	Fuel Wood Production
World	2,500.5	46	1.57	0.86
Developed	807.1	8	0.93	−5.95
Developing	1,029.3	81	2.38	1.81
Centrally planned	664.0	38	1.21	0.61
Africa	309.3	86	2.15	1.85
Latin America	278.4	81	1.77[c]	1.48
Middle East and Asia	691.3	71	2.41	1.81
North America	479.9	4	1.68	−6.34
Europe	331.8	17	0.41	−3.68
USSR	383.0	22	0.69	−1.06
Oceania	26.8	22	1.45	−2.04

Source. United Nations Food and Agriculture Organization, *1973 Yearbook of Forest Products* (Rome, 1974).

[a] Includes coniferous and nonconiferous "wood in the rough."

[b] Includes "wood in the rough to be used as fuel for purposes such as cooking, heating, or power production." FAO's estimates for fuel wood use are considered by many to be considerably understated.

[c] Excludes Central America.

and the destruction of or at least damage to local agricultural production. Also, although per capita noncommercial consumption probably will continue to decline, the increased absolute demand may magnify pressure to use manure and vegetable wastes. Both of these latter substances, particularly manure, play a vital agricultural role as a mulch and fertilizer.[58] Although manure is not extensively used in many regions in the tropics, the absolute rise in noncommercial energy demands (because of high population growth rates), including the use of dried dung for fuel, robs the agricultural sector of a potential nutrient and erosion-control substance.[59] It should be remembered, of course, that the tropical world is potentially at an advantage compared to the temperate regions because of the much greater growth rate of burnable products, either forest or crop residues.[60]

Although noncommercial fuel use per capita may not increase, the potential for increased deforestation and erosion will probably be heightened if there is continued growth in noncommercial fuel use. In those areas with low per capita incomes and high population growth rates, such fuel use will probably increase. The abrupt and massive oil price increases virtually ensure strong fuel demand for wood, dried manures, and vegetable wastes in many developing countries.

THE HUMAN ENVIRONMENT

As discussed earlier, the compass of environmental concerns has been expanded to include at least some of the attributes of poverty. Accordingly, a description of the environmental landscape in developing countries should go beyond a compilation of material covering the physical landscape and the demographic and economic structures that place stress on the physical environment—deterioration of soils, water and air quality, and ecological systems. The extension should include comparative data on the aspects of poverty now considered to be aspects of the human environment. However, this is open ended—malnutrition and overcrowded housing are certainly measurable aspects of poverty. The presence or absence of parks, playgrounds, green space, and quiet areas are determinants of the quality of the urban environment, with an impact on the level of human welfare. But an inclusive descriptive becomes unmanagable, and comparisons are lost in details.

We resolve this problem by generally restricting comments to two areas, urbanization and water-borne disease vectors. The choice is based on two considerations. The first is the enormous magnitude of the urbanization process in developing countries and the magnitude of the water-borne disease vector problems. Second, both these areas retain a link with the quality of the physical environment—urbanization through its demand for sanitary water supplies and sewage disposal systems, and water-borne disease vectors, because of the direct link to water use.

Urbanization

Even in the best circumstances, with good land-use planning, a reasonable tax base, and an adequate initial water, sewage, and transportation infrastructure, rapid urbanization is difficult to accomplish without environmental stress. Unfortunately, almost all developing countries start from a much less satisfactory base—chaotic land use, inadequate municipal water and sewage facilities, and overextended transport systems. Yet rapid urbanization of the developing countries is a fact and will continue.

Tables 2.32 and 2.33 present the broad patterns. According to these estimates, urban population in developing countries increased ninefold from 1920 to 1960, 67 to 605 million, and will reach 1250 million by the year 2000. The

Table 2.32 Urbanization Trends and Projections in Developing Countries[a]

Year	Millions			Urban Population as Percentage of Total	Annual Growth Rate of Urban Population
	Total Population	Total Urban Population	Population in Cities over 100,000		
1920	800.7	67.0	30.3	8	
1940	1054.7	122.8	63.7	12	3.1
1950	1493.0	277.8	NA	19	8.3
1960	2424.5	604.7	166.4	25	8.1
2000	3750.8	1249.2	NA	33	1.8

Source. Data from UN Population Study No. 44, *Growth of the World's Urban and Rural Population, 1920–2000,* as modified by IBRD, *Urbanization Sector Working Paper,* The data rely on regional definitions of urban areas.

[a] Mainland China not included, Spain and Italy included.

Table 2.33 Urban Population by Region

Region	Total Population[a] 1975 (millions)	Percentage Urban[a]		As Percentage of Total Population of Cities 100,000 and Over 1970[b]			Percentage of Countries in Region Covered[b]
		1950	1975	For Region	High Country	Low Country	
World	4147	28.6	39.3	NA	NA	NA	NA
Africa	420	13.2	24.5	11	32	0	81
Asia	2319	NA	25.9	38	56	10	50
Middle East	89	23.3	43.7	21	52	18	50
Latin America	328	40.9	60.4	17	51	6	86
North America	242	63.7	76.5	66	68	54	100
Western Europe	368	NA	70.0	44	69	20	100
Eastern Europe	360	NA	59.0	29	31	9	100
Oceania	21	64.5	71.6	53	64	45	100

Source. [a]*1975 World Population Estimates* (Washington, D.C.: The Environmental Fund 1975). The Fund's source for urban data is *Trends and Prospects in Urban and Rural Populations, 1950–2000*, as Assessed in 1973–74 (Population Division, Department of Economic and Social Affairs of the U.N. Secretariat, April 25, 1975).

[b] United Nations Research Institute for Social Development, (UNRISD), *1970 Data Bank*, 1975.

Note that the discrepencies between table 2.32, table 2.33 and the IBRD as quoted on page 86 are accounted for by differing projected rates of population growth and the exclusion in 2.32 of the People's Republic of China.

ratio of urban to total population is expected to increase to 33% by 2000. Table 2.33 shows estimates of urban ratios for 1950 and 1975 by region. There are major differences among regions, ranging from 76% for North America to 24% for Africa, but all regions exhibit substantial growth over the period.

The IBRD, by including China, provides even more dramatic estimates:

> In the next 25 years, the developing countries will add 1.3 *billion* inhabitants to their urban populations: that is, almost twice as many people as presently inhabit the cities of the developed countries. In 1975 there are 90 cities in the developing world with populations of over a million; by the year 2000, there will be close to 300 cities. In this period, the urban populations of these countries will grow from 28 percent (21 percent in 1950) of the total population to over 42 percent. For the first time in history, the increase in the urban population of the developing world will exceed that of the rural population.
>
> Almost two-thirds of the increase in the urban populations of the developing world by the year 2000 are likely to occur in Asia where two countries, India and China, between them will account for nearly 60 percent. In Latin America the urban population will grow to 75 percent of the total population; that is, the increase in the urban population alone will be more than twice the rural population today. In Africa the urban population will grow from 25 percent of the total population to 38 percent which means a more than tripling of the urban population in 25 years.[61]

Urbanization is not a uniform phenomenon in developing countries. The eventual ability or inability to cope successfully with urban growth depends in part on the causes of urbanization and the economic circumstances of the country. Some regions experience an acute shortage of arable land; some experience the pull of rapid industrialization and jobs. For some, a sophisticated public service sector is currently in place; for others not. For some urban areas the critical question will be the provision of basic sanitary facilities to prevent large-scale and frequent epidemics. For others, the problems may be more similar to those of industrial countries—increasing air pollution from industrial production and transportation, congestion interfering with urban movement of goods and people, and the absence of any urban amenities. In all this, the scale of urban centers is central.

The IBRD has classified developing country urbanization patterns as follows: type 1, characterized by relatively high income levels, high initial urbanization, low pressure on natural resources; type 2, semi-industrialized countries with rapid industrial growth and relative scarcity of arable land; type 3, characterized by low income levels, low initial urbanization levels, and modest pressure on agricultural resources; type 4, rural and poor with moderate to severe agricultural land pressures and industrial growth insufficient to employ the increasing labor force. Further information, by selected country and city, using this classification is presented in Tables 2.34 and 2.35. Current and prospective urban ratios for type 1 and 2 countries are high. The largest recent growth rates are in type 2 and 3 countries. The projected absolute size of individual cities is striking—31 million for Mexico City, 26 million for Sao Paulo; two cities in China and two in India will have populations near or above 20 million.[62]

Urban areas in the developing world have grown at a far higher pace than the country's aggregate rate of population growth. The migration into cities has often led to severe overcrowding and the unrestrained spread of slums and

Table 2.34 Populations of Selected Urban Areas 1950–2000, in Millions

Country	1950	Average Annual Rate of Growth (percent)	1975	Average Annual Rate of Growth (percent)	2000
Type 1					
Mexico City	2.9	5.4	10.9	4.4	31.5
Buenos Aires	4.5	2.9	9.3	1.5	13.7
Sao Paulo	2.5	5.7	9.9	3.9	26.0
Rio de Janeiro	2.9	4.4	8.3	3.4	19.3
Bogota	0.7	6.5	3.4	4.2	9.5
Type 2					
Cairo	2.4	4.3	6.9	3.6	16.9
Seoul	1.0	8.3	7.3	3.8	18.7
Manila	1.5	4.4	4.4	4.3	12.8
Type 3					
Kinshasa	0.2	9.7	2.0	5.6	7.8
Lagos	0.3	8.1	2.1	6.2	9.4
Type 4					
Shanghai	5.8	2.8	11.5	2.6	22.1
Peking	2.2	5.8	8.9	3.7	22.0
Djakarta	1.6	5.1	5.6	4.7	17.8
Calcutta	4.5	2.4	8.1	3.7	20.4
Bombay	2.9	3.7	7.1	4.2	19.8
Karachi	1.0	6.2	4.5	5.4	16.6
Developed countries					
New York	12.3	1.3	17.0	1.3	22.2
London	10.2	0.2	10.7	0.7	12.7
Paris	5.4	2.1	9.2	1.2	12.4
Tokyo	6.7	3.9	17.5	2.0	28.7

Source. UN, City Projections, medium tempo, medium variant (December 1974), International Bank for Reconstruction and Development, "The Task Ahead for the Cities of the Developing Countries," World Bank Staff Working Paper, No. 209, July 1975.

squatter settlements. It is difficult to compare data from city to city on the growth of these "substandard" housing sectors because of problems of definition, but Table 2.36 presents some illustrative data from a recent UN world housing study that suggests the problem's scale.

Finally, to complete the observations, Appendix Table A2.13 contains information by country on certain environmental indicators bearing on the quality of housing and sanitation. They are the percentage of dwellings with three or more persons per room, the percentage of dwellings with piped water, and the percentage of population with "reasonable access"[63] to sanitary water supplies. The appendix table also contains available information on infant mortality rates by country. Although these rates are determined by overall conditions—availability of medical services, nutritional levels, and so on—they are also reflections of the prevailing sanitary conditions and practices.

Some regional summaries of sewage facilities in developing countries are

Table 2.35 Urbanization Patterns in a Sample of Developing Countries

Country	Per Capita GNP Level in 1972 US$	Size of Population (in thousands) 1975 Urban	1975 Rural	2000 Urban	2000 Rural	Percentage of Urban Population 1975	2000	Compound Urban Growth Rate 1970–1975	1995–2000	Compound Rural Growth Rate 1970–1975	1995–2000
Type 1											
Argentina	1290	20,293	5,091	29,288	3,573	79.9	89.1	2.19	1.11	−2.46	−1.66
Mexico	750	37,349	21,855	103,287	28,957	63.1	78.1	4.86	3.60	1.19	0.82
Colombia	400	15,938	9,952	40,115	11,349	61.6	78.0	5.24	2.96	2.58	0.13
Brazil	530	65,128	44,602	161,604	50,903	59.4	76.1	4.72	3.13	1.67	0.31
Type 2											
Algeria	430	8,432	8,455	27,205	11,199	49.9	70.8	6.78	3.85	1.52	0.94
Egypt	240	17,822	19,546	42,716	23,726	47.7	64.3	4.20	3.24	1.15	0.49
Korea	310	16,074	17,875	36,019	15,979	47.4	69.3	6.66	2.26	−1.36	−0.68
Philippines	220	15,837	29,468	46,068	47,956	35.0	49.0	4.25	3.66	3.02	0.99
Malaysia	430	3,641	8,666	9,888	12,589	29.6	44.0	3.34	3.28	2.09	0.58
Type 3											
Senegal	260	1,262	3,190	3,740	5,013	28.4	42.7	3.89	4.18	1.83	1.47
Ivory Coast	340	994	3,891	3,718	5,899	20.4	38.7	7.02	4.46	1.51	1.54
Nigeria	130	11,419	51,511	40,953	94,008	18.2	30.3	4.67	5.10	2.07	2.36
Sudan	120	2,400	15,782	9,438	31,704	13.2	22.9	6.10	5.43	2.57	2.69
Kenya	170	1,483	11,625	6,458	24,743	11.3	20.7	6.48	5.61	3.38	2.83
Upper Volta	70	502	5,556	1,827	9,828	8.3	15.7	5.01	4.87	1.84	2.10
Type 4											
Pakistan	130	18,939	53,418	65,357	93,170	26.2	41.2	4.45	4.28	2.42	1.53
India	110	132,367	488,742	354,872	748,834	21.3	32.2	3.62	3.92	2.09	1.27
Indonesia	90	26,232	110,284	78,433	171,519	19.2	31.4	4.54	4.01	2.32	1.29
China (Mainland)	170	207,510	630,406	478,404	673,555	24.8	41.5	4.31	2.75	0.84	−0.07

Source. International Bank for Reconstruction and Development, "The Task Ahead for the Cities of the Developing Countries," World Bank Staff Working Paper, No. 209, July 1975.

Table 2.36 Population in Slums and Squatter Settlements as Percentage of Population for Selected Cities, 1970

City	Country	Slum and Squatter[a] Population Percentage of City	Annual Growth Rate of Slums and Squatter Settlements (%)
Accra	Ghana[b]	61	NA
Nairobi	Kenya	33	22.5
Ibadan	Nigeria[c]	75	NA
Dar-es-Salaam	Tanzania	50	35.7
Kinshasa	Zaire[d]	60	NA
Buenos Aires	Argentina	5	NA
Rio de Janeiro	Brazil	30	5.5
Santiago	Chile[e]	25	NA
Mexico City	Mexico	46	12.0
Lima	Peru	40	13.7
Caracas	Venezuela[f]	42	5.7
Seoul	Korea[d]	29	56.6
Dacca	Bangladesh[g]	18[h]	NA
Phnom Penh	Khmer Republic[i]	46	16.4
Calcutta	India[c]	67	9.1
Bombay	India[c]	45	17.4
Delhi	India	36	NA
Djakarta	Indonesia[i]	26	4.6
Kuala Lumpur	Malaysia[d]	37	8.0
Katmandu	Nepal	22	NA
Karachi	Pakistan[c]	23	10.0
Manila	Philippines[i]	35	5.5
Bangkok	Thailand[f]	8–15	NA

Source. United Nations, Department of Economic and Social Affairs, *World Housing Survey, 1974* (New York: United Nations, 1976) Table 48, pp. 159–163.

[a] See p. 29 of the UN Report for definition. These data are not strictly comparable because of the vagueness of the terms slum and squatter settlements and should be viewed as illustrative.

[b] 1968.

[c] 1971.

[d] 1969.

[e] 1964.

[f] 1974.

[g] 1973.

[h] Forty-two percent for total urban population in Bangladesh.

[i] 1972.

also available and are presented in Table 2.37. The table displays data on the percentage of the urban population served by public and household sewage disposal systems and the percentage of the rural population with "adequate" disposal. For the developing world as a whole, the data show that 69% of the urban population have "sewage disposal" (of which disposal by buckets is 13%, and untreated public systems account for 24%) and that 8% of the rural population has "adequate" disposal.

There is no way to fully catalogue the urban environmental problems of developing countries. However, studies of specific cities can point out both universal and unique problems. A case study of Seoul, Korea, prepared by the Office of International and Environmental Programs of the Smithsonian Institution for U.S. AID, is an excellent example.[64]

Seoul is instructive in part because of its extremely rapid growth. Its population has increased from 1.7 million in 1950 to 2.4 million in 1960 to 6.3 million in 1973. The IBRD projects the population to be 18.7 million in 2000.[65] This was literally unplanned and unanticipated growth—1963 population projections for water consumption anticipated a population of 3.8 million for 1973, but this was reached in 1966. The current population density is over 10,000 persons/km^2. It is atypical of developing countries because of its temperate zone location.

Interestingly, two of the most serious environmental problems result from transferring activities appropriate to rural areas to an urban setting in which they are no longer appropriate. The two practices are the "ondol" heating and cooking system and the disposal of night soil. They also illustrate the unique rather than the universal character of Seoul's environmental problems. The ondol system comprises an excavated kitchen/furnace room with flues to spaces underneath other rooms. Heat and combustion gases provide radiant heating before being vented to chimneys. The fuel is anthracite briquets in the city, and wood and charcoal in extreme rural areas. Although apparently providing efficient and pleasant heating, the environmental problems are numerous: provision of a good medium for tuberculosis bacilli (overall Korean incidence 4.2% in 1970, but 64.8% for nonvaccinated persons); carbon monoxide poisoning from improper house ventilation (levels of 100 ppm CO for 62% of all living rooms sampled; EPA standards set levels above 10 ppm as unsafe); ambient air pollution by carbon monoxide (accounting for 38% of all fuel combustion derived emissions, and the implication of excessive ambient CO levels in the extraordinarily high industrial and auto accident rate); and 30,000 metric tons of dust per year from the manufacture, transport, and use of anthracite briquets. There is also a solid waste disposal problem—4200 tons of anthracite ash per day, representing 60% of all solid wastes, must be collected and disposed of. A comparison of the composition of solid wastes between Seoul and Tokyo (Table 2.38) is illuminating.

A total of 6356 kiloliters of night soil per day are collected, of which 4269 receive some form of treatment, and 10% is directly discharged into the Han River. Environmental problems include intestinal infection; pollution of the Han River with consequent loss of recreational value, destruction of commercial fisheries, and downstream pollution in the Inchon area; increased expenditure on water purification facilities; and contamination of shallow wells and other ground water sources. Even the portion of sewage that is treated remains

Table 2.37 Sewage Disposal Facilities in Developing Countries

	Africa	Americas	Eastern Mediter-ranean	European Region	South East Asia	West Pacific	Total Developing World
Percentage of urban population served by:							
Public sewage system	11	34	8	27	26	26	27
Treated	(7)	(3)	(5)	(2)	(3)	(4)	(3)
Untreated	(3)	(31)	(3)	(25)	(23)	(22)	(24)
Household systems	40	31	86	13	48	53	42
Privey and septic tank	(31)	(31)	(85)	(10)	(20)	(37)	(29)
Buckets	(9)	(0)	(1)	(3)	(28)	(16)	(13)
Total public and household systems	51	65	94	40	74	80	69
Percentage rural population with adequate disposal	18	22	21	5	3	5	8
Percentage total population (urban and rural) with sewage disposal facilities	22	46	40	19	16	8	25

Source. Derived from F. van der Leeden, *Water Resources of the World* (Water Information Center, 1975) Table 7.38.

Table 2.38 Percentage Composition of Solid Wastes, 1971

	Seoul	Tokyo
Combustible		
Paper	9.0	33.3
Plastics	3.0	9.7
Garbage	10.0	31.8
Fibers	4.6	3.6
Wood		1.6
Others		7.5
Total combustible	26.6	87.5
Incombustible		
Glass and china	1.7	5.0
Metal	2.9	2.9
Soil	7.0	4.6
Anthracite ash	61.8	
Total incombustible	73.4	12.5
Total solid wastes	100.0	100.0

Source. The Urban Environment of Seoul, Korea, A Case Study of the Impact of Rapid Urbanization, Report for Office of Science and Technology, Agency for International Development, Peter H. Freeman, editor (Washington, D.C.: November 1974).

a health hazard—fermentation at disposal basins is not sufficient to kill parasite eggs, and the treated sewage may be unsafe when used for fertilizer. The data on intestinal infections, acute and chronic, are sobering, with an 80% infection rate. This is clearly linked to the manner in which night soil is collected and disposed of. It is also related to another unique feature—the almost daily consumption of kimchi, a pickled and partially fermented vegetable dish that is "undoubtedly responsible for much of the prevalence of intestinal parasitism in the population of Korea."[66] Interestingly, a sewage collector system has not been installed, but the natural drainage system has been used for this purpose. It is gradually converted by ditching, lining, and in some cases by paving over the channel.

Atmospheric pollution is a serious problem to which home heating, transportation, and industry all contribute. Of sulfur dioxide emissions, 32% came from anthracite (mostly home heating) and 66% from bunker-c type oil (mostly industry). Forty-one percent of carbon monoxide comes from anthracite and 57% from gasoline consumption. Seoul is a major manufacturing center—in 1966, 45% of national production took place in that area. In 1972, 4300 industries and enterprises were subject to emission controls. The Smithsonian study states that nitrogen oxide had risen to dangerously high levels throughout the city by 1969 and that sulfur dioxide, carbon monoxide, and dust levels were all excessive, at least by United States standards.

The number of automobiles in Seoul is extremely low, around 10 per thousand, but they create serious problems of air pollution (57% of CO loading, 41% of hydrocarbon loading), congestion, and traffic safety. Traffic deaths were reported at 748 (1972) and auto accidents at 20,168 (1972), or almost one accident for every three cars. The number of autos per thousand is a very crude indication of pollution, because much depends on use hours per day, maintenance, fuel grade, time spent idling, and so on. In fact, the number of autos could be adjusted upward by a factor of 10 to reflect the high trip and mileage rate per day. Table 2.39 presents some comparative data on auto use. What appears significant is the exceptionally low rate for Seoul in comparison to other developing country cities in light of the documented problems that autos create in that city.

The final point to be made is that the physical environment does seem to play an important role, as suggested elsewhere in this chapter. The Smithsonian report observes that "a major ingredient in the Seoul air pollution problem is the extremely seasonal rainfall . . . Temperature inversions are common in the late fall and winter."[67] Also, the river flow of the Han is highly seasonal, ranging from about 110 m^3/sec to nearly 2,000 m^3/sec (for the period 1965–1968). A comparison of Han variability with other rivers is found in the earlier Table 2.4. In view of the multipurpose use of the Han—irrigation, municipal and

Table 2.39 Automobiles in Selected Urban Areas

	Number of Automobiles per 1000 Population, 1970	Rates of Growth of Autos, 1960–1970	Rate of Population Growth, 1960–1970
Type 1			
Buenos Aires	78.9	(12.1)	2.4
Caracas	91.0	8.3	5.4
Sao Paulo	62.3	NA	6.4
Mexico City	78.3	10.5	5.8
Type 2			
Seoul	6.3	22.0	8.5
Tehran	44.4	(15.4)	7.0
Beirut	153.0	9.1	2.9
Type 3			
Lagos	22.8	15.5	7.9
Nairobi	52.7	(6.8)	8.1
Dar-es-Salam	33.0	NA	9.0
Type 4			
Bombay	13.5	8.2	3.7
Calcutta	13.0	7.2	2.2
Madras	7.9	5.8	4.5
Karachi	10.4	(0.6)	5.6
Bangkok	49.7	12.0	6.2
Tokyo	83.3	16.0	3.4
London	222.0	5.2	−0.7
Washington	316.0	2.0	−0.1

Source. IBRD Sector Paper, *Urban Transport* (Washington, D.C.: International Bank for Reconstruction and Development, May 1975).

Parentheses indicate IBRD estimates. NA — not available.

industrial water, commercial fishing, and the short distance to its estuary—and its pervasive use for waste disposal, the extreme seasonal variation in water flow must present special pollution control difficulties.[68]

Water-related Disease Vectors

The incidence of parasitic disease is related in a complicated fashion to climate, per capita income levels, and sanitation practices. Some observers stress the role of climate, even with regard to disease spread by human wastes. They argue that climate, as a control of disease, encouraged the northward movement of civilization: "The precarious balance between increasing technology, increasing population density, increasing parasitic infections dictated that the coldward course of progress must continue until a latitude of permanent climatic control of parasites was reached."[69] This of course is not true for all such diseases. Malaria, for example, was widespread around the Lake Michigan region of the United States before drainage projects.

Whatever the historic role of climate, technological advances in disease vector control and sanitation suggest that income and sanitation practices have become relatively more important in determining incidence. Climatic differences between North and South may limit the spread of certain diseases and intensify the problem in the tropics, but they need not be a barrier to eradication. Three illustrative diseases of great importance in developing countries are schistosomiasis, hookworm, and onchocerciasis (river blindness).

Schistosomiasis affects nearly 200 million individuals and exists almost entirely within the tropical world, with scattered pockets in Japan and Portugal. Map 2.8 displays the affected areas. It is a debilitating but not usually fatal disease that is spread by the schistosome parasite that requires a snail vector. According to one publication, it is "a pre-eminent example of the relationship between health and environment. It depends upon an absence of sanitation and the presence of a particular species of water-borne snail."[70] Table 2.40 shows estimates of the distribution of the disease in developing countries.

Table 2.40 Schistosomiasis Distribution, 1968

Region	Number of Countries	Total Population (millions)	Percentage Believed Infected
Africa	43	301.7	25
Southwest Asia	9	84.4	4
"The Orient"[a]	6	857.8	4
Latin America	11	97.0	6

Source: F. E. McJunkin, *Engineering Measures for Control of Schistosomiasis,* AID, 1970, p. 7.

McJunkin (1970) suggests that although moderate organic pollution greatly favors the snail population, chemical pollution from industry is harmful to the snail host. No one has yet suggested from this fact an extremely perverse method of controlling the disease.

[a] Excludes India, where incidence is minor.

SCHISTOSOMIASIS DISTRIBUTION

Map 2.8. Schistosomiasis distribution.

What makes it particularly interesting is that the snail vector is often unintentionally spread by the development of irrigation projects "raising the incidence of schistosomiasis from zero or a negligible level to rates of 75 or even 90 percent of the population in some areas of Egypt, West Africa, the Philippines, China and other places."[71] One control measure is to limit weeds within irrigation systems and streams so that the water velocity is increased and to spray with some molluscicides and herbicides. These may also cause pollution problems and need care in their application. The development of biodegradable substances as well as biological controls is also needed. The need for an integrated pesticide management program to control parasites and insect-vectored diseases will be just as great (if not greater) as the need for crop protection, particularly since much of the chemicals are applied near or on bodies of water. Another method to control this disease, of course, is to break human contact with the transmission sites through eliminating snail habitats, providing clean drinking water, or moving the population out of the infected regions. The first two would seem to have fewer environmental consequences than pesticide use.[72]

Hookworm affects over 500 million persons. The infestation of this worm parasite, which can enter its human host via contaminated ground, is related to levels of health care, which in the last century were related to levels of per capita GNP. However, pollution from human settlements and lack of toilets are only two factors. In 1929 Chandler stated that "hookworm infestation is primarily controlled in its distribution by climate. . . . In general favorable temperature conditions exist in a great belt encircling the globe, taking in all of the tropical and subtropical regions of the world . . . it is bounded approximately by the 36th parallel in the north and the 30th parallel in the south."[73] Berenson notes that hookworms are "widely endemic in those tropical and subtropical countries where disposal of human feces is inadequate and soil, moisture, and temperature favor development of infective larvae." The two varieties are found in various parts of the tropics and subtropics.[74]

In another article, distressingly entitled "This Wormy World,"[75] Norman Stoll stated that, as of 1947, the intensity of hookworm and similar parasitic infestations, although different for the temperate and tropical regions, did not abruptly cease in temperate regions. "Some people in the USA and Canada . . . have a way of feeling that we are a relatively helminth-free people. It is the rest of the world that is really parasitized. Well, part of such a statement is partly true. Actually, Northern America shares with Oceania and Europe, exclusive of the USSR, a status of about 1/3 as many helminthiases as people; for the USSR in both Europe and Asia this rises to 2/3; for Asia and (Latin) America, it is not far from 4/3; for Africa over 6/3"[76]

Onchocerciasis (river blindness) affects around 20 million people, mostly in the tropics of Africa and Latin America. The fly-borne disease causes blindness but not death; although it is not a major killer, the debilitating economic and social consequences severely affect the development prospects of a series of countries, particularly those of the Volta River Basin. Kamark remarks that "In Upper Volta, the river valleys, notably those . . . which roughly run from north to south across the central plateau, are practically deserted although they are potentially rich for agriculture. The reason is the presence of river-blindness (and sleeping sickness). Over half of the country's population live on less than one-fourth the country's area, the central plateau—which is on the whole the most poorly endowed in terms of natural resources."[77] The black fly needs flowing or turbulent water for egg laying. Increased agricultural production has unwittingly aided the fly. According to a joint World Bank–United Nations Development Program booklet on river blindness, "during the last two or three decades, man has constructed hundreds of artificial breeding sites, irrigation sluices and waterways that precisely suit the black fly's needs. Today, most government authorities realize the dangers. They consult with onchocerciasis experts when planning new irrigation works."[78]

Onchocerciasis in the Volta River Basin of West Africa illustrates more than the incidental adverse effects of agricultural projects on the disease vector. The severe depopulation of river valleys following black fly infestation has placed an intolerable burden on the soils of upland and watershed areas. According to the mission report (UNDP, IBRD, FAO, WHO), upland areas with an inherent agricultural capacity of 20–30 persons/km^2 are populated at 100 persons/km^2. The traditional agricultural system of semishifting cultivation has been forced into continual cropping with consequent soil degradation, erosion, and declining yields. According to the mission report, the indirect cost of yield reductions in noninfested areas exceeds the costs of maintaining the blind victims of the disease.

Precautionary design may help to limit black fly breeding areas, yet this does not control the natural breeding sites. To do this, insecticides, particularly DDT, have been used. This has been effective in parts of East Africa and the Congo basin. However, DDT has not been entirely successful because of the great range of the black fly, the need for coordinated international programs (since the fly need not breed in the same country that its offspring eventually infect), and the tendency of the fly to develop a tolerance to DDT.

Unlike pesticides used in agriculture, those designed to eliminate health hazards often are introduced directly into rivers, streams, ponds, and irrigation systems. However, such substances need not be added to rivers forever to eliminate the disease. In theory, once the pool of infection dries up, pesticide needs go down. Still, the time required to eliminate such disease pools is not trivial. With river blindness, for instance, the life span of the worm within its final host (man) is about 20 years. Although the black fly would no longer be a threat after 20 years if the worm were effectively removed, during that time there could conceivably be considerable damage arising from the massive use of pesticides directly into the river system. The World Bank-UNDP report continues, "ecological considerations would forbid such protracted use of DDT, as most rivers in the region now flow into two new man-made lakes, Volta and Ghana, and Kossou in Ivory Coast."[79]

One solution may be the development of less toxic substances that eliminate the vector and the parasite and at the same time have limited after-effects. This is not an easy task, and it is possible that the environmental effects of pesticides used in health programs may be ignored, or at least played down, while attempts are made to eliminate the serious scourges that have held back agricultural and industrial growth in the tropics as they once did in subtropic regions. It is impossible to tell what the environmental costs arising from the use of disease-controlling pesticides in the tropics will be, but it is important at least to consider the problem.

NOTES

1. Concerning environmental indices see Council on Environmental Quality, *Environmental Quality* (Washington, D. C.: GPO, 1972) pp. 3–50.
2. An alternative approach with some value would have been to select key developing countries and concentrate on them. For example, six developing countries (India, Mexico, Nigeria, Brazil, Indonesia, and China) together account for 72% of the population of the South and 56% of the land area (the six have a combined population of 1.8 billion and a land area of 26 million square kilometers).
3. Reference information on land area and coast line by country is in Appendix Table 2.1.
4. See the Introduction of Andrew Kamarck's *Climate and Economic Development*, The World Bank Seminar Papers Series, 1975, particularly the Kenneth Boulding quotation on p. 5 from Boulding's article, "Is Economics Culture-Bound?" *American Economic Review*, 50, No. 2 (May 1970).
5. Map 2.2 and Table 2.1 use the climatic zones devised by Troll (1966), the complete descriptions of which are given as follows:

   Tropical zones:

   a. Tropical rainy climates: regions with or without short interruptions of the rainy season (12–9½ humid months): evergreen tropical rain forests and half-deciduous transition wood.
   b. Tropical humid climates: with 9½–7 humid and 2½–5 arid months: rainy green humid forest and humid grass savanna, or tropical winter humid climate with 9½–7 humid and 2½–5 arid months: half-deciduous wood.
   c. Wet and dry tropical climates: areas with 7–4½ humid and 5–7½ arid months, rainy green dry wood and dry savanna.
   d. Tropical dry climates: areas with 4½–2 humid and 7½–10 arid months, tropical thorn succulent wood and savanna, or tropical dry climates with humid months in winter.
   e. Tropical semidesert and desert climates: areas with less than 2 humid and more than 10 arid months, tropical to semidesert and desert.

   Warm temperate subtropical zones are defined as all areas with mild winters, the coldest months being 2°–13° C or 6°–13° C in the Southern Hemisphere. H. E. Landsberg, Troll, et al., *World Maps of Climatology*, 3rd ed. (Berlin: Springer Verlag, 1966) p. 27.
6. See David Grigg, *The Harsh Lands* (London: St. Martins Press, 1970) for a discussion of the differences between various methods of climate divisions as well as a description of his own climatic zones. There are major differences between Troll and Grigg; the greatest is that Grigg tends to include regions often listed as subtropical or even temperate within Troll's classifications, since Grigg is often more interested in divisions that cut across tropical and temperate rather than simply tropical climates. An example of this is Grigg's inclusion in arid zones of the upper northwest regions of the United States. Data on percentage distribution of climate zones by country is not detailed enough to develop population estimates using the Troll divisions.
7. David Grigg, *The Harsh Lands;* Erik Eckholm, *Losing Ground* (New York: Norton, 1976); Raymond F. Dasman, John P. Milton, and Peter H. Freeman, *Ecological Principles for Economic Development* (New York: Wiley, 1972); William G. McGinnies and Brian J. Goldman, Eds., *Arid Lands in Perspective* (Tucson, University of Arizona Press, 1969); and *Arid Lands: A Geographical Appraisal* (Paris: UNESCO, 1970).
8. The concentration index follows the Gini coefficient method, where the degree of concentration C_i for the ith country is given by

   $$C_i = \sqrt{\sum\left(\frac{Rij}{R_i}\right)^2}$$

   where Rij is the rainfall in the ith country and the jth month, and R_i is total (12 months) rainfall for the ith country. With the number of months equal to 12, C ranges from .288 (equal distribution) to 1.0 (perfect concentration, or all rainfall within 1 month). For some purposes the absolute rainfall in 1 month is of interest, and the index described does not capture this. With low average rainfall, the concentration coefficient tends to be large (even if absolute variations are small). The measure does not give the number of dry seasons per year, an important aspect of climate.

9. V. P. Subrahmanyam, "Water Balance of India," *Annals of the Association of American Geographers*, 1956, p. 23.
10. See pp. 46–50, 72–75.
11. Climate differences between regions, as well as differences within regions caused by urban centers, bodies of water, and other factors, affect pollution dispersion. For a good summary of the significance of differential wind patterns, particularly as they are affected by cities, see William R. Frisken, *The Atmospheric Environment*, Resources for the Future (Baltimore: Johns Hopkins Press, 1973) particularly pp. 10–18 and 20.
12. See Eckholm, *Losing Ground*, pp. 96–98.
13. See Eckholm, *Losing Ground*, p. 41; H. C. Pereira, *Land Use and Water Resources in Temperate and Tropical Climates* (Cambridge: Cambridge University Press, 1973) pp. 182–183 and B. C. Raymahashay, "Characteristics of Stream Erosion in the Himalayan Region of India," *Proceedings of the Symposium of Hydrogeochemists and Biogeochemists* (Tokyo, September 9–9, 1970) pp. 82–92.
14. This was suggested by Dr. Gordon Wolman.
15. John N. Holeman, "The Sediment Yield of Major Rivers of the World," *Water Resources Research*, **4**, No. 4 (August 1968).
16. *Ibid.*, p. 740.
17. *Ibid.*, p. 745.
18. *Ibid.*, p. 742.
19. See pp. 46–50, Chapter 2, for more on sediment erosion.
20. Holeman, "The Sediment Yields of Major Rivers," p. 746.
21. This section relies on Charles E. Kellog and Arnold C. Orvedahl, *Potentially Arable Soils of the World* (Washington, D. C.: United States Department of Agriculture, 1969).
22. One bright hope in the management of tropical latisols is the example of the Southeastern United States where crop yields have increased quite substantially. Although the tropics incur heavier and more variable rains than the subtemperate regions and receive more potentially nutrient-leaching solar energy, they also are capable of growing more than one crop per year with proper management.
23. Kamarck, *Climate and Economic Development*, p. 15.
24. Theodore Morgan, *Economic Development: Concept and Strategy* (New York: Harper and Row, 1975) pp. 183–184.
25. Grigg, *The Harsh Lands*, p. 207.
26. P. A. Sanchez and S. W. Buol, "Soils of the Tropics and the World Food Crisis," *Science*, **188**, No. 4188 (May 9, 1975) p. 598.
27. *Ibid.*, p. 601.
28. *Ibid.*, p. 601.
29. *Ibid.*, p. 600.
30. *Ibid.*, p. 600.
31. The interrelation between climate, population growth, spatial location, and economic production has been a fertile field for speculation. See for example Kamarck, *Climate and Economic Development* and Robert Clairbourne, *Climate, Man, and History* (New York: Norton, 1970).
32. Population projections depend on alternative assumptions. For example, the United Nations' high, medium, and low world population projections for the year 2075 are 15.8, 12.2, and 9.5 billion persons, respectively. Source: United Nations, *World and Regional Population Prospects*, E/CONF. 60/BP/3 and BP/3/add. 1, 1973.
33. One method of presenting the distribution of industry would be to show it spatially using maps. For our scale, such a map is far too imprecise, although an example can be found in the *Oxford Economic Atlas*, 4th ed. (Oxford: Oxford University Press, 1972) p. 7. A more useful exercise would be a regional, or at the least continental, examination of industrial location. Two interesting examples of this are the *National Atlas of the United States of America* (Washington, D. C.: United States Department of the Interior, Geological Survey, 1970) pp. 200–216, as well as H. R. Davies, *Tropical Africa: An Atlas for Rural Development* (Cardiff: University of Wales Press, 1973). See also Alan Gilbert, "Industrial Location Theory: Its

Relevance to an Industrializing Nation," in B. S. Hoyle, Ed., *Spatial Aspects of Development* (London: Wiley, 1974).

34. See notes to appendix tables for more detailed definitions.
35. United States Department of Agriculture, *Perspectives on Prime Lands* (Washington, D. C., GPO, July 16, 1975).
36. David Grigg, *History of Agricultural Systems: An Evolutionary Approach* (Cambridge: Cambridge University Press, 1974) pp. 75–112.
37. See Chapter 6, pp. 317–318, 320–321.
38. F. E. McJunkin, *Engineering Measures for Control of Schistosomiasis* (Washington, D. C.: AID, 1976).
39. Suggested by Frederick Hotes.
40. See Tables 6.12 and 6.13, fertilizer and pesticide use by crop in the United States. Note that the concentration per hectare is greatest on nongrain crops—vegetables, fruits, cotton, and tobacco.
41. Eckholm, *Losing Ground.*
42. There have been studies that examine the relation of sediment load and land use practices in watershed areas. See Pereira, *Land Use and Water Resources in Temperate and Tropical Climates.*
43. *Report of the Irrigation Commission,* Vol. I (New Delhi: Government of India, Ministry of Irrigation and Power, 1972) pp. 325–331 includes a good discussion of the need for watershed management similar to that of the TVA in the United States.
44. This subject is discussed in Eckholm's *Losing Ground,* as well as in J. S. Bali, *Soil Degradation and Conservation Problems in India* (New Delhi: Ministry of Agriculture and Irrigation of the Government of India, 1974).
45. See the chapter on "The Effects of Croplands on Water Resources," in Pereira, *Land Use and Water Resources,* pp. 167–183 and G. U. Jacks and R. O. Whyte, *Vanishing Lands: A World Survey of Soil Erosion* (New York: Doubleday, Doran and Co., 1939).
46. Pierre Birot, *Cycle of Erosion in Different Climates* (Berkeley: University of California Press, 1968) pp. 44–73.
47. Birot, *Cycle of Erosion,* pp. 98–99.
48. J. M. L. Jansen and R. B. Painter, "Predicting Sediment Yield from Climate and Topography," *Journal of Hydrology,* **21** (1974) p. 379.
49. *Ibid.*
50. *Ibid.*
51. The data should be treated with caution. There are differences between countries in industrial classification systems that are not fully adjusted. Also, the latest year for which United Nations data is available ranges from 1969–1972; thus the material is not fully current. Local currencies converted to dollars at official rates are another source of error.
52. Spatial concentration measures on industrial activities suffer in comparison to income distribution measures because units of land surface, such as square kilometers, are quite arbitrary compared to income per capita, where the individual is a natural unit.
53. New Jersey is the most heavily industrialized state at $804,000/km^2; Wyoming is the least (excluding Alaska) at $583/km^2.
54. The list of environmental problems associated with energy production and use is extensive; strip mining for coal, oil well blowouts and spills, auto emissions, refinery effluence, nuclear safety, and utility emissions of sulfur dioxide are some of the more important.
55. Joel Darmstadter, *Energy and the World Economy,* Resources for the Future (Baltimore: The Johns Hopkins University Press, 1971).
56. Arjon Mahhijani, *Energy and Agriculture in the Third World,* A Report to the Energy Policy Project of the Ford Foundation (Cambridge, Mass.: Ballinger, 1975) p. 23.
57. International Bank for Reconstruction and Development, *Economic Situation and Prospects for India: The Energy Sector* (Washington, D. C.: IBRD, 1974).
58. See pp. 309–310 of Chapter 6.

59. See Eckholm, *Losing Ground*, pp. 105–106. See also Jacks and Whyte, *Vanishing Lands*, pp. 159–172; M. S. Swaminathan, "Organic Manures and Integrated Approaches to Plant Nutrition," paper given to the Technical Advisory Committee, Consultative Group on International Agricultural Research, 8th meeting, Washington, D. C., July 1974; as well as Chapter 6 of this book, pp. 309–310.
60. See Derek Earl, *Forest Energy and Economic Development* (Oxford: Clarendon Press, 1975).
61. International Bank for Reconstruction and Development, *The Task Ahead for the Cities of Developing Countries*, Working Paper No. 209, July 1975.
62. *Ibid.*
63. The World Health Organization defines reasonable access: "In an urban area, a public fountain, or standpost located not farther than 200 meters away from a house may be considered as within reasonable access to that house. In rural areas, reasonable access would imply that the housewife or members of the household do not have to spend a disproportionate part of the day in fetching the families' water needs." This definition is from the WHO's *World Health Statistics Report*, 1973.
64. The Smithsonian Institution, Office of International and Environmental Programs, Peter Freeman, Ed., *The Urban Environment of Seoul, Korea* (Washington, D.C.: GPO, November 1974). This section relies on that report and observations by one of the authors during a visit in 1975.
65. Korea falls within type 2 of the IBRD classification by virtue of its rapid industrialization and scarcity of agricultural land. Seoul is atypical because of its temperate climate.
66. Smithsonian Institution, *The Urban Environment of Seoul, Korea*, p. 183.
67. Smithsonian Institution, *The Urban Environment of Seoul, Korea*, p. 121.
68. This summary is not meant to imply that Seoul has neglected its environment. As the Smithsonian report makes quite clear, the problems have been recognized, and measures ranging from subway construction to sewage treatment plans are being undertaken.
69. D. Lambert, "The Role of Climate and the Economic Development of Nations," *Land Economics*, **47** (November 1971) p. 341.
70. *World Environment Newsletter*, April 24, 1975, p. 41.
71. *Ibid.*
72. See Patricia L. Rosenfield, *Development and Verification of a Schistosomiasis Transmission Model* (Washington, D. C. United States Government, Agency for International Development, GPO, 1975).
73. Lambert, "The Role of Climate."
74. Abram S. Berenson, Ed., *Control of Communicable Diseases in Man*, 11th ed. (Washington, D. C.: American Public Health Association, 1970).
75. Lambert, "The Role of Climate," p. 342.
76. *Ibid.*
77. Kamarck, *Climate and Economic Development*, pp. 52–53.
78. International Bank for Reconstruction and Development and the United Nations Development Programme, *Stemming the River of Blindness* (Washington, D. C.) p. 8.
79. *Ibid.*, p. 13.

Notes and Sources to Appendix Tables

Table A2.1, Area and Coastline
Columns

I. Food and Agriculture Organization of the United Nations, *Production Yearbook*, 1974.
II. Calculated by the authors.
III. Calculated by the authors.
IV. Office of the Geographer, United States Department of State.

Table A2.2, Columns — Climate Zones

I–VII — Approximate distribution calculated by the authors from Troll et al., *World Maps of Climatology* (Berlin: Springer-Verlag, 1966).

Table A2.3, Rainfall

Data from H. M. Conway, Ed., *The Weather Handbook* (Atlanta: Conway Research, 1974). Thirty-year average.

Table A2.4, Water Balances

Data for Indian cities from U. P. Subrahmanyam, "Water Balance of India According to Thornwaite's Concept of Potential Transevaporation," *Annals of the Association of American Geographers,* 1956. Other data from *Publications in Climatology,* Vol. XI (Centerton, New Jersey: Drexel Institute of Technology, Laboratory of Climatology, 1958).

Table A2.5, Columns — Population

I. Population Reference Bureau, *1975 World Population Data Sheet.*

II. *Ibid.*

III. *Ibid.*

IV. Environmental Fund, *1975 World Population Estimates.*

V. *Ibid.*

VI. Calculated by the authors from appendix tables.

Table A2.6, Columns — GNP and GDP from Agriculture

I. IBRD, *1975 Atlas.*

II. *Ibid.*

III. Calculated by the authors from appendix tables.

IV. *United Nations Statistical Yearbook, 1974* (1976).

Table A2.7, Columns — Agriculture

I. FAO, *Production Yearbook, 1975* (1976). Arable land and land under permanent crops.

II. Calculated by the authors from appendix tables.

III. FAO, *Production Yearbook, 1975* (1976). Arable land, permanent crops, and permanent meadows.

IV. Calculated from appendix tables and FAO, *Production Yearbook 1975* (1976).

Land-use definitions are those used by the Food and Agriculture Organizations in their 1974 Production Yearbook: *arable land* refers to "land under temporary crops (double-cropped areas are counted only once), temporary meadows for mowing or pasture, land under market and kitchen gardens . . . and land temporarily fallow (less than 5 years) or lying idle."

Land under permanent crops refers to "land cultivated with crops which occupy the land for long periods and need not be replanted after each harvest . . . it includes land under shrub, fruit trees, nut trees and vines, but excludes trees grown for wood or timber."

Permanent meadows and pastures refers to "land used permanently (5 years or more) for herbaceous forage crops, either cultivated or growing wild . . ."

See pp. 273–274 of the 1974 *Production Yearbook* for more details.

Table A2.8, Fertilizer and Pesticides
Columns

I. FAO, *Production Yearbook, 1975* (1976). Fertilizer defined as N_2; P_2O_5; and K_2O.

II. Calculated by the authors from appendix tables.

III. FAO, *Production Yearbook, 1974* (1975). Insecticide defined as "DDT, BHC, Lindane, Aldrin and similar insecticides parathian, malathian, pyrethrums, arsenicals and all other insecticides, Tables 124–129 *excluding* fungicides."

IV. Calculated by the authors from appendix tables.

V. FAO, *Production Yearbook, 1974* (1975), "2.4-D, MCPA and others, Tables 132, 133, and 134 excluding fumigants."

VI. Calculated by the authors from appendix tables.

These data do not distinguish between agricultural and nonagricultural uses.

Table A2.9, Irrigation and Agricultural Workers
Columns

I. FAO, *Production Yearbook, 1975* (1976).

II. Calculated by the authors from appendix tables.

III. United Nations Research Institute for Social Development, *1970 Data Bank*, 1975. Indicator #61.

UNRISD Data is "compiled and processed for comparative research purposes by the United Nations Research Institute for Social Development, and based largely on United Nations and specialized agency sources."

Table A2.10, Value Added
Columns

I–IV Value added data, by sector, from United Nations, *The Growth of World Industry*, 1973 Edition, volume I (1975). Converted to United States dollars according to IMF, *International Financial Statistics* and United Nations, *Statistical Yearbook 1974* (1975) at year-end exchange rates.

V. Computed by the authors.

Table A2.11, Commercial Energy Use
Columns

I. United Nations, *World Energy Supplies 1969–1972*, ST/STAT/SER. J/17 (New York: United Nations, 1974).

II. Calculated by the authors from 1972 population data and A2.11, I.

III. Calculated by the authors from appendix tables.

IV. United Nations, *World Energy Supplies, 1969–1972*.

V. United Nations, *World Energy Supplies, 1969–1972*.

Table A2.12, Gasoline Consumption and Petroleum Refining
Columns

I. *1975 International Petroleum Encyclopedia* (Tulsa, Oklahoma: The Petroleum Publishing Company, 1975).

II. Calculated by the authors from 1973 population data (1975 IBRD *World Atlas*) and A2.12, I.

III. *1975 International Petroleum Encyclopedia*,

Table A2.13, Health
Columns

I. *United Nations World Economic Survey, 1969–70.*

II. *UNRISD 1970 Data Bank,* April 1975, #35.

III. *UNRISD 1970 Data Bank,* April 1975, #37.
According to the World Health Organization, "reasonable access" in rural areas implies "that the housewife or members of the household do not have to spend a disproportionate part of the day in fetching the family's water needs."
"In urban areas a public fountain or standpost located not farther than 200 meters away from the house may be considered as within reasonable access to that house." WHO, *World Health Statistics Report,* 1973.

IV. *UNRISD 1975 Data Bank,* April 1975, #1.

Map Sources

Map 2.1 World Political Divisions. U.S. Central Intelligence Agency, 1975.

Map 2.2 Principal Classes of Landforms. U. S. Department of Agriculture, 1965. USDA Neg. ERS2401-63.

Map 2.3 Climatic Zones. Adapted from map in Landsberg, Troll, et al., *World Maps of Climatology* (Berlin: Springer-Verlag, 1966).

Map 2.4 Primary Groups of Soils. Adapted from USDA map, USDA Neg. ERS2402-63, 1965.

Map 2.5 Rainfall. Adapted from USDA map, USDA neg. ERS2402-63, 1965.

Map 2.6 World Population Distribution. Adapted from USDA map, USDA neg. ERS2408-63, 1965.

Map 2.7 Approximate Cropland Area. USDA map, USDA neg. ERS2405-63, 1965.

Map 2.8 Schistosomiasis Distribution. Adapted from World Health Organization maps, in N. Ansari, *Epidemiology and Control of Schistosomiasis (Bilharzia)*, published on behalf of the WHO by University Park Press, 1973.

We would like to specially thank Mr. James O'Brian of *Federal Graphics*, Washington, D.C. for his professional production and revision of these maps and his enthusiastic suggestions concerning the project's graphic material.

Appendix Table A2.1 Area and Coastline

Region and Country	Total Area 1974 (millions of km²)	Percentage of Regional Area	Size Rank in World	Length of Coastline (miles)
Africa				
Angola	1.246	4.5	21	NA
Burundi	0.028	0.1	113	0
Cameroon	0.475	1.7	46	187
Central African Republic	0.622	2.2	40	0
Chad	1.284	4.6	19	0
Dahomey (Benin Republic)	0.112	0.4	88	65
Ethiopia	1.221	4.4	23	546
Ghana	0.238	0.8	69	285
Guinea	0.246	0.9	67	190

Appendix Table A2.1 (Continued)

Region and Country	Total Area 1974 (millions of km²)	Percentage of Regional Area	Size Rank in World	Length of Coastline (miles)
Ivory Coast	0.322	1.1	55	274
Kenya	0.587	2.1	42	247
Liberia	0.111	0.4	90	290
Malagasy Republic	0.587	2.1	41	2,155
Malawi	0.118	0.4	86	0
Mali	1.240	4.4	22	0
Mauritania	1.031	3.7	27	360
Mozambique	0.783	2.8	33	NA
Niger	1.267	4.5	20	0
Nigeria	0.924	3.3	31	415
Rhodesia	0.391	1.4	52	0
Rwanda	0.026	0.1	112	0
Senegal	0.196	0.7	73	241
Sierre Leone	0.071	0.2	100	219
Somalia	0.638	2.3	39	1,596
South Africa	1.221	4.4	24	1,462
Tanzania	0.945	3.4	30	669
Togo	0.056	0.2	103	26
Uganda	0.236	0.8	72	0
Upper Volta	0.274	1.0	62	0
Zaire	2.345	8.4	11	22
Zambia	0.753	2.7	36	0
Algeria	2.382	8.5	10	596
Egypt	1.002	3.6	28	1,307
Libya	1.769	6.3	15	910
Morocco	0.446	1.6	50	895
Sudan	2.506	9.0	9	387
Tunisia	0.164	0.6	79	555
Total available Africa	27,854	100.0		13,899
North America				
Canada	9.976	51.6	2	11,129
USA	9.363	48.4	4	11,650
Total available North America	19.339	100.0		22,779
Latin America				
Costa Rica	0.051	0.2	104	446
Cuba	0.114	0.6	87	1,747
Dominican Republic	0.049	0.2	105	325
El Salvador	0.021	0.1	114	164
Guatemala	0.108	0.5	93	178
Haiti	0.028	0.1	111	584
Honduras	0.112	0.5	89	374
Jamaica	0.011	<0.1	116	280
Mexico	1.972	9.8	13	4,848
Nicaragua	0.130	0.6	83	445
Panama	0.076	0.4	99	979
Puerto Rico	0.009	<0.1	118	NA

Appendix Table A2.1 (Continued)

Region and Country	Total Area 1974 (millions of km²)	Percentage of Regional Area	Size Rank in World	Length of Coastline (miles)
Argentina	2.777	13.9	8	2,120
Bolivia	1.099	5.5	26	0
Brazil	8.512	42.5	5	3,692
Chile	0.757	3.8	35	2,882
Colombia	1.139	5.7	25	1,022
Ecuador	0.284	1.4	61	458
Paraguay	0.407	2.0	51	0
Peru	1.285	6.4	18	1,258
Uruguay	0.178	0.9	77	305
Venezuela	0.915	4.6	32	1,081
Total available Latin America	20.033	100.0		23,188
Middle East (excluding N. Africa)				
Iran	1.648	27.8	16	790
Iraq	0.449	7.6	49	10
Israel	0.021	0.3	115	124
Jordan	0.098	1.6	95	15
Lebanon	0.010	0.2	117	105
Saudi Arabia	2.253	38.0	12	1,316
Syria	0.185	3.1	75	82
Turkey	0.781	13.2	34	1,921
Yemen (A.R.)	0.195	3.3	74	654
Yemen (P.D.R.)	0.287	4.8	60	244
Total available Middle East	5.927	100.0		5,461
Asia				
Afghanistan	0.648	3.0	38	0
Burma	0.678	3.2	36	1,230
China	9.597	45.0	3	3,492
Hong Kong	0.001	0.1	119	
India	3.268	15.0	7	2,759
Indonesia	1.904	8.9	14	19,784
Japan	0.370	1.7	53	4,842
Khmer Republic	0.181	0.8	75	210
Korea (D.P.R)	0.121	0.5	85	578
Korea (Rep)	0.098	0.4	94	712
Laos	0.237	1.1	70	0
Malaysia	0.333	1.5	55	1,853
Mongolia	1.565	7.3	17	0
Nepal	0.141	0.6	81	0
Bangladesh and Pakistan	0.947	4.4	29	750
Philippines	0.300	1.4	60	6,997
Singapore	0.001	0.1	120	28
Sri Lanka	0.065	0.3	102	650
Thailand	0.514	2.4	44	1,299
North Vietnam	0.159	0.7	80	382

Appendix Table A2.1 (Continued)

Region and Country	Total Area 1974 (millions of km²)	Percentage of Regional Area	Size Rank in World	Length of Coastline (miles)
South Vietnam	0.174	0.8	78	865
Taiwan	0.036	0.1		470
Total available Asia	21.335	100.0		46,901
Western Europe				
Austria	0.084	2.4	98	0
Belgium	0.031	0.9	109	34
Denmark	0.043	1.2	106	686
Finland	0.337	9.6	53	735
France	0.547	15.7	43	1,373
Germany (West)	0.248	7.1	66	308
Greece	0.132	3.8	82	1,645
Ireland	0.070	2.0	101	663
Italy	0.301	8.6	59	2,451
Netherlands	0.041	1.1	107	198
Norway	0.324	9.3	56	1,650
Portugal	0.092	2.6	97	743
Spain	0.505	14.5	45	2,038
Sweden	0.450	12.9	48	1,359
Switzerland	0.041	1.2	108	0
United Kingdom	0.244	7.0	68	2,790
Total available Western Europe	3.390	100.0		16,673
Eastern Europe and USSR				
Albania	0.029	0.1	110	155
Bulgaria	0.111	0.5	91	134
Czechoslovakia	0.128	0.5	84	0
Germany (D.D.R)	0.108	0.5	92	191
Hungary	0.093	0.4	96	0
Poland	0.313	1.3	58	241
Romania	0.238	1.0	71	113
Yugoslavia	0.256	1.1	65	426
USSR	22.402	94.6	1	23,098
Total available Eastern Europe and USSR	23.677	100.0		24,358
Oceania				
Australia	7.687	91.3	6	15,091
Papua-New Guinea	0.462	5.5	47	
New Zealand	0.269	3.2	64	2,770
Total available Oceania	8.417	100.0		17,861
Total "world"	130.072			171,120

Appendix Table A2.2 Climate Zones: Percentage Distribution

Country and Region	Temperate Cold and Cool	Temperate Subtropical		Tropical Desert	Tropical Dry and Wet Dry	Tropical Humid	Tropical Rainy
		Arid	Humid				
Africa							
Angola					60		40
Burundi						100	
Cameroon					25	25	50
Central African Republic					19	51	30
Chad				60	40		
Dahomey (Benin Rep.)					50	50	
Ethiopia				20	50	30	
Ghana					39	50	11
Guinea					100		
Ivory Coast						80	20
Kenya					90	10	
Liberia						18	82
Malagasy Republic					50	20	30
Malawi					75	25	
Mali		4		21	75	<1	
Mauritania		49		30	21		
Mozambique					70	30	
Niger		25		40	35		
Nigeria					40	45	15
Rhodesia					100		
Rwanda						100	
Senegal					100		
Sierre Leone						60	40
Somalia				50	50		
South Africa		54	36		10		

Tanzania					60	40	
Togo					20	80	
Uganda						90	10
Upper Volta					100		
Zaire					10	50	40
Zambia					100		
Algeria		74	4	2	20		
Egypt		90			10		
Libya		90			10		
Morocco		25			75		
Sudan		5		20	60	15	
Tunisia				40	60		
Total available Africa	0	22	2	11	40	16	9
North America							
Canada	100						
USA	80	5	15				
Total available North America	90	2	8	0	0	0	0
Latin America							
Costa Rica						25	75
Cuba						70	30
Dominican Republic						15	85
El Salvador							
Guatemala						40	60
Haiti						10	90
Honduras						55	45
Jamaica						100	
Mexico	12	30			50	2	4
Nicaragua					25	45	30
Panama						60	40
Puerto Rico							100
Argentina	25	33	27		15		
Bolivia					20	65	15

Appendix Table A2.2 (Continued)

Country and Region	Temperate Cold and Cool	Temperate Subtropical Arid	Temperate Subtropical Humid	Tropical Desert	Tropical Dry and Wet Dry	Tropical Humid	Tropical Rainy
Brazil			5		12	43	40
Chile							
Colombia						30	70
Ecuador					15	15	70
Paraguay					50	10	40
Peru				5	5	15	75
Uruguay			100				
Venezuela					10	60	30
Total available Latin America	1	8	15	<1	16	30	30
Middle East (excluding N. Africa)							
Iran		90	10				
Iraq		55	45				
Israel		60	40				
Jordan		50	50				
Lebanon			100				
Saudi Arabia		73		22	2	3	
Syria							
Turkey	80		20				
Yemen (A.R.)				45	30	25	
Yemen (P.D.R.)				80	20		
Total available Middle East	11	58	10	16	3	2	0
Asia							
Afghanistan							

Burma					25	15	60
China	60		35			5	<1
Hong Kong						100	
India					54	40	6
Indonesia						20	80
Japan	50		50				
Khmer Republic						100	
Korea (D.P.R.)			100				
Korea (Rep.)			80			20	
Laos			20			65	15
Malaysia							100
Mongolia	100						
Nepal	40					60	10
Bangladesh and Pakistan		38	2		5	30	25
Philippines						50	50
Singapore							100
Sri Lanka					50	20	30
Thailand					60	30	10
North Vietnam			20		15	65	
South Vietnam						100	
Taiwan						50	50
Total available Asia	35	2	18	0	11	20	14
Western Europe							
Austria	100						
Belgium	100						
Denmark	100						
Finland	100						
France	100						
Germany (West)	100						
Greece	35		65				
Ireland	100						
Italy	50		50				
Netherlands	100						

Appendix Table A2.2 (Continued)

Country and Region	Temperate Cold and Cool	Temperate Subtropical Arid	Temperate Subtropical Humid	Tropical Desert	Tropical Dry and Wet Dry	Tropical Humid	Tropical Rainy
Norway	100						
Portugal		100	100				
Spain	15	8	77				
Sweden	100						
Switzerland	100						
United Kingdom	100						
Total available Western Europe	78	1	21	0	0	0	0
Eastern Europe and USSR							
Albania	50		40				
Bulgaria	100						
Czechoslovakia	100						
Germany (D.D.R.)	100						
Hungary	100						
Poland	100						
Romania	100						
Yugoslavia	90		10				
USSR	100						
Total available Eastern Europe and USSR	95		5				
Oceania							
Australia		47	8	20	25		
Papua-New Guinea						50	50
New Zealand	55		45				
Total available Oceania	2	43	8	18	23	3	3

Appendix Table A2.3 Rainfall

Region and Country	Rainfall Concentration Index[a]	Average Annual Rainfall (mm)
Africa		
Algeria		
Algiers	.352	752
Bene	.354	775
Angola, Luanda	.463	320
Cameroon, Yaounde	.337	1530
Central African Republic		
N'Dele	.384	1395
Bangui	.329	1535
Chad, Fort Lamy	.524	732
Dahomey, Cotonou	.391	1290
Egypt		
Alexandria	.499	130
Aswan	.500	10
Cairo	.353	32
Ethiopia, Addis Ababa	.400	1203
Ghana, Accra	.375	712
Guinea, Conakrie	.451	4225
Ivory Coast, Abidjan	.372	1920
Kenya, Nairobi	.369	1182
Liberia, Monrovia	.369	4372
Libya, Benghazi	.423	268
Malawi, Zambia	.420	1322
Mali Timbuktu	.460	1108
Mauritania, Nouakekott	.654	162
Morocco		
Casablanca	.357	400
Tangiers	.353	880
Mozambique, Laurenco Marques	.351	748
Niger, Niamey	.474	5378
Nigeria, Lagos	.372	1815
Rhodesia, Salisbury	.421	812
Senegal, Dakar	.555	538
Sierre Leone, Freetown	.412	3440
Somalia	.372	422
South Africa		
Cape Town	.350	500
Durban	.317	990
Sudan, Khartoum	.562	160
Tanzania, Dar es Salaam	.380	1048
Tunisia, Tunis	.335	412
Uganda, Kampala	.310	1155
Zaire, Leopoldville	.350	1332
Zambia, Lucasa	.448	825
Total Africa	.410	1070
Standard Deviation (S.D.)	±.077	±992

Appendix Table A2.3 (Continued)

Region and Country	Rainfall Concentration Index[a]	Average Annual Rainfall (mm)
North America		
Canada		
Ottawa	.291	858
Vancouver	.328	1435
USA		
New York, New York	.292	1050
Helena, Montana	.328	288
Topeka, Kansas	.322	800
Los Angeles, California	.418	318
Chicago, Illinois	.302	825
Total North America	.326	795
S.D.	±.044	±400
Latin America		
Costa Rica, San José	.361	1770
Cuba, Havana	.316	1205
Dominican Republic, Santo Domingo	.316	1495
El Salvador, San Salvador	.380	1750
Guatemala, Guatemala City	.391	1295
Haiti, Port-au-Prince	.327	1332
Mexico		
La Paz	.449	115
Mexico City	.388	575
Mazatlan	.463	990
Panama, Panama City	.335	3258
Puerto Rico	.301	1605
Argentina		
Parana	.329	1165
Santiago	.368	512
Bolivia		
Concepcion	.360	1020
La Paz	.365	565
Brazil		
Belem	.327	2422
Corumbá	.328	1212
Rio de Janeiro	.307	1060
Chile, Santiago	.426	355
Colombia, Bogota	.313	1045
Ecuador, Quito	.329	1098
Paraguay, Ascuncian	.306	1296
Peru		
Cuzco	.376	800
Lima	.351	270
Uruguay, Montevideo	.294	935
Venezuela, Caracas	.331	820
Total Latin America	.351	1119
S.D.	±.044	±912

Appendix Table A2.3 (Continued)

Region and Country	Rainfall Concentration Index[a]	Average Annual Rainfall (mm)
Middle East (excluding North Africa)		
Iran, Tehran	.374	242
Iraq, Baghdad	.397	140
Israel, Jerusalem	.436	495
Lebanon, Beirut	.400	880
Saudi Arabia, Riyadh	.465	88
Syria, Damascus	.397	218
Turkey, Ankara	.311	340
Yemen (A.R.), Sana	.401	82
Total Middle East	.396	332
S.D.	±.038	±292
Asia		
Afghanistan		
Kabul	.428	318
Kanadhur	.512	182
Burma, Mandalay	.377	815
China		
Canton	.347	1590
Shanghai	.316	1125
India		
Bombay	.496	1782
Calcutta	.396	1572
Hyderabad	.394	745
Indonesia, Djakarta	.330	1770
Japan, Tokyo	.313	1540
Korea (Republic), Seoul	.410	1230
Laos, Vientienne	.359	1888
Malaysia, Kuala Lumpur	.299	2402
Mongolia, Vlan Bator	.478	198
Nepal, Katmandu	.464	1405
Bangladesh and Pakistan, Karachi	.487	192
Philippines, Manila	.303	2050
Sri Lanka, Colombo	.323	2308
Thailand, Bangkok	.381	1468
North Vietnam, Hanoi	.371	1735
South Vietnam, Saigon	.368	1952
Taiwan, Taipei	.305	1808
Total Asia	.389	1368
S.D.	±.055	±685
Western Europe		
Austria		
Innsbruck	.310	845
Vienna	.297	645
Denmark, Copenhagen	.298	582
Finland, Helsinki	.295	688
France, Paris	.292	560

Appendix Table A2.3 (Continued)

Region and Country	Rainfall Concentration Index[a]	Average Annual Rainfall (mm)
Germany (West), Frankfurt	.295	602
Greece, Athens	.345	398
Ireland, Dublin	.292	742
Italy, Rome	.330	738
Netherlands, Amsterdam	.298	640
Norway, Oslo	.302	670
Portugal, Lisbon	.334	678
Spain		
Barcelona	.303	588
Mardrid	.311	412
Sweden, Stockholm	.302	565
Switzerland, Geneva	.296	848
United Kingdom, London	.293	572
Total Western Europe	.305	638
S.D.	±.016	±131
Eastern Europe and USSR		
Albania, Durres	.353	1072
Bulgaria, Sofia	.303	625
Czechoslovakia, Prague	.314	482
Hungary, Budapest	.293	780
Poland, Warsaw	.306	550
Romania, Bucharest	.300	570
Yugoslavia, Belgrade	.296	615
USSR		
Astrakan	.293	160
Moscow	.300	600
Sverdbu	.353	392
Total Eastern Europe and USSR	.311	578
S.D.	±.017	±235
Oceania		
Australia		
Melbourne	.290	642
Perth	.382	968
New Zealand, Wellington	.295	1228
Total Oceania	.322	948
S.D.	±.051	±292

[a] See footnote 8, Chapter 2.

Appendix Table A2.4 Water Balances for Selected Stations (mm)

	Potential Evaporation	Precipi-tation	Actual Evaporation	Storage	Deficit	Surplus
Calcutta, India						
January	48	10	31	195	10	0
February	58	25	45	175	13	0
March	141	33	87	121	54	0
April	171	53	92	82	79	0
May	185	140	152	70	33	0
June	179	297	179	188	0	0
July	180	323	180	300	0	31
August	168	338	168	300	0	170
September	153	254	153	300	0	101
October	135	124	135	289	0	0
November	72	18	66	241	6	0
December	37	5	30	216	7	0
Year	1520	1620	1318		202	302
Kodaikanal, India						
January	47	81	47	300	0	34
February	46	38	46	292	0	0
March	61	46	60	278	1	0
April	69	122	69	300	0	31
May	75	163	75	300	0	88
June	65	107	65	300	0	42
July	60	119	60	300	0	59
August	60	178	60	300	0	118
September	57	185	57	300	0	128
October	55	259	55	300	0	204
November	49	259	49	300	0	210
December	45	132	45	300	0	87
Year	689	1689	688		1	1001
Sukkur, India						
January	12.0	5	5	0	7	0
February	28.0	7	7	0	21	0
March	82.0	6	6	0	76	0
April	16.5	3	3	0	162	0
May	21.0	4	4	0	206	0
June	21.3	4	4	0	209	0
July	21.4	4	4	0	210	0
August	19.9	28	28	0	171	0
September	17.6	1	1	0	175	0
October	14.4	0	0	0	144	0
November	6.0	0	0	0	60	0
December	2.0	1	1	0	19	0
Year	1523	63	63	0	146	0
Rangoon, Burma						
January	108	3	55	122	53	0
February	123	6	46	82	77	0
March	158	8	41	49	117	0
April	172	50	67	32	105	0
May	176	308	176	164	0	0

Appendix Table A2.4 (Continued)

	Potential Evaporation	Precipi-tation	Actual Evaporation	Storage	Deficit	Surplus
June	156	481	156	300	0	189
July	157	580	157	300	0	423
August	151	529	151	300	0	378
September	145	393	145	300	0	248
October	147	181	147	300	0	34
November	132	68	126	242	6	0
December	110	11	79	174	31	0
Year	1735	2618	1346		389	1272
Paris, France						
January	9	43	9	260	0	0
February	13	39	13	286	0	0
March	29	46	29	300	0	3
April	51	47	51	296	0	0
May	87	54	85	265	2	0
June	109	53	99	219	10	0
July	124	58	102	175	22	0
August	110	48	81	142	29	0
September	78	47	61	128	17	0
October	44	62	44	146	0	0
November	19	52	19	179	0	0
December	11	58	11	226	0	0
Year	684	607	604		80	3
Rome, Italy						
January	12	82	12	300	0	79
February	17	68	17	300	0	117
March	32	73	32	300	0	83
April	53	66	53	300	0	20
May	91	55	89	273	1	0
June	124	40	106	178	33	0
July	152	17	90	96	101	0
August	140	26	66	55	123	0
September	99	65	75	43	64	0
October	60	128	60	93	0	0
November	30	112	30	178	0	0
December	15	98	15	272	0	0
Year	825	830	645		322	299
Chicago, USA						
January	0	49	0	339	0	0
February	0	48	0	387	0	0
March	6	68	6	300	0	62
April	37	74	37	300	0	37
May	79	90	79	300	0	11
June	122	93	121	272	1	0
July	146	84	135	221	11	0
August	132	80	115	186	17	0
September	90	76	85	177	5	0
October	51	67	51	193	0	0
November	12	59	12	240	0	0

Appendix Table A2.4 (Continued)

	Potential Evaporation	Precipi-tation	Actual Evaporation	Storage	Deficit	Surplus
December	0	50	0	290	0	0
Year	675	838	641		0	0
New York, USA						
January	0	89	0	300	0	89
February	0	86	0	300	0	86
March	12	98	12	300	0	86
April	40	86	40	300	0	46
May	86	84	86	298	0	0
June	125	85	123	260	2	0
July	149	106	141	225	8	0
August	132	113	126	212	6	0
September	94	88	93	207	1	0
October	55	88	55	240	0	0
November	22	82	20	300	0	0
December	2	85	2	300	0	83
Year	717	1090	700		17	390

Appendix Table A2.5 Population, Urbanization and Density

Region and Country	Total Population, Mid 1975 (millions)	Current Rate of Population Growth (% p.a.)	Projected Population, 2000 (millions)	Percentage Urban, 1950	Percentage Urban, 1975	Population Density 1975 (persons/km^2)
Africa						
Angola	6.4	2.3	12.5	5.8	18.3	6.1
Burundi	3.8	2.3	7.3	1.4	3.8	135.7
Cameroon	6.4	1.8	11.6	9.0	23.8	13.5
Central African Republic	1.8	2.1	3.4	10.6	35.9	2.9
Chad	4.0	2.0	6.9	4.0	13.9	3.1
Dahomey (Benin Rep.)	3.1	2.7	5.9	5.9	18.0	27.7
Ethiopia	28.0	2.4	53.7	4.8	11.2	22.9
Ghana	9.9	2.7	21.2	14.5	32.4	41.6
Guinea	4.4	2.4	8.5	5.6	19.5	17.9
Ivory Coast	4.9	2.5	9.6	6.3	20.4	15.2
Kenya	13.3	3.3	31.0	5.6	11.3	22.7
Liberia	1.7	2.3	3.2	5.7	15.2	15.3
Malagasy Rep.	8.0	2.9	17.8	7.8	17.8	13.6
Malawi	4.9	2.4	9.5	3.2	6.4	41.5
Mali	5.7	2.4	11.3	8.1	13.5	4.6
Mauritania	1.3	2.0	2.3	4.9	11.1	1.3
Mozambique	9.2	2.3	17.6	2.3	6.3	11.7
Niger	4.6	2.7	9.6	4.8	9.4	3.6
Nigeria	62.9	2.7	134.9	10.4	18.2	68.1
Rhodesia	6.3	3.4	15.1	10.2	19.7	16.1
Rwanda	4.2	2.6	8.7	0.9	3.8	161.5
Senegal	4.4	2.4	8.2	18.9	28.3	22.4
Sierre Leone	3.0	2.4	5.7	9.8	15.0	42.3
Somalia	3.2	2.7	6.5	16.5	28.3	5.0

South Africa	24.7	2.7	50.0	41.4	50.0	20.2
Tanzania	15.4	3.0	34.0	3.6	6.8	16.3
Togo	2.2	2.7	4.6	7.9	13.5	39.3
Uganda	11.4	2.9	24.2	2.9	8.4	48.3
Upper Volta	6.0	2.3	11.0	4.0	8.3	21.9
Zaire	24.5	2.5	49.4	7.9	26.2	10.4
Zambia	5.0	3.1	11.6	11.0	36.6	6.6
Algeria	16.8	3.2	36.7	21.4	49.9	7.1
Egypt	37.5	2.4	64.6	31.9	47.7	37.4
Libya	2.3	3.0	4.7	18.7	30.5	1.3
Morocco	17.5	2.9	35.9	20.6	38.0	39.2
Sudan	18.3	3.0	39.0	7.4	13.2	7.3
Tunisia	5.7	2.2	10.9	25.9	46.9	34.8
Total available Africa	392.7	2.6	798.4	13.2	24.5	14.1
North America						
Canada	22.8	1.3	31.6	60.7	78.4	2.3
USA	213.9	0.9	264.4	63.9	76.3	22.8
Total available North America	236.7	0.9	296.0	63.7	76.5	12.2
Latin America						
Costa Rica	2.0	2.8	3.7	32.8	39.9	39.2
Cuba	9.5	2.0	15.3	49.8	61.6	83.3
Dominican Republic	5.1	3.3	11.8	23.3	44.0	104.1
El Salvador	4.1	3.1	8.8	36.3	40.1	195.2
Guatemala	6.1	2.9	12.4	29.5	35.1	56.5
Haiti	4.6	1.4	7.0	12.1	20.8	164.3
Honduras	3.0	3.5	6.9	24.5	28.0	26.8
Jamaica	2.0	1.5	2.7	22.2	45.1	181.8
Mexico	59.2	3.2	132.2	42.1	63.2	30.0
Nicaragua	2.3	3.3	5.2	35.7	47.9	17.7
Panama	1.7	2.8	3.2	35.5	51.4	22.4
Puerto Rico	2.9	1.1	3.7	40.6	65.4	322.2
Argentina	25.4	1.3	32.9	64.2	80.0	9.1
Bolivia	5.4	2.5	10.3	25.8	37.2	4.9

Appendix Table A2.5 (Continued)

Region and Country	Total Population, Mid 1975 (millions)	Current Rate of Population Growth (% p.a.)	Projected Population, 2000 (millions)	Percentage Urban, 1950	Percentage Urban, 1975	Population Density 1975 (persons/km²)
Brazil	109.7	2.8	212.5	35.4	59.5	12.9
Chile	10.3	1.8	15.4	58.1	83.0	13.6
Colombia	25.9	3.2	51.5	36.0	61.8	22.7
Ecuador	7.1	3.2	14.8	28.4	41.6	25.0
Paraguay	2.6	2.8	5.3	33.2	37.4	6.4
Peru	15.3	2.9	30.6	41.3	57.0	11.9
Uruguay	3.1	1.0	3.9	80.6	65.4	17.4
Venezuela	12.2	2.9	23.6	55.2	82.4	13.3
Total available Latin America	319.5	2.7	613.7	40.9	60.4	15.9
Middle East (excluding N. Africa)						
Iran	32.9	3.0	66.6	28.7	44.3	20.0
Iraq	11.1	3.4	24.4	36.4	61.9	24.7
Israel	3.4	2.9	5.6	74.4	83.6	161.9
Jordan	2.7	3.3	5.9	34.6	56.1	27.6
Lebanon	2.9	3.0	6.1	24.5	59.8	290.0
Saudi Arabia	9.0	2.9	18.6	8.2	20.8	4.0
Syria	7.3	3.0	15.8	34.8	45.5	39.4
Turkey	39.9	2.5	72.6	21.3	43.1	83.0
Yemen (A.R.)	6.7	2.9	13.8	2.1	8.9	34.4
Yemen (P.D.R.)	1.7	2.9	3.4	14.4	29.0	5.9
Total available Middle East	117.6		232.8			19.8
Asia						
Afghanistan	19.3	2.5	36.7	6.0	12.3	29.8

Bangladesh	73.7	2.7	144.3	4.2	6.8	519.0
Burma	31.2	2.4	54.9	11.9	22.3	46.0
China	822.8	1.7	1,126.2	11.1	23.5	85.7
Hong Kong	4.2	1.4	5.6	79.1	94.9	4,200.0
India	613.2	2.4	1,059.4	17.0	21.5	187.6
Indonesia	136.0	2.6	237.5	11.8	19.3	71.4
Japan	111.1	1.3	132.9	50.3	75.2	300.3
Khmer Republic	8.1	2.8	15.8	8.7	22.5	44.8
Korea (D.P.R.)	15.9	2.6	27.5	20.5	42.7	131.4
Korea (Rep.)	33.9	2.0	52.0	18.4	47.4	345.9
Laos	3.3	2.2	5.7	5.7	11.2	13.9
Malaysia	12.1	2.9	22.1	20.0	30.2	36.3
Mongolia	1.4	3.0	2.7	22.4	51.5	0.9
Nepal	12.6	2.2	32.0	2.1	4.8	89.4
Pakistan	70.6	3.1	146.9	15.4	26.9	87.7
Philippines	44.4	3.3	89.7	26.3	36.0	148.0
Singapore	2.2	1.6	3.1	47.4	90.2	3,666.6
Sri Lanka	14.0	2.2	21.3	14.4	24.3	215.4
Thailand	42.1	3.3	85.6	10.3	16.5	81.9
North Vietnam	23.8	2.4	43.1	5.1	14.3	149.7
South Vietnam	19.7	1.8	32.7	14.3	20.2	113.2
Taiwan	16.0	1.9	21.8			444.4
Total available Asia	2,131.6		3,399.5			99.9
Western Europe						
Austria	7.5	0.2	8.1	49.4	53.0	89.3
Belgium	9.8	0.4	10.8	63.4	71.8	316.1
Denmark	5.0	0.4	5.4	67.9	82.0	116.3
Finland	4.7	0.2	4.7	32.0	55.1	13.9
France	52.9	0.9	62.1	56.0	76.1	96.7
Germany (West)	61.9	0.3	66.2	70.8	83.4	249.6
Greece	8.9	0.3	9.6	37.3	56.9	67.4
Ireland	3.1	1.2	4.0	41.1	55.3	44.3
Italy	55.0	0.5	60.9	54.4	66.7	182.7
Netherlands	13.6	0.8	16.0	73.2	79.4	331.7

Appendix Table A2.5 (Continued)

Region and Country	Total Population, Mid 1975 (millions)	Current Rate of Population Growth (% p.a.)	Projected Population, 2000 (millions)	Percentage Urban, 1950	Percentage Urban, 1975	Population Density 1975 (persons/km²)
Norway	4.0	0.7	4.5	32.6	45.5	12.3
Portugal	8.8	0.3	9.9	21.3	28.8	95.6
Spain	35.4	1.0	44.9	52.6	69.5	70.1
Sweden	8.3	0.6	9.4	65.9	83.7	18.4
Switzerland	6.5	0.8	7.4	44.2	57.4	158.5
United Kingdom	56.4	0.3	62.8	79.1	78.2	231.1
Total available Western Europe	341.8		386.7			100.8
Eastern Europe and USSR						
Albania	2.5	2.7	4.3	20.4	37.4	86.2
Bulgaria	8.8	0.7	10.0	27.6	57.9	79.3
Czechoslovakia	14.8	0.6	16.8	42.6	58.1	115.6
Germany (G.D.R.)	17.2	0.2	18.2	70.8	74.9	159.2
Hungary	10.5	0.4	11.1	36.9	47.7	112.9
Poland	33.8	0.8	39.8	38.0	56.7	107.9
Romania	21.2	0.9	25.8	25.6	44.8	89.1
Yugoslavia	21.3	0.9	25.7	22.0	38.7	83.2
USSR	255.0	1.0	315.0	39.4	60.5	11.4
Total available Eastern Europe and USSR	385.1		466.7			16.3
Oceania						
Australia	13.8	1.9	20.2	80.2	86.0	1.8
Papua-New Guinea	2.7	2.4	5.0	1.2	12.9	5.8
New Zealand	3.0	1.4	4.3	72.2	83.4	11.2
Total available Oceania	19.5		29.5	64.5	71.6	2.3
Total "world"	3,944.5		6,223.3			30.3

Appendix Table A2.6 GNP, GNP Per Capita, GNP/km²

Region and Country	GNP 1974 (Million US $)	GNP Per Capita 1974 (US $)	GNP/km² 1974 (US $)	Percentage GDP from Agri-culture
Africa				
Angola	3,370	580	2,703.1	
Burundi	300	80	10,791.4	
Cameroon	1,650	260	3,470.8	50
Central African Republic	350	200	561.4	31
Chad	360	90	280.9	
Dahomey (Benin Rep.)	370	120	3,285.9	36
Ethiopia	2,550	90	2,086.9	51
Ghana	3,310	350	13,878.4	47
Guinea	660	120	2,685.1	30
Ivory Coast	2,570	420	7,968.9	
Kenya	2,580	200	4,395.2	31
Liberia	500	330	4,488.3	19
Malagasy Republic	1,440	170	2,453.2	29
Malawi	630	130	5,316.5	46
Mali	410	70	330.7	
Mauritania	290	230	281.4	
Mozanbique	3,590	420	4,584.9	
Niger	470	100	370.9	51
Nigeria	17,830	240	19,302.8	45
Rhodesia	2,930	480	7,501.3	16
Rwanda	330	80	12,500.0	
Senegal	1,310	320	6,676.9	
Sierre Leone	520	180	7,252.4	
Somalia	260	80	408.2	
South Africa	29,210	1,200	23,929.0	10
Tanzania	2,060	140	2,179.7	36
Togo	460	210	8,214.3	43
Uganda	1,780	160	7,542.4	48
Upper Volta	470	50	1,715.3	44
Zaire	3,650	150	1,556.5	50
Zambia	2,310	480	3,071.8	49
Algeria	9,840	650	4,131.5	
Egypt	10,090	280	10,074.9	25
Libya	7,530	3,360	4,279.6	2
Morocco	6,940	430	15,543.1	31
Sudan	2,560	150	1,021.9	35
Tunisia	3,080	550	18,826.4	17
Total available Africa	128,560.0	348	4,615.0	31
North America				
Canada	136,570	6,080	13,689.7	4
USA	1,406,610	6,640	150,229.1	3
Total available North America	1,543,180.0	6,584	79,795.0	4
Latin America				
Costa Rica	1,520	790	29,980.3	22
Cuba	5,780	640	50,657.3	

Appendix Table A2.6 (Continued)

Region and Country	GNP 1974 (Million US $)	GNP Per Capita 1974 (US $)	GNP/km² 1974 (US $)	Percentage GDP from Agri-culture
Dominican Republic	2,710	590	55,645.8	22
El Salvador	1,540	390	71,962.6	26
Guatemala	3,010	570	27,844.6	28
Haiti	640	140	23,529.4	51
Honduras	990	340	8,831.4	32
Jamaica	2,270	1,140	208,256.9	8
Mexico	58,130	1,000	29,470.2	11
Nicaragua	1,310	650	10,076.9	24
Panama	1,640	1,010	21,693.1	23
Puerto Rico	7,260	2,400	815,730.3	3
Argentina	46,900	1,900	16,889.3	11
Bolivia	1,390	250	1,265.2	16
Brazil	93,180	900	10,947.0	13
Chile	8,490	820	11,216.8	8
Colombia	11,630	510	10,211.6	27
Ecuador	3,200	460	11,283.5	24
Paraguay	1,200	480	2,950.6	34
Peru	10,670	710	8,302.2	18
Uruguay	3,210	1,060	18,084.5	11
Venezuela	19,830	1,710	21,669.8	7
Total available	286,500.0			
Latin America	276,500.0	936	13,802.0	20
Middle East (excluding N. Africa)				
Iran	3,500	1,060	21,310.7	19
Iraq	10,400	970	23,178.1	18
Israel	11,150	3,380	538,647.3	6
Jordan	1,040	400	10,644.8	16
Lebanon	3,300	1,080	317,307.7	9
Saudi Arabia	16,690	2,080	7,406.9	6
Syria	3,480	490	18,790.5	26
Turkey	26,800	690	34,319.4	26
Yemen (A.R.)	740	120	3,794.9	71
Yemen (P.D.R.)	200	120	696.9	19
Total available				
Middle East	108,920.0	1,066	18,377.2	22
Asia				
Afghanistan	1,620	100	2,501.9	
Burma	2,710	90	3,997.1	34
China	245,840	340	25,616.6	
Hong Kong	6,550	1,540	655,000.0	
India	78,990	130	24,170.0	45
Indonesia	18,600	150	9,768.0	41
Japan	425,880	3,880	1,151,649.5	6
Khmer Republic	570	70	3,149.2	44
Korea (D.P.R.)	5,960	390	49,460.6	

Appendix Table A2.6 (Continued)

Region and Country	GNP 1974 (Million US $)	GNP Per Capita 1974 (US $)	GNP/km² 1974 (US $)	Percentage GDP from Agri-culture
Korea (Rep.)	15,800	470	160,406.1	29
Laos	220	70	929.1	
Malaysia	7,610	660	22,880.3	31
Mongolia	860	620	549.4	
Nepal	1,310	110	9,303.9	69
Bangladesh and	7,260	100	16,932.5	34
Pakistan	8,770	130		
Philippines	13,030	310	43,433.3	29
Singapore	4,700	2,120	7,833,333.3	6
Sri Lanka	1,140	130	26,067.1	32
Thailand	12,140	300	23,618.7	30
North Vietnam	3,000	130	18,898.0	
South Vietnam	3,400	170	20,000.0	31
Taiwan	11,370	720	315,833.3	
Total available Asia	452,020	242	21,029.0	23
Western Europe				
Austria	30,480	4,050	48,329.4	6
Belgium	51,080	5,210	1,674,754.1	4
Denmark	29,390	5,820	681,902.6	7
Finland	19,350	4,130	57,418.4	12
France	272,410	5,190	498,007.3	6
Germany (West)	365,220	5,890	1,469,698.2	4
Greece	17,680	1,970	134,040.9	16
Ireland	7,330	2,370	103,385.1	14
Italy	153,300	2,770	508,964.1	8
Netherlands	66,060	4,880	1,619,117.6	7
Norway	21,070	5,280	64,990.8	6
Portugal	13,930	1,540	151,248.6	15
Spain	68,650	1,960	135,994.5	12
Sweden	54,850	6,730	121,498.4	4
Switzerland	43,110	6,650	1,043,825.7	
United Kingdom	188,630	3,360	773.073.8	3
Total available Western Europe	1,402,540	4,108	413,729.0	8
Eastern Europe and USSR				
Albania	1,260	530	43,902.4	
Bulgaria	15,390	1,770	138,773.7	23
Czechoslovakia	47,270	3,220	369,874.8	11
Germany (G.D.R.)	58,880	3,430	544,177.5	12
Hungary	22,410	2,140	240,968.0	17
Poland	82,440	2,450	263,639.3	19
Romania				22
Yugoslavia	25,430	1,200	99,413.6	18
USSR	580,750	2,300	25,923.8	19

Appendix Table A2.6 (Continued)

Region and Country	GNP 1974 (Million US $)	GNP Per Capita 1974 (US $)	GNP/km² 1974 (US $)	Percentage GDP from Agri-culture
Total available Eastern Europe and USSR	833,830.0	1,975	35,217.0	23
Oceania				
Australia	63,450	4,760	8,255.3	6
Papua-New Guinea	1,150	440	2,490.8	
New Zealand	12,440	4,100	46,297.0	
Total available Oceania	77,040.0	4,050	9,153.0	6
Total "world"	5,321,890	1,349	40,915.0	

Appendix Table A2.7 Arable and Agricultural Land

Region and Country	Arable Land and Land Under Permanent Crops 1974 (1000 km²)	Arable Land as % Total Land 1974	Agricultural Land 1974 (1000 km²)	Population per km² Arable Land 1974
Africa				
Angola	13.1	1.1	303.1	473.6
Burundi	12.6	49.2	17.0	291.1
Cameroon	73.4	15.6	156.4	85.5
Central African Republic	59.0	9.5	60.0	29.7
Chad	70.0	5.6	520.0	56.3
Dahomey (Benin Rep.)	29.5	26.2	33.9	101.4
Ethiopia	137.3	12.5	786.3	198.9
Ghana	27.1	11.8	135.1	354.2
Guinea	41.5	16.9	71.5	103.8
Ivory Coast	91.0	28.6	171.0	52.3
Kenya	17.6	3.1	55.6	728.4
Liberia	3.8	3.4	6.2	438.7
Malagosy Republic	29.5	5.0	369.5	263.9
Malawi	28.9	30.7	47.3	166.0
Mali	117.0	9.6	417.0	47.5
Mauritania	10.0	1.0	402.5	125.7
Mozambique	30.8	3.9	470.8	293.2
Niger	150.0	11.8	180.0	29.8
Nigeria	253.0	27.4	460.2	242.0
Rhodesia	24.8	6.4	73.4	254.0
Rwanda	8.8	35.1	16.9	164.8
Senegal	23.0	12.0	80.0	187.6
Sierre Leone	37.4	52.2	59.4	77.8
Somalia	10.5	1.7	299.0	293.9
South Africa	144.7	11.9	964.7	165.8

Appendix Table A2.7 (Continued)

Region and Country	Arable Land and Land Under Permanent Crops 1974 (1000 km²)	Arable Land as % Total Land 1974	Agricultural Land 1974 (1000 km²)	Population per km² Arable Land 1974
Tanzania	123.3	13.9	517.3	121.4
Togo	22.8	40.8	24.8	96.0
Uganda	51.3	26.5	101.3	214.8
Upper Volta	53.8	19.6	191.4	109.6
Zaire	77.5	3.3	325.5	308.2
Zambia	49.8	6.6	349.8	97.7
Algeria	70.0	2.9	454.5	232.4
Egypt	28.6	2.9	NA	1,282.3
Libya	25.4	1.4	93.9	86.1
Morocco	76.3	17.1	201.3	222.7
Sudan	71.9	3.0	311.9	246.3
Tunisia	43.6	28.1	76.1	128.7
Total available Africa	2,138.6	7.6	8,804.6	162.9
North America				
Canada	431.0	4.7	681.0	52.2
USA	2,069.2	22.7	4,269.2	102.4
Total available North America	2,490.2	13.6	4,950.2	94.1
Latin America				
Costa Rica	5.0	10.2	20.7	388.0
Cuba	37.2	32.5	64.2	249.6
Dominican Republic	10.0	20.7	24.5	495.1
El Salvador	6.7	33.7	13.4	594.5
Guatemala	17.0	15.8	26.0	350.1
Haiti	9.1	33.7	14.7	492.6
Honduras	8.7	7.8	28.7	337.1
Jamaica	2.6	23.9	4.8	788.8
Mexico	273.9	13.9	948.9	209.2
Nicaragua	9.6	7.9	27.6	233.6
Panama	5.6	7.5	17.1	291.3
Puerto Rico	2.0	22.6	5.3	1,434.0
Argentina	344.2	12.4	1,782.2	72.8
Bolivia	32.2	3.0	33.0	163.8
Brazil	360.6	4.3	2,029.6	295.8
Chile	57.4	7.7	59.5	175.4
Colombia	50.9	4.9	223.9	492.9
Ecuador	43.2	15.2	65.2	159.0
Paraguay	9.7	2.4	159.7	265.2
Peru	28.8	2.2	300.0	516.9
Uruguay	18.6	10.5	154.0	165.4
Venezuela	51.8	5.9	221.0	229.0
Total available Latin America	1,384.8	7.5	6,224.0	225.6

Appendix Table A2.7 (Continued)

Region and Country	Arable Land and Land Under Permanent Crops 1974 (1000 km^2)	Arable Land as % Total Land 1974	Agricultural Land 1974 (1000 km^2)	Population per km^2 Arable Land 1974
Middle East (excluding N. Africa)				
Iran	162.8	10.0	272.8	196.1
Iraq	52.8	12.2	92.8	202.6
Israel	4.3	21.2	12.5	767.4
Jordan	13.6	14.0	13.7	191.2
Lebanon	3.5	34.0	3.6	794.9
Saudi Arabia	7.8	0.4	857.8	1,115.6
Syria	60.3	32.7	124.2	116.7
Turkey	279.0	36.2	555.0	139.4
Yemen (A.R.)	12.4	6.5	82.4	522.1
Yemen (P.D.R.)	3.3	1.2	93.9	488.5
Total available Middle East	599.8	10.4	2,108.7	233.9
Asia				
Afghanistan	84.7	13.0	144.3	221.8
Bangladesh	91.1	63.0	97.2	789.8
Burma	103.7	16.0	107.5	294.2
China	1,300.0[a]	14.0[a]	3,424.0[a]	634.7[a]
Hong Kong	0.1	9.4	0.1	41,660.0
India	1,650.7	50.0	1,780.7	362.5
Indonesia	185.0	10.0	283.8	716.5
Japan	56.2	15.0	58.6	1,951.4
Khmer Republic	30.5	17.0	36.2	258.4
Korea (D.P.R)	21.0	17.0	21.5	735.7
Korea (Rep.)	24.2	25.0	24.4	1,404.0
Laos	9.6	4.1	17.6	336.4
Malaysia	59.8	18.0	60.3	196.4
Mongolia	8.0	5.0	1,406.8	175.6
Nepal	20.0	14.0	40.0	613.9
Pakistan	194.5	24.2	244.5	351.4
Philippines	103.1	35.0	109.6	416.9
Singapore	0.1	15.5	0.2	22,190.0
Sri Lanka	19.8	30.6	24.2	689.9
Thailand	141.0	27.6	144.1	288.9
Vietnam, North	21.5	13.5	41.5	1,080.8
Vietnam, South	33.5	19.3	62.2	575.9
Total available Asia	4,158.1	19.3	8,129.3	500.0
Western Europe				
Austria	16.1	19.5	37.9	467.6
Belgium	8.2	27.0	15.5	1,058.5
Denmark	26.6	62.7	29.3	189.8
Finland	26.5	8.7	28.1	176.6
France	188.4	34.4	324.4	278.7

Appendix Table A2.7 (Continued)

Region and Country	Arable Land and Land Under Permanent Crops 1974 (1000 km²)	Arable Land as % Total Land 1974	Agricultural Land 1974 (1000 km²)	Population per km² Arable Land 1974
Germany (West)	80.8	33.3	133.4	761.7
Greece	39.0	29.8	91.6	228.3
Ireland	10.5	15.3	48.5	294.7
Italy	122.9	41.8	175.0	450.4
Netherlands	8.4	24.8	20.9	1,611.9
Norway	7.9	2.6	9.0	505.1
Portugal	36.4	41.1	42.3	577.0
Spain	208.9	41.8	320.8	167.2
Sweden	30.3	7.4	37.3	269.3
Switzerland	3.8	9.6	20.1	1,707.6
United Kingdom	71.5	29.7	186.4	786.4
Total available Western Europe	886.2	26.0	1,520.5	374.5
Eastern Europe & USSR				
Albania	6.4	22.0	7.3	377.5
Bulgaria	44.9	40.6	59.9	193.9
Czechoslovakia	52.9	42.1	70.4	277.9
Germany (D.D.R)	48.9	46.1	62.9	350.0
Hungary	55.0	59.2	67.8	190.2
Poland	150.8	22.3	192.6	223.4
Romania	104.7	45.5	149.3	200.7
Yugoslavia	80.7	31.6	144.2	262.2
U.S.S.R	2,327.0	10.4	6,078.0	108.3
Total available Eastern Europe & USSR	2,871.3	12.2	6,832.4	129.1
Oceania				
Australia	449.8	5.9	4,989.8	29.7
Papua-New Guinea	3.5	0.8	4.5	757.4
New Zealand	8.3	3.1	139.2	43.9
Total available Oceania	461.6	5.5	5,133.5	41.2

[a] For 1972. Excludes Taiwan.

Appendix Table A2.8 Fertilizer and Pesticide Consumption, 1972

Region and Country	Fertilizer Consumption: (1000 metric tons of N, P_2O_5,K_2O)	Fertilizer Consumption: (Metric tons/km^2 Arable Land)	Insecticide Consumption:[a] (1000 metric tons)	Insecticide Consumption: (kg/km^2 Arable Land)	Herbicide Consumption:[a] (1000 metric tons)	Herbicide Consumption: (kg/km^2 Arable land)
Africa						
Angola	28.2					
Burundi	1.1	0.09	0.26	22.7		
Cameroon	16.2	0.22				
Central African Republic	1.6					
Chad	4.8		0.15			
Dahomey (Benin Rep.)	4.4					
Ethiopia	19.3	0.15				
Ghana	5.7	0.22	0.025	1.0		
Guinea	1.0					
Ivory Coast	28.2	0.32	.13	1.5		
Kenya	43.6					
Liberia	3.3	0.9				
Malagasy Republic	13.1	0.46	1.09	38.6	0.015	0.5
Malawi	14.5					
Mali	8.9					
Mauritania	0.2					
Mozambique	14.0					
Niger	0.4	<0.1	0.04	0.3		
Nigeria	215.7		0.1			
Rhodesia	146.0					
Rwanda	1.1	0.14				
Senegal	23.1	0.41				
Sierre Leone	2.8	0.07				
Somalia	2.3					

South Africa	684.3	5.60				
Tanzania	19.4	0.12				
Togo	0.6	.03				
Uganda	7.2	.15				
Upper Volta	0.6	0.01				
Zaire	6.6					
Zambia	40.1	0.83				
Algeria	215.8	3.12				
Egypt	458.0	16.40	25.9	924.30		
Libya	14.2	.58				
Morocco	137.0	2.09				
Sudan	70.2	1.00	0.30	4.30	0.050	0.70
Tunisia	43.4	0.97				
Total available Africa		1.3		70.0		0.70
North America						
Canada	1,183.0	2.69	3.07	7.00	11.5	26.20
USA	17,490.5	9.16	161.42	84.50	163.6	85.60
Total available North America	18,673.5	7.8		70.3		74.6
Latin America						
Costa Rica	64.0	6.59				
Cuba	277.3	7.81				
Dominican Republic	78.5	8.18				
El Salvador	107.8	16.58	3.54	544.60	0.20	30.80
Guatemala	49.4	4.26	4.00	344.80	0.40	34.50
Haiti	1.4	0.39				
Honduras	24.0					
Jamaica	21.6					
Mexico	747.5	2.79	19.7	73.40	1.65	6.20
Nicaragua	54.5	7.57	0.08	11.10		
Panama	30.3	5.61				
Puerto Rico			0.79	359.1	0.94	427.3
Argentina	95.6	0.37	10.90	41.8	4.68	17.6

Appendix Table A2.8 (Continued)

Region and Country	Fertilizer Consumption: (1000 metric tons of N, P_2O_5,K_2O)	Fertilizer Consumption: (Metric tons/km^2 Arable Land)	Insecticide Consumption: (1000 metric tons)	Insecticide Consumption: (kg/km^2 Arable Land)	Herbicide Consumption: (1000 metric tons)	Herbicide Consumption: (kg/km^2 Arable land)
Bolivia	8.1	0.29				
Brazil	1,673.2	4.88				
Chile	188.7	4.08				
Colombia	311.9	6.23	6.34	126.5	0.30	6.0
Ecuador	52.4	1.37				
Paraguay	3.0	0.28				
Peru	9.8	0.35				
Uruguay	48.1	2.60	0.18	9.7	0.12	6.5
Venezuela	85.1					
Total available Latin America		3.2		72.8		13.5
Middle East (excluding N. Africa)						
Iran	291.7	1.80				
Iraq	41.3	0.39				
Israel	56.8	13.52				
Jordan	2.1	0.16	0.05	3.90	0.65	50.2
Lebanon	72.7	23.01				
Saudi Arabia	8.4	1.04				
Syria	42.6	0.72				
Turkey	722.6	2.62				
Yemen (A.R.)	0.4					
Yemen (P.D.R.)						

Total available Middle East	1,238.6	2.0		3.9		50.2
Asia						
Afghanistan	37.5					
Burma	56.8		0.08			
China	5,732.5					
Hong Kong						
India	2,783.0	1.69	6.05	3.7	0.15	0.1
Indonesia	475.3	2.63	0.43	2.4		
Japan	2,298.8	43.87	29.12	555.7	4.18	79.8
Khmer Republic	2.0		0.17			
Korea (D.P.R.)	396.6					
Korea (Rep.)	757.1	32.63				
Laos	0.2					
Malaysia	255.8	7.19				
Mongolia	5.5					
Nepal	14.0					
Bangalesh and Pakistan	402.7	1.78				
Philippines	236.1	2.63				
Singapore	3.0	27.27				
Sri Lanka	94.9	4.79	0.10	5.0		
Thailand	154.7	1.36				
North Vietnam						
South Vietnam	70.3	2.23				
Taiwan	b	b				
Total available Asia		3.1		18.7		2.7
Western Europe						
Austria	406.9	24.36	0.33	19.8	1.42	85.0
Belgium	523.8	67.36				
Denmark	736.0	27.67				
Finland	562.9	20.62	0.06	2.2	1.33	48.7
France	5,804.3	30.40				
Germany (West)	3,180.9	38.93	1.79	21.9	12.99	158.9
Greece	394.9	10.88	0.94	25.9		
Ireland	501.2	43.58				

Appendix Table A2.8 (Continued)

Region and Country	Fertilizer Consumption: (1000 metric tons of N, P_2O_5,K_2O)	Fertilizer Consumption: (Metric tons/km^2 Arable Land)	Insecticide Consumption: (1000 metric tons)	Insecticide Consumption: (kg/km^2 Arable Land)	Herbicide Consumption: (1000 metric tons)	Herbicide Consumption: (kg/km^2 Arable land)
Italy	1.411.8	11.49			12.60	102.5
Netherlands	617.7	66.44				
Norway	207.5	26.94			2.18	283.1
Portugal	247.9	6.18				
Spain	1,462.1	6.91				
Sweden	567.9	15.73			6.18	171.2
Switzerland	147.8	41.05			1.24	344.4
United Kingdom	1,850.4	25.63				
Total available Western Europe	18,624.0	20.6		19.7		128.2
Eastern Europe and USSR						
Albania	58.1	10.56				
Bulgaria	632.9	14.03				
Czechoslovakia	1,416.9	26.63	1.5	28.2	4.67	87.8
Germany (G.D.R.)	1,755.0	32.26				
Hungary	1,202.1	21.54	17.5	313.6	13.51	242.1
Poland	3,329.7	22.01			2.09	13.8
Romania	792.8	7.56				
Yugoslavia	734.9	9.03			4.36	53.6
USSR	12,560.0	5.49				
Total available Eastern Europe and USSR	22,482.4	7.9		174.5		72.1
Oceania						
Australia	1,450.9	3.25				
Papua-New Guinea	6.6					
New Zealand	657.7					
Total available Oceania	2,115.2	3.3				

[a] See note, p. 103.

[b] Taiwan is included in the total for Mainland China.

Appendix Table A2.9 Irrigation and Agricultural Workers

Region and Country	Irrigated Land km² (100 ha) 1974	Irrigated Land as Percentage Arable Land	Agricultural Workers per km² Arable Land 1970
Africa			
Angola	NA		
Burundi	50	0.43	
Cameroon	70	0.09	
Central African Republic	NA		
Chad	10	0.01	
Dahomey (Benin Rep.)	50	0.16	
Ethiopia	550	0.41	8.0
Ghana	180	0.69	7.0
Guinea	450	1.09	
Ivory Coast	230	0.25	6.0
Kenya	200	1.14	
Liberia	30	0.81	
Madagascar	3,500	12.41	
Malawi	50	0.18	
Mali	700	0.60	
Mauritania	30	0.30	
Mozambique	20	0.08	3.0
Niger	60	0.04	
Nigeria	150	0.06	
Rwanda	10	0.12	50.0
Senegal	1,250	2.24	6.0
Sierre Leone	30	0.08	
Somalia	1,620	15.57	
South Africa	10,170	8.33	2.0
Rhodesia	500	2.05	
Tanzania	500	0.30	5.0
Togo	30	0.13	21.0
Uganda	80	0.16	
Upper Volta	20	0.03	6.0
Zaire			
Zambia	30	0.06	1.0
Algeria	300	0.43	3.0
Egypt	28,550	100.0	161.0
Libya	1,300	5.28	
Morocco	8,500	11.33	11.0
Sudan	8,700	12.39	
Tunisia	900	2.00	5.0
Total available Africa	6,882.0	3.45	
North America			
Canada	4,500	1.02	1.0
USA	164,000	8.58	1.0
Total available North America	168,500	6.62	

Appendix Table A2.9 (Continued)

Region and Country	Irrigated Land km² (100 ha) 1974	Irrigated Land as Percentage Arable Land	Agricultural Workers per km² Arable Land 1970
Latin America			
Costa Rica	260	5.30	8.0
Cuba	5,300	14.92	36.0
Dominican Republic	1,300	26.53	21.0
El Salvador	260	4.0	42.0
Guatemala	600	5.17	
Haiti	480	13.33	
Honduras	750	8.82	12.0
Jamaica	300	12.0	
Mexico	43,400	16.17	
Nicaragua	290	4.02	8
Panama	230	4.25	11.0
Puerto Rico	390	17.72	9.0
Argentina	17,800	6.81	1.0
Bolivia	1,100	3.87	
Brazil	9,900	2.88	
Chile	12,300	26.62	4.0
Colombia	2,700	5.38	11.0
Ecuador	5,000	13.05	16.0
Paraguay	500	4.71	3.0
Peru	11,200	39.57	5.0
Uruguay	300	1.62	1.0
Venezuela	2,350	4.58	
Total available Latin America	11,670	8.3	
Middle East (excluding N. Africa)			
Iran	53,500	33.12	13.0
Iraq	41,000	39.04	
Israel	1,770	42.14	5.0
Jordan	600	4.65	
Lebanon	850	26.56	26.0
Saudi Arabia	1,850	22.83	
Syria	5,780	9.78	6.0
Turkey	19,700	7.12	9.0
Yemen (A.R.)	1,000	8.19	
Yemen (P.D.R.)	50	1.66	
Total available Middle East	126,100	15.6	
Asia			
Afghanistan	24,200	28.63	
Bangladesh	12,120	13.30	
Burma	9,870	9.57	
China	842,000	65.27	
Hong Kong	60	60	

Appendix Table A2.9 (Continued)

Region and Country	Irrigated Land km² (100 ha) 1974	Irrigated Land as Percentage Arable Land	Agricultural Workers per km² Arable Land 1970
India	320,000	19.38	57.0
Indonesia	43,800	24.21	96.0
Japan	26,750	51.04	74.0
Khmer Republic	890	2.91	
Korea (D.P.R.)	5,000	24.39	
Korea (Rep.)	11,300	48.70	129.0
Laos	850	8.98	
Malaysia	2,840	7.97	30.0
Mongolia			
Nepal	1,850	9.34	
Pakistan	141,000	73.82	
Philippines	13,510	15.06	
Singapore			
Sri Lanka	4,300	21.71	54.0
Thailand	30,180	26.45	52.0
North Vietnam			
South Vietnam			
Taiwan			
Total available Asia	1,495,390	37.6	
Western Europe			
Austria	40	0.23	6.0
Belgium	10	0.11	8.0
Denmark	10	0.03	6.0
Finland	90	0.32	10.0
France	5,500	2.88	6.0
Germany (West)	3,000	3.67	8.0
Greece	8,790	24.21	9.0
Ireland			5.0
Italy	35,500	28.88	11.0
Netherlands	720	7.74	
Norway	250	3.24	11.0
Portugal	6,250	15.58	17.0
Spain	27,830	13.15	7.0
Sweden	300	0.83	6.0
Switzerland	300	8.33	8.0
United Kingdom	860	1.19	3.0
Total available Western Europe	89,450	9.3	
Eastern Europe & USSR			
Albania	2,350	42.72	
Bulgaria	11,010	24.41	12.0
Czechoslovakia	920	1.72	8.0
Germany (G.D.R.)	1,650	3.41	8.0
Hungary	3,080	5.52	11.0
Poland	2,090	1.38	15.0

Appendix Table A2.9 (Continued)

Region and Country	Irrigated Land km² (100 ha) 1974	Irrigated Land as Percentage Arable Land	Agricultural Workers per km² Arable Land 1970
Romania	13,960	13.30	
Yugoslavia	1,330	1.63	15.0
U.S.S.R.	137,000	5.99	2.0
Total available Eastern Europe & USSR	173,390	6.2	
Oceania			
Australia	17,500	3.92	
Papua-New Guinea			
New Zealand	1,350	16.27	1.0
Total available Oceania	18,850		
Total "world"	2,257,210		

Appendix Table A2.10 Value Added by Sector, 1973 (millions US$)

Region and Country	Total Industry	Manufacturing	Mining and Quarrying	Selected Polluting Industries[a]	Value Added in Manufacturing per km² ($)
Africa					
Angola					
Burundi					
Cameroon					
Central African Republic		14.9			24
Chad					
Dahomey (Benin Rep.)					
Ethiopia					
Ghana		159.8	43.7	13.6	671
Guinea					
Ivory Coast					
Kenya	193.6	161.5	7.4	27.4	275
Liberia					
Malagasy Republic		66.9		10.1	114
Malawi	37.9	33.8	0.2	4.6	286
Mali					
Mauritania					
Mozambique	159.1	142.9	5.5	7.7	183
Niger					
Nigeria		752.7		35.2	815
Rhodesia	414.4	302.7	77.1	55.5	774
Rwanda			40.5		
Senegal					

Appendix Table A2.10 (Continued)

Region and Country	Total Industry	Manufac-turing	Mining and Quarry-ing	Selected Polluting Indus-tries[a]	Value Added in Manufac-turing per km² ($)
Sierre Leone					
Somalia		17.2	14.3		27
South Africa	6,042.3	4,231.2	1,684.7	793.7	3,465
Tanzania		90.0	13.7	9.0	95
Togo					
Uganda		73.4		6.5	311
Upper Volta					
Zaire	566.8	164.5	389.8	27.6	70
Zambia	736.6	233.5	470.9	10.7	310
Algeria	559.6	494.6	20.7	86.9	208
Egypt		702.1	124.6	95.7	701
Libya		54.9	2,782.2		31
Morocco	562.1	377.9	119.5	62.1	847
Sudan	172.1	123.3	4.6	24.6	49
Tunisia	320.5	181.6	104.9	49.8	1,107
North America					
Canada		26,149	4,312	4,987	2,621
USA		351,710	26,580	56,730	37,564
Latin America					
Costa Rica					
Cuba					
Dominican Republic		341.7		20.7	6,973
El Salvador					
Guatemala		220.0		45.2	2,037
Haiti					
Honduras		173.9		8.1	1,553
Jamaica	337.3	174.7	141.1	15.3	15,882
Mexico					
Nicaragua					
Panama		174.3		10.0	2,293
Puerto Rico					
Argentina					
Bolivia					
Brazil		8,263.2		2,018.4	971
Chile		2,273.0		682.6	3,003
Colombia		1,694.5		245.0	1,488
Ecuador		195.5		21.0	688
Paraguay					
Peru		1,230.5		237.0	958
Uruguay					
Venezuela					
Middle East (excluding N. Africa)					
Iran		1,760.5		710.2	1,068
Iraq	283.0	223.6		45.5	498

Appendix Table A2.10 (Continued)

Region and Country	Total Industry	Manufacturing	Mining and Quarrying	Selected Polluting Industries[a]	Value Added in Manufacturing per km² ($)
Israel		1,658.6	60.9	169.8	78,981
Jordan		26.8	4.6	11.7	273
Lebanon					
Saudi Arabia					
Syria	445.0	337.6	78		1,825
Turkey		2,479.2	156.7	596.1	3,174
Yemen (A.R.)					
Yemen (P.D.R.)					
Asia					
Afghanistan					
Burma					
China					
Hong Kong					
India		3,983.9	394.9	1,124.2	1,219
Indonesia		493.0		10.1	259
Japan		90,521.0	759.0	17,341.0	244,651
Khmer Republic					
Korea (D.P.R.)					
Korea (Rep.)		2,253.9	107.8	393.7	22,999
Laos					
Malaysia		480.4			1,443
Mongolia					
Nepal					
Bangladesh					
Singapore		640.1		129.4	1,066,833
Sri Lanka		151.6		15.6	2,297
Thailand		430.2		12.9	837
North Vietnam					
South Vietnam					
Taiwan					
Western Europe					
Austria		5,174	215	872	61,595
Belgium	10,999	9,610	414	2,077	310,000
Denmark		4,351	3.1	357	101,186
Finland	3,856	3,463	66	865	10,276
France	70,993	67,258		16,450	122,957
Germany (West)	114,900	105,512	3,323		425,452
Greece		1,447	97	246	10,962
Ireland	1,491	1,265	91	202	18,071
Italy	27,389	24,454	522	6,370	81,242
Netherlands	11,555	10,488	181	7,243	255,805
Norway	3,961	3,450	152	689	10,648
Portugal		1,670	40	225	18,152
Spain		9,234		1,532	18,285
Sweden	12,864	11,491	332	2,136	25,535

Appendix Table A2.10 (Continued)

Region and Country	Total Industry	Manufacturing	Mining and Quarrying	Selected Polluting Industries[a]	Value Added in Manufacturing per km² ($)
Switzerland					
United Kingdom	60,010	52,668	2,266	8,427	21,585
Eastern Europe and USSR					
Albania					
Bulgaria					
Czechoslovakia	21,324	18,846	1,858	4,222	147,239
Germany (G.D.R)					
Hungary	16,301	14,014	1,367	2,569	150,688
Poland					
Romania					
Yugoslavia	5,183	4,506	328	800	17,601
USSR	197,346	179,238			8,001
Oceania					
Australia	15,407	12,354	1,839	1,965	1,607
Papua-New Guinea		67	6		145
New Zealand		1,724		120	6,409

[a] Pulp and paper, industrial chemicals, petroleum refining, iron and steel, non-ferrous metals.

Appendix Table A2.11 Commercial Energy Use

Region and Country	Commercial Energy Use, 1972 (million metric ton coal equivalent)	Energy Use per capita 1972 (kg coal equivalent)	Energy Use per km² 1972 (metric tons)	Solid Fuels Share of Total Energy Use 1972 (Percent)	Liquid Fuels Share of Total Energy Use 1972 (Percent)
Africa					
Angola	1.02	218.5	0.95	0.2	93
Burundi	0.03	9.4	1.08	0	100
Cameroon	0.60	105.8	1.26	0	78
Central African Republic	0.90	57.5	0.14	0	89
Chad	0.07	19.7	0.05	0	100
Dahomey (Benin Rep.)	0.09	33.5	0.80	0	100
Ethiopia	0.90	37.0	0.74	0.7	94
Ghana	1.38	161.9	5.79	0.005	70
Guinea	0.40	103.8	1.63	0	98
Ivory Coast	1.39	327.3	4.31	0	98

Appendix Table A2.11 (Continued)

Region and Country	Commercial Energy Use, 1972 (million metric ton coal equivalent)	Energy Use per capita 1972 (kg coal equivalent)	Energy Use per km^2 1972 (metric tons)	Solid Fuels Share of Total Energy Use 1972 (Percent)	Liquid Fuels Share of Total Energy Use 1972 (Percent)
Kenya	1.99	175.9	3.39	2	93
Liberia	0.60	392.7	5.26	0	95
Malagasy Republic	0.49	74.2	0.83	4	92
Malawi	0.24	54.8	2.03	0.23	77
Mali	0.12	24.3	0.10	0	100
Mauritania	0.12	104.1	0.12	0	
Mozambique	1.20	150.4	1.53	45	55
Niger	0.12	30.4	0.09	0	100
Nigeria	3.83	70.4	4.15	9	80
Rhodesia	3.30	618.7	8.45	7.5	10
Rwanda	0.05	13.7	1.87	0	60
Senegal	0.64	165.7	3.27	0	100
Sierre Leone	0.35	141.9	4.88	0	100
Somalia	0.09	32.7	0.14	0	100
South Africa					
Tanzania	0.97	73.9	1.03	1	96
Togo					
Uganda	0.69	70.4	2.92	0	91
Upper Volta	0.06	11.4	0.22	0	100
Zaire	1.98	42.4	0.84	22	57
Zambia	2.24	540.7	2.98	44	32
Algeria	8.10	565.9	3.40	3	68
Egypt	11.25	344.5	11.23	5	88
Libya	9.18	4,708.6	5.21	0	18
Morocco	3.53	237.9	7.91	18	74
Sudan	1.97	127.5	0.79	0.6	99
Tunisia	1.88	372.8	11.53	7	91
Total available Africa	61.01	181.8	2.3		
North America					
Canada	235.01	11,474.8	23.56	11	49
USA	2,426.08	12,393.8	259.11	20	43
Total available North America	2,661.09	11,627.2	137.6		
Latin America					
Costa Rica	0.88	510.2	17.36	0	84
Cuba	10.22	1,246.0	89.10	1	99
Dominican Republic	1.13	280.4	23.20	1	99
El Salvador	0.75	212.8	35.05	0	92
Guatemala					

Appendix Table A2.11 (Continued)

Region and Country	Commercial Energy Use, 1972 (million metric ton coal equivalent)	Energy Use per capita 1972 (kg coal equivalent)	Energy Use, per km² 1972 (metric tons)	Solid Fuels Share of Total Energy Use 1972 (Percent)	Liquid Fuels Share of Total Energy Use 1972 (Percent)
Haiti	0.14	29.5	5.05	0	100
Honduras					
Jamaica	3.02	1,678.1	277.06	0	99
Mexico	69.12	1,400.9	35.05	4	57
Nicaragua					
Panama	0.36	252.7	4.76	0	86
Puerto Rico	11.77	4,468.7	1,322.47	0	100
Argentina	41.34	1,843.8	14.89	1.3	57
Bolivia	1.09	224.0	0.99	1	86
Brazil	52.54	567.1	6.13	9	77
Chile	15.22	1,780.4	20.13	10	50
Colombia	13.72	650.8	12.06	20	57
Ecuador	1.93	316.3	6.82	0	97
Paraguay	0.31	128.0	0.76	0	90
Peru	8.99	663.0	7.00	3	84
Uruguay	2.68	966.0	15.10	1	92
Venezuela	27.13	2,638.0	29.65	1	50
Total available Latin America	262.34	961.6	13.3		
Middle East (excluding N. Africa)					
Iran	29.14	1018.0	17.68	3	54
Iraq	6.46	684.0	14.42	0	85
Israel					
Jordan					
Levanon	2.64	952.0	253.85	0	100
Saudi Arabia	7.38	960.0	3.28	0	43
Syria	3.04	249.0	16.43	0	100
Turkey	22.88	660.0	29.33	28	61
Yemen (A.R.)	0.08	57.0	0.41	0	100
Yemen (P.D.R.)					
Total available Middle East	71.62	697.2	13.0		
Asia					
Afghanistan	0.67	40.0	1.03	19	52
Burma	1.66	61.0	2.45	10	84
China					
Hong Kong	4.21	1101.0	4,210.00	1	99
India	104.82	198.0	32.07	71	25

Appendix Table A2.11 (Continued)

Region and Country	Commercial Energy Use, 1972 (million metric ton coal equivalent)	Energy Use Use per capita 1972 (kg coal equivalent)	Energy Use per km² 1972 (metric tons)	Solid Fuels Share of Total Energy Use 1972 (Percent)	Liquid Fuels Share of Total Energy Use 1972 (Percent)
Indonesia	16.13	141.0	8.07	1	64
Japan	344.55	3468.0	933.74	22	73
Khmer Republic	0.18	27.0	0.99	6	94
Korea (D.P.R.)					
Korea (Rep.)	26.76	878.0	271.68	46	53
Laos	0.25	86.0	1.08	0	92
Malaysia	4.85	473.6	14.58	0.4	97
Mongolia					
Nepal	0.17	15.8	1.21	18	76
Bangladesh and Pakistan	13.70	37.0	14.47	3	52
Philippines	9.70	184.7		10	47
Singapore	1.90	942.8	3,166.67	0.5	99
Sri Lanka	1.91	156.4	29.12	0.5	94
Thailand	11.05	324.9	21.50	1	96
North Vietnam	3.08	149.1	17.80	79	20
South Vietnam	5.48	302.9	34.68	0	100
Taiwan					
Total available Asia excluding Japan	552.02	193.4	54.9		
Western Europe					
Austria	26.96	3,840.2	321.72	22	53
Belgium	65.00	7,141.8	2,131.14	30	56
Denmark	27.79	5,941.6	643.29	8	92
Finland	22.79	5,251.4	67.63	15	77
France	214.93	4,435.3	392.93	20	66
Germany (West)	332.78	5,756.9	1,341.85	35	52
Greece	14.32	1,712.7	108.57	29	70
Ireland	9.96	3,530.2	141.08	34	66
Italy	151.93	2,982.3	504.42	7	75
Netherlands	76.13	6,093.0	1,865.93	5	36
Norway	18.24	4,951.6	56.30	7	50
Portugal	7.80	942.4	84.78	7	79
Spain	60.89	1,883.5	120.81	26	64
Sweden	46.61	6,123.9	103.81	4	80
Switzerland	22.80	3,787.9	552.05	2	82
United Kingdom	301.83	5,771.9	1,237.01	40	46
Total available Western Europe	1,400.76	4,650.0	413.2		

Appendix Table A2.11 (Continued)

Region and Country	Commercial Energy Use, 1972 (million metric ton coal equivalent)	Energy Use per capita 1972 (kg coal equivalent)	Energy Use per km² 1972 (metric tons)	Solid Fuels Share of Total Energy Use 1972 (Percent)	Liquid Fuels Share of Total Energy Use 1972 (Percent)
Eastern Europe and USSR					
Albania	1.53	712.8	53.31	25	57
Bulgaria	35.43	4,405.5	319.48	56	42
Czechoslovakia	99.10	7,301.9	775.43	79	16
Germany (G.D.R.)	102.18	6,347.5	946.11	83	14
Hungary	34.10	3,498.1	365.59	52	30
Poland	150.66	4,860.4	482.88	85	8
Romania	65.32	3,355.2	275.61	23	23
Yugoslavia	33.44	1,717.8	130.73	53	36
USSR	1,179.60	5,087.6	52.66	39	34
Total available Eastern Europe and USSR	1,701.36	4,575.5	71.9		
Oceania					
Australia	73.88	6,081.8	9.61	47	45
Papua-New Guinea					
New Zealand	8.39	3,086.6	31.31	19	54
Total available Oceania	82.27	5,189.4	10.3		

Appendix Table A2.12 Gasoline Consumption and Refining

Region and Country	Gasoline Consumption 1973 (millions U.S. gal per yr)	Gasoline Consumption per capita 1973 (U.S. gal per year)	Petroleum Refining Capacity 1975 (1000 bbl/day)
Africa			
Angola			36
Burundi			
Cameroon			
Central African Republic			
Chad			
Dahomey (Benin Rep.)			
Ethiopia	31.0	1.2	14
Ghana	76.0	8.2	28
Guinea			

Appendix Table A2.12 (Continued)

Region and Country	Gasoline Consumption 1973 (millions U.S. gal per yr)	Gasoline Consumption per capita 1973 (U.S. gal per year)	Petroleum Refining Capacity 1975 (1000 bbl/day)
Ivory Coast			
Kenya	77.0	6.2	48
Liberia	15.0	10.3	10
Malagasy Republic	32.0	3.8	15
Malawi			
Mali			
Mauritania			
Mozambique	30.0	3.6	17
Niger			
Nigeria	245.0	3.4	60
Rhodesia			
Rwanda			
Senegal			
Sierre Leone	15.0	5.4	10
Somalia			
South Africa	1,486.0	61.2	397
Tanzania	30.0	2.1	16
Togo			
Uganda			
Upper Volta			
Zaire	77.0	3.3	16
Zambia			
Algeria	155.0	10.5	115
Egypt	108.0	3.0	118
Libya	76.0	35.2	76
Morocco	123.0	7.7	59
Sudan	31.0	1.8	22
Tunisia	30.0	5.5	25
Total available Africa	2,637.0	9.0	
North America			
Canada	7,797.0	352.3	2,024
USA	101,000.0	480.0	14,843
Total available North America	108,797.0	467.9	
Latin America			
Costa Rica	31.0	16.6	11
Cuba	491.0	55.0	122
Dominican Republic			
El Salvador	30.0	8.0	14
Guatemala	77.0	14.9	25
Haiti			
Honduras	30.0	10.8	14
Jamaica	92.0	46.8	33
Mexico			760
Nicaragua	46.0	23.3	13

Appendix Table A2.12 (Continued)

Region and Country	Gasoline Consumption 1973 (millions U.S. gal per yr)	Gasoline Consumption per capita 1973 (U.S. gal per year)	Petroleum Refining Capacity 1975 (1000 bbl/day)
Panama	92.0	58.6	100
Puerto Rico			283
Argentina	1671.0	68.8	721
Bolivia	107.0	20.1	26
Brazil	3,388.0	33.5	962
Chile	521.0	50.9	124
Colombia	797.0	35.4	172
Ecuador	154.0	22.7	44
Paraguay			5
Peru	521.0	35.8	130
Uruguay	77.0	25.7	43
Venezuela	1,287.0	114.1	1,532
Total available Latin America	9,412.0	43.4	
Middle East (excluding N. Africa)			
Iran	475.0	14.8	755
Iraq	168.0	16.1	169
Israel	130.0	40.5	201
Jordan	52.0	20.4	21
Lebanon	68.0	22.8	54
Saudi Arabia	219.0	28.2	610
Syria	153.0	22.0	50
Turkey	445.0	11.7	316
Yemen (A.R.)	45.0	28.8	169
Yemen (P.D.R.)			
Total available Middle East	1,755.0	15.9	
Asia			
Afghanistan			
Burma	61.0	2.0	28
China			265
Hong Kong	46.0	11.1	
India	628.0	1.1	555
Indonesia	521.0	4.2	428
Japan	6,868.0	63.4	5,134
Khmer Republic			
Korea (D.P.R.)			
Korea (Rep.)	353.0	10.7	425
Laos			
Malaysia	276.0	24.4	969
Mongolia			
Nepal			
Bangladesh	31.0	0.41	120
Pakistan	107.0	1.5	

Appendix Table A2.12 (Continued)

Region and Country	Gasoline Consumption 1973 (millions U.S. gal per yr)	Gasoline Consumption per capita 1973 (U.S. gal per year)	Petroleum Refining Capacity 1975 (1000 bbl/day)
Philippines	736.0	16.6	274
Singapore			
Sri Lanka	62.0	4.7	34
Thailand	366.0	9.3	166
North Vietnam			
South Vietnam			
Taiwan	276.0	17.9	210
Total available Asia excluding Japan	10,357.0	3.4	
Western Europe			
Austria	721.0	95.8	220
Belgium	966.0	98.9	867
Denmark	613.0	122.1	220
Finland	475.0	101.4	196
France	5,488.0	105.2	3,342
Germany (West)	6,975.0	112.6	2,987
Greece	322.0	36.1	411
Ireland	291.0	96.0	56
Italy	3,925.0	71.5	3,953
Netherlands	1,334.0	99.3	1,841
Norway	383.0	96.7	168
Portugal	245.0	27.2	110
Spain	1,287.0	37.0	1,165
Sweden	1,134.0	139.3	248
Switzerland	935.0	145.4	138
United Kingdom	5,887.0	105.1	2,783
Total available Western Europe	30,981	101.2	
Eastern Europe and USSR			
Albania			
Bulgaria			
Czechoslovakia			250
Germany (G.D.R.)			
Hungary			210
Poland			146
Romania			320
Yugoslavia	612	29.2	288
USSR			6,750
Total Available Eastern Europe and USSR		29.2	
Oceania			
Australia	3,157	240.4	722
Papua-New Guinea			
New Zealand	566	191.2	54
Total available Oceania	3,723	231.1	

Appendix Table A2.13 Health Indicators

Region and Country	Percentage Dwellings with 3 or More Persons/ Room 1970	Percentage Dwellings with Piped Water 1970	Percentage Population with "Reasonable Access" to Sanitary Water Supply 1970	Infant Mortality 1970 (Deaths per 1000 Births)
Africa				
Angola				
Burundi			2	
Cameroon			32	
Central African Republic			3	
Chad			26	
Dahomey (Benin Rep.)			29	
Ethiopia			6	155.0
Ghana			33	122.0
Guinea			11	
Ivory Coast			44	
Kenya	41		12	119.0
Liberia			17	137.3
Malagasy Republic			12	
Malawi				
Mali			3	
Mauritania			17	
Mozambique				
Niger			20	
Nigeria	41		20	
Rhodesia				
Rwanda				127.0
Senegal			81	
Sierre Leone			12	
Somalia			15	
South Africa				
Tanzania			13	
Togo			18	
Uganda			25	120.0
Upper Volta			25	
Zaire			13	
Zambia		27	37	
Algeria			39	140.0
Egypt	16		93	116.3
Libya	31		60	
Morocco		52	51	
Sudan			18	
Tunisia			49	125.0
North America				
Canada		96	100	18.8
USA		98	100	19.8

Appendix Table A2.13 (Continued)

Region and Country	Percentage Dwellings with 3 or More Persons/ Room 1970	Percentage Dwellings with Piped Water 1970	Percentage Population with "Reasonable Access" to Sanitary Water Supply 1970	Infant Mortality 1970 (Deaths per 1000 Births)
Latin America				
Costa Rica			71	61.5
Cuba				40.1
Dominican Republic			34	
El Salvador		38	40	66.6
Guatemala			39	87.1
Haiti			12	146.9
Honduras	26		33	117.2
Jamaica	34	38	57	32.2
Mexico	47	49	54	68.5
Nicaragua	42		34	
Panama	38	64	66	40.5
Puerto Rico		77		28.6
Argentina	12		55	63.3
Bolivia			34	
Brazil	5	39	57	
Chile	19	78		79.2
Colombia			65	80.6
Ecuador	40		33	76.6
Paraguay	53		11	
Peru	34		34	
Uruguay			77	42.6
Venezuela	21	72.7	75	49.3
Middle East (excluding N. Africa)				
Iran			40	
Iraq			49	104.0
Israel	11	96	100	22.9
Jordan			77	
Lebanon			92	67.3
Saudi Arabia			49	
Syria	36		71	
Turkey		36	63	
Yemen (A.R.)			4	
Yemen (P.D.R.)			57	
Asia				
Afghanistan				
Burma				
China				
Hong Kong		95	90	19.6
India				140.2

Appendix Table A2.13 (Continued)

Region and Country	Percentage Dwellings with 3 or More Persons/ Room 1970	Percentage Dwellings with Piped Water 1970	Percentage Population with "Reasonable Access" to Sanitary Water Supply 1970	Infant Mortality 1970 (Deaths per 1000 Births)
Indonesia		11	61	137.0
Japan	7			13.1
Khmer Republic			45	
Korea (D.P.R.)				
Korea (Rep.)	59	38	55	41.0
Laos			48	
Malaysia	51		38	
Mongolia		3	21	
Nepal	20		3	
Bangladesh and Pakistan	59		20	128.4
Philippines		23	35	96.9
Singapore			74	20.5
Sri Lanka		14	14	53.0
Thailand		12	17	62.0
North Vietnam				
South Vietnam				
Taiwan				16.8
Western Europe				
Austria		100	100	25.9
Belgium		87	100	20.5
Denmark		99	100	14.2
Finland	7	72		13.2
France	5	94	100	18.2
Germany (West)		100	100	23.6
Greece	14	81		29.6
Ireland	2	79		19.5
Italy		89		29.6
Netherlands				12.7
Norway	1	97	100	12.7
Portugal	7	82		58.0
Spain				28.0
Sweden		98	100	11.0
Switzerland		100	100	15.1
United Kingdom		100	100	18.5
Eastern Europe and USSR				
Albania				
Bulgaria	9			27.3
Czechoslovakia		77		22.1
Germany (G.D.R.)		100	100	18.5
Hungary		58		35.9
Poland	12	52		33.2

Appendix Table A2.13 (Continued)

Region and Country	Percentage Dwellings with 3 or More Persons/ Room 1970	Percentage Dwellings with Piped Water 1970	Percentage Population with "Reasonable Access" to Sanitary Water Supply 1970	Infant Mortality 1970 (Deaths per 1000 Births)
Romania				49.4
Yugoslavia		42		55.5
USSR				24.4
Oceania				
Australia				17.9
Papua-New Guinea				
New Zealand				16.7

Chapter 3

TRADE AND INVESTMENT IMPACTS

INTRODUCTION

The impact of environmental controls on the foreign trade and investment position of developing countries has been a prominent issue since preparations were first started for the Stockholm Conference. Some of the effects are seen as positive and others negative.[1] Unfortunately, analysis of the issue has suffered from a confusion of concepts and a lack of empirical research. Most discussion has been on a speculative level. Consequently, the effect of environmental controls on the trade and investment links between North and South remains a controversial and contentious subject.

The purpose of this chapter is to set forth the issues as clearly as possible and to assess the importance of environmental control policies for the trade and investment position of developing countries. If the trade and investment effects appear important, the material presented here will be useful for policy formation. If the effects appear trivial, developing countries should turn their attention to other trade and investment questions of greater importance. A special effort has been made to review, assemble, and interpret empirical material. The data are not adequate for very strong conclusions, but tentative estimates and conclusions are presented.

The impacts on developing countries are part of the larger question of the international economic effects of environmental controls. Economists have attempted to incorporate environmental resources and controls into the current theory of international trade and to develop an economic theory for transnational pollution.[2] Equally important, the industrial countries have agreed to a set of principles to guide their trade policy with regard to environmental control measures. These were formalized in 1972 with the adoption by the Organization for Economic Cooperation and Development (OECD) of the "Guiding Principles Concerning International Economic Aspects of Environmental Policies." The developing countries have not subscribed to these principles nor developed their own. However, the trade prospects of developing countries are determined in large measure by the trade policies of industrial countries. Therefore, the Guiding Principles are important in analyzing North–South trade impact.

The order of exposition is as follows: the following section presents some useful analytical distinctions; the next section describes the various channels through which the trade and investment impact is transmitted; the third section develops the necessary analytical theory, including modification of the theory of comparative advantage. The fourth section describes the trade/environment policies undertaken by industrial countries as they effect developing countries. The next five sections consider, respectively, macroeconomic effects, microeconomic effects, product standards, resource recovery, and foreign direct investment.

CONCEPTS

It is useful to begin by distinguishing between production (process) pollution and product (consumption) pollution.[3] Production pollution involves wastes generated during the process of producing goods and services and corresponds to the a_{11} and a_{12} type externalities described in Chapter 1. Product pollution involves environmental damages associated with the use and disposal of final products. It corresponds to the a_{21} and a_{22} types. Examples are auto emissions and roadside litter.[4]

The distinction is particularly useful in the context of international trade. Both types of pollution cause environmental damages, but the location of damages differs. Barring transnational pollution, production pollution damages are borne by the country of production and export. Product pollution damages are borne by the country of destination and final consumption.

A country with no environmental controls on the production of goods and services forces its residents to bear the social costs of environmental damages, but the market price of its exports reflects only private production costs. The country's exports are given an implicit subsidy. At the same time, the importing country receives subsidized imports. This introduces a distortion into international trade and results in a misallocation of resources. In contrast to production pollution, the costs of *product* pollution are borne by the country of consumption. The market price of the good crossing the border will reflect the full social costs of production in the exporting country, but consumer prices will not include environmental use and disposal costs.[5] Since consumer prices are distorted, the consumption pattern departs from its optimum, and resources are again misallocated.

It follows that environmental control measures can be classified according to whether they are designed to abate production or product pollution. Each will have fundamentally different trade and investment effects. Controls on production, including related occupational health and safety regulations, will increase production costs. Unless offset by government subsidy, the supplier will suffer a deterioration in his international competitive position. The increased costs will result regardless of the type of environmental control measure—emission and effluent charges, discharge limits, or production facility design standards. Assuming for the moment that environmental control (EC) costs will be higher in industrial countries, either because they select higher environmental quality standards or because they have more fully exhausted the assimilative capacity of their environment, some competitive advantage in international trade may accrue to developing countries. Also, investment may be reallocated toward the lower environmental control cost countries. Stated crudely, the important factors for developing countries are (1) the magnitude of the trade advantage they might gain by keeping their EC costs low, (2) the environmental damage that would result to them, and (3) whether they wish to accept investments from industrial countries seeking low EC cost locations.

Environmental controls on products pose different problems for developing countries. Most product controls will take the form of product design and operating standards, although occasionally consumption and discard taxes may be employed. Although production costs and prices may increase as a result of design and operating standards for the product (as is the case for auto emission control devices), the price increase is not the result of deliberately closing the gap between private and social production costs, as is the case for production pollution controls. Rather, the increased price reflects a changed and improved product. Also, both the exporter and the import competing firms will presumably have to meet the same standards; therefore, both will have product cost increases. The critical trade issue for developing countries is whether the product standards applied by industrial countries will be a barrier to their exports. The question is one of market access for developing countries. It merges with the venerable issue of health, safety, and sanitary regulations applied to articles moving in international trade. As such, it falls logically in the category of non-tariff trade barriers (NTBs) and can be analyzed from that perspective.[6]

In summary, production pollution controls will change production costs, international competitive position of suppliers, and hence international trade and investment patterns. Developing countries may improve their trade position if their EC costs are low relative to industrial countries. They must weigh the trade gain against the associated environmental damages. Product pollution controls are mainly product standards and can act as traditional NTBs, possibly harming market access for developing countries. Whether either of these involves serious trade amounts is a question requiring further investigation.

It cannot be stressed too strongly that some alteration in the level and pattern of international trade is both expected and desirable as countries incorporate environmental control costs into production costs and establish product standards. International trade has started from a distorted situation in which market prices do not reflect social production costs. The fundamental purpose of environmental controls is to correct these distortions, both domestically and internationally. Since environmental resources and the demand for environmental quality are recognized as determinants of comparative advantage, some reallocation of economic activity toward environmentally less damaging locations is a necessary part of the correction process.

Another useful distinction in analyzing the international economic effects of environmental controls is to separate macroeconomic and microeconomic effects. Macro effects include the impact of environmental controls on aggregate variables—price levels, employment, national income, and the trade balance. The direction of causation runs both ways—an environmental control program may deteriorate a country's trade balance by making it less competitive, but an environmentally induced slowdown in GNP may improve the trade balance.

Micro effects include the impact on production, employment, prices, profits, and trade of specific industries and firms. Even if macro effects are small or easily offset, the effects on individual industries can be substantial. We can demonstrate this by assuming a major pollution abatement program undertaken in a floating exchange rate regime. The abatement expenditures will increase production costs and erode the competitive position of export and import competing firms. However, the macroeconomic problem of trade balance deterioration does not arise, because the loss of international competitiveness triggers a depreciation of the currency and a restoration of the trade balance.

However, the currency depreciation does not restore individual industries in the export and import competing sector to their original position. Those industries with relatively low EC costs will find that the exchange rate change more than offsets their abatement costs, and their competitive position improves. Conversely, relatively high EC cost industries will find some relief through currency depreciation, but not sufficient to restore them to their original competitive position. Accordingly, the composition of both production and trade will change. The shift will be environmentally beneficial to the country, with the clean industries accounting for a larger share of production. These propositions are discussed more fully in the theory section.

CHANNELS

We can now list the channels through which environmental control programs undertaken in industrial countries may affect the trade prospects of developing countries. The first two are implied in the previous discussion. The first channel is increased production costs as industrial countries impose more stringent abatement regulations. Environmentally related occupational health and safety regulations, such as exposure standards to asbestos dust and vinyl chloride, can also be included, even though the environmental damages are internal to the workplace. Assuming that control costs are higher in industrial countries, the direction of the effect is clear. Developing countries will receive some competitive advantage for their exports from lower control costs. However, they will pay higher prices for imports from advanced countries, because the latter include all social production costs in product price.

Second, the imposition of environmentally related product standards in industrial countries may adversely affect market access for developing countries. The important questions are similar to those posed by other types of standards: Do the standards reflect legitimate social objectives for the importing country, or are they covertly used as trade barriers? Are the standards applied to domestic and imported products in a nondiscriminatory fashion? Should standards be harmonized among importing countries? Will the trade effect be important or trivial?

Third, waste disposal problems in industrial countries have increased the desirability of recycling and resource recovery. By adding the social cost of waste disposal, the economics of resource recovery become more attractive. This will affect the demand for virgin raw materials. Developing countries that export raw materials will be adversely affected.

Fourth, environmentally related shifts in consumption patterns in industrial countries may shift trade in selected items or in intermediate inputs to these items. One example is the phasing out of leaded gasoline, with impact on the lead trade. A second, until the oil crisis, was the premium placed on low-sulfur oil from North Africa and the reduced demand for high-sulfur Venezuelan oil.

Fifth, if rigorous environmental control programs divert resources away from traditional production and decrease investment, industrial country growth rates will slacken. Hence demand for imports from developing countries might be reduced. Note that the mere diversion of resources toward abatement expenditures need not reduce import demand, because these expenditures will also have an import component. Only if the resource diversion also leads to a reduced rate of investment will there be a direct connection with demand for developing country exports.

Finally, environmental controls will affect shipping costs and hence marine freight rates. One example is the design standards for oil tankers established by the International Convention for the Prevention of Pollution from Ships. Increased freight rates will generally discourage trade. However, further processing of raw materials in developing countries might be stimulated if the processing involves significant weight loss and therefore higher product value per ton shipped.

This listing is neither exhaustive, nor are the categories mutually exclusive. More important, nothing has been said about the importance or magnitude of the effects anticipated. However, the listing does provide a useful method for organizing the subsequent material.

THEORY

The effects of international differences in production pollution control costs can be readily illustrated in a partial equilibrium context. If industrial countries have higher environmental standards leading to higher production costs than developing countries, *ceterius paribus,* this will result in higher prices, some displacement of domestic production, and increased imports into industrial countries. Developing countries will experience an increase in the volume and price of exports and hence foreign exchange earnings. The size of the price, production, and import effects will depend on the differences in control costs between countries, the elasticity of demand for the product, and the supply elasticities of the exporters and domestic producers.

Consider Diagram 3.1.[7] *DD* is domestic demand in the importing country, S_f foreign export supply, S_d domestic supply, and $S_d + S_f$ total supply to the market. Initial equilibrium is at price P_1, with OQ_6 consumed, OQ_2 supplied by domestic producers, and OQ_3 the amount of imports. An increase in environmental control costs, C, shifts the domestic supply to S'_d and total market supply to $S'_d + S_f$. Equilibrium is reestablished at P_2.

Price is neither constant, as would be the case with either infinitely elastic demand or infinitely elastic foreign supply, nor does it rise the full amount of the increase in control costs. The initial increase in domestic production costs increases the demand for imports, but because imports are not perfectly elastic, price starts to rise, consumption is reduced, and some of the initial displacement of domestic supply is restored through the induced increase in price. At

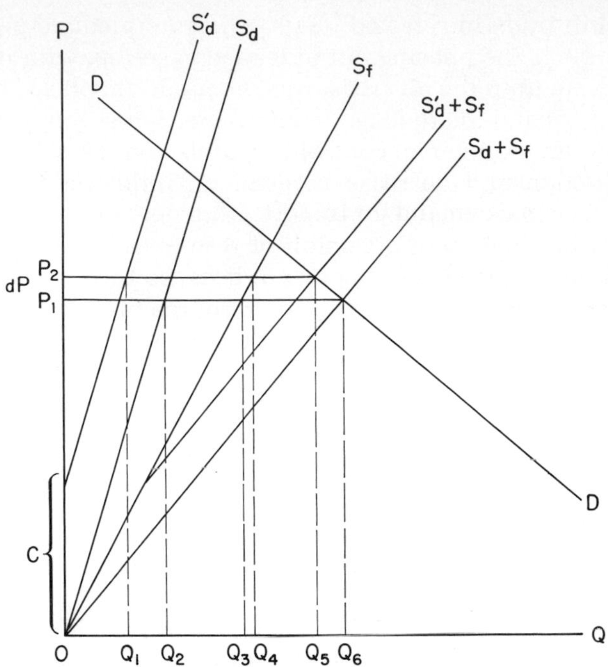

Diagram 3.1. Price and trade effects, partial equilibrium.

equilibrium, consumption has fallen from OQ_6 to OQ_5, imports have increased from OQ_3 to OQ_4, and domestic production has fallen from OQ_2 to OQ_1.

The percentage price change resulting from the imposition of environmental control costs can be stated as follows:

$$\frac{dp}{p} = \frac{C}{p}\left(\frac{E_{sd} \cdot Q_{sd}}{E_{sx} Q_x + E_{sd} Q_{sd} - E_d Q_d}\right) \tag{1}$$

where: C is the environmental control cost difference
p is the price of the product
E_{sd} is domestic supply elasticity
E_{sx} is foreign supply (export) elasticity
E_d is domestic demand elasticity
Q_{sd} is domestic supply
Q_d is domestic demand
Q_x is quantity exported (imported).

The percentage change in the value of imports (exports) is the combination of the positive price and quantity effect and can be expressed:

$$\frac{dV_x}{V_x} = \frac{dP}{P}(E_{sx} + 1) \tag{2}$$

Note that both the negative consumption effect and the induced increase in domestic production work to limit the increased foreign exchange earnings for developing countries. For example, if E_{sx}, E_{sd} and E_d are 2, 1, and 1, respectively, and total consumption is initially shared equally between imports and domestic production, and the control costs, C, are 10% of product price, the price will rise only 2%, and the total foreign exchange earnings will rise only 6%. Substantial increases in production costs because of pollution abatement may lead to more modest changes in export earnings for developing countries, a conclusion that they should bear in mind when formulating their own environment policies.

It should also be noted that the relevant environmental cost concept includes not only abatement costs imposed on the process of manufacture, but all control costs passed along through higher prices on purchased inputs to the production process.[8] For example, the relevant cost for hardwood plywood suppliers in the United States market is not only the direct controls placed on plywood manufacture, but control costs on all inputs including peeler logs, transport to mill, power, and so on. Control costs can be stated more formally as

$$C_j = C_j^* + \sum_{i=1}^{n} a_{ij} C_i$$

where C_j is the total direct and indirect costs for the output of industry j, C_j^* is the direct cost on the process of manufacturing j; a_{ij} is the input output coefficient from industry i to industry j, and C_i is the abatement cost in industry i. Of course, to calculate the trade effect, it is the *difference* between control costs in the importing and exporting country that is relevant. Because developing countries already have some abatement measures, analysis based only on industrial country control costs will overstate the trade effect.

The trade effects of environmental controls on developing countries can also be investigated using general equilibrium techniques and modifying the existing theory of comparative advantage. We analyze two different cases and then present a more general discussion of assimilative capacity and comparative advantage.

First consider case 1, a situation in which an industrial country has a strong preference for the "good" environmental quality that is currently being damaged by the production of its export good A. To keep the initial analysis simple, assume that the only available method for improving environmental quality is to change the composition of output. Expenditure on pollution abatement is not an option.[9]

The situation is depicted in Diagram 3.2. The top panel shows the transformation function (production possibility frontier) for goods A and B, and the international terms of trade shown by the slope of the line T. Demand for A and B is represented by community indifference curves U_1 and U_2. (Homothetic utility function assumed for convenience.) Initial production is at point P, consumption is at point C, and the trade triangle PNC is formed. PN of good A is exported; NC of good B is imported. Because there are now three elements in the utility function—goods A and B and environmental quality—consumption points in the AB space no longer measure welfare levels. For this reason the bottom panel, vertically aligned with the top panel, is introduced. Each point on the transformation curve is associated with one level of B production and one level of welfare derived from the consumption of A and B. Therefore, we draw the welfare function W_{A+B} as a function of the level of production of B. As the production point moves to the right, sliding down the transformation curve and assuming constant terms of trade, welfare derived from the con-

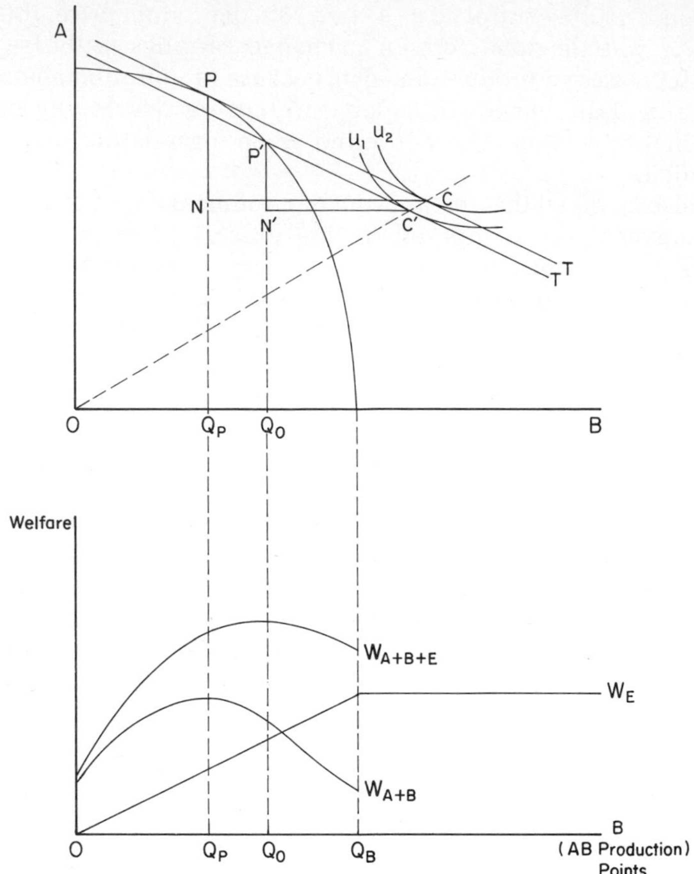

Diagram 3.2. Welfare and trade effects of environmental controls, Case 1.

sumption of A and B first increases, reaches a maximum of Q_p, and then declines. W_{A+B} includes the welfare derived from being able to trade along the price line T (the gains from trade). Without introducing environmental quality, welfare is maximized at Q_p, where the international terms of trade T are just tangent to the transformation curve at P and the highest possible indifference curve at C.

To represent the assumed deterioration of environmental quality from the production of the export good A, the welfare function for environmental services, W_E is introduced. The exact shape is unknown, but it should be inversely associated with A production and hence positively associated with B production. Hence it is drawn positive over the range OQ_B and constant thereafter, since A is no longer produced. Total welfare W_{A+B+E} is the vertical sum of welfare derived from conventional goods, W_{A+B}, and from environmental services W_E.

Neither the initial production point Q_p nor the complete elimination of A production at Q_B maximizes welfare. Rather, the optimal production point is at Q_0 where the marginal losses from departing from the free trade equilibrium point are just equal to the marginal gains from increasing the flow of environmental services. In effect, the country is equating the marginal utility derived from goods A and B with the marginal utility derived from environmental services. To do this it alters the composition of production away from good A toward the environmentally neutral good B, accepts smaller gains from trade, but increases welfare derived from environmental services.

As a result of rearranging production, output of A has decreased, B has increased (production moving to point P'), consumption of both goods has shrunk to point C', and trade has declined from PNC to $P'N'C'$. If the country is a large supplier, its terms of trade may improve, and some reverse movement of the production point occurs (not shown on the diagram).

If, on the other hand, the production of the import competing good B is more environmentally damaging, opposite conclusions would obtain. Production of A would increase, strengthening international specialization, the volume of trade would increase, and the industrial country terms of trade would tend to deteriorate. Accordingly, we conclude that the effect on trade partners (developing countries) will be a decline in the volume of trade and their terms of trade if industrial country exports are environmentally more damaging than import competing goods and an expansion of trade at improved terms if industrial country imports are more damaging than their exports. One study of the United States concluded that pollution control costs, a proxy for damages, were approximately equal for export and import competing industries (1.75% vs. 1.52% of sales price); thus the effect may be neutral.[10] The data, however, are no longer current and should not be generalized to other industrial countries.

Whether the production shift in industrial countries is toward the export or import competing sectors is important in identifying the trade volume and terms of trade effect on developing countries. In both cases, however, there will be some shift at the margin away from environmentally damaging activities toward cleaner ones. If we assume for the moment that developing countries have a lower effective demand for environmental quality, they will increase their comparative advantage (reduce their disadvantage) in dirty industries.

This conclusion is built on the assumption that the only abatement measure available is changing the composition of production. However, similar conclusions emerge if expenditures on pollution abatement are allowed. It will generally be less costly to combine production composition shifts with abatement expenditures to achieve a desired improvement in environmental quality, rather than relying totally on production composition changes. Still, the most damaging activities will be those with greatest abatement costs (invoking the marginal principle for determining optimal abatement levels), and for this reason comparative advantage in relatively dirty industries will again shift toward areas with low environmental standards—by assumption, developing countries.

Abatement cost data by industry is examined later. Here we simply note that the most highly polluting industries seem to be those which transform basic raw materials into intermediate inputs—manufacture of pulp and paper, nonferrous metal smelting and refining, iron and steel production, petroleum refining, and electrical energy production. The location of some of these industries may be determined by raw material supplies or proximity to markets for transport cost and other reasons. However, in other industries, initial processing can be shifted from one location to another. We conclude that environmental considerations should encourage local processing of raw materials originating in developing countries. This is in harmony with the export policies of most developing countries. Transport costs and capital requirements will limit the movement of developed country raw materials to developing countries for processing and reexport.

The analysis so far is deficient because it does not include the resource-using aspect of pollution abatement, nor does it recognize the possible productivity gains from preserving environmental resources, a point that is stressed in this study. Case 2 assumes that abatement involves the use of real resources, and that the activity of abatement uses intensively the same factor input as the export sector (say capital). Diagram 3.3 assumes that the economy is capital abundant in the Heckscher-Olin sense, export good *X* is capital intensive relative to import good *M*, and pollution abatement has a relatively high capital to labor ratio. The initial transformation function is given by *XM*, terms of trade (assumed constant) by *T*; production is at point *P*, consumption at *C*; exports are seen in the trade triangle as *PN* and imports as *NC*.[11]

Following Walter, welfare will be improved by diverting resources away from conventional goods *X* and *M* into pollution abatement. Again, consumption points in the *XM* space no longer measure welfare because the contribution of environmental services is not represented. The resource diversion away from *X* and *M* will shrink the transformation curve inwards. The shrinkage will be proportionately greater for the export good, *X*, because by assumption

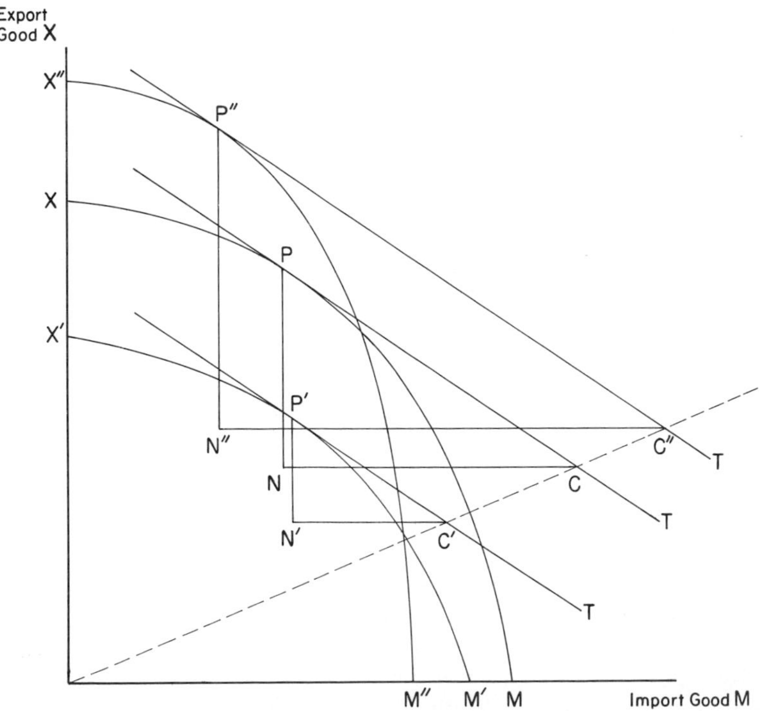

Diagram 3.3. Trade effects of environmental controls, Case 2.

both it and pollution abatement use the same factor (capital) intensively. This is represented by the shrunken transformation curve $X'M'$. Production of conventional goods decline to P', consumption declines to C', and trade volume is reduced to $P'N'$ for exports and $N'C'$ for imports. If the foreign offer curve is less than infinitely elastic, home country terms of trade improve on a smaller trade volume. Conversely, if pollution abatement were intensive in the country's scarce factor, resource diversion toward abatement would shrink production of the M good disproportionately, the terms of trade of the home country would worsen, and trade volume might increase.

There have not been any systematic studies of the factor intensity of pollution abatement. Casual observation suggests that it varies according to type of pollutant and industry but may be capital intensive relative to most manufacturing operations. However, when abatement is achieved by process change, the concept of factor intensity loses most of its meaning. Even if pollution abatement proves to be capital intensive, the conclusions from case 2—reduced comparative advantage for countries exporting capital-intensive goods—will be extremely difficult to verify from trade data. The changes will be long in coming and will be reduced to the extent that developing countries also impose pollution abatement regulations on their own industry and industrial country governments subvent private sector environmental control costs.

Moreover, the analysis of case 2 is incomplete, because it fails to account for improvements in the productivity of factor inputs that arise from environmental control measures. As explained in Chapter 1, these measures increase both the flow of environmental services that are directly consumed and in some instances maintain or increase the productivity of conventional resource inputs. Accordingly, the shift of the transformation curve to $X'M'$ in Diagram 3.3 reflects only the resource diversion effect, but a second, outward shift from increased resource productivity is also likely. One hypothetical transformation function is $X''M''$ in Diagram 3.3. Its shape and position are the result of the initial resource diversion effect and a second, outward shift from improved productivity. The skewness of the outward shift depends on the extent to which a reduction in environmental damages assists the production of the X and M goods. Little can be said a priori, but certainly the results could be the opposite of the earlier conclusions—increased trade volume and a decline in the home country's terms of trade. The trade triangle $P''N''C''$ illustrates the possible increase in trade volume.

Past some point these speculations may be of interest to trade theorists, but it is difficult to see why development planners should give them much attention. The ambiguity of the conclusions in the face of extreme difficulties in measuring the variables suggests that this particular approach becomes a dead end. An analysis of trade shifts in a partial equilibrium context is more practical. When developing countries are considering attracting high-pollution industries, they should weigh the expansion of production against the social costs in terms of health, productivity, and amenity losses.

There is another approach to environment and comparative advantage that has a persuasive surface appeal and some merit if stated carefully. This involves the concept of assimilative capacity, or the ability of environmental media to absorb wastes and render them harmless. It also involves differences among countries in their demands for environmental quality. The basic thrust of the argument is that it is economically and environmentally rational to locate high waste discharge industries where the assimilative capacity is large and the demand for environmental quality is low.

The international trade theory extension of this proposition can be stated simply. The supply of assimilative capacity is viewed as another factor of production that helps determine the spatial allocation of economic activity. Also, international differences in the demand for environmental quality affect the spatial allocation of production. If countries differ in their endowments of assimilative capacity and the extent to which the capacity is exploited and if demand patterns differ, it is efficient to allocate some waste-producing activities to countries and regions in which excess capacity exists and demand for environmental quality is low. Further, countries will tend to specialize in the production and export of those commodities that use intensively the factor they have in relative abundance (assimilative capacity), whereas other countries will import these commodities because for them assimilative capacity is a relatively scarce factor of production. In short, this is a simple extension of the Heckscher-Olin factor endowment theory of comparative advantage, in which trade is the vehicle through which the gains from specialization are realized.

On the surface this sounds rational and is often followed by the assertion that developing countries, by virtue of their endowments of assimilative capacity and an assumed low demand for environmental quality, may have a comparative advantage in high waste production industries (subject to their suitability in terms of other factor endowments). However, this is actually a more subtle proposition than it appears at first and must be treated quite carefully.

We must first examine the term assimilative capacity, or the ability to absorb wastes and render them harmless. The concept implies that up to some threshold level waste loads cause no perceptible damage. Only after the threshold is breached do wastes become pollutants and the waste disposal capacity of the environment becomes an economically valuable resource.[12] It remains unclear whether a range of zero damages is a frequent occurrence. One might suggest, for example, a river with a high constant flow rate capable of dissipating heat and organic material without biological damage. However, for other wastes such as toxic materials, there may be no zero damage range.

An operational definition of relative endowments of assimilative capacity that can be used to predict trade patterns has not yet been devised. In Chapter 2 we investigated some climatic and topographical indicators of assimilative capacity. The regularity and level of rainfall and river runoff and the strength and regularity of prevailing winds are measures of flushing and dispersal characteristics. These vary considerably among regions and countries. To this must be added special physical features that make one region more fragile than another. The slow rate of biodegradation in cold climates and the propensity in some airsheds for thermal inversions are examples. Although no comprehensive measures of assimilative capacity have yet been devised, there is no evidence that developing countries have a generally greater endowment of waste disposal capacity than industrial countries. Indeed, as discussed in Chapter 2, there is some evidence to the contrary.

On closer inspection, the argument that developing countries have a comparative advantage in waste-producing industries really turns on the degree to which their assimilative capacity is being exploited, and not that their endowment is necessarily large. One very rough measure of the extent of exploitation of assimilative capacity is GNP per square kilometer. Except for certain city states such as Hong Kong and Singapore, it is easy to show that economic activity per unit of land surface is higher in industrial countries and, by implication, waste loads per square kilometer are higher. For example, Chapter 2 shows GNP/km^2 as $1,151,649 for Japan, $150,229 for the United States, and only $9768 for, say, Indonesia.

But here again caution is needed before drawing conclusions regarding comparative advantage. It is the spatial concentration of economic activity within countries that determines the exhaustion of local assimilative capacity. Judging from urbanization and industrialization patterns in developing countries to date, it is unlikely that most of the reallocated production would be placed in remote rural areas. Data in Chapter 2 indicate that industrial production in developing countries is concentrated in highly urbanized areas and in small highly urbanized countries. Moreover, the remote rural areas of industrial countries would also exhibit this "comparative advantage."

If the reallocation of industrial activity to developing countries would not go to countries and areas in which there is unused waste disposal capacity, an analysis of supply alone as a determinant of comparative advantage is not sufficient. Most cases would involve environmental damages. The question then becomes, is there is a systematic difference between North and South in damage functions and in abatement cost functions? Abatement costs are heavily influenced by the physical landscape (air pollution dispersal by prevailing winds or high smoke stacks) and the level of pollution present; however, as discussed previously, it is difficult to support the contention of a generally higher cost pattern in industrial countries.

Chapter 4 examines the concept of damage functions in some detail. It does seem reasonable that the demand for certain types of environmental services, particularly those which are directly consumed, is income elastic. If so, there is a justification for introducing environmental concerns into the theory of comparative advantage, and there is some global welfare gain from a reallocation of production toward its least damaging sites. However, as argued throughout this study, damages to productive resources and perhaps to health, should not be neglected in developing countries. In any event, the proposition has shifted from a narrow view of assimilative capacity endowment to its proper focus, relative economic damages. The attributes of assimilative capacity—river discharge flows, rainfall, wind velocity, incidence of thermal inversions, vulnerability of water bodies to eutrophication, sensitivity of crops to air pollutants, stability or fragility of soil systems, and so on—are too complex to be measured and weighted for the purpose of distinguishing North and South.

None of this suggests that environmental factors are unimportant in determining industrial location. On the contrary, siting decisions for industries is an important function for planning ministries, and consideration of the ecological and physical characteristics of alternative sites should be an integral part of establishing development plans and sector goals. Heat discharges from a nuclear power plant on Lake Cayauga can destroy the highly valued lake trout; the same discharge at Oswego on Lake Ontario might not. Thermal inversions in Los Angeles, Mexico City, and Santiago make these cities poor choices for plants that emit air pollutants.

POLICY RESPONSE

The impact of environmental controls on the trade and investment positions of developing countries is determined in part by specific policies adopted by the developed countries. These policies are for the most part already established and can be identified.

The major tools for implementing environmental legislation throughout the OECD region are the establishment of mandatory design standards and specific effluent and emission limits. Despite the advantages often claimed by economists for the use of effluent and emission fees as the more efficient method of controlling the discharge of pollutants, fee systems are in quite limited use.[13] There are exceptions; the Netherlands has a tax on water pollution discharges, and in the United States some municipal waste-treatment plants charge their industrial customers on the basis of waste loads and toxicity. Still, the thrust is strongly in the direction of regulation by standards. For developing countries, the difference between the two approaches is not crucial. Both the fee and standards approaches are consistent with private-sector financing of its own abatement. Both can affect industrial production costs and hence international trade.

More important is the distribution of environmental control (EC) costs between government and industry. Government subsidies to industry to offset industrial pollution abatement costs will neutralize production cost increases and erode a potential trade advantage for developing countries. The guiding principle with respect to the financing of pollution abatement in the private sector is the so-called polluter-pays principle, subscribed to by industrial countries through the OECD.[14] The principle requires that pollution abatement costs incurred in the private sector be borne there either through higher product prices or reduced wages and profits. This makes good economic sense because the distance between social costs and private costs is closed and market prices more accurately reflect the social costs of production. It also makes sense from the point of view of international trade: one country will not gain a competitive advantage over another because of government subsidies to producers that offset their environmental control costs. Adherence to this principle would be a step in the direction of rational use of global environmental resources. Developing countries would find that if indeed they have a competitive advantage in some products based on lower EC costs, this advantage will not be offset by government subsidies to producers in industrial countries. Developing countries will, however, pay higher prices for their imports.

In practice, the polluter-pays principle is not strictly followed. Some departures are authorized under the OECD Guiding Principles and subsequent clarifications. All OECD countries assist their industrial sectors with environmental control costs in some fashion. The instruments include:

- Direct subsidies and grants for pollution abatement capital or operating expenses.
- Tax relief by special accelerated depreciation and sales tax remission.
- Loan subsidies and guarantees for the purchase of abatement equipment.
- Provision of municipal waste-treatment plant facilities at less than full cost.

Estimates have been made of the extent to which government assistance programs reduced control costs in the private sector, and descriptions of the programs are available.[15] Probably the single most important form of assistance in the United States is the use of industrial revenue bonds for financing abatement expenditures by private industry. The bonds are issued by local governments for financing abatement facilities which in turn are leased to private firms. The interest on the bonds is exempt from federal tax; thus the bond interest rate is considerably less than market rates. The financing cost to industry is reduced accordingly. The amount financed by these bond issues has grown rapidly, reaching perhaps $3 billion in 1974. One estimate is that ultimately one-half of all air and water pollution control will be financed by this method.[16]

However, when calculated as a proportion of production costs or sales, the value of subsidies appears very small. We calculate the annual value of subsidy (interest savings) from the industrial revenue bond system for the United States as about $373 million in 1975, and this value might approach $933 million by 1985.[17] As a percentage of sales this is less than 0.04% in 1975, and fails to reach 0.1% by 1980. We conclude that general adherence to the polluter-pays principle by the OECD countries is in the interests of the developing countries, and that in aggregate departures from the principle are not now significant in terms of international trade. Still, the impact on individual industries may be noticeable.

In addition to giving official sanction to the polluter-pays principle, the OECD Guiding Principles sets forth two other trade–environment principles that are relevant to developing countries. The first concerns the use of border tax adjustments (export rebates and import surcharges) to offset international differences in environmental control costs.[18] Border adjustments could either compensate exporters for international differences in environmental control costs with export rebates or, more likely, assist import competing firms through some form of import surcharges offsetting lower foreign control costs.

The idea of border adjustments can be faulted on many grounds. On the level of basic theory, it is precisely international differences in costs that make trade possible and give rise to gains from trade through specialization. Accordingly, border adjustments would frustrate a desirable reallocation of economic activity on the basis of environmental endowments and would inhibit environmentally desirable modifications in production within countries. To be effective they would have to be applied by country and thereby violate the nondiscriminatory principle of Most Favored Nation (MFN) treatment. They would provide an invitation for covert protectionism.

Despite powerful theoretical and practical arguments against border adjustments, developing countries have retained suspicions that they might be used against their interests. Some grounds exist for these suspicions. Certainly one can imagine an alliance between environmentalists and protection-oriented industry that argues that if United States industry pays the price for clean-up, it should not be placed at a trade disadvantage vis a vis environmentally irresponsible countries. Indeed, using trade as an instrument for forcing others to improve their clean-up has been suggested by academics and is embodied as a possibility in United States legislation.[19] Section 6 of the 1972 Federal Water Pollution Control legislation specifically requested that the Commerce Department study the trade disadvantage that United States industry might face as a result of EC costs and the possibilities for using border adjustments to force a higher level of foreign environmental controls. To date, three reports of that study have not concluded that border adjustments are warranted. To our knowledge, no such schemes exist in other industrial countries. One reason was the early agreement within the OECD Guiding Principles in which members renounced the use of border adjustments. The renouncement was made easier by the uniform financing rule of the polluter-pays principle.

We conclude that border adjustments for differences in environmental control costs are possible but unlikely. For most industrial countries, anticipated increases in imports resulting from environmental control costs will be small relative to domestic dislocations caused by control measures. The probable response to domestic dislocations will be a combination of direct assistance to affected industries, temporary relaxation of environmental control measures, and reliance on general trade adjustment assistance programs. Judging from recent experience, including the response to the energy crisis, when stringent environmental controls threaten substantial economic disruption, governments will relax initial control directives and timetables.[20] Still, developing countries should be aware that an argument for border adjustments may surface and may be supported by protectionist elements and environmentalists. This will be more likely as environmental control costs rise over the rest of the decade and if developing countries establish open and visible "pollution havens," attracting industry on the basis of zero or low environmental control costs.

The final trade-related environmental policy undertaken by industrial countries that bears on the trade prospects for the South concerns product standards. Industrial countries have pledged through the Guiding Principles to avoid using environmental standards on products as covert trade barriers and to harmonize product standards to the extent feasible to prevent disruption to international trade. As discussed later, there are no known situations in which environmentally related product standards have been deliberately used for covert protection purposes. However, the incidental effect of product standards when legitimately used may hinder the access of developing countries to industrial country markets.

In summary, the trade policy response of industrial countries to the environmental control cost issue has been threefold: uniform private financing through the polluter-pays principle, renouncing the use of border adjustments, and a commitment to avoid using product standards for protection. The interests of the developing countries have been supported in each of these areas. These principles provide no grounds for controversy between North and South.

AGGREGATE CONTROL COSTS AND MACROECONOMIC EFFECTS

The trade and investment impact on developing countries of environmental control measures will be determined by the relative costs of controls and their allocation among industrial sectors. There are almost no data on control costs in developing countries, but some estimates are available for industrial countries.[21] Before examining estimates it is worth noting that environmental control cost data are exceptionally difficult to collect and interpret.

Three groups of problems can be identified. First, what should be included as an environmental control cost? In theory, additional production costs from locating in commercially less attractive but environmentally less damaging sites could be included. However, evaluating the economic cost of alternative sites is difficult and not included in aggregate cost data. Also, abatement investment and technological improvements in production often go hand in hand, and allocating expenditures between them is arbitrary. So-called "end-of-pipe" treatment can be costed quite easily, but abatement can also involve process and product modification. For example, environmental considerations have accelerated the shift from sulfite to sulfate pulp, but the shift was under way in any event, and the "cost" attributable to environmental concerns alone cannot be determined. The U.S. Department of Commerce estimates that process changes contributed 21% to total industry capital expenditures on pollution abatement in 1974, whereas end-of-pipe treatment accounted for 79% of expenditures.[22] Environmental control costs should also be net of the market value of recovered resources. For example, evaporation of the waste liquor from pulp and paper manufacture yields processing chemicals and commercially valuable heat. The value of both recovered resources should be subtracted from initial pollution abatement expenditures.[23]

A second set of problems centers on the differences among plants as to their pollution loads and abatement costs. For example, hardboard produced by a wet process ("wet felting") generates far more water pollution than hardboard produced by a dry process.[24] Therefore, hardboard production capacity should be broken down by process—63% dry and 37% wet—and separate control cost estimates should be made for each. Along this same line, plant size and age are factors in pollution loads and abatement costs. Finally, environmental standards often vary from plant to plant and region to region. All this suggests that a full survey of all plants in an industry might be desirable. This is seldom possible, and compromises are made.

Third, as mentioned previously, the total cost for a product is the sum of the direct costs and indirect costs passed along on purchased inputs. Input–output production coefficients assist in evaluating indirect costs, but problems remain. The extent to which costs on inputs are absorbed or passed forward in price may be unknown. Also, the fixed-input coefficient assumption of input–output analysis does not permit adjustment for the change in the relative costs and prices of purchased inputs. Finally, the pass-through of EC costs on imported inputs is generally unknown.

Table 3.1 presents U.S. Department of Commerce estimates for pollution abatement costs as a percentage of GNP for 10 industrial countries. Tables 3.2 and 3.3 present recent OECD estimates for several industrial countries. New expenditures are given as a percentage of GNP, as a percentage of GNP growth over the period, and as a percentage of investment. With the exception of the OECD estimate for Japan, EC expenditures represent less than 2% of GNP, sometimes substantially less. As a percentage of GNP growth or investment during the period, the percentage rises substantially. In absolute terms (not shown) the magnitudes are very large indeed.

Table 3.1 Pollution Abatement Cost Estimates in Ten Industrialized Countries

Country	Percentage of GNP	Time Period
United States	0.7–1	1973–1982
Belgium	1.0	1974
Canada	2.0	1974–1980
France	0.4	1974
Germany	1.8	1971–1975
Italy	0.6	1971–1975
Japan	1.2	FY 1973
Netherlands	0.5	1974
Sweden	1.0	1974
United Kingdom	1.0	1974

Source. U.S. Department of Commerce, *The Effects of Pollution Abatement on International Trade—III* (Washington, D.C.: GPO, April 1975).

Table 3.2 Total Expenditure on New Programs of Pollution Control After Adjustments as a Percentage of Total GNP Over the Program Period and as a Percentage of the Growth in Total GNP Over the Program Period

Period and Country	New Program Total Expenditure (% of total GNP)	New Program Total Expenditure (% of total growth of GNP)
1971–1975		
United States	0.8	7.0
Germany	0.8	6.0
Sweden	0.5–0.9	4.9–9.0
Italy	0.4	3.0
Japan	3.0–5.5	11.1–20.6
Netherlands	0.4	3.8
1976–1980		
United States	1.7	13.5
Italy	1.3	7.5
Netherlands	1.3	10.6
1971–1980		
United States	1.4	7.0
Netherlands	0.9	7.6
United Kingdom	0.3–0.5	1.3–2.6
Italy	0.9	3.0

Source. Organization for Economic Cooperation and Development, *Economic Implications of Pollution Control* (Paris: OECD, February 1974).

Table 3.3 Pollution Control Investment as a Percentage of Total Projected Investment Over the Program Period, 1971–1980

Country	Percent of Investment
United States	3.7
Germany	4.3
Sweden	2.1
Netherlands	4.1
United Kingdom	0.9
Italy	2.0
Japan	6.9

Source. OECD, *Economic Implications of Pollution Control* (Paris: OECD, February 1974).

A better perspective is gained by examining pollution control cost estimates for one country in greater detail. This is done for the United States in Tables 3.4 and 3.5. The data are broken down by the nature of the pollutant (air, water, noise, etc.), the source (public, private), and capital and operating and maintenance expenditures. Costs are annualized for 1975 and 1984 and are cumulated for the period 1975–1984. Table 3.4 contains *total* pollution control expenditures, whereas Table 3.5 presents data on *incremental* expenditures, or those expenditures to be made in compliance with Federal legislation that go beyond those which would have been made in the absence of that legislation. From the trade viewpoint, total expenditures are more relevant.

The United States tables indicate:

- Air and water pollution abatement account for 87% of total cumulative environmental control costs for the period 1975–1984.
- Total expenditures on water pollution control are 42% higher than on air pollution control.
- For private air and water pollution abatement expenditures, 77% of costs are incremental or attributable to Federal regulations.
- Sixty-one percent of the total costs for air, water, and solid wastes over the period will be in the private sector and 39% in the public sector.
- For total air and water abatement expenditures over the period, 58% will be for capital costs and 42% for operation and maintenance.
- The total annual private cost for air and water pollution abatement, excluding mobile sources, is expected to climb from $11.1 billion in 1975 to $32.8 billion in 1983. This implies that industry has not yet felt the full burden of environmental regulations, and the full trade impacts have yet to be felt.

To place these costs in perspective, the Council on Environmental Quality estimated that the real resource cost for incremental abatement (i.e., in response to Federal regulations and standards) is 1.1% of GNP in 1974 and would rise to 1.5% of GNP in 1979. Estimated private *incremental* pollution control investments (excluding mobile sources) were less than 2.5% of gross private

Table 3.4 Estimated Total Pollution Control Expenditures (in billions of 1975 dollars), 1975–1984

Pollutant/Source	1975			1984			Cumulative (1975–1984)			
	Operation and Maintenance Costs	Capital Costs[a]	Total Annual Costs[b]	Operation and Maintenance Costs	Capital Costs[a]	Total Annual Costs[b]	Capital Investment	Operation and Maintenance Costs	Capital Costs[a]	Total Annual Costs[b]
Air pollution										
Public	0.1	0.1	0.2	0.6	0.2	0.8	1.9	4.2	1.8	6.0
Private										
Mobile	3.4	1.5	4.9	1.3	4.4	5.7	29.0	20.9	31.7	52.6
Industrial	2.1	2.4	4.5	4.9	5.6	10.5	24.0	34.8	39.5	74.3
Utilities	1.0	1.0	2.0	3.5	3.5	7.0	19.0	21.0	21.0	42.0
Subtotal	6.6	5.0	11.6	10.3	13.7	24.0	74.0	80.9	94.0	174.9
Water pollution										
Public										
Federal	0.2	<0.05	0.2	0.2	0.1	0.3	2.0	2.1	0.4	2.5
State and local	2.3	7.6	9.9	6.2	15.1	21.3	56.9	41.7	113.7	155.4
Private										
Industrial	1.9	1.7	3.6	7.4	5.7	13.1	41.4	40.6	33.0	73.6
Utilities	0.6	0.4	1.0	1.4	0.8	2.2	3.8	10.5	6.3	16.8
Subtotal	5.0	9.7	14.7	15.2	21.7	36.9	104.1	94.9	153.4	248.3
Radiation										
Nuclear power plants	<0.05	<0.05	<0.05	<0.05	<0.05	<0.05	0.2	0.1	<0.05	0.2
Solid waste										
Public	1.5	0.3	1.8	2.1	0.6	2.7	4.6	18.2	4.2	22.4
Private	2.9	0.7	3.6	3.9	1.1	5.0	5.6	28.4	8.8	37.2
Subtotal	4.4	1.0	5.4	6.0	1.7	7.7	10.2	46.6	13.0	59.6
Land reclamation										
Surface mining[c]										
Noise	NA	NA	NA	0.3	0.3	0.6	1.7	1.8	1.6	3.4
Total	16.0	15.7	31.7	31.8	37.4	69.2	190.0	224.2	262.0	486.2

Source. Council on Environmental Quality, *Environmental Quality*, Seventh Annual Report (Washington, D.C.: GPO, 1976) Table 1–37.

[a] Interest and depreciation.

[b] Operation and maintenance plus capital costs.

[c] Not included in this year's estimate.

NA, not available.

Table 3.5 Estimated Incremental Pollution Control Expenditures (in billions of 1975 dollars), 1975–1984[a]

Pollutant/Source	1975			1984			Cumulative (1975–1984)			
	Operation and Maintenance Costs	Capital Costs[b]	Total Annual Costs[c]	Operation and Maintenance Costs	Capital Costs[b]	Total Annual Costs[c]	Capital Investment	Operation and Maintenance Costs	Capital Costs[b]	Total Annual Costs[c]
Air pollution										
Public	0.1	0.1	0.2	0.6	0.2	0.8	1.9	4.2	1.8	6.0
Private										
Mobile	3.4	1.5	4.9	1.3	4.4	5.7	29.1	20.9	31.7	52.6
Industrial	1.2	1.5	2.7	3.1	3.6	6.7	15.1	21.7	25.4	47.1
Utilities	0.6	0.6	1.2	2.7	2.7	5.4	15.6	15.4	15.4	30.8
Subtotal	5.3	3.7	9.0	7.7	10.9	18.6	61.7	62.2	74.3	136.5
Water pollution										
Public										
Federal	0.2	<0.05	0.2	0.2	0.1	0.3	2.0	2.1	0.4	2.5
State and local	1.1	0.2	1.3	4.8	2.3	7.1	24.2	28.6	11.2	39.8
Private										
Industrial	1.3	1.2	2.5	6.0	4.7	10.7	36.5	30.9	26.1	57.0
Utilities	0.4	0.3	0.7	0.9	0.5	1.4	2.3	7.2	4.3	11.5
Subtotal	3.0	1.7	4.7	11.9	7.6	19.5	65.0	68.8	42.0	110.8
Radiation										
Nuclear power plants	<0.05	<0.05	<0.05	<0.05	<0.05	<0.05	0.2	0.1	<0.05	0.2
Solid waste										
Public	0.2	0.1	0.3	0.3	0.1	0.4	1.1	2.6	0.8	3.4
Private	0.3	0.1	0.4	0.7	0.2	0.9	0.8	4.3	0.2	4.5
Subtotal	0.5	0.2	0.7	1.0	0.3	1.3	1.9	6.9	1.0	7.9
Land reclamation										
Surface mining[d]										
Noise	NA	NA	NA	0.3	0.3	0.6	1.7	1.8	1.6	3.4
Total	8.8	5.6	14.4	20.9	19.1	40.0	130.5	139.8	118.9	258.8

Source. Council on Environmental Quality, *Environmental Quality*, Seventh Annual Report (Washington, D.C.: GPO, 1976) Table 1–35.
[a] Incremental costs are expenditures made pursuant to federal environmental legislation beyond those which would have been made in the absence of this legislation.
[b] Interest and depreciation.
[c] Operation and maintenance plus capital costs.
[d] Not included in this year's estimate.
NA, not available.

domestic investment in 1975 and 4.5% of business investment in plant equipment. If *total* private pollution control investments (excluding mobile sources) were used, these would increase to 5% and 10%, respectively. Individual industries face higher ratios, and the ratios themselves are expected to climb slightly through 1979.

Attempts have been made to predict the aggregate economic impact of these expenditures. The estimated impact on real GNP growth and the trade balance is of special interest to developing countries. A slackening of growth rates within industrial countries reduces their import demand from developing countries. A deterioration of the trade balance indicates a loss of competitive position because of environmental control costs and indirectly indicates trade advantage secured by other countries.

One forecast was made in the 1976 run of the Chase Econometric models for the CEQ. The results are reported in Table 3.6. The general procedure was to estimate the impact of pollution abatement expenditures on a variety of macroeconomic variables by comparing an economic forecast including the pollution abatement expenditure with a forecast that excluded the abatement expenditures. For the historical portion, 1970–1975, the actual values of the variables were compared to values that would have obtained had there been no incremental abatement expenditures.

The table indicates that real GNP growth was slightly higher in most of the 1970–1976 period with abatement expenditures, but thereafter the expenditures led to modestly lower real GNP growth rates. The reason that EC measures increased growth rates early in the period is their contribution to aggregate demand during a slack period in the economy. After 1976 they divert resources and increase production costs, dampening growth. However, the amounts are quite modest. By 1983 real GNP is projected to be 2.2% less than the baseline (without) forecast. With regard to prices, by 1983 the cumulative effect will be that the consumer price index will be up 4.7% and the GNP deflator up 3.6% over what they otherwise would have been. This is equivalent to an average annual rate of increase of the CPI of 0.4% and the GNP deflator of 0.3% because of incremental pollution abatement expenditures.

These estimates depend strongly on the quality of the EC cost data, the structural reliability of the model (which includes input–output coefficients for cumulating direct and indirect EC costs), and an assumed configuration of governmental policies. The data fed in were for incremental costs or those attributable to Federal regulations; total costs would have had greater impact. Also, the model was run before the pause in the United States economy in mid-1976. Although they must be treated with great caution, the estimates provide some reassurance to developing countries that environmental control expenditures will not exert a strong downward pressure on industrial country growth rates and hence depress the export markets of developing countries. Cyclical fluctuations, such as the 1972–1975 boom–bust in industrial countries, are of far greater importance to the exports of developing countries.

The Chase projections for the United States trade balance are of little direct use for inferring the export prospects of developing countries. One reason is that the model does not appear to account for the new managed floating exchange regime. A second reason is that there is no sector disaggregation for the trade balance effect. Without knowledge of the commodity composition of

Table 3.6 Estimated Macroeconomic Impacts of Incremental United States Pollution Abatement Expenditures

	1970	1971	1972	1973	1974	1975	1976	1977	1978	1979	1980	1981	1982	1983
Gross national product, current dollars														
Without pollution control costs	979.4	1060.2	1168.4	1304.8	1405.1	1495.2	1683.5	1875.7	2002.2	2118.4	2346.6	2629.2	2904.3	3186.1
With pollution control costs	981.4	1063.2	1173.8	1312.1	1413.9	1505.8	1703.7	1897.7	2022.0	2142.7	2373.8	2660.4	2939.2	3226.6
% difference	0.20	0.28	0.46	0.56	0.63	0.71	1.20	1.17	0.99	1.15	1.16	1.19	1.20	1.27
Gross national product, 1974 dollars														
Without pollution control costs	1254.1	1292.0	1367.7	1442.2	1416.3	1387.4	1479.3	1550.5	1559.1	1573.9	1660.4	1766.8	1855.6	1934.3
With pollution control costs	1256.0	1293.4	1369.9	1443.1	1414.8	1384.4	1480.6	1543.0	1543.1	1555.7	1636.9	1736.8	1819.0	1892.4
% difference	0.15	0.11	0.16	0.06	−0.11	−0.22	0.09	−0.48	−1.03	−1.16	−1.42	−1.70	−1.97	−2.17
Implicit GNP deflator, 1974 = 100														
Without pollution control costs	78.0	82.1	85.6	90.4	99.2	107.8	113.7	120.9	128.4	134.6	141.3	148.8	156.5	164.7
With pollution control costs	78.1	82.2	85.7	90.9	100.0	108.7	115.0	122.9	131.0	137.7	145.0	153.2	161.6	170.6
% difference	0.13	0.12	0.12	0.55	0.81	0.83	1.14	1.65	2.02	2.30	2.62	2.96	3.26	3.58
Consumer price index, 1974 = 100														
Without pollution control costs	78.6	81.8	84.4	89.5	99.2	108.0	115.6	123.9	132.4	138.6	145.7	153.2	161.1	169.9
With pollution control costs	78.6	82.0	84.7	90.0	100.0	109.3	117.4	126.7	136.0	143.0	151.0	159.4	168.3	177.9
% difference	0.00	0.24	0.36	0.56	0.81	1.20	1.56	2.26	2.72	3.17	3.64	4.05	4.47	4.71
Trade balance, 1974 dollars														
Without pollution control costs	−11.1	−14.1	−19.6	−4.9	8.5	21.7	7.9	4.4	8.5	11.6	8.3	7.3	12.8	18.1
With pollution control costs	−11.4	−14.4	−20.0	−5.4	8.5	21.5	7.3	3.9	9.3	11.8	8.2	8.3	14.0	19.5
% difference	−2.70	−2.13	−2.04	−10.20	.00	−.92	−7.59	−11.36	9.41	1.72	4.82	13.70	9.38	7.73
Corporate profits before taxes, current dollars														
Without pollution control costs	72.2	83.1	97.9	118.9	133.5	118.3	151.1	175.4	161.9	170.8	198.7	217.0	240.8	266.4
With pollution control costs	72.0	82.7	97.3	118.1	132.5	117.1	148.4	172.4	158.6	167.2	194.3	212.8	236.3	261.6
% difference	−0.28	−0.48	−0.61	−0.67	−0.75	−1.01	−1.79	−2.04	−1.71	−2.11	−1.96	−1.94	−1.87	−1.80
Index of industrial production, 1974 = 100														
Without pollution control costs	84.9	84.4	91.3	100.2	99.4	89.2	100.9	110.5	109.4	106.9	114.2	126.3	135.9	143.6
With pollution control costs	85.2	84.8	92.0	101.1	100.0	89.8	102.5	111.7	109.5	107.1	114.0	125.5	134.2	141.5
% difference	0.35	0.47	0.77	0.90	0.60	0.67	1.59	1.09	0.09	0.19	−0.18	−0.63	−1.25	−1.46

Source. Chase Econometric Associates, Inc., "The Economic Impact of Pollution Control: Macroeconomic and Industry Reports," prepared for the Council on Environmental Quality, August 1976, Table 2.

changes, little can be said about the impact on a particular group of countries, the Third World. At this stage of our knowledge, disaggregation by industrial sector offers better insight than macro models.

IMPACT BY INDUSTRY

Macroeconomic modeling of the trade effect of environmental controls is inadequate because substantial variations among industries can be concealed. Therefore, disaggregation by industrial sector is preferable. However, disaggregated environmental control (EC) cost studies differ widely in their timeliness, coverage, and methodology. Moreover, most stop short of estimating trade impacts. Finally, we are aware of only one (Pearson for UNCTAD) that is directly concerned with the impact of environmental controls on the trade of developing countries.

Despite these limitations, the studies do provide information on control costs by industry and therefore suggest the industries that may face sharper competition from foreign suppliers with low EC costs. The appendix to this chapter provides a brief review of the results of seven studies that have examined environmental control costs by industry. Several conclusions emerge from the review.

First, the Walter and the Yezer and Philipson studies confirm the importance of cumulating the EC costs on purchased inputs and adding them to the direct abatement costs in the industry under consideration. In the Walter study indirect costs account for an average of 39% of the total costs, and for Yezer, indirect costs were an average of 52% of the total costs of the industries studied in 1973. EC costs on purchased inputs, or indirect costs, were estimated using input–output coefficients.

Second, the studies indicate that the utilities sector, mainly electric power, will be one of the most heavily affected. This can be seen in Tables A3.1, A3.2, and A3.7. In another study not reported here, abatement costs were estimated to lead to a 9% increase in utility prices by 1977.[25] However, utilities are seldom traded; thus these costs are important only as they are passed on in the form of input prices in the production of other commodities.

Third, with respect to traded commodities the studies suggest that certain raw materials processing industries will be most heavily affected by direct EC costs (Tables A3.1–A3.4 and A3.7). These include primary metals (iron and steel and nonferrous metals), pulp and paper, basic chemicals, petroleum refining, and perhaps cement. When indirect costs are also included, the picture is less striking. Still, all other things being equal, these industries will be subject to more intense pressure from low EC costs suppliers. The further processing of raw materials is of course in harmony with the trade policies of developing countries. Other studies indicate that there are substantial cost differences among products within broad industrial sectors.[26]

Finally, the magnitude of the cost increases do not look especially large. Most fall below 2% of production costs, occasionally reaching 5%. Recall that any competitive disadvantage initially apparent for the high EC cost country may be offset in part by EC costs among trade partners and by compensatory exchange rate changes. Only one of the studies reviewed attempted to collect foreign EC cost data, and none apparently took into account compensatory exchange rate changes.

As noted previously, the Pearson study addressed the question of anticipated trade impact on developing countries. The starting point was direct average annual incremental air and water pollution control costs in the United States, as presented in Table 3.7. Fifteen industrial sectors are included. Costs are those reported by Chase Econometrics to the CEQ and EPA, who supplied primary cost data to Chase. Costs for lumber and wood products are apparently in error, as they are too high. Two major adjustments were made to these costs. The first adjusted for the fact that the data were incremental costs; for trade analysis purposes, total costs, not only those related to Federal regulations, are more appropriate. This adjustment was made by computing total to incremental cost coefficients. The coefficients are computed separately for each industrial sector, reflecting the relative size of air and water pollution control costs in each sector, and separate coefficients for the 1973–1977 and 1978–1982 periods are also calculated. The adjustment coefficients are reported in columns 5 and 6 of Table 3.7. The second adjustment was to incorporate indirect costs working through the input–output structure or those EC costs which increase the costs of purchased inputs. The ratios of direct to total (direct plus indirect) costs are taken from Yezer and from the 1967 U.S. Input Output Table.[27] The results are reported in columns 7 and 8. Columns 9 and 10 present the estimated average annual total direct and indirect environmental control costs expressed as a percentage of the value of shipments for the periods 1973–1977 and 1978–1982.

The costs as reported in columns 9 and 10 appear reasonable and are generally consistent with other estimates. The average total costs for all industry, 2.08% and 2.36%, should not be taken too seriously, because they are computed as the simple average of the column ratios. Except for the higher-stage processing industries the percentage increases generally fall between 1 and 2%. Those industries with relatively high direct costs tend to have lower indirect costs; thus total costs show less dispersion. Costs in the two time periods are quite similar. This reflects the offsetting effects of high remedial expenditures in the first period and more stringent standards in the second period. Capital costs, which are "lumpy," have been annualized, and this smooths costs over time.

The next step is quite speculative. Ideally, the study would have obtained data on EC cost increases for other industrial countries and developing countries, together with supply elasticities by country of origin and industrial sector. These were unavailable. As an alternative, hypothetical price elasticities of demand for imports to the United States were used, together with data on current levels of United States imports by industry sector. The elasticities, which increase from crude materials through semimanufactured products to finished manufactures, conform to various estimates that have appeared in the literature.[28] The elasticities and import data were then used to estimate the potential increase in imports if foreign environmental control costs were zero.

The share of the potential increase in imports that is captured by developing countries depends on their control costs relative to industrial country suppliers and the supply capabilities of the developing countries. The latter is reflected in part by the ability of developing countries to compete with other industrial

Table 3.7 Estimation of Environmental Control Costs

Industry	Average Direct Incremental Control Costs (millions 1973 $)		Average Direct Annual Incremental Environmental Control Costs as Percentage Value of Shipments (%)		Weighted Adjustment Coefficients to Determine Total Direct Environmental Control Costs		Ratio of Total Direct Plus Indirect Costs to Direct Costs		Estimated Annual Total Direct Plus Indirect Environmental Control Costs as Percentage Value of Shipments (%)	
	1973–1977	1978–1982	1973–1977	1978–1982	1973–1977	1978–1982	1973–1977	1978–1982	1973–1977	1978–1982
	(1)	(2)	(3)	(4)	(5)	(6)	(7)	(8)	(9)	(10)
Food and kindred products[a]	448.4	597.4	0.30	0.31	1.53	1.57	3.00	1.87	1.377	0.910
Textile mill products	97.2	145.2	0.28	0.33	1.65	1.65	2.71	2.57	1.252	1.399
Lumber and wood products	192.8	293.2	0.74	0.89	1.65	1.65	2.52	2.03	3.077	2.981
Paper and paper products	191.0	266.4	0.53	0.58	1.55	1.57	1.67	2.01	1.372	1.830
Chemicals	233.2	313.2	0.36	0.38	1.52	1.54	2.90	1.75	1.587	1.024
Petroleum[b]	252.4	325.0	0.63	0.64	1.44	1.47	1.49	1.33	1.352	1.251
Rubber and misc. plastics	79.8	121.6	0.35	0.42	1.65	1.65	2.40	2.28	1.386	1.580
Leather	28.6	42.8	0.45	0.43	1.65	1.65	1.55	1.51	1.151	1.071
Stone, clay and glass	104.2	127.8	0.37	0.36	1.38	1.33	3.36	2.61	1.716	1.250
Primary metals	628.4	676.2	.79	0.66	1.24	1.26	1.30	1.43	1.273	1.189
Iron and steel	336.2	331.8	0.86	0.67	1.22	1.26	1.30	1.43	1.364	1.207
Primary non-ferrous metals	292.2	334.4	0.99	0.92	1.22	1.26	1.30	1.43	1.570	1.658
Fabricated metals	50.6	66.4	0.08	0.08	1.65	1.65	9.42	11.77	1.243	1.554
Nonelectrical machinery	42.0	59.0	0.05	0.05	1.65	1.65	7.25	6.78	0.598	0.559
Electrical machinery	29.0	40.0	0.04	0.04	1.65	1.65	7.00	6.52	0.462	0.437
Transportation equipment	20.6	28.0	0.01	0.01	1.65	1.65	11.50	27.00	0.322	0.446
Total industrial	2440.2	3111.0	0.30	0.30	1.47	1.51	4.72	5.21	2.081	2.360
Utilities[c]	2225.8	3951.8	4.00	5.58						

Sources. For cost data, 1974 Chase Econometrics Report to EPA/CEQ. For Value of Shipments, U.S. Department of Commerce, *Survey of Current Business* annual percent increase of 5% assumed. For explanation of other entries, see text. Originally reported in Pearson, *Implications for the Trade of Developing Countries of U.S. Environmental Control,* UNCTAD TD/B/C.2 (New York: United Nations, 1976).

[a] Includes feedlots and grain handling; does *not* include restrictions on pesticides and herbicides.

[b] Includes coal cleaning and natural gas production.

[c] Includes residential, industrial, and commercial heating.

countries in the United States market. Accordingly, the current share of developing countries of the United States import market, by sector, is used to estimate a plausible range of increase in the exports of developing countries to the United States market. Specifically, the "low" estimate of the increase in the exports of developing countries assumes that developing countries maintain their current market share of the estimated increase in United States imports for each commodity category. This corresponds to a situation in which other industrial countries do not bear substantial environmental control costs, and all suppliers maintain their market shares. The "high" estimate assumes that developing countries share disproportionately in the estimated increase in United States imports. This would be expected if other industrial country suppliers do bear significant environmental control costs and if developing countries have a moderate capacity to expand exports and partially displace other suppliers. The displacement impact is assumed to be equal to a doubling of the current markets share of developing countries and applies only to the additional imports resulting from higher production costs in the United States.

These steps are reported in Tables 3.8 and 3.9 for the 1973–1977 and 1978–1982 periods. Column 1 gives the assumed elasticity (increasing as one moves from crude materials to intermediate to finished products); column 2 gives the estimated increase in United States imports; column 3 the current share of developing countries in the United States import market; columns 4 and 5 the minimum and maximum likely impact on the exports of developing countries (annual basis). To put the numbers into perspective, the minimum and maximum estimates are expressed as a percentage of the current exports of developing countries to the United States in columns 6 and 7.

The analysis suggests that for the 1973–1977 period, the minimum likely increase in the exports of developing countries of these manufactures to the United States market will be $129 million per year, and the maximum likely increase will be $257 million. The annual minimum and maximum for the 1978–1982 period are estimated to be $116 million and $232 million. These increases represent between 2.1 and 4.6% of current developing country exports of these products to the United States market (columns 6 and 7, Tables 3.8 and 3.9). The industries showing the largest absolute increases in the 1978–1982 period are petroleum refining (minimum $31 million, maximum $63 million) and primary metals, especially nonferrous metals (minimum $14 million, maximum $28 million). These are also the industries exhibiting the largest increases in the 1973–1977 period. In terms of percentage increases, the strongest impacts are felt by lumber and wood products (5.4–10.8%) and primary nonferrous metals (2.9–5.8%), but as noted, EC costs for lumber and wood were apparently in error. In the pulp and paper and nonelectrical machinery industries, the current low share of imports from developing countries has sharply limited the estimated increase in the exports of developing countries. If in the next decade the supply capabilities of the developing countries improve, these industries may also record substantial environmental cost-related increases in exports. There is little variation between the two time periods regarding the absolute or percentage increase in developing country exports, either in total or for specific industries. Finally, the EC-related increases in developing country exports are small in comparison to the recent growth of their manufactures exports to the United States market.

Table 3.8 Estimated Average Annual Trade Impact on Developing Countries, 1973–1977

Industry	Assumed Elasticity[a]	Potential Increase in Imports[b] (millions $)	Current LDC Share of U.S. Import Market[b]	Minimum Likely Impact on Developing Countries[c] (millions $)	Maximum Likely Impact on Developing Countries[d] (millions $)	Minimum Estimate as Percentage Current LDC Exports to U.S.%	Maximum Estimate as Percentage Current LDC Exports to U.S. %
	(1)	(2)	(3)	(4)	(5)	(6)	(7)
Food and kindred products	1.0	28.49	0.58	16.52	33.04	1.4	2.7
Textile mill products	1.8	34.44	0.33	11.36	22.76	2.2	4.5
Lumber and wood products	1.8	36.29	0.39	14.15	28.31	5.7	11.1
Paper and paper products	1.8	31.14	0.01	0.44	0.88	2.5	5.0
Chemicals	1.8	57.30	0.13	7.45	14.90	2.8	5.7
Petroleum refining	1.8	41.20	0.82	33.78	67.57	2.4	4.8
Rubber and misc. plastics	1.8	9.99	0.04	0.40	0.80	2.3	4.7
Leather	1.8	3.65	0.39	1.42	2.85	4.0	2.0
Stone, clay, and glass	1.8	43.00	0.19	8.17	16.34	3.1	6.2
Primary metals	1.8	111.34	0.14	15.59	31.17	2.2	4.4
Iron and steel	1.8	71.84	0.07	5.03	10.06	2.3	4.6
Primary non-ferrous metals	1.8	54.63	0.25	13.66	27.32	2.8	5.6
Fabricated metals	3.0	42.56	0.06	2.55	5.11	3.6	7.2
Nonelectrical machinery	4.0	105.50	0.03	3.16	6.33	2.4	4.8
Electrical machinery	4.0	62.37	0.21	13.10	26.20	1.8	3.6
Transport equipment	4.0	123.81	0.005	0.62	1.22	1.3	2.6
Total		857.55		128.71 .1580	257.48	2.3	4.6

[a] See text.
[b] Trade data from OECD Trade Statistics, Series C. Note that only imports of prepared foods are used. Crude petroleum imports are excluded.
[c] Assumes that developing countries maintain their current market share of potential increase in imports.
[d] Assumes that developing countries double their current market share of potential increase in imports.

Table 3.9 Estimated Average Annual Trade Impact on Developing Countries, 1978–1982

Industry	Assumed Elasticity[a]	Potential Increase in Imports[b] (millions $)	Current LDC Share of U.S. Import Market[b]	Minimum Likely Impact on Developing Countries[c] (millions $)	Maximum Likely Impact on Developing Countries[d] (millions $)	Minimum Estimate as Percentage Current LDC Exports to U.S. (%)	Maximum Estimate as Percentage Current LDC Exports to U.S. (%)
	(1)	(2)	(3)	(4)	(5)	(6)	(7)
Food and kindred products	1.0	18.83	0.58	10.92	21.84	0.9	1.8
Textile mill products	1.8	38.48	0.33	12.70	25.40	2.5	5.0
Lumber and wood products	1.8	35.16	0.39	13.71	27.42	5.4	10.8
Paper and paper products	1.8	41.53	0.01	0.58	1.16	3.2	6.4
Chemicals	1.8	36.97	0.13	5.20	10.39	2.0	4.0
Petroleum refining	1.8	38.20	0.82	31.25	62.52	2.2	2.4
Rubber and misc. plastics	1.8	11.39	0.04	0.46	0.91	2.7	5.4
Leather	1.8	3.40	0.39	1.33	2.65	1.9	3.8
Stone, clay, and glass	1.8	31.32	0.19	5.95	11.90	2.3	4.6
Primary metals	1.8	103.99	0.14	14.56	29.12	2.1	4.1
Iron and steel	1.8	63.57	0.07	4.45	8.90	2.1	4.1
Primary non-ferrous metal	1.8	57.65	0.25	14.31	28.63	2.9	5.8
Fabricated metals	3.0	53.21	0.06	3.19	6.38	4.6	9.3
Nonelectrical machinery	4.0	98.61	0.03	2.96	5.92	2.2	4.5
Electrical machinery	4.0	58.99	0.21	12.39	24.78	1.7	3.5
Transport equipment	4.0	171.48	0.005	0.86	1.71	1.8	3.6
Total				116.1	232.1	2.1	4.1

[a] See text.
[b] Trade data from OECD Trade Statistics, Series C. Note that only imports of prepared foods are used. Crude petroleum imports are excluded.
[c] Assumes that developing countries maintain their current market share of potential increase in imports.
[d] Assumes that developing countries double their current market share of potential increase in imports.

Although these estimates should be treated with great caution and more detailed analysis of individual products is indicated, they do provide some indication of the magnitude of the shift in trade flows that will arise from differences in environmental control costs in production. The absolute magnitudes are not trivial, but they are certainly not overwhelming. They of course refer only to developing country exports to the United States market. The United States absorbs 23% of developing country exports to the OECD region and about 38% of manufactured exports. The estimates suggest that developing countries will wish to consider the trade impact when establishing their own environmental control programs, but the estimates do not appear to justify policies of deliberate exploitation of the environment to gain an advantage in international trade. Furthermore, if deliberate "pollution havens" were established for trade advantage, some form of compensatory protection in industrial countries might be introduced.

ENVIRONMENTAL PRODUCT STANDARDS

Although developing countries may gain some competitive advantage based on low EC costs in production, they have been concerned that environmental standards applied to products may impair market access for their exports. As noted earlier, the two types of environmental regulations are quite dissimilar. Production pollution controls protect the supplying country; product pollution controls protect the environment and residents of the consuming country. Production pollution control affects trade through changes in relative production costs. Product pollution controls can be analyzed as an extension of one form of traditional nontariff trade barriers (NTBs)—national health, safety, and sanitary regulations.

It is difficult to determine if environmental standards will become serious trade barriers for developing countries. One reason is that they merge with traditional health and safety standards, and separate identification is somewhat arbitrary. Another reason is that environmental product standards are still in the process of evolution in industrial countries. Their ultimate form and the degree of harmonization among countries are still matters of conjecture. Also, trade flow data do not necessarily indicate the seriousness of the barrier, because restrictive standards reduce imports and discourage potential suppliers from entering the market. Therefore, an analysis of existing trade may understate the effect. Finally, the manner in which product standards are publicized and implemented by customs officials is often critical, but little can be said a priori.

How can product standards impair market access for exporters? To summarize the discussion, there are four ways: standards may be used as covert trade barriers; they fragment markets and may entail shorter production runs and higher per unit costs; they may require knowledge that is expensive for exporters to acquire; they may require testing and verification procedures that place the exporter at a disadvantage.

Developing countries are interested in three questions. What is the justification for environmental product standards in industrial countries? How important will they be, and for which products? What policies can developing countries adopt or support that would minimize adverse effects on their exports?

Unquestionably, countries have the right to establish health, sanitary, and safety standards for products consumed within their territory. This right extends to imported goods. Article 20 of the General Agreement on Tariffs and Trade states:

> Subject to the requirement that such measures are not applied in a manner which would constitute a means of arbitrary or unjustifiable discrimination between countries where the same conditions prevail, or a disguised restriction on international trade, nothing in this Agreement shall be construed to prevent the adoption or enforcement by any contracting party of measures . . . necessary to protect human, animal or plant life or health [or] . . . relating to the conservation of exhaustible natural resources if such measures are made effective in conjunction with restrictions on domestic production or consumption.

Although environmentally related product standards are not explicitly included in the GATT formulation, many are virtually indistinguishable from the broader group of health, safety, and sanitary standards. Accordingly, environmental product standards can be imposed on imports.

As with other product standards, environmental standards are legitimate if two criteria are met: their purpose is to contribute toward a domestic social goal (in this case environmental quality), and they are applied in a nondiscriminatory fashion to imports and domestic goods alike (national treatment). Conversely, they are not legitimate if their purpose is a disguised restriction on international trade or if imports are subject to more stringent standards than domestic goods. These criteria are sometimes ambiguous. For example, the very process of inspection may delay agricultural imports from clearing customs and result in spoilage. Despite some gray areas, these two criteria do offer a distinguishing test for legitimate and illegitimate product standards.

There is no evidence that current United States environmental standards on products are illegitimate in the sense that they are discriminatory or used for covert trade restriction. Indeed, there is evidence to the contrary. The GATT has had machinery in place to accept and examine complaints of environment-related trade distortions, but none has been received. The same is true for the OECD. Moreover, UNCTAD has recently surveyed both developed and developing countries to determine if problems exist. Although a few countries indicated that their exports were affected by environmental regulations in importing countries, no examples of explicit discrimination were uncovered.[29]

Even if all environmental standards are legitimate, developing countries remain concerned about market access. Standards create additional costs and difficulties for exporters. A multiplicity of standards in export markets means that products must be adapted to specific markets. Production runs are shorter, and unit costs are higher. Small suppliers may become uncompetitive or may avoid entering the market altogether. Even if standards were fully harmonized among export markets, the delay, expense, and uncertainty of testing and inspection by customs officials becomes a barrier. Occasionally, standards require that inspection take place during the manufacturing process, and this is either expensive or not feasible. Two examples are the French requirement that pharmaceuticals be inspected during their manufacture and the United States requirement that compressed gas cylinders be inspected for flaws while being produced. Neither regulation makes provision for foreign on-site inspection, and the markets are effectively closed to exporters.[30] Finally, imported products may be subject to stricter standards than domestic products simply because the foreign manufacturer is beyond the reach of penalties and sanctions. Alternately, the importer may have to post bonds against product defects, with the effect of discouraging imports.[31]

The trade effects of environmental product standards are also a concern of industrial countries, and the policies they adopt influence the market access of developing countries. The relevant provisions of the OECD Guiding Principles quoted as follows reflect three objectives: to avoid using environmental standards as covert trade barriers, to provide nondiscriminatory treatment of imports, and to minimize the economic costs of differing standards through harmonization and improved inspection procedures:

9. Measures taken to protect the environment should be framed as far as possible in such a manner as to avoid the creation of non-tariff barriers to trade.

10. Where products are traded internationally and where there could be significant obstacles to trade, Governments should seek common standards for polluting products and agree on the timing and general scope of regulations for particular products.

National Treatment and Non-Discrimination

11. In conformity with the provisions of the GATT, measures taken within an environmental policy, regarding polluting products, should be applied in accordance with the principle of national treatment (i.e., identical treatment for imported products and similar domestic products) and with the principle of non-discrimination (identical treatment for imported products regardless of their national origin).

Procedures of Control

12. It is highly desirable to define in common, as rapidly as possible, procedures for checking conformity to product standards established for the purpose of environmental control. Procedures for checking conformity to standards should be mutually agreed so as to be applied by an exporting country to the satisfaction of the importing country.

Examining different types of standards provides an indication of their importance as trade barriers. With some overlap, seven groups can be identified:

- Motor vehicle emission standards.
- Product noise standards.
- Product radiation standards.
- Regulations on agricultural products.
- Packaging requirements.
- Toxic substances.
- Standards on products that contribute directly to trans-national pollution.

Although motor vehicle emission standards are a major pollution control instrument and will be costly to achieve, it is unlikely that they will become a serious problem for developing countries in the next 5 or 10 years. (However, uncontrolled auto emissions in developing countries are a serious problem.) One reason is the negligible value of auto exports from developing countries, currently less than 0.01% of United States imports. Auto standards may become a significant trade barrier, but the problem will be for industrial country exporters. If a few developing countries attempted auto exports on a significant scale, it would be done through multinational firms. The firms would have available to them information on the standards and testing procedures and would be familiar with technology for compliance. Therefore, developing countries would not be at any special disadvantage.

Regulation of noise pollution from products is still in its infancy.[32] In the United States, the Noise Control Act of 1972 requires the Environmental Protection Agency to identify and regulate noise sources.[33] Products most likely affected are construction equipment, transportation equipment, engines and motors, electrical and electronic equipment, and certain consumer items such as chain saws and motor bikes. Proposed noise standards have been published for portable air compressors, medium and heavy duty trucks, railroad trains, and aircraft. Again, it does not appear likely that developing countries will have serious problems with noise standards. Export levels from developing countries for these items are currently low, and in many instances the modifications necessary to meet standards are not complicated or expensive—improved mufflers, acoustical absorption material, and so on. Abatement of noise from aircraft and airports, which is ultimately regulated by the Federal Aviation Agency, may prove to be quite expensive. Estimates range from $1 billion to $20 billion, depending on the noise levels and control methods selected. Although these will have some effect on developing country airlines using United States airports, the aircraft themselves will not be supplied by developing countries, and their export prospects will be unaffected.[34]

Radiation-emitting products are regulated by the Department of Health, Education and Welfare through the Radiation Control for Health and Safety Act of 1968. Products include both consumer items and devices used in industry and in the health sector—for example, television receivers, microwave ovens and dryers, x-ray machines, electronic microscopes, infrared dryers and ovens, laser devices, and ultrasonic devices. The current level of imports from developing countries appears low for some items (x-ray apparatus, 2.5% United States imports, microwave ovens, 0.3%) but very substantial for other items (television receivers, $231 million, or 28% total United States imports in 1976). Even if current levels are low, rapid growth is possible. The procedure that exporters must follow illustrate the typical way in which product standards are applied to imports. The prospective exporter first obtains a certificate of conformity from HEW. To do this a sample is delivered to the Director of Customs or HEW for testing by the radiological division of HEW. If the product conforms, a certificate is issued to the exporter, and the Director of Customs is notified. The exporter guarantees the conformity of each item in his shipment by labeling. The shipment is then subject to random testing at customs. Regulations and procedures are published in the *Federal Register*. Even if strict national treatment is accorded, there is opportunity for delay and increased costs.

Environmental regulations on agricultural products are perhaps most important to developing countries because of the trade importance of agriculture. The United States maintains a rather complex set of regulations.[35] The extent of these regulations will probably increase with the growing concern for health and the environmental consequences of food additives and pesticide residues. Meat and meat products can only be imported from processing plants in countries whose inspection systems have been approved by the United States, and the foreign government has certified the plant as meeting United States standards. USDA officials conduct on-site inspections. The Food and Drug Administration (FDA) regulates additives and pesticide residues. Additives "Generally Recognized as Safe" (GRAS) are listed by the FDA but are subject to delisting. Imported meats and poultry products are sampled by the USDA for residues at the time of inspection. Most analyses are for chlorinated hydrocarbon pesticides (aldrin, DDT, etc.) and heavy metals (mercury, cadmium, etc.). Tolerance levels are published by USDA. Plants and plant products are inspected on entry into the United States. Tolerances for pesticide residues are published in the *Federal Register,* as are approved additives (GRAS).

The problem of agriculture is complicated by several factors. First, delay at customs can and has resulted in spoilage and the loss of an entire shipment. Second, detailed and current knowledge of tolerance levels is required. Third, there have been allegations that inspection is arbitrary or capricious. Fourth, not all developing countries have available to them the expertise for testing prior to shipment. Finally, residues will vary from lot to lot, and uncertainty will discourage some exporters. Work is being done through FAO and WHO to establish internationally uniform standards.

Packaging requirements are of two kinds, those to control litter and reduce solid wastes and those designed to prevent product contamination. The first appears mainly to be return/deposit schemes for bottles and cans. Because of high transport costs for beer and soft drinks, most are bottled close to the final market, and the problem for developing countries should be minimal. The major case in product contamination now involves the use of polyvinyl chloride for packaging food products.[36] The Food and Drug Administration proposed stringent regulations when it became clear that potentially carcinogenic substances were being transferred from the packaging material to the food contents. The extent to which developing countries are exporting food products with polyvinyl chloride packaging is not known, but it is probably small.

Controls on toxic substances are described to some extent in other categories. Examples include heavy metals (cadmium, lead, zinc, etc.), polychlorinated biphenyls (PCB), asbestos, and vinyl chloride. Broad regulation of toxic substances is contained in the Toxic Substances Control Act, which has just been enacted. Controls will cover production, distribution, and use, and they may impede imports. For example, testing requirements for new compounds may work against foreign suppliers. Current information on tolerance levels is required. Manufacturing and distribution records, labeling requirements, and possible arbitrary action by customs officials present further difficulties to exporters.

A final category of standards is national or international regulations on products that contribute directly to transnational pollution. The major example is the design and equipment standards for oil tankers found in the 1973 Prevention of Pollution from Ships Convention. One provision calls for segregated ballast tanks for tankers over 70,000 DWT to insure the physical separation of sea water ballast and cargo. The purpose is to prevent the discharge of dirty ballast. As a nontariff barrier, this should not present any particular difficulties to developing countries. Their shipyards can construct tankers in compliance with regulations as easily as other shipyards. It will, however, increase ocean transport rates modestly, and presumably this cost will ultimately be passed along to importing countries.

What conclusions can be drawn from this review? If broadly defined, environmentally related product standards cover a wide range of developing country exports and will increase in the next decade as industrial countries apply increasing controls and developing countries diversify their exports. One study concluded that OECD imports of "environmentally sensitive products" was $129 billion, or 34% of total imports (excluding petroleum). Excluding petroleum, developing countries supplied 15.2% of OECD imports, but only 13.3% of OECD imports of environmentally sensitive products.[37] These numbers may overdramatize the problem, because the existence of product standards does not automatically place imports at a competitive disadvantage. Also, although there is scope for arbitrary action on the part of customs officials, there is no indication that standards have been used as covert trade restrictions. Finally, in those instances in which compliance with standards requires sophisticated technology, the knowledge may be transferred through multinational corporations with manufacturing subsidiaries in developing countries. It does not appear that environmentally motivated product standards are now a serious problem for developing country exporters.

Even so, when agreement is possible, developing countries would benefit from harmonization of standards among industrial countries. This would permit increased production runs and scale economics, decrease information requirements, and limit delay and uncertainty during inspection and certification procedures. Prospects for harmonization are brightest when the threat is to human health, for example, pesticide residues and radiation emission levels. There is no conflict between industrial and developing country exporters in working toward harmonization, and the provisions of OECD's Guiding Principles serve the interests of both.

From another perspective, the need for detailed, timely information is apparent. When products are manufactured by multinational firms in developing countries, the information will be available to them. In other cases it may be inadequate. There have been suggestions for an "early warning system" in which industrial countries would publicize impending changes in environmental regulations on products to give advance notice to suppliers. Although the idea has merit, the need for information extends to all product standards, not only environmental standards. Also, knowledge of the procedures for testing and certification is important. Finally, for the United States, both the EPA and the FDA do go through a procedure of publishing proposed regulations that does provide some advance warning. Environmental standards appear to be little different in principle from other product standards that have international trade implications.[38]

MATERIALS RECOVERY[39]

Measures to protect the environment affect the use of virgin versus recovered materials in two ways, and each favors recovered over virgin materials. The first is the increased cost of extracting and initial processing of virgin materials as measures are taken to protect the natural environment. Familiar examples are regulations requiring reclamation of lands that have been strip mined and regulations covering techniques for log harvesting. As virgin and recovered materials compete as production inputs, the increased cost of virgin materials shifts demand toward recovered materials. If developing countries choose lower protective standards for extractive industries (and it is not clear that they should), demand shifts away from virgin materials supplied by industrial countries toward both virgin materials supplied by developing countries and increased materials recovery. The situation is similar to the differential changes in production costs examined earlier.

The more interesting effect arises from the increased cost of waste disposal resulting from environmental controls and the consequent incentive to recycle materials back into productive use, rather than discarding them.[40] As the social cost of waste disposal is brought into private decisions (or to municipal authorities), the recovery and recycling of materials becomes economically more attractive. In turn, increased supplies of recovered materials depress the demand and price of virgin materials, and developing country export markets for virgin materials will be somewhat less buoyant. Accordingly, developing countries will lose some foreign exchange earnings as compared to what they would have earned without restrictions on waste disposal. The magnitude of this effect is unknown, but as noted later, it may be substantial.[41]

It is useful to consider resource recovery from both production and consumption activities.[42] Even if disposal were free, it would be profitable in many industries to capture scrap or "wastes" and return them to the production process (termed "home" scrap) or to deliver them to a secondary materials market (termed "prompt" scrap). For example, in an integrated forest products complex, wastes from plywood manufacture may be delivered to hardboard or particle board mills for chipping into raw material. In some industries the recovery pattern is so firmly established that they are not considered wastes, but marketable by-products, such as hides from slaughter houses. Increased materials recovery is not an exotic activity that was born with the environmental movement, but an intensification brought about by change in the relative costs of disposal versus reuse.

Resource recovery from consumption activities has also been around for some time, especially when virgin materials are scarce and expensive. Auto junkyards are part of this process even if they are visually offensive. Retreading tires and the scrap paper market are other examples. The most difficult aspects of resource recovery from consumption appear to be (1) the dispersal and dilution of materials, which means higher collection costs for reuse than for industrial wastes, (2) the contamination or mixing of materials in waste flows, especially in municipal garbage but also in consumer durables such as autos, and (3) the perverse incentives confronting consumers. On this last point, incentives are inadequate to bring consumer behavior into socially desirable patterns. Roadside litter and the abuse of common property resources is one example. Even if households collected all wastes as garbage, collection fees are seldom pegged to volume or adjusted for preliminary sorting. Kitchen garbage disposals are a free good to the household, but the organic wastes place heavy demands on municipal treatment plants. Given the effective free disposal of consumer wastes, it is understandable that volume in the United States continues to climb (1971, 133 million tons; 1973, 144 million tons), and that only 6.2% of postconsumer solid waste is currently recovered.[43]

Although wastes vary in their volume and the environmental problems they create, the general effect of environmental protection measures is to restrict free disposal. Industry, households, and municipalities will then face the decision of accepting higher disposal costs or increasing the recovery of materials for reuse. To cite but one example, the 1972 Ocean Dumping Convention and implementing United States legislation limit the types and amounts of wastes that can be barged to sea and dumped. Although the EPA appears slow in implementing the legislation (total tonnage dumped in 1974 was 14.1 million tons, up 18% from 1973), ultimately the practice of dumping sewage sludge offshore (6.5 million tons) should be eliminated. Together with increasing scarcity of land disposal sites near urban centers and the costs and environmental restrictions on incineration, the economics will be more favorable for processing sludge into fertilizers, thus reducing the demand for primary raw materials used as inputs in chemical fertilizers.[44] The example of sludge illustrates the major determinants of resource recovery: the price of virgin material inputs (phosphate), decreased opportunity for traditional disposal (ocean dumping), increased costs of alternative disposal methods (incineration, sanitary land fill), and improvements in the technology of recovery and reuse (transforming sludge to fertilizer or soil conditioners).

The final point to make in this connection is that the material recovered need not be similar in form or purpose to the materials that generated wastes. Indeed, it appears that the major valuable output from municipal resource recovery systems is energy, either by feeding wastes directly into utility boilers or by pyrolysis, which converts municipal solid wastes into gaseous and liquid fuels.[45] Another example is the production of sulfuric acid by trapping SO_2 emissions during the process of smelting copper. Consequently, a full analysis of the trade consequences of resource recovery should consider the "cross-commodity" effects on the demand for virgin materials from developing countries.

No comprehensive study has been done of the trade effects of resource recovery. There is, however, scattered evidence that suggests that the impact may be substantial. For example, the Council on Environmental Quality estimates that the theoretical energy value of solid wastes produced in the United States in 1980 will be equivalent to 385 million barrels of oil per year. If this figure is adjusted downward to include only wastes in more densely populated areas, where centralized municipal waste collection is feasible, the figure is reduced to 225 million barrels.[46] This latter figure represents 10% of current United States oil imports and, at an international price of $11 per bbl, is equal to $2.47 billion. At moderately high oil prices and land values, the economics of energy recovery also appear favorable. The CEQ estimated that at a price of $0.80/million BTUs of energy recovered (equivalent to an oil price of just under $5/bbl), recovery is more economic than sanitary landfill, even if land costs were zero. With positive land prices, energy recovery would become even more attractive. However, on the basis of projects actually planned in 1974, the oil displacement effect in 1980 would be much less—15 billion bbl or about $169 million. Developing countries currently supply 87% of the United States oil import market. Note also that any oil import displacement by solid waste energy recovery is the combined result of environmental constraints on waste disposal and the sharp increase in the price of imported oil.

In another study Walter and Maltezou concluded that substantial recycling opportunities exist for waste lubrication oil.[47] They estimate that if all collectable waste oil in 1972 had been collected and rerefined, it would have been equivalent to a crude oil content value of $35–59 million at 1972 crude oil prices. At 1974 prices, the crude oil value would have been $112–189 million. The rerefined lube oil itself would have been worth $161–270 million at 1972 prices, or 103–172% of United States lube oil imports in 1972. Walter and Maltezou estimate that only 25% of lube oil consumption is actually recycled.

There is also indirect evidence that the recovery of nonferrous metals could increase. Pearce estimates a recovery effort index for three metals (aluminum, copper, and lead) for six industrial countries.[48] The index is the ratio of recovered materials to total materials used, and for the six countries it ranges from a low of .200 to a high of .285 for aluminum, from .270 to .447 for copper, and from .180 to .616 for lead. Intercountry differences in the recovery index are not conclusive evidence of unexploited opportunity for materials recovery, because end-use patterns may differ and the amount in dissipative uses vary, but they are still suggestive. In another study, Clay computed the ratio of scrap to total consumption for four nonferrous metals (aluminum, zinc, lead, and copper) for the same six industrial countries, and the low/high range is even larger: .158–.346 for aluminum, .121–.291 for zinc, .167–.672 for lead, .299–.475 for copper.[49] One way to get a feel for the trade magnitudes involved is to assume that each country is able to achieve at least as high a scrap use ratio as the highest country, and that the additional materials recovered would displace imports. We have done this using the Clay data and estimate that the import displacement effect for the six countries combined would be $446 million for aluminum, $87 million for zinc, $250 million for lead, and $344 for copper. None of these numbers should be considered projections, but they do illustrate that resource recovery efforts may have considerable impact over time on LDC export levels. From a trade policy viewpoint, there is nothing special that should be done. Increased resource recovery, either in response to higher prices of virgin materials or higher waste disposal costs, is economically and environmentally desirable.

FOREIGN INVESTMENT

No aspect of North–South environmental relations is more sensitive than the issue of direct foreign investment. The critical questions are, will differences in environmental control costs draw industries from industrial countries to developing countries, and should this process be encouraged or discouraged? A definitive estimate of environmentally motivated investment cannot be made, and the issue will remain controversial.

Developing countries are in an awkward position. They are reluctant to become the dumping grounds for the dirty industries of the North. More generally, their political sensitivity to direct foreign investment and the behavior of multinational corporations (MNCs) is involved. At the same time, most developing countries are committed to industrialization, and foreign investment can bring income, jobs, technology, and foreign exchange, even if the investment is on the basis of low environmental control costs.[50]

Industrial countries also display some ambivalence. The "export" of jobs by MNCs is a frequent allegation, and the export of jobs to escape rigorous domestic environmental controls would be especially objectionable. Both labor and environmentalists (with a global perspective) have an interest in limiting foreign investments in "sweated" environments, yet for many individuals it is better to locate a smelter or refinery where they are not personally inconvenienced. When sites in industrial countries become scarce and controls too expensive, operations may shift abroad.

There is no empirical evidence that environmental considerations have led to major investment flows from North to South. Three surveys of the business literature have failed to document relocation for this reason.[51] This is not surprising. As noted earlier, EC regulations are just beginning to put major cost pressure on firms in industrial countries, and it may be too soon to observe relocation. Moreover, firms that deliberately invested abroad to escape domestic abatement costs would not wish to publicly state their motives. Candor would offend their hosts and strengthen their critics in industrial countries. Nor does it appear likely that ex post statistical examination of aggregate investment flows will be of much help in identifying the impact. Differences in environmental control costs will be small relative to other determinants of investment location—labor quality and cost, transport costs, tax rates, political stability, and so on. Although analysis of individual industries might yield firm conclusions, the separation and identification of an EC cost factor in aggregate investment data does not appear promising. This does not mean it is inconsequential, but rather that empirical identification will be quite difficult.

In the absence of a useful methodology and statistical evidence, most discussion has been based on more casual observation and a general knowledge of MNC behavior. For example, Gladwin and Wells conclude that "flows of foreign direct investment do not appear as yet to differ substantially from what would be expected in the absence of environment-induced locational shifts except in a few instances. More importantly, we do not expect a flow of environmentally induced FDI of any real significance to materialize in the future."[52] In a related conclusion, they state that most MNCs do not adopt identical environmental policies for their global operations, but interpret and implement policies tailored to the local situation. However, Gladwin and Wells are not consistent; they state that "process technology selection for overseas plants has been found to be rather insensitive to leniency of environmental regulations—MNC's generally move abroad with 'off the shelf' plant designs and with their newest, most efficient process technologies."[53]

Which industries might be most likely to relocate in developing countries for EC purposes? Higher stage manufacturing and assembly operations would probably be least likely to, because the ratio of EC costs to value added tends to be relatively low, and the manufacture of sophisticated products often is located close to markets or requires skills that are unavailable in developing countries. Also, it seems unlikely that processing industries for raw materials supplied by industrial countries would find it economic to ship the materials abroad and reimport the processed material back to industrial country markets. For example, certain operations in food processing are subject to considerable EC costs, particularly for water pollution abatement, but the operations are tied to food input supplies.

The most likely general category would be the early stage or basic processing of raw materials for which the ratio of EC costs to value added is high, and for which raw materials are located in developing countries. Candidates include metal smelting operations, petroleum refining, manufacture of hardboard and other manufactured woods, pulp and paper, fertilizers, production of aluminum, and perhaps basic iron and steel production and some petrochemicals. There would be additional incentive in these industries if (1) developing countries deliberately encourage processing to increase domestic value added, (2) the production of the raw material itself were subject to costly environmental controls in industrial countries (for example, a ban on "clear-cut" logging and expensive controls on wet storage of logs), (3) processing reduced bulk and saved shipping costs, and (4) the processing were part of a vertically integrated industry in which MNCs were a major force (for example, aluminum). Even if all these characteristics are favorable, the extent of relocation for EC purposes remains uncertain.

The petroleum refining industry fulfills several of these criteria, yet casual examination of capacity expansion data over the past 10 years does not support a relocation hypothesis. Table 3.10 provides expansion figures for the periods

Table 3.10 Expansion of Petroleum Refining Capacity 1965–1970 and 1970–1975

	Capacity (1000 bbl/day)			Percentage Increase	
	1965	1970	1975	1965–1970	1970–1975
Industrial Countries	21791	31640	42115	45	33
United States	10800	12079	14845	12	23
Canada	1150	1355	2024	18	49
Western Europe	7502	14651	18993	95	30
Japan	1856	2796	5134	51	84
Developing Countries	7083	10438	15335	47	47
Latin America	2724	3716	5391	36	45
Caribbean[a]	1199	1618	2270	35	40
Africa[b]	399	614	849	54	38
Middle East	1801	2686	3283	49	22
Asia[b]	960	1804	3542	88	96

Source. Derived from *International Petroleum Encyclopedia 1975* (Tulsa, Oklahoma, 1975).

[a] Includes Barbados, Jamaica, Netherlands Antilles, Puerto Rico, Trinidad and Tobago, Virgin Islands.

[b] Developing countries only.

1965–1970 and 1970–1975 by major country or geographical region. In absolute terms most of the expansion occurred in industrial countries in both periods. Although the growth rate has been more rapid in developing areas (47%), there does not appear to be a break in recent years that might mark an environmental factor. The United States capacity expanded more rapidly in the second period (23% vs. 12%). Interestingly, most expansion was to existing capacity, not the construction of new refineries.[54] The situation may change, however, if the "no significant deterioration" of air quality currently being considered by Congress is enacted.

There is another group of industries, characterized by hazardous workplace conditions as well as possible neighborhood effects, that may have incentive to relocate abroad. These industries include asbestos textiles, benzidine dyes, vinyl chloride, lead smelting and lead batteries, and perhaps synthetic rubber production. Increasingly stringent workplace standards may make foreign location attractive. At a minimum, it would be desirable that the host governments be given full and detailed information on the occupational dangers associated with the production of these products. Stronger measures might also be needed to prevent "runaway" hazardous industries.

The principle on which developing countries should base their policy toward environmentally motivated investment is simple enough. Foreign investments should be neither favored nor discriminated against compared to domestic industry, but should be subject to the same level of environmental controls as equivalent domestic firms. Again, in principle, the level should reflect both the real resource costs of abatement and the benefits or social damages avoided. If this leads to some incremental inflow of investments from industrial countries, well and good. If not, fine, for the environmental costs would have exceeded abatement expenditures. In practice it will be more difficult to make these decisions. One reason is that MNCs may have far better information on the amount of pollutants emitted and the techniques and costs of abatement.[55] This will be especially true when abatement involves process and product changes instead of end-of-pipe treatment. Negotiating with MNCs under these circumstances places the host government at a disadvantage, but the issue is no different in principle from other examples of unequal access to information.

It has also been suggested that developing countries may be forced into a pernicious competition, one with the other, to attract foreign investment on the basis of lenient EC standards. The pollution haven argument is analogous to the tax holiday competition. We doubt, however, if the absence of environmental controls becomes a serious basis for competing for direct investments except perhaps in the extractive industries such as forest products and extensive agriculture. EC costs will generally be minor locational determinants. Also, if the likely sectors are certain raw material processing industries, competition would be confined to a fairly small number of countries. Developing countries have the option of adopting a uniform EC financing principle similar to that set out by the OECD, and this would reduce competition based on the degree of government subsidies. The economic justification for private sector financing of its own abatement costs holds for developing as well as developed countries. Furthermore, an exchange of information among experts in specific industries as to the techniques for controls and the levels chosen in various developing countries might be useful in formulating overall environmental policies in developing countries. Incidentally it might lead to some coordination and improvement in their negotiating position with foreign investors.

The preceding observations place the primary burden of controlling the environmental behavior of MNCs on the host countries. If one were confident that transnational pollution was minimal, and that developing countries would establish EC regulations that were optimal from their perspective, there would be little justification for environmental controls on the overseas activities of MNCs by investor governments.[56] Indeed, the extension of United States environmental standards to foreign subsidiaries of United States firms in developing countries, as has been suggested, would frustrate the efficient allocation of environmental resources and would infringe on the sovereignty of developing countries.[57]

However, we are not sanguine about the capacity of developing countries to formulate and implement effective environmental policies toward foreign investors. In part this is because developing countries often do not have the technical information concerning the effects of pollution and the techniques of abatement that are available to the MNC. One possibility worth serious thought is the establishment of an environmental code of conduct for MNCs. One aspect of such a code would be the obligation of the investor to provide a detailed statement to the environmental authorities of the host country of the pollution and pollution abatement techniques available for its operations. This transfer of knowledge would assist the authorities of the developing countries to establish rational control policies.

NOTES

1. The relevant literature includes Ingo Walter, *International Economics of Pollution* (London: Macmillan, 1975); Ingo Walter, "Environmental Control and Economic Development: The Issue Reconsidered," *Intereconomics* (March 1974) p. 43; Charles Pearson, *Implications for the Trade and Investment of Developing Countries of United States Environmental Controls*, United Nations Conference on Trade and Development TD/B/C.2 (New York: United Nations, 1976); Jaleel Ahmad, "Environmental Aspects of International Income Distribution," and Thomas N. Gladwin and John G. Wells, "Environmental Policy and Multinational Corporate Strategy," in Ingo Walter, Ed., *Studies in International Environmental Economics* (New York: Wiley-Interscience, 1976) p. 225 and p. 177; and United Nations Conference on Trade and Development, "Impact of Environmental Policies on Trade and Development in Particular of the Developing Countries," (Geneva: UNCTAD Document TD/130, 13 March 1972).
2. See Walter, *International Economics of Pollution;* Herbert G. Grubel, "Some Effects of Environmental Controls on International Trade: The Heckscher-Ohlin Model" and Horst Siebert, "Environmental Control, Economic Structure, and International Trade," in Ingo Walter, Ed., *International Environmental Economics*, p. 9 and p. 29; Stephen P. Magee and William F. Ford, "Environmental Pollution, the Terms of Trade and Balance of Payments of the United States," *Kyklos*, **25**, No. 1 (1972) p. 101; Anthony C. Koo, "Environmental Repercussion and Trade Theory," *Review of Economics and Statistics*, **56**, No. 2 (May 1974) p. 235; and also the contributions to Organization for Economic Cooperation and Development, *Transfrontier Pollution* (Paris: OECD, 1975).
3. GATT, *Industrial Pollution Control and Trade;* Walter, *International Economics of Pollution;* Pearson, *Implications for Developing Countries of U.S. Environmental Controls.*
4. The distinction should not be pressed too far. Some products are used for both final consumption and as intermediate production inputs. Commercially operated trucks are one example.

5. Assuming no transnational pollution and no other price distortions.
6. Another question is, will equipment imported into developing countries be environmentally "overengineered" and not suited to their circumstances?
7. This partial equilibrium diagram does not account for possible offsetting effects of induced exchange rate changes.
8. Walter uses the terms "direct environmental control loading" (DECL) and "overall environmental control loading" (OECL) to describe the direct and direct plus indirect costs. Walter, *International Economics of Pollution,* Chapter 3. In theory, imported inputs not subject to environmental controls will have no pass-through of price increase.
9. For example, the United States might choose to discourage the production of coal, an export item, if it is not possible to avoid direct environmental damages from mining.
10. Ingo Walter, "The Pollution Content of American Trade," *Western Economic Journal,* **11,** No. 1 (March 1973) p. 61.
11. The original diagram was by Ingo Walter, "International Trade and Resource Diversion: The Case of Environmental Management," *Weltwirtschaftliches Archives,* Bd. 110 (1974) p. 482. It was modified by Charles Pearson in "International Trade and Environmental Controls: Comment," *Weltwirtschaftliches Archive,* Bd. 111 (1975) p. 564.
12. Grubel, for example, assumes a zero damage range for wastes. Grubel, "Effects of Environmental Controls on Trade." Note also that traditional trade theory relies heavily on comparative static analysis, and this technique is not particularly well suited to analyzing losses that are delayed in time.
13. The argument in favor of effluent and emission fees is that abatement cost functions differ among polluters; for efficient abatement the marginal abatement cost for each polluter should be equalized. A fee system, based on a tax per unit pollutant emitted, is said to accomplish this more readily, because each polluter is most familiar with his own abatement cost function. For a discharge standard system to be efficient the authorities would have to know the abatement cost functions for each polluter, and set individual standards accordingly. For proponents, see Charles L. Schultz and Alan V. Kneese, *Pollution, Prices, and Public Policy* (Washington D.C.: Brookings Institution, 1975). For a summary of environmental regulations in industrial countries see U.S. Department of Commerce, *The Effects of Pollution Abatement on International Trade III* (Washington, D.C.: GPO, 1975). The EPA is also building a collection of foreign environmental reports and documents. See the monthly bulletin, United States Environmental Protection Agency, Office of International Activities, *Summaries of Foreign Government Environmental Reports.*
14. See "Recommendations of the Council on Guiding Principles Concerning International Economic Aspects of Environmental Policies" C(72)128, OECD, Paris, June 6, 1972; *The Polluter Pays Principle-Definition-Analysis-Implementation* (Paris: OECD, 1975); Jean-Philippe Barde, "National and International Policy Alternatives for Environmental Control and Their Economic Implications," in Ingo Walter, Ed., *Studies in International Environmental Economics,* p. 137.
15. U.S. Department of Commerce, *The Effects of Abatement on Trade III.* The OECD is also doing work in this area.
16. Edward F. Renshaw, "Should the Federal Government Subsidize Industrial Pollution Control Investments?" *Journal of Environmental Economics and Management,* **1,** No. 1 (May 1974) p. 84.
17. The calculations are made by cumulating the flow of pollution investment subject to industrial development bond financing from 1970 to 1975 and multiplying by 2.5%, the estimated amount of interest subsidy residing in the tax-free feature of the bonds.
18. Charles S. Pearson, "Environmental Control Costs and Border Adjustments," *National Tax Journal,* **27,** No. 4 (December 1974) p. 599.
19. Eugene V. Coan, Julia N. Hillis, and Michael McCloskey, "Strategies for International Environmental Action: The Case for an Environmentally Oriented Foreign Policy," *Natural Resources Journal,* **14,** No. 1 (January 1974) p. 87.
20. For example, the timetable for auto emission standards for hydrocarbon and carbon monoxide emissions was relaxed in the 1974 U.S. Energy Supply and Environmental Coordination Act.

21. Expenditures should not be used for international comparisons of commitment to environmental quality, because they do not account for differences in remedial clean-up, industrial structure, assimilative capacity, and so on.
22. John E. Cremeans, Frank W. Segel, and Gary Rutledge, "Capital Expenditures by Business for Air, Water, and Solid Waste Pollution Abatement, 1974 and Planned 1975," *Survey of Current Business,* **55,** No. 7 (July 1975) p. 15.
23. The U.S. Department of Commerce attempts to do this in their primary data collection. John R. Cremeans, "Capital Expenditure by Business for Air and Water Pollution Abatement, 1973 and Planned 1974," *Survey of Current Business,* **54,** No. 7 (July 1974) p. 58.
24. U.S. Environmental Protection Agency, *Plywood, Hardboard, and Wood Preserving Segment of the Timber Products Processing Point Source Category,* Development Document EPA 440/1-74-023-a (Washington: EPA, April 1974) Section V.
25. Organization for Economic Cooperation and Development, *Economic Implications of Pollution Control* (Paris: OECD, 1974) Table VIII.
26. See for example *The Economics of Clean Water–1973,* Annual Report of the EPA to the Congress (Washington: GPO, 1974) Table VII–10.
27. U.S. Department of Commerce, "The Input-Output Structure of the U.S. Economy: 1967," *Survey of Current Business,* **54,** No. 2 (February 1974) p. 24.
28. Specifically, see Sung Y. Kwack, "Determination of U.S. Imports and Exports," *Southern Economic Journal,* January 1972 p. 309 for a review of empirical work on United States trade elasticities.
29. See Ingo Walter, "Implications of Environmental Policies for the Trade Prospects of Developing Countries: Analysis Based on an UNCTAD Questionnaire," Report to UNCTAD Secretariat, December 1975. It has been alleged, however, that the 1973 Canadian restrictions on beef imports from the United States, which obstensibly were directed against residuals of the growth hormone DES, were actually to limit a sharp upsurge of United States beef destined for Canadian markets. *Washington Post,* April 10, 1974 and subsequent editorials.
30. Bart S. Fisher, "U.S. Safety Standards as Non-Tariff Trade Barriers: The Case of Compressed Gas Cylinders," *SAIS Review,* **19,** No. 4 (Fall 1975) p. 42.
31. Harald B. Malmgren, "Environmental Management and the International Economy," in Allen V. Kneese, Sidney E. Rolfe, and Joseph W. Harned, Eds., *Managing the Environment* (New York: Praeger, 1971) p. 53.
32. Noise abatement within the workplace is receiving greater attention. Abatement measures will change production costs and should be analyzed along with other environmental production costs. The costs may be large. One study concluded that the cost of moving from a 90 dB standard to a 85 dB standard would be $8 billion over 5 years. CEQ *Environmental Quality, Seventh Annual Report,* p. 55.
33. Local governments have long had noise ordinances and have recently prepared noise standards for specific products used within their jurisdiction.
34. Aircraft noise has been a serious issue in granting landing rights in the United States to the Concorde, the British/French supersonic transport.
35. For a convenient but no longer current survey see "Information on U.S. Quarantine, Sanitary, and Health Laws and Regulations" (document CIES/CECONSANIT (8)) prepared by the United States Delegation to the Meeting of Governmental Experts on Sanitary, Quarantine, and Health Regulations, Organization of American States (February 28–March 3, 1972).
36. *Washington Post,* August 29, 1975, p. A3.
37. Walter, "Analysis of UNCTAD Questionnaire," p. 34.
38. Both the OECD and the GATT have done considerable work on the issue of international trade and product standards. This issue is also part of UNCTAD's work program.
39. For surveys of the theory, technology, and trade aspects see, respectively, Walter O. Spofford, "Solid Residuals Management: Some Economic Considerations," *Natural Resources Journal,* **11,** No. 3 (July 1971); Midwest Research Institute for the CEQ, *Resource Recovery: The State of Technology* (Washington, D.C.: GPO, 1973); and Ingo Walter, "A Discussion of Secondary Materials Recovery," *International Economic Studies Institute,* Contemporary Issues No. 2, December 1975.

40. Resource recovery itself can generate pollutants.
41. Both cartel action by virgin material producers and stricter environmental regulations on waste disposal will stimulate the market for recovered materials. However, they should have opposite effects on the earnings of virgin materials producers. Cartel action will only be undertaken with the expectation of higher earnings (restricting supply with inelastic demand), but increased recovered material will shift down the demand for virgin material and depress earnings.
42. Spofford terms the first "recycling" and the second "reclamation."
43. Council on Environmental Quality, *Environmental Quality: Sixth Annual Report* (Washington, D.C.: GPO, 1975) p. 92.
44. Sewage sludge used as fertilizer can present hazards with respect to traces of PCBs, toxic metals and viruses. T. D. Hinesly, "Practices, Economics, and Effects of Municipal Sludge Utilization or Land as an Alternative to Ocean Dumping," in *Ocean Disposal Practices and Effects,* Report to the Environmental Protection Agency by the President's Water Pollution Control Advisory Board (Washington, D.C.: EPA, 1972).
45. CEQ, *Annual Report 1975,* p. 94.
46. CEQ, *Annual Report 1974,* p. 137.
47. Ingo Walter and Sonia P. Maltezou, "Resource Recovery and U.S. International Trade: The Case of Waste Oil," *Environmental Affairs,* **3,** No. 3 (July 1974).
48. David Pearce, "Environmental Protection, Recycling and the International Materials Economy," in Ingo Walter, Ed., *Studies in International Environmental Economics,* p. 319.
49. J. A. Clay, "Future Developments—A Primary View of the Secondary Non-Ferrous Scrap Industry," as cited by Ingo Walter in "International Economic Dimensions of Secondary Materials Recovery."
50. UNIDO has endorsed the objective that developing countries produce 25% of world industrial output by 2000.
51. Gladwin and Wells, "Environmental Policy and Multinational Strategy"; Anthony Yezer and Amy Philipson, "Influence of Environmental Considerations on Agriculture Decisions to Locate Outside of the Continental United States," prepared by the Public Interest Economics Center for the CEQ, 1974 (mimeo); E. Dennis Conroy, "Will 'Dirty' Industries Seek Pollution Havens Abroad?," *SAIS Review,* **18,** No. 3 (Fall 1974) p. 48.
52. Gladwin and Wells, "Environmental Policy and Multinational Strategy," p. 202.
53. Gladwin and Wells, "Environmental Policy and Multinational Strategy," p. 200.
54. For refining capacity data see *Oil and Gas Journal,* various issues.
55. MNCs are also the major vehicle for transferring pollution abatement technology to developing countries.
56. Gladwin and Wells reach similar conclusions.
57. Suggested by Coan et al. in "Strategies for International Environmental Action."

APPENDIX. DISAGGREGATED ENVIRONMENTAL CONTROL COST AND TRADE STUDIES

The purpose of this appendix is to review briefly several EC control cost and trade studies to

- Indicate the magnitude of environmental control costs;
- Indicate their distribution among industries;
- Summarize trade conclusions when available.

The studies vary considerably in scope and purpose, ranging from survey data of pollution abatement expenditures actually made to studies of individual commodities markets.

(1) *U.S. Department of Commerce, Capital Expenditures for Pollution Abatement*

Table A3.1 presents data on capital expenditures by industry for 1975 and planned 1976. The estimates include air and water pollution abatement and solid waste disposal expenditures. Expressed as a percentage of total capital expenditures, the most heavily impacted sectors for 1975 are primary metals (17.2%), stone, clay, and glass (14.2%), paper (16.8%), chemicals (10.8%), petroleum (11.8%), and electric utilities (9.7%). These data are not directly useful for trade analysis, because they do not annualize costs, include operation and maintenance expenses, or include indirect costs on purchased inputs.

(2) *Japanese Capital Expenditures for Pollution Abatement*

As a comparison, Table A3.2 provides data on capital investment, by sector, for pollution abatement in Japan. In general, the same industries as in the United States are most heavily impacted—iron and steel, petroleum, thermal power, pulp and paper, chemicals, and mining all rank high—but the ratios of abatement expenditure to total investment are considerably higher. This illustrates the urgent remedial nature of the Japanese pollution abatement program. Again, the data are not directly useful for trade analysis purposes.

(3) *Study by Professor Ingo Walter*

Table A3.3 provides the direct and total (direct and indirect) EC costs estimated by Professor Walter. Costs are given as costs per dollar of final sales for 64 Input-Output industry categories. The study has the considerable advantage of cumulating EC costs through the I-O structure to capture both direct and indirect costs. The data base, however, is no longer current. In principle this approach may overstate EC costs as it does not consider input coefficient changes in response to EC related relative price changes. The size of this bias is not known.

(4) *Study by Professor Anthony Yezer and Amy Philipson*

Tables A3.4a and A3.4b contain estimates made by Yezer and Philipson for the CEQ. Fourteen industrial sectors are included. The original data source for control costs was the EPA, and similar to Walter, both direct and indirect costs were included and expressed as a percentage of value of shipments. The final column shows the estimated output effect on United States production. With the exception of petroleum refining, the output decrease is generally less than 1%. The study includes only incremental costs (those attributable to federal legislation) and thus underestimates the output effect. Also, it appears that indirect costs working through utilities were not included.

(5) *U.S. Department of Commerce; The Effects of Pollution Abatement on Trade in the Copper Smelting, Kraft Woodpulp, Phosphate Fertilizer, and Primary Aluminum Industries*

Table A3.5 reports the results of a recent intensive study undertaken by the Commerce Department of four industries. With the exception of the OECD pulp and paper study, this is the only attempt to develop cost data for other major producing countries as a first step in estimating the trade impact of environmental controls. The results of a detailed study such as this are difficult to summarize, and the original document should also be consulted. Note that air pollution controls alone were considered and that indirect EC costs working through purchased inputs are not included.

For the three copper smelting countries there is a wide range of abatement levels, from 88.2% sulfur removal for the United States to 29.5% for Chile and Peru (certain facilities only). The estimated industry average EC cost for the United States (6.6 cents/lb.) conceals a broad range among refiners (4.3–10.5 cents/lb.) and is substantial compared to the current spot price (65 cents/lb.). Within the phosphate fertilizer industry, the impact of EC costs as a percentage of price varies from product to product (0–2%). Concerning kraft pulp production, the study concluded that cost differentials in international markets were less important than securing financial capital for pollution abatement expenditures. Note that one must be quite careful in interpreting the estimates. For example, the estimated cost per ton of $2.45 applies to incremental air pollution costs only and does not include very large expenditures to meet state air pollution controls. Nor does it include the estimated $6.50/ton cost of meeting water pollution controls.

(6) *Public Research Institute's Estimates of Trade Impact in Selected Industries*

The Public Research Institute, under contract to the National Commission on Water Quality, has recently completed a study of the price, output, and trade impacts expected from the 1972 Federal Water Pollution Control legislation. The study covered five industries—metals (steel, copper and aluminum), pulp and paper, textiles, leather, and red meats. The results, as related to percentage increases in imports, are summarized in Table A3.6. The results show very modest import penetration except for wood pulp.

The method employed was to construct econometric models of each industry (or subindustry), simulate baseline projections for prices, output, and trade, and compare the baseline projections to a second simulation including the costs of pollution control. The results should not be taken as trade estimates of pollution abatement, because only incremental water pollution control costs were included. Also, it does not appear that indirect costs were systematically included, and increases in foreign production costs arising from foreign environmental control programs were not considered. Original cost estimates were supplied by the National Bureau of Economic Research and Development Planning and Research Associates. It is not known if these were based on engineering cost estimates.

(7) *Study by Richardson and Mutti*

Professors Richardson and Mutti have attempted to measure the price and output effects by industry of United States environmental controls. Some of their results are reported in Table A3.7. One interesting feature of their work, which explicitly took account of increased competition through the foreign sector, was to estimate the effects under different financing regimes: polluter pays; government subsidies financed by a value added tax, and subsidies financed by a production tax.

The results show generally modest price and output effects. The range for price increases under the polluter-pays regime was 0.19–5.12% with the weighted average being 1.7% or 1.2%, depending on elasticity assumptions. Interestingly, the negative output effects under the value added tax regime and the production tax regime were 1.51%, and these were almost as large as the negative effect on output under the polluter-pays regime of 1.75%.

Again, the results have limited value for trade prediction purposes. EC cost estimates were based mostly on Walter's study and are no longer current. Furthermore, the study did not include foreign EC costs or the indirect effect of compensatory exchange rate changes.

Table A3.1 United States Pollution Abatement Capital Expenditures by Industry, 1975 and 1976

	Abatement Capital Expenditures (millions $)		Abatement Capital Expenditures as Percentage of Total Capital Expenditures	
Industries	1975	Planned 1976	1975	Planned 1976
All industries	6549	7346	5.8	6.1
Manufacturing	4475	4488	9.3	8.8
Durable goods	1775	1762	8.0	7.9
Primary metals	1012	1007	17.2	17.3
Blast furnaces, steel works	396	540	13.5	18.8
Nonferrous metals	546	396	24.1	18.7
Electrical machinery	136	158	5.8	6.6
Machinery, except elect.	83	106	1.7	2.2
Transportation equipment	116	137	3.4	4.1
Motor vehicles	86	114	3.9	4.8
Aircraft	26	20	2.8	2.8
Stone, clay, and glass	198	164	14.2	11.5
Other durables	229	191	5.3	4.3
Nondurable goods	2700	2726	10.3	11.1
Food including beverage	175	203	5.2	5.4
Textiles	31	46	4.6	5.8
Paper	489	502	16.8	15.0
Chemicals	684	786	10.8	11.5
Petroleum	1239	1100	11.8	9.8
Rubber	41	54	3.9	4.6
Other nondurables	41	34	2.8	2.5
Nonmanufacturing	2074	2859	3.2	4.1
Mining	73	99	1.9	2.7
Railroad	35	35	1.4	1.5
Air transportation	11	14	.6	1.1
Other transportation	41	58	1.4	2.0
Public utilities	1700	2431	8.4	10.1
Electric	1650	2386	9.7	11.9
Gas and other	50	45	1.5	1.1
Communication, commercial, and other	214	221	.6	.6

Source. Derived from Frank W. Segel and Gary L. Rutledge, "Capital Expenditures by Business for Air, Water, and Solid Waste Abatement, 1975 and Planned 1976," *Survey of Current Business,* July 1976, p. 14, Table 1.

Table A3.2 Japanese Pollution Abatement Capital Expenditure, by Industry, 1973–1975

	Abatement Capital Expenditure as Percentage of Total Capital Expenditure		
Industry	Fiscal Year 1973 (actual)	Fiscal Year 1974 (prospect)	Fiscal Year 1975 (plan)
All Industries	10.3	16.4	18.9
Iron and steel	17.0	18.5	19.9
Petroleum	19.8	32.0	39.9
Thermal power generation	26.5	44.8	39.9
Pulp and paper	21.8	29.2	31.0
Nonferrous metal	10.0	13.8	14.5
Chemicals (exc. petrochemicals)	17.8	28.8	32.9
Machinery	3.8	5.5	5.3
Petrochemicals	16.1	23.1	19.6
Mining (except coal)	26.0	38.0	43.1
Textile	10.4	16.5	17.3
Cement	10.9	15.6	15.0
Ceramics (except cement)	10.8	16.3	11.7
City gas	2.1	3.8	3.5
Coal	3.8	3.7	14.3
General merchandise	7.0	8.8	15.8
Construction materials	5.2	6.4	6.6
Power generation (except thermal)	1.1	1.1	1.2

Source. Japan Society of Industrial Machinery Manufacturers as cited in U.S. Department of Commerce, *The Effects of Pollution Abatement on International Trade III* (April 1975) pp. g–89.

Table A.3.3 Direct and Total Environmental Control Costs as Reported by Ingo Walter

Estimated Direct (DECL) and Overall (OECL) Environmental-Control Loadings Entering United States International Trade Flows, 1968–1970

I/O Product or Service Group	(1) DECL [a]	(2) OECL [a]
1. Livestock and products	1.28	1.98
2. Other agricultural products	1.92	2.46
3. Forestry and fishery products	0.64	1.05
5. Iron and ferroalloy ores mining	0.82	1.16
6. Nonferrous metal ores mining	0.82	1.29
7. Coal mining	1.76	2.21
8. Crude petroleum and natural gas	0.41	0.64
9. Stone and clay mining and quarrying	0.41	0.95
10. Chemical and fertilizer mining	0.82	1.31
13. Ordnance and accessories	0.53	2.36
14. Food and kindred products	0.36	1.01
15. Tobacco manufactures	0.18	0.51
16. Broad and narrow fabrics, yard, thread	0.38	1.02
17. Misc. textile goods and floor covering	0.38	1.10
18. Apparel	0.19	0.50
19. Misc. fabricated textile products	0.19	0.55
20. Lumber and wood products except containers	0.10	0.45
21. Wooden containers	0.05	0.56
22–23. Furniture and fixtures	0.05	0.59
24. Paper and allied products except containers	1.63	2.33
25. Paperboard containers and boxes	1.63	2.50
26. Printing and publishing	0.08	0.56
27. Chemicals and selected chemical prods.	2.19	3.25
28. Plastics and synthetic materials	2.19	3.34
29. Drugs, cleaning, toilet preparations	1.10	1.78
30. Paints and allied products	3.29	4.27
31. Petroleum refining and related products	3.73	4.58
32. Rubber and misc. plastic products	0.63	1.38
33. Leather tanning and industrial leather	0.95	1.38
34. Footwear and other leather products	0.32	0.57
35. Glass and glass products	0.86	1.55
36. Stone and clay products	1.72	2.40
37. Primary iron and steel	1.47	2.16
38. Primary nonferrous metals	1.76	3.09
39. Metal containers	0.53	1.35
40. Heating, plumbing, structural metal	0.53	1.28
41. Stamping, screw machine products	0.53	1.21
42. Other fabr. metal products	0.53	1.23
43. Engines and turbines	1.03	1.66
44. Farm machinery and equipment	1.03	1.66
45. Construction, mining, oil field equipt.	1.03	1.94
46. Metals handling mach. and equipt.	1.03	1.75
47. Metalworking mach. and equipt.	1.03	1.53
48. Special industrial mach. and equipt.	1.03	1.61
49. General industrial mach. and equipt.	1.03	1.63

Table A3.3 (Continued)

Estimated Direct (DECL) and Overall (OECL) Environmental-Control Loadings Entering United States International Trade Flows, 1968–1970

IO Product or Service Group	(1) DECL[a]	(2) OECL[A]
50. Machine shop products	1.03	1.58
51. Office computing and acct. machines	0.49	0.89
52. Service industry machines	1.03	1.63
53. Electric industrial equipt.	0.49	1.07
54. Household appliances	0.49	1.22
55. Electric lighting and wiring equipt.	0.49	1.14
56. Radio, TV, commun. equipt.	0.49	0.84
57. Electronic components and access.	0.49	1.04
58. Misc. elect. mach. and supplies	0.49	1.11
59. Motor vehicles and equipt.	1.19	2.04
60. Aircraft and parts	0.57	1.06
61. Other transportation equipment	0.72	1.31
62. Scientific and controlling instr.	3.37	4.03
63. Optical, ophthalmic, photographic equipt.	3.37	3.96
64. Misc. manufacturing	1.17	1.67
65. Transportation and warehousing	0.53	0.85
70. Finance and insurance	0.16	0.38
77. Medical, educational nonprofit	0.01	0.29
RR. Misc. services[b]	0.69	1.16

Source. Ingo Walter, "The Pollution Content of American Trade," *Western Economic Journal*, **XI**, No. 1 (March 1973) Table 2.

[a] Cents per dollar of final sales.

[b] Includes I/O Nos. 4, 11, 12, 66, 67, 68, 69, 71, 72, 73, 75, 76.

Table A3.4a Environmental Control Costs and Output Effects as Estimated by Yezer and Philipson, 1973

SIC	Classification of Industrial Products	Indirect Control Cost as a Percentage of Value of Shipments	Direct Control Cost as a Percentage of Value of Shipments	Total Control Cost as a Percentage of Value of Shipments	Price Elasticity	Output Effect (% decrease)
20	Food and kindred products	0.281	0.18	0.461	0.65	0.299
22	Textile mill products	0.388	0.19	0.578	0.99	0.572
24	Lumber and wood products	0.566	0.44	1.006	0.81	0.815
26	Paper and allied products	0.123	0.42	0.543	0.53	0.288
28	Chemical products	0.521	0.40	0.921	0.46	0.424
29	Petroleum refining	0.063	0.43	0.493	4.32	2.117
30	Rubber and misc. plastics	0.147	0.20	0.347	0.55	0.191
31	Leather products	0.078	0.29	0.368	0.23	0.084
32	Stone, clay, and glass products	0.346	0.25	0.596	1.10	0.656
33	Primary metals	0.042	0.80	0.842	0.51	0.429
34	Fabricated metals	0.508	0.07	0.578	0.33	0.191
35	Nonelectrical machinery	0.161	0.04	0.201	0.33	0.066
36	Electrical machinery	0.144	0.04	0.184	0.92	0.169
37	Transportation equipment	0.27	0.02	0.29		

Table A3.4b 1980

SIC	Classification of Industrial Products	Indirect Control Cost as a Percentage of Value of Shipments	Direct Control Cost as a Percentage of Value of Shipments	Total Control Cost as a Percentage of Value of Shipments	Price Elasticity	Output Effect (% decrease)
20	Food and kindred products	0.223	0.39	0.613	0.65	0.398
22	Textile mill products	0.424	0.40	0.824	0.99	0.816
24	Lumber and wood products	0.766	0.88	1.646	0.81	1.33
26	Paper and allied products	0.666	0.88	1.546	0.53	0.819
28	Chemical products	0.311	0.86	1.171	0.46	0.539
29	Petroleum refining	0.125	0.99	1.115	4.32	4.821
30	Rubber and misc. products	0.317	0.39	0.707	0.55	0.389
31	Leather products	0.183	0.57	0.753	0.23	0.173
32	Stone, clay, and glass products	0.499	0.56	0.809	1.1	0.890
33	Primary metals	0.595	2.0	2.595	0.51	1.323
34	Fabricated metals	1.368	0.13	1.498	0.33	0.494
35	Nonelectrical machinery	0.392	0.09	0.482	0.33	0.159
36	Electrical machinery	0.339	0.08	0.419	0.92	0.385
37	Transportation equipment	0.638	0.03	0.668		

Source. Anthony Yezer and Amy Philipson, "Influence of Environmental Considerations on Agricultural and Industrial Decisions to Locate Outside of the Continental United States," prepared for the CEQ by the Public Interest Economics Center, 1974.

Table A3.5 Pollution Abatement Costs in Four Industries

Copper Smelting
(air pollution control only)

Country	EC Costs	Level of Abatement
United States	6.6¢/lb. industry average 4.3–10.5¢/lb. range	88.2% sulfur input removed
Canada	2.7¢/lb. industry average 2.2–7.4¢/lb. range	66.3% sulfur removed
Peru and Chile	0.5¢/lb. industry average 0–1.4¢/lb.[a] range	29.5% sulfur removed[a]

Historic peak copper price:	$1.50/lb.
Current spot price (Aug. 1975):	0.65/lb.

Phosphate Fertilizers
(air pollution control only)

Country	Process (Product)	EC Control Cost as Percentage of Price
United States	Wet process phosphoric acid	0.05
	Granular triple superphosphate	2.0
	Diammonium phosphate	0.82
	Ammonia	0
	Normal superphosphate	0.7
Canada	EC costs currently less than U.S.	
Brazil	EC costs currently virtually nil	

Kraft (Sulfate) Wood Pulp
(air pollution control only)

Country	Annual EC Costs for Control of Particulates and Sulfur by Mill Size (tons per day)		
	500	1000	1500
		(thousands $)	
United States	$494	$777	$1,002
Canada	13	17	21
Finland	None	None	None

Cost per Ton		Percent Selling Price	
United States	$2.45	United States	less than 1%
Canada	0.07	Canada	negligible
Finland	None	Finland	None

Table A3.5 (Continued)

Country	Air Pollution Abatement Capital Expenditure (millions $)	Air Pollution Abatement Capital Expenditure per Ton Capacity	Range of Abatement Capital Expenditure per Ton Capacity	Average Operating Costs (¢ per lb.)	Range of Operating Costs (¢ per lb.)
	Aluminum (air pollution control only)				
United States	$616	$125	$258–80	2.7	5.5–1.7
Canada	151	118	157–70	2.5	3.0–2.1
Norway	102	134		2.5	
Germany	93	110	190–80	2.3	4.1–1.7
Japan	204	130	250–50	2.8	5.4–1.1

Average total investment cost per ton of capacity: $1600
Average production cost per pound aluminum: 30¢

Source. U.S. Department of Commerce, *The Effects of Pollution Abatement on International Trade III* (Washington, D.C.: GPO, July 1975).
[a] Average of four firms.

Table A3.6 Percentage Increase in Imports Arising from Incremental Water Pollution Control Expenditures

Industry	1973	1974	1975	1976	1977	1978	1979	1980	1981	1982	1983	1984	1985
Shoes	0	0	0	0	0.09	0.16	0.24	0.32	0.39	0.46	0.52	0.57	0.61
Steel		0	0	0	0.83	1.52	2.26	2.97	3.60	4.17	4.86	5.46	6.00
Copper													
Low-cost case	0	0	0	0	0.069	0.070	0.123	0.159	0.181	0.197	0.206	0.307	0.382
High-cost case	0	0	0	0	0.343	0.347	0.614	0.792	0.906	0.981	1.030	1.532	1.908
Aluminum													
Low-cost case	0	0	0	0	0.606	0.506	0.449	0.403	0.352	0.330	0.737	0.573	0.467
High-cost case	0	0	0	0	2.981	2.478	2.187	1.956	1.704	1.591	3.471	2.663	2.122
Beef and Veal	0	0	0	0	0.256	0.414	0.76	1.142	1.324	1.372	1.482	1.626	1.612
Pork	0	0	0	0	0.328	0.635	0.926	1.186	1.311	1.286	1.284	1.428	1.525
Wood pulp													
Low-cost case		0	0	0	4.67	4.05	3.60	3.31	3.17	3.20	4.49	4.77	10.19
High-cost case		0	0	0	5.40	4.67	4.16	3.83	3.66	3.70	2.21	7.20	5.61
Newsprint													
Low-cost case		0	0	0	0.46	0.45	0.45	0.44	0.42	0.44	0.52	0.52	0.94
High-cost case		0	0	0	0.54	0.53	0.52	0.51	0.49	0.51	0.82	0.81	1.26
Paper board													
Low-cost case		0	0	0	1.74	1.54	1.34	1.15	0.94	0.77	0.65	0.49	0.43
High-cost case		0	0	0	2.03	1.79	1.55	1.32	1.08	0.89	0.89	0.68	0.57
Other paper													
Low-cost case		0	0	0	0.69	0.94	1.12	1.30	1.33	1.39	1.54	1.64	2.23
High-cost case		0	0	0	0.80	1.10	1.31	1.52	1.55	1.62	2.04	2.25	2.97

Source. Derived from Public Research Institute, *The Effects of Effluent Discharge Limitations on Foreign Trade in Selected Industries*, Report to the U.S. National Commission on Water Quality (Arlington, Virginia, February 1976).

Table A3.7 Price and Output Effect of United States Environmental Controls (Following Polluter-Pays Principle)

Industry Number and Title	Percentage Increase[a] in Domestic Prices	Percentage Decrease[a] in Domestic Output
Agriculture, Forestry, and Fisheries		
1. Livestock and livestock products	3.03	3.06
	0.50	0.51
2. Other agricultural products	2.94	2.71
	0.63	0.58
3. Forestry and fishery products	1.53	2.13
	0.19	0.26
4. Agricultural, forestry, and fishery services	1.37	1.37
	0.67	0.67
Mining		
5. Iron and ferroalloy ores mining	1.72	1.76
	0.25	0.25
6. Nonferrous metal ores mining	1.76	1.85
	0.23	0.25
7. Coal mining	2.62	2.36
	0.41	0.37
8. Crude petroleum and natural gas	0.88	0.90
	0.13	0.13
9. Stone and clay mining and quarrying	1.33	1.38
	0.18	0.19
10. Chemical and fertilizer mineral mining	1.55	1.61
	0.22	0.23
Construction		
11. New construction	1.63	1.63
	1.39	1.39
12. Maintenance and repair construction	1.26	1.26
	1.07	1.07
Manufacturing		
13. Ordinance and accessories	1.50	1.50
	1.32	1.32
14. Food and kindred products	1.95	1.99
	0.80	0.81
15. Tobacco manufactures	1.13	1.04
	0.49	0.45
16. Broad and narrow fabrics, yarn and thread mills	2.01	2.07
	1.15	1.18
17. Miscellaneous textile goods and floor coverings	2.09	2.28
	1.28	1.40
18. Apparel	1.21	1.29
	0.75	0.81
19. Miscellaneous fabricated textile products	1.50	1.50
	0.90	0.90
20. Lumber and wood products except containers	0.84	0.90
	0.51	0.55

Table A3.7 (Continued)

Industry Number and Title	Percentage Increase[a] in Domestic Prices	Percentage Decrease[a] in Domestic Output
21. Wooden containers	1.14	1.14
	0.87	0.87
22. Household furniture	1.37	1.37
	1.14	1.14
23. Other furniture and fixtures	1.47	1.47
	1.26	1.26
24. Paper and allied products except containers	2.85	2.82
	1.70	1.68
25. Paperboard containers and boxes	3.08	3.08
	1.75	1.75
26. Printing and publishing	0.92	0.93
	0.68	0.68
27. Chemicals and selected chemical products	4.00	3.84
	3.39	3.25
28. Plastics and synthetic materials	4.18	4.35
	3.62	3.77
29. Drugs, cleaning, and toilet preparations	2.29	2.22
	1.95	1.89
30. Paints and allied products	5.12	5.12
	4.51	4.51
31. Petroleum refining and related industries	4.78	4.74
	2.41	2.38
32. Rubber and miscellaneous plastics products	2.02	2.10
	1.41	1.47
33. Leather tanning and industrial products	2.23	2.23
	1.78	1.78
34. Footwear and other leather products	1.31	1.68
	1.06	1.35
35. Glass and glass products	1.79	1.87
	1.55	1.61
36. Stone and clay products	2.84	2.95
	2.50	2.60
37. Primary iron and steel manufacturing	2.66	2.85
	2.23	2.39
38. Primary nonferrous metal manufacturing	3.36	3.69
	1.75	1.93
39. Metal containers	2.05	2.05
	1.63	1.63
40. Heating, plumbing, and structural metal products	1.89	1.88
	1.49	1.47
41. Stampings, screw machine products, and bolts	1.74	1.74
	1.38	1.38
42. Other fabricated metal products	1.75	1.78
	1.36	1.39
43. Engines and turbines	2.29	2.41
	1.92	2.01

Table A3.7 (Continued)

Industry Number and Title	Percentage Increase[a] in Domestic Prices	Percentage Decrease[a] in Domestic Output
44. Farm machinery and equipment	2.23	2.40
	1.88	2.03
45. Construction, mining, and oil field	2.17	1.67
machinery	1.89	1.45
46. Materials handling machinery and	2.19	2.08
equipment	1.86	1.77
47. Metalworking machinery and equipment	1.94	2.09
	1.65	1.78
48. Special industry machinery and	2.00	2.08
equipment	1.70	1.77
49. General industrial machinery and	2.09	2.09
equipment	1.77	1.77
50. Machine shop products	1.92	1.92
	1.63	1.63
51. Office, computing, and accounting	1.27	1.87
machines	1.01	1.50
52. Service industry machines	2.35	2.35
	1.95	1.95
53. Electric industrial equipment and	1.50	1.49
apparatus	1.20	1.19
54. Household appliances	1.79	1.77
	1.43	1.41
55. Electric lighting and wiring equipment	1.54	1.86
	1.20	1.46
56. Radio, television, and communication	1.23	1.22
equipment	1.02	1.01
57. Electronic components and accessories	1.39	1.67
	1.12	1.34
58. Miscellaneous electrical machinery,	1.69	1.69
equipment, and supplies	1.30	1.30
59. Motor vehicles and equipment	2.66	2.88
	2.42	2.62
60. Aircraft and parts	1.51	1.47
	1.34	1.30
61. Other transportation equipment	1.89	2.01
	1.66	1.76
62. Scientific and controlling instruments	4.54	4.72
	4.01	4.17
63. Optical, ophthalmic, and photographic	4.31	4.44
equipment	3.84	3.95
64. Miscellaneous manufacturing	2.22	2.71
	1.95	2.38
Services, Government, Dummy, and Special Industries		
65. Transportation and warehousing	1.12	1.36
	0.97	1.18

Table A3.7 (Continued)

Industry Number and Title	Percentage Increase[a] in Domestic Prices	Percentage Decrease[a] in Domestic Output
66. Communications except radio and	0.29	0.29
TV broadcasting	0.25	0.25
67. Radio and TV broadcasting	0.58	0.58
	0.51	0.51
68. Electric, gas, water, and sanitary	5.37	5.37
services	5.18	5.18
69. Wholesale and retail trade	0.71	0.71
	0.63	0.64
70. Finance and insurance	0.55	0.55
	0.50	0.50
71. Real estate and rental	0.61	0.66
	0.56	0.56
72. Hotels; personal and repair services	0.93	0.93
except auto	0.82	0.82
73. Business services	0.84	0.84
	0.74	0.74
75. Automobile repair and services	1.06	1.06
	0.93	0.93
76. Amusements	0.88	0.88
	0.74	0.74
77. Medical, educational services, and	0.52	0.52
nonprofit organizations	0.44	0.44
78. Federal government enterprises	0.91	0.91
	0.70	0.70
79. State and local government enterprises	1.18	1.18
	1.05	1.05
80. Business travel, entertainment,	1.83	1.83
and gifts	1.39	1.39
81. Office supplies	3.17	3.17
	2.76	2.76

Source. J. David Richardson and John H. Mutti, "Industrial Displacement through Environmental Controls: The International Competitive Aspects," in Ingo Walter, Ed., *Studies in International Environmental Economics.*

[a] The first number for each line entry assumes infinitely elastic domestic supply; the second assumes a finite supply elasticity.

Chapter 4

ENVIRONMENT AND DEVELOPMENT PROJECT APPRAISAL

APPROACHES

The basic framework for integrating environmental considerations in development project appraisal can be simply stated. Project evaluation should be conducted so that the external social costs of environmental deterioration resulting from the project are identified, quantified, given monetary value, and entered into the project's cost stream. If protective measures can be accommodated in the project, they should be costed and compared to the prospective benefits or damages avoided. The full social cost of the project, including protective measures and residual damages, should then be compared to the benefits, and a decision to accept or reject should be made. The distributional consequences of the project, including any residual environmental damages, should also be considered.

Each step presents considerable difficulties. Even in the United States, where the usefulness of cost benefit work is generally understood, neither the air nor water pollution control legislation is explicitly grounded on cost–benefit analysis. Because of the difficulties, some less ambitious and perhaps more practical approaches should be mentioned first. One approach is an ex post evaluation of development projects. Using a case study method, unanticipated adverse environmental consequences can be identified and described. This is especially useful in the initial stage of environmental awareness, when attention continues to be focused on traditional and narrow measures of project costs and benefits. Dramatic examples of environmental negligence or oversight can compel the attention of project planners and funding agencies.[1] Moreover, a systematic search for and consideration of past neglect can provide an empirical base for determining the effects of projects and can provide guidance for planners in forthcoming analysis. One result would be an increased sensitivity to possible environmental damages and an awareness of methods for minimizing damages. Ex post evaluation also highlights the need for baseline environmental data.

Another approach, closely related, is the preparation of an inventory or checklist of environmental disturbances that are likely to occur. The basis for the inventory would be information from past projects, combined with reasoned speculation on anticipated effects. Presumably, the inventory would be prepared by project sector; thus problems typical of different types of projects would be grouped together. For example, for river basin development projects, the inventory would include disturbances to downstream fisheries, changes in downstream channel erosion, sedimentation, aquatic weed infestation, change in disease vector patterns, and so on. For a manufacturing operation, the air, water, and solid waste pollution flows typical of the operation would be listed. In all instances the listing would be made more useful if there were also a discussion of control techniques and abatement technologies. If well done, this approach can provide useful guidance for planners and project analysts. At a minimum, a checklist of anticipated environmental effects provides a systematic method for identifying consequences and improves the probability that they will be entered in the analysis. It can also be used as a framework to assemble data on the environmental features of specific projects and to spot areas for further data collection. Both U.S. AID and the World Bank have put together environmental checklists for projects. The complexity of the checklist approach is illustrated in the joint case studies undertaken by the Smithsonian Institution and AID, especially the study of river basin development. Also along these lines, the Institute for Ecology has sponsored workshops that attempt to integrate ecological planning into resource development.[2]

Another approach is to adapt the environmental impact statement technique for use in development projects. Again, the advantage is that explicit consideration of environmental consequences may increase sensitivity to the problems, force consideration of alternatives, and improve the chances for entering damage costs in the project appraisal. There are potential disadvantages, however. The preparation of impact statements can cause unjustified delay. The statements can be costly to compile. Without some rudimentary national environmental policies, isolated project impact statements may be inconsistent or irrelevant.

In fact, none of these approaches is sufficient. The mere recitation of unanticipated damages that arose from past projects, no matter how striking, is not enough to condemn the projects. The questions that must be examined are, could the projects have been modified to reduce damages, how much would that modification have cost, and would the project have been justified on the basis of a comprehensive accounting of all benefits and costs, including environmental damage costs. In similar fashion, a detailed checklist of anticipated effects or an environmental impact statement is still not sufficient. There must also be methods for incorporating the effects into project analysis and a reconsideration of traditional project evaluation criteria in light of environmental consequences. Environmental assessment is a first, but not final, step.

Both the literature on project appraisal in developing countries and the material on environmental resource management in industrial countries is relevant to the task of incorporating environmental considerations in project analysis. Very considerable advances have been made in both areas in recent years. However, there has been little work that explicitly relates the two. It can be argued that on a very general level the principles of project appraisal are universal, and principles for rational resource management are equally valid in rich and poor countries. We contend that the conditions under which projects are undertaken in industrial and developing countries differ sharply, and some adaptation of methodologies is needed to conform to the special conditions in developing countries.

Some of these special conditions that may require adaptation of methods and instruments are as follows: First, market prices in developing countries frequently fail to reflect economic scarcity, and it is then necessary to estimate shadow or accounting prices. In this respect developing country project analysis is well placed to include environmental effects, for the failure of market prices to reflect social costs provides the rationale for using accounting prices to value factor inputs, and the failure of market prices is also a major characteristic of environmental externalities. Second, development projects in poor countries are more apt to be large relative to the total economy, and the partial equilibrium assumptions of traditional benefit cost analysis, including benefit cost analysis of environmental effects, are less defensible. In addition, developing countries often lack national pollution standards and policies within which projects can be evaluated. Also, administration and enforcement is frequently less effective, and social rates of time discount are higher.

On a more fundamental level, one response to environmental externalities in industrial countries that have well-developed markets in which the private sector dominates could be to encourage negotiation between polluters and damaged parties, using either bribes or compensation to achieve a socially optimum level of pollution abatement. This approach, which has not been extensively used in developed countries, would have little merit in developing countries in which the government is the principal sponsor of development projects with environmental spillovers. There is no evidence that governments enter into abatement bargains with the private sector to curtail their own polluting activities. Nor can we rely on a highly developed network of private environmental groups to monitor development projects in most poor countries. For these reasons, both the methodology by which environmental considerations are entered into project analysis and the instruments for pollution control may need adaptation in the developing country context. The explicit synthesis of techniques for project evaluation in developing countries and advances in the economics of environmental resource management has not yet been accomplished.

Recent methodological work on project analysis in developing countries has been concerned with such topics as alternative approaches to shadow pricing project inputs, methods for incorporating distributional objectives, spatial location theory, and evaluating nonmarket project services such as health and education. None of this is irrelevant for environmental analysis, but specific procedures for incorporating environmental effects and controls are not addressed in this literature.[3] At the same time, the valuable practical manuals on sector project analysis prepared by the World Bank are almost silent on environmental issues. Gittinger correctly notes that a conservation project designed to prevent loss, such as a soil erosion control program, is as legitimate as a project designed to increase output. He also notes that adverse ecological effects can result from agricultural production, and their costs (or preventive costs) should be included as part of direct projects costs, but there is no further discussion.[4]

The environmental unit of the World Bank has published a short discussion of the issues in *Environment and Development*. A brief section considers interesting issues—benefit measurement techniques such as "willingness to pay" and the merits of using discharge standards versus effluent fee and subsidy schemes—but how the Bank uses these in developing countries is not described. The publication is also vague with respect to World Bank criteria for setting pollution standards. For example, World Bank policy is to "adapt the standards of protection to the circumstances of the country." Control costs on World Bank-financed projects have been kept low thus far by using standards that are "appropriate to the current stage of development and the requirements of the project."[5] The Bank asserts that conditions in developing countries permit more liberal effluent and emission standards than can be tolerated in industrial countries. This does not indicate that the Bank is doing an inadequate job. Rather, the interesting questions are left unanswered. How liberal should standards be in developing countries, and how is that determined? How are future environmental damages, subject to great uncertainty, evaluated? How much reliance can be placed on willingness to pay as a technique for measuring benefits in societies with great income inequality?

At the same time, there has been a great flowering of literature in the industrial countries on environmental cost–benefit analysis and the larger topic of environmental resource management. Examples include the work by Kneese and Bower and more recently Kneese and Schultze on the use of effluent and emission charges to correct environmental externalities, an analysis by Fisher and Krutilla of the economics of natural resources, the OECD-sponsored work on environmental damage costs, and the recent papers edited by Seskin and Peskin on cost–benefit analysis of water pollution control policies.[6] However, for the reasons noted earlier, this material may require modification when used in developing country situations.

A final approach would be to examine the experience and operations of national and international development assistance agencies in the environmental aspects of development assistance. The interesting questions are, the extent to which assistance agencies fund environmental conservation and improvement projects, how the agencies go about incorporating controls in other projects they fund, how the financial burden of controls is allocated between the agency and the recipient, and whether the establishment of project environmental standards is a contentious issue between donors and recipients.

Environmental checklists for projects have been prepared elsewhere. Also, no new case studies of completed projects were done for this book. Therefore, little more is said in the remainder of this chapter about these two approaches. Instead, we discuss some principles and difficulties in modifying project evaluation to account for environmental impact, take up the subject of additionality, or the allocation of the financial burden of abatement between the lender and the borrower, and comment briefly on US AID and IBRD experience.

MODIFYING PROJECT ANALYSIS

The basic function of project analysis is to guide the allocation of scarce resources into activities that yield the largest net benefits for society. Project analysis is a collection of techniques for evaluating projects according to specific criteria such as the net present value or the internal rate of economic return. In so doing, the costs of the project are the opportunity costs of the resources employed (capital, labor, etc.), and the benefits are the additional output of goods and services made possible by the project. Benefits can be defined to include the contribution of the project to greater income equality as well as greater income. That is, the distribution of project output among income groups can be explicitly included in the analysis.[7] For a correct evaluation of projects, it is also necessary that the social costs of environmental damages, or the environmental externalities associated with the project, be included in the analysis. To ignore the cost of environmental damages would be to understate the full costs of the project and would lead to a misallocation of resources. How is this to be done?

It is useful for expositional purposes to begin by distinguishing between two broad groups of projects—those whose primary purpose is to directly preserve or improve the quality of the environment and projects for other purposes that incidentally have adverse environmental consequences. Using an expanded definition of environment to include features associated with poverty, the first group includes projects in three areas: provision of sanitary water supplies and sewage disposal systems, programs to eliminate or reduce environmental disease, and soil conservation projects.[8] Obviously, multipurpose projects can overlap the two groups as, for example, swamp drainage to control disease vectors and to add arable land.

The distinction is analytically useful because the central question for evaluation differs. For the first group the main purpose and the source of project benefits is an improvement in the quality of environmental resources and services. The problem is to select among competing projects on the basis of rational criteria when resources are scarce. In contrast, the purpose of the second group of projects is to improve physical infrastructure (roads, harbor facilities) or economic productive capacity (e.g., steel mills, plantation forests) or perhaps human skills through training. The problem for the second group is to identify and evaluate incidental environmental consequences and incorporate the consequences into the cost–benefit calculus for the project as a whole. This second group can be divided into two subgroups. First are projects in which environmental damage cannot be avoided except by scrapping the entire project. Prominent among these are projects representing incompatible use of resources. Examples are the destruction of a fishery spawning bed incidental to harbor dredging for port enlargement and the loss of a unique scenic area as the result of a hydroelectric power dam and reservoir. In one respect, this type of project is easier to analyze. Secondary decisions concerning the level and efficiency of damage avoidance measures are absent. The time stream of services lost (e.g., rental value of fisheries or amenity losses) are opportunity costs and are considered part of the project cost.

More frequently, projects with adverse environmental consequences can be modified to reduce damages. For industrial projects, process change and "end-of-pipe" treatment for pollution abatement are generally known, and the technology for abatement is readily available at a cost. Damage avoidance techniques are also available outside the industrial area. For example, log harvesting in a forestry development project may, if left unregulated, produce soil erosion and compaction. Damage avoidance measures can include regulations on the harvesting system (clearcut vs. selection), the harvesting technique (tractor skidding, high lead, helicopter), the construction of logging roads, and other activities. These avoidance measures, however, generally have costs. The analysis can become quite complex. Benefit cost analysis should be done for the project as a whole. To accomplish this, it is necessary to analyze various damage avoidance techniques (or pollution abatement systems) and to determine the level or standard to which that technique must comply. For example, it will not be enough to decide that boiler stack emissions for plywood mills require emission controls. The degree of emission control and its cost should also be considered. Only after the optimal abatement decision has been made can a rational decision be taken concerning the costs and benefits of the mill as a whole.

Several other useful distinctions are discussed later in the chapter. One is to classify environmental damages according to the type of damage receptor as was done in Chapter 1—natural resources, physical capital, health, and amenity services directly consumed. Each type presents special valuation difficulties. One can also distinguish among damages on the basis of environmental media—air, water, and land effects. Finally, for some purposes it is useful to distinguish between environmental damages that are reversible and those which are permanent or irreversible.

We now illustrate the process for incorporating environmental effects in greater detail. Assume a typical industrial project with incidental damage from uncontrolled pollution. Assume that pollution abatement measures are available at a cost. The procedure is to first determine the optimal level of pollution abatement. On the basis of that level, the costs and benefits for the project as a whole are estimated. Occasionally when plant scale or design has an important impact on abatement techniques, the analysis must be done simultaneously.

To select the optimum level of abatement it is necessary, in theory, to construct abatement cost and benefit functions in which costs and benefits are estimated over a range of abatement levels. The guiding principle is to select that abatement level at which the marginal cost of abatement is equal to the marginal benefit (damages avoided). The principle underlying the selection of the optimal level of abatement is illustrated in Diagram 4.1. Consider costs first. In quadrant 1 an arbitrary abatement cost function, $C = f(A)$, has been drawn. Its shape corresponds to the widely accepted assumption of increasing marginal abatement costs. Abatement cost functions are normally easier to construct than benefit functions because they rely on engineering cost data and usually involve purchased inputs. Abatement techniques and technology include process change, in-plant recycling of water, and end-of-pipe treatment. The technology for most emission and effluent control systems is not highly sophisticated. Lagooning of waste water with evaporation and mechanical cyclones for removal of air particles are two illustrations of standard techniques. The technology and techniques should be appropriate to developing country conditions. In particular, lower labor costs, possibly lower land costs for wastewater disposal, and the scarcity of technicians to operate abatement equipment should be recognized. Additionally, the possibility of shunting wastes from one medium to another needs attention. Restriction on the open burning of waste materials that simply leads to dumping it in the nearest stream is not desirable. Also, abatement techniques should consider enforcement problems. It is of little merit to install costly abatement equipment if, in

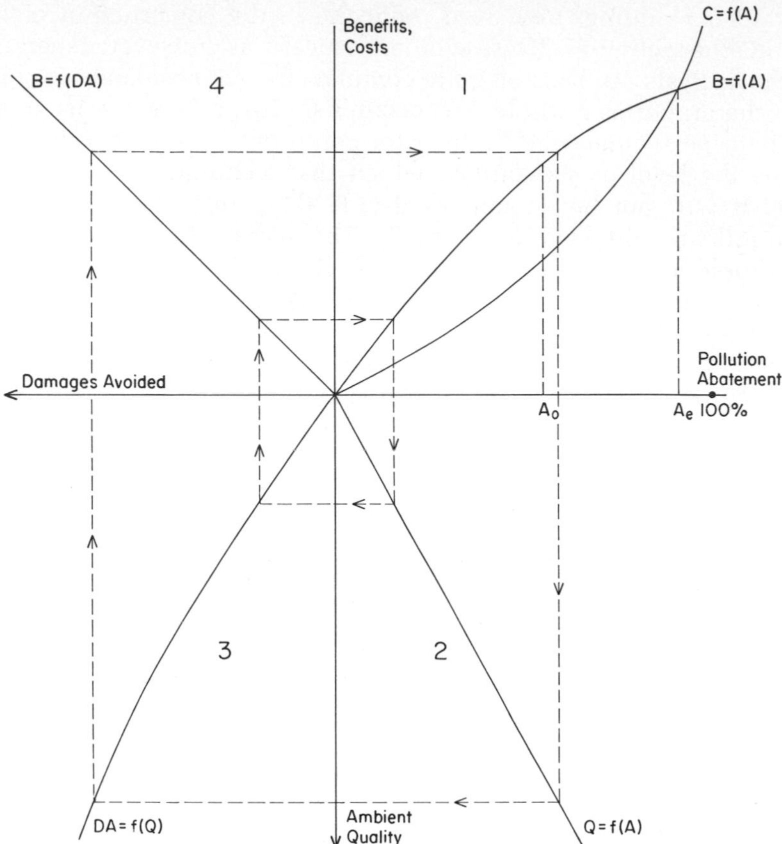

Diagram 4.1. Benefit cost analysis of pollution abatement.

operating, it is misused or bypassed. Developing countries have an acute shortage of enforcement personnel, and abatement devices that are automatic because of equipment design are preferable.

The construction of benefit functions is more difficult in theory and practice. What is desired is a relation between different levels of abatement and the resulting benefits or the economic value of damages avoided. Three steps may be involved: moving from abatement levels to ambient environmental quality levels, estimating biological and other physical damages avoided at different ambient quality levels, and placing an economic value on damages avoided. These steps are illustrated in quadrants 2, 3, and 4 of the diagram.

In quadrant 2 an arbitrary functional relation between abatement levels and ambient quality levels, $Q = f(A)$, has been drawn. To establish this relation, uncontrolled emissions are taken as a benchmark, and the effect of these emissions (measured, say, in milligrams of pollutant per cubic meter per day discharged or per unit output) on an index of ambient air or water quality is estimated. This requires close knowledge of the production process and physical diffusion and dispersion properties to establish dilution factors. Abatement is then hypothetically increased and improvements in ambient quality estimated; thus $Q = f(A)$ is traced out. Quadrant 3 relates improvements in ambient quality to reductions in biological and other physical damages, $DA = f(Q)$. This relation is not self-evident when complex ecological relations are poorly known and may involve discontinuities and thresholds. There also may be an important time dimension. The curve is drawn to reflect an assumed decreasing marginal reduction in physical damages as ambient environmental quality improves. In quadrant 4, a monetary value is placed on damages avoided, or benefits, $B = f(DA)$. In this fashion the three functional relations trace out a pollution abatement benefit function, $B = F(A)$, in quadrant 1. This can be seen by following the dotted lines in a clockwise fashion. By assumption, marginal benefits of abatement decline.

At each step the uncertainties are large. The economist makes his contribution in quadrant 4, placing monetary value on damages avoided, and in quadrant 1, selecting the optional abatement level. Damage valuation is discussed presently. Here we note that, if the damages (avoided) are to productive resources that enter factors markets, for example, soil deterioration, costing may be easier. The value of damages can then be taken as the reduced capitalized value of the resource or the reduced rent it commands. If the damage is to an environmental service that is directly consumed without passing through markets, such as recreation, or directly affects human health, valuation is less direct and more complicated. In any event, the discrepancies between market prices and opportunity costs that characterize developing countries should be recognized, and accounting prices should be used to correct for market price distortions.

If the cost and benefit functions illustrated in quadrant 1 are known, the optimal level of abatement is where marginal costs equal marginal benefits, or the slopes of the curves are equal. This is illustrated by A_0 in the diagram. To proceed to the higher level of abatement at A_e, where benefits equal costs, would be uneconomic. The incremental costs of moving from A_0 to A_e exceed the incremental benefits, and total welfare declines. If only a small number of points are known, that level of abatement with highest net benefits should be chosen. We are aware that, to some, this exercise in marginalism is irrelevant, because the data supporting the damage avoidance function are often unavailable. Nevertheless, these decisions will be made in some fashion as long as projects are undertaken. The preferred criterion should be stated even if it is not fully operational. More work can and should be done on the identification and valuation of externalities.

Once the technique and levels of environmental controls are selected, their costs are entered into the cost stream for the project as a whole. Control costs will include capital expenditure on abatement and annual operation and maintenance charges. The benefits from pollution abatement remain damages avoided. For projects whose purpose is not environmental improvement or preservation, the benefits cannot be included in the benefit stream for the project as a whole. This would be double counting and would inflate the social value of the project beyond its true value.

Also, if the optimal level of abatement selected does not eliminate environmental damages, as is likely, the project benefit stream should be deflated by the amount of residual damages. For example, if measures are taken in an irrigation project that reduce but do not eliminate the incremental spread of schistosomiasis, the residual increase should be costed and entered as a negative benefit for the entire project. Assuming that the full procedure described here can be carried out, then normal project selection criteria—either net present value or internal rate of economic return—can be used. If the inclusion of environmental protection costs and the deflation of the benefit stream for residual environmental damages brings the net present value below zero or the internal rate of return below the cut-off point, the project should not be selected.

A few remarks on the proper interpretation of environmental control costs and benefits are in order. First, if abatement leads to materials recovery, abatement costs should be entered net of the economic value of recovered materials, regardless of whether they are returned to the manufacturing operation or sold as a by-product. Taking plywood manufacture as an example, if bark and other wastes had been dumped in nearby waters but are now recycled to the boiler or sold in local markets for fuel, abatement costs should be net of the bunker oil fuel saved or receipts from scrap sales. Second, in estimating abatement costs and choosing least-cost techniques, it may be less costly in some cases for "victims" to avoid damage rather than controlling the pollutant. Damage avoidance costs incurred by "victims" should be included as a cost in the cost–benefit calculus for the project.[9] Third, it is important to include only the abatement component of capital expenditures as a cost. Often capital expenditures simultaneously improve productivity and reduce pollution loads. Expenditures that would have been made for productivity reasons and that have incidental beneficial environmental effects should not be considered abatement expenditures. To do so would exaggerate abatement costs. As a practical matter it may be difficult to disentangle the two. Fourth, the economic benefits of pollution damages avoided should be net, not gross. For example, if discharge effluents reduce the productivity of a downstream fishery, the damage is not the number of fish killed times their market price, but an estimate of the rental value of the fishery lost. The market price of fish include the costs of cooperant resources—labor, fishing boats, and transport. Unless these have a zero opportunity cost (economic value), the economic damage will be less than the market value loss. Also, welfare transfers from one group to another are not included in net costs unless distributional objectives are explicitly entered into the analysis.

The process of incorporating environmental damage costs into project analysis will be much easier if national effluent and emission standards have been established. In that case the project analyst need only consider alternative techniques for meeting standards and select the least-cost method. The responsibility for establishing standards has not evaporated; it is simply shifted to another location. Some developing countries have regulations concerning conditions in the workplace, including noise exposure standards, exposure to toxic materials, ambient dust levels, and so on. Without judging whether the standards are adequate or adequately enforced, the project analyst need only cost out the expenditures on compliance. Comprehensive effluent and emission standards in developing countries are less frequent, and the project analyst will have to confront the abatement level decision as well as the choice of the least-cost technique.

VALUING DAMAGES

The great diversity of projects and their environmental damages makes it difficult to say anything general and useful about valuation. However, by classifying damages as suggested earlier—deterioration in productive resources, health effects, and loss of directly consumed environmental services—a start can be made.[10]

Damages to productive resources include a wide variety of effects. Some of the more obvious are soil quality deterioration, reduced fisheries yield, increased irregularity of stream flows (making irrigation more expensive), erosion of embankments, siltation of reservoirs and irrigation systems, cost of industrial water purification, corrosion, and increased cleaning costs. In one respect, these types of damages are easiest to value. Either the resources themselves or the products of the resources generally enter markets, and a market price is established. This provides a first approximation to the value of damages or the benefit value from damage avoidance. Of course, if market prices are distorted away from efficiency prices, a correction should be made, but project analysts in developing countries have considerable experience in making the appropriate adjustments. Also, expenditures by potential victims in damage avoidance measures may not be obvious, but they should be included.

An almost universal characteristic of developing countries is their scarcity of physical capital. Also, there is often a scarcity of accessible, good-quality agricultural land. This suggests that a high price should be attached to damages of this type. In turn, a high value placed on damages will, *ceteris paribus*, justify stringent environmental control efforts, or perhaps force scrapping of environmentally disruptive projects. One cannot assert that developing countries need necessarily seek higher environmental standards than industrial countries, but when damages are clearly associated with a reduction in resource productivity, they should not be neglected.

The economic evaluation of damages to human health presents major problems for both industrial and developing countries. One issue common to both is how to find a monetary valuation for the preservation of health so that investment funds can be efficiently allocated among competing uses. However, the types of environmentally related health problems may be quite different between the rich and the poor.

Estimates have been made for the United States and a few other industrial countries of the absolute and relative health cost of pollution. These should not be taken too seriously because of major defects in definition, methodology, and data. One estimate for the United States placed the total annual air pollution damages to residential property, materials, health, and vegetation at $19–$25 billion (1968 dollars). Of this, health costs are 60% and 47%, respectively. An estimate of air pollution costs in the United Kingdom (1970) that included amenity losses placed annual losses at £ 1.2 billion (US $2.86 billion) with health costs comprising 54%. Air pollution costs in Italy (1968) were estimated to be 350 billion lire (US $560 million) with direct damage to human health at 17%, and work efficiency losses including sick time at 6% of the total.[11]

Health costs from water pollution have not been comprehensively and accurately estimated. It is probable, however, that the major damage from water pollution in the United States is to recreation and other amenities. Fisher estimated that 6% of water pollution damages in the United States were to human health, 31% to property values, and 62% to recreation. Commercial fisheries accounted for less than 2% of damages.[12] The relative importance of recreation damages is given some confirmation in three local studies in which recreation losses ranged from 23 to 78% of total water damages.[13] There are several reasons why health damages from water pollution may be less important in industrial countries than developing countries relative to other types of damages. One is that recreation expenditures represent a larger fraction of consumer budgets in rich countries, and hence there is more exposure to recreational losses from water pollution. Another reason is that sanitary water supply and sewage disposal infrastructure is mostly in place in industrial countries. Consequently, contamination of drinking water supplies by sewage wastes is less frequent. Finally, water-borne disease vectors appear to be a more serious problem in tropical countries.

In any event, the focus at the project analysis level is not on the overall health damages to the country but the health consequences of specific projects. There are at least five different types that can be identified. The first includes projects designed specifically to improve environmental health conditions—mainly the provision of sanitary water supplies and sewage disposal systems and disease eradication. If total investment funds for the country are limited and public health programs of this type are forced to compete for project funds with other sector development programs on the basis of rigorous cost–benefit analysis, the need to estimate benefit functions and to place a monetary value on the improvement in human health cannot be escaped. This is usually not the case. In most countries the public health and public works budget is set in a political process in which the economic productivity of funds allocated to the sector is simply not computed and measured against funds allocated to other sectors. Accordingly, the project design and selection process deals with a more homogenous product—improvements in health. Since the total funds available to the sector are given and the output more comparable (say in terms of deaths prevented), it is no longer necessary to place a monetary value on health improvement to rationally allocate funds to projects within the sector. Rather, the problem is one of the cost effectiveness of alternative projects. Which projects provide the greatest number of people with clean water and sewers per million dollars of funds invested? Even as an exercise in cost effectiveness, the problems for the analyst are not trivial. One stubborn problem is the synergistic effects of poor nutrition and a variety of endemic diseases. Also, projects for improvements in environmental health are apt to be site specific and directed toward an identifiable group of people. Consequently, the selection of projects is likely to be quite political.

The other types of health consequences of development projects involve incidental (but not unanticipated) negative effects. One is the increased incidence of water-borne disease vectors sometimes associated with reservoirs and irrigation schemes. Placing a monetary value on the estimated increase of such diseases is arbitrary and unsatisfactory. One method that would yield a minimum damage cost is to estimate the productivity loss of labor from chronic diseases plus the cost of treatment.[14] However, this would not capture the disutility from being sick nor the loss of agricultural land because of disease vector infestation. Also, the synergistic effects of various diseases and widespread malnutrition in developing countries make it difficult to determine the productivity effect of eliminating just one disease. Probably the best that can now be done in project analysis is to set down the likely impact of the project on disease incidence and to discuss the availability, effectiveness, and cost of alternative measures to reduce the potential increase in disease.

Toxic wastes from industrial projects that contaminate drinking water supplies or enter the food chain are another incidental effect. These wastes may be toxic metals, carcinogenic substances, or, occasionally, disease-carrying bacteria. One solution would be the removal of the substances or containment on premises by lagooning. If this is feasible and the cost appears reasonable, the problem of placing a monetary value on adverse health effects can be sidestepped. More frequently, some dilution of toxic material will enter wastewater streams, and, as illustrated by the taconite dumping case in the United States, the problem will be compounded by uncertainty among scientists as to the long-run health implications.[15] Closely related to this are the occupational health and safety aspects of development projects. In many instances, for example dust removal from sanding operations or noise abatement, there is a wide range of abatement levels that can be chosen. Project design and appraisal in developing countries is placed in a very uncomfortable position. Workplace abatement equipment can become expensive as standards are increased. Yet no one wishes to unnecessarily place workers in danger. Also, the experiences of the polyvinyl chloride and synthetic rubber industries in the United States suggest that dangers are not always foreseen, and information is not always communicated.

A final health consequence of development projects is their contribution to the deterioration of ambient air quality. The projects are mainly in the industrial and utilities sectors. Because air pollutants from various sources comingle, it is usually not possible to associate particular damages with a particular source. The partial equilibrium approach of project analysis breaks down. An abatement policy must be formulated on the regional and not the project level. This is examined in a subsequent section.

In addition to damages to productive resources and health, development projects can adversely effect environmental services that are directly consumed and thereby reduce welfare. Environmental amenities is a general term used, and recreational opportunities is a frequent example. Valuing damages to these services is similar to estimating the demand for public goods to determine the optimal supply. There is a substantial literature on this subject, and we restrict our comments to those relevant to developing countries.

There is evidence that the demand for environmental amenities, especially recreation, is income elastic. If so, amenity damages from development projects should be valued lower in poor countries, and less should be spent on their protection. Also, the demand for recreation will depend on the internal distribution of income. Therefore, the incidence of benefits and the costs of damage avoidance measures in development projects should be explicitly addressed. It seems reasonable that funds spent on preserving environmental amenities will often benefit the elite in developing countries, and this direct provision of nonmarket services will worsen rather than improve the existing inequality of income distribution. Also, an inequitable distribution of income that departs from the social objective means that a popular technique for estimating the demand for public goods—survey data on "willingness to pay"—is no longer as useful. The reason is that the full term is "willingness *and ability* to pay." One cannot accurately determine the value of environmental services to a society using willingness to pay if the ability to pay (reflecting the distribution of income) is seriously distorted.

Notwithstanding these arguments, amenity damages from projects in developing countries should not be given a zero value. One reason is that as incomes increase and the supply of these environmental amenities remains rather constant (or declines) they will increase in relative value. Also, some services may not be skewed toward the elite. Beaches near urban areas are one example. Finally, some amenities may pass through markets, particularly those associated with international tourism. The increasing relative scarcity of amenities from unique environments, including cultural artifacts, historical sites, and wildlife and wilderness areas, is global in nature. Their accessibility and exploitability improves with transportation improvements. Even if developing countries do not contemplate large-scale domestic tourism, they should be aware of the increasing value of their historical and wildlife resources to foreign tourists. Environmental damage to these resources is, in many respects, similar to damage to any productive resource, and funds spent on maintaining the amenities for current and prospective tourists can be evaluated with traditional cost–benefit measures. Of course, we recognize that even with international tourism these services often have a public goods character that makes it difficult to extract from the consumer a payment that is equal to the value received. This is especially true when the consumption is vicarious by individuals in rich countries who do not undertake travel. However, where possible, tourist income foregone as a result of a particular development project should be included in the analysis.

DISCOUNT RATE, RISK, AND UNCERTAINTY

Any incidental environmental damages from a development project should be entered in the analysis of the total costs and benefits of the project. Generally, environmental damages and damage avoidance measures will have a time dimension. For this reason, discounting should be applied to future environmental damages and damage avoidance costs, just as the time streams of other project benefits and costs are discounted to determine their present value. The appropriate rate at which future costs and benefits are discounted is, in theory, determined by the marginal productivity of the investment within the economy and the social preference for current over future consumption. With the reasonable assumptions that resources for investment are relatively scarce in developing countries and that poverty implies a high preference for current over future consumption, discount rates in poor countries should be higher than in rich countries. How should future environmental costs and benefits be discounted, and what are the environmental implications of high discount rates?

For those development projects for which environmental protection measures are unavailable (e.g., incompatible use of resources), the time profile of the damages should be determined, a monetary value placed on them, and the net present value of the project reduced accordingly. This can be done either by discounting the damage stream separately and subtracting it from the net present value of the project or by deflating the stream of project net benefits by the stream of damages before discounting. For irreversible losses that cannot be prevented, for example, the unavoidable extermination of a species, the damages are in perpetuity. If the inclusion of damages results in a negative net present value (or forces the internal rate of return below the cut-off), the project should be scrapped.

If damage avoidance measures are available, the capital and the operating and maintenance costs of the avoidance measures increase the time profile of project costs (increase project costs throughout the time period). Residual environmental damages are also additions to the projects cost stream (or can be treated as negative benefits). Hence these costs should be included and discounted to determine the adjusted net present value. The benefits from damage avoidance measures are in fact damages avoided and therefore should not be entered as additional benefits of the project.

The time profiles of the economic losses from environmental damages must be identified, just as they are for any other project cost or benefit. The losses should be included as a cost at the point in time at which the loss occurs, not when a pollutant is initially released or the environment is disturbed. These losses can be immediate and temporary (1 year reduction in fish yields because of temporary construction activity), sustained at a uniform level (permanent need for downstream water purification), or could cumulate to a delayed loss (siltation of navigational channels).

Whether the inclusion of these losses and the cost of prevention measures forces scrapping or redesign of the project depends on a number of factors—the initial attractiveness of the project, the magnitude of abatement costs and residual damages, the time profile of abatement costs and residual damages, and the discount rate applied. In general, the incorporation of environmental considerations will make projects less attractive (1) the larger the abatement costs (and by implication the larger the environmental damages that would have occurred), (2) the larger the residual damages, (3) the closer in time (shorter time profile) of abatement costs, (4) the closer in time (shorter time profile) of residual damages, and (5) the lower the discount rate. Conversely, the effect on the attractiveness of a project will be less (1) the smaller the abatement costs and residual damages, (2) the further in time abatement costs and residual damages occur, and (3) the higher the discount rate.

The reasons are clear. Large abatement costs and residual damages reduce the net present value of the project and may make it negative. The closer the costs and damages occur in time, the less they are diminished by the discounting process. At the extreme, an initial abatement expenditure for capital equipment with no operating expenses will not be discounted at all and will enter in full as an increase in project cost. If some of the abatement expenditures are in the future or if residual damages occur in the future, the lower the discount rate the greater is their present value, and hence the more they reduce the net present value of the project. For developing countries in which high discount rates are the rule, this implies a greater tolerance for environment damages in project selection, provided the damages are equally valued in rich and poor countries and the time profiles of damages are the same. However, as stressed elsewhere, damages to productive resources may be valued higher in poor countries because of their scarcity, and one cannot make any general assertions about the acceptability of environmentally disruptive projects in rich versus poor countries. We can say, however, that when project selection does not consider incidental environmental costs, it is skewed toward projects that have large and near-term environmental damage profiles. We can also say that, by virtue of their higher discount rates, developing countries that take environmental considerations into account in project analysis will be more likely to accept projects with long-term environmental damages than will richer countries with lower discount rates.

This points to a critical and fundamental dilemma for poor countries. On one hand, their low income reflects the low level of productivity of their resources, and sustained economic growth will require the conservation and augmentation of their resource base. On the other hand, extreme poverty implies a strong preference for present production and consumption and a temptation to exploit resources for short-term gain without regard for long-term sustained yields. The pressure for rapid resource exploitation is perhaps most evident in the forest resource sector, responding to current industrial country market demand, and in the food production sector, in which the population pressure and food needs create increasing pressure on a fragile soil resource base.

The appendix to this chapter provides a model of subsistence agriculture that illustrates how the strong preference for current consumption can lead to a deterioration in the productivity of soils and an undermining of long-term yields. This process is quite independent of and additional to any environmental damages resulting from externalities and inappropriate property rights such as upstream watershed disturbances causing downstream erosion. The important conclusions from the model are

- It can be optimal to shorten the fallow period for land below its biological maximum output level, even without discounting.
- If future yields are discounted, the optimal fallow period is even shorter and soil quality is depleted further.
- The higher the discount rate, the greater the incentive to mine the soil for immediate output rather than sustained yields.

When one also considers that individual farmers, with expanding families and virtually no access to either credit or additional land, can have implicit discount rates much higher than the social rate for the country as a whole, the potential for destructive agricultural practices becomes very serious.

Discount rates also enter forcefully in projects that involve irreversible change in unique physical environments.[16]

Resource development projects can reduce or eliminate amenity services provided by undisturbed natural environments. Moreover, potentially valuable genetic and biological resources useful for plant breeding and pharmaceuticals can be lost. These losses can be irreversible in the sense that once development is undertaken it is technically impossible to repair, restore, or replace the unique environmental features, the ecological systems of the area, or the lost genetic and biological reserves. In considering resource development projects, the environmental services foregone by development should be counted as an opportunity cost of the project and should be subtracted from net development benefits. If irreversible, the losses continue in perpetuity.

It has been shown in a formal model by Smith that if unique environments yielding amenity services are in fixed supply, demand for these services corresponds to reasonable assumptions, and technical change can improve productivity for conventional goods but not the services of unique environments, the price of these services will rise over time relative to the price of the conventional products of development. The assumption of biased technical change is reasonable, because the services of unique environments are not produced in the traditional sense; they are gifts of nature.

The implication of these propositions is straightforward. Including the environmental services forgone in resource development project analysis reduces the net present value of the project. If the benefits from the preservation of the unique environment are increasing relative to the benefits from resource development, the inclusion of the opportunity cost of amenity services forgone has an even stronger impact. The net present value of the resource development project is reduced even more. Indeed, if the rate of growth of amenity benefits exceeds the discount rate, the opportunity cost of the project will grow over time even when it has been discounted. The increasing relative value of undisturbed environments will reduce the attractiveness of the resource development alternative.[17]

These conclusions hold for both industrial and developing countries. However, there are three special considerations. First, one can argue a priori that amenity services are less highly valued in developing countries because of their lower income levels. Therefore, all other things being equal, the loss of these services will have less effect on the attractiveness of resource development projects. Second, the higher discount rates prevailing in developing countries will also tend to reduce the impact of including future environmental amenities forgone. Third, there is no evidence pro or con about whether the rate of increase of the value of amenity services relative to conventional goods is higher or lower in rich countries than poor countries. Even if amenity services have a lower value at the moment in developing countries, their rate of increase may equal or exceed that of industrial countries. It is therefore appropriate to include the possibility of increasing relative prices of amenity services in project analysis in developing countries even if the current absolute values are small.

A closely related question asks whether the discount rate that is appropriate for evaluating conventional investments is also appropriate for discounting environmental damages. There is a durable argument that asserts that the social rate of discount is less than the private rate as formed by the marginal productivity of capital and the time preferences of individuals for present over future consumption. It is based on the contention that individuals have a limited time horizon and therefore a relatively high discount rate, whereas society has a stronger interest in continuity and the well-being of future generations.[18] If this argument is accepted for conventional investment, it should also hold for evaluating environmental damages. The effect of a lower discount rate would be to increase the attractiveness of marginal projects and therefore perhaps to encourage greater environmental disruption. However, if damages are included in the analysis, the lower discount rate also increases the present value of future environmental damages and will therefore justify greater abatement measures or scrapping projects with heavy damages.

The most satisfactory solution is to accept the social rate of discount used for conventional investments as the appropriate rate for environmental effects provided (1) ultimate waste disposal costs are incorporated in product price, (2) optimal preventive measures are taken during extraction, and residual damages are included, and (3) the possibility that the threatened productive resources might increase in relative value is considered. If these conditions do not hold, some tinkering with the discount rate might be useful. It is true that waste disposal problems are positively related to the rate of extraction of raw materials, and that extraction itself can often be environmentally disruptive. If the social costs of extraction and waste disposal are not included in market price, these costs could be reduced by slowing the rate of extraction. This could be accomplished by increasing the discount rate applied to resource extraction projects (or applying a severence tax to the extraction of virgin materials), making recycling and conservation of materials more attractive. However, this appears to be a second best approach. Specifically, slowing the rate of extraction, and thus wastes to be disposed of, by means of discount rate manipulation will do nothing to improve the allocation of the wastes to their least damaging sites.

There are also questions that turn on risk and uncertainty. One argument asserts that the market rates of interest used as proxies for establishing the discount rate in project analysis include a risk premium that is appropriate for individuals but inappropriate for society as a whole.[19] Public projects should be risk neutral, implying a lower discount rate. It is questionable whether this is relevant to projects and programs that are characterized by a very low probability of catastrophic environmental damages. Indeed, the usefulness of cost–benefit techniques can be challenged for these decisions.

The notion of option value is also relevant to the evaluation of environmental damages that are subject to great uncertainty and possible irreversibility. In its simplest formulation, the notion of option value merely asserts that, in the face of an uncertain outcome that is irreversible, a separate value can be given to the course of action that preserves future choices or options. To accomplish this, projects with potentially disruptive environmental effects can be evaluated at a higher discount rate, or, alternately, the environmental damages can be discounted at a lower rate, giving them an inflated present value. A more sophisticated argument can be made for option values if information improves with the passage of time.[20] The idea is simple. Decisions taken under uncertainty involve subjective probabilities. If a decision concerning an irreversible action can be deferred, the information base for establishing the probabilities improves, and a better quality decision is possible. These last arguments are quite general and apply to public projects in both industrial and developing countries.

The use of benefit cost analysis for pollution control decisions and, by implication, the modification of traditional project evaluation to include the costs and benefits of pollution abatement have been challenged on more fundamental grounds. Pearce argues that there are fundamental conceptual problems, especially for pollutants that cumulate over time as a stock.[21] The essence of his argument is that what appears to be an optimal point, at which marginal abatement costs equal marginal damages avoided, may prove to be ecologically unstable over time if waste disposal exceeds assimilative capacity. In that case, the excess of undegraded waste accumulates as a stock, and the assimilative capacity (which he views in biological terms) diminishes over time. Consequently, the optimal level of abatement increases over time and converges at zero ecological disturbance, a result that is overlooked in the initial, conventional, application of cost–benefit analysis.

ADDITIONAL CONSIDERATIONS

Alternative Techniques

Full-scale cost–benefit analysis can be expensive, time consuming, and sometimes impossible with available data. When the analysis is partial, in the sense that some but not all benefits and costs are given a monetary value, it can convey an erroneous aura of precision. However, it is not always necessary to reduce intangibles and externalities to a common monetary unit. Assume, for example, a port development project that must necessarily destroy an urban beach. Assume also that, with the exception of the amenity services of the beach, all costs and benefits can be given monetary value, and they have been properly discounted to give a positive net present value. In this situation the decision maker does not require a precise estimate of the amenity services forgone. He need only decide whether the calculated net present value of the port project is larger or smaller than the present value of amenity services lost. Presenting the question in this fashion may be superior to using a questionable monetary value for beach use. Also, a minimum but defensible estimate of beach use value may be sufficient to decide against the port development project.

Cost effectiveness is another technique that sometimes can be used to avoid the difficulties of benefit evaluation. If the project analyst is provided with a pollution abatement objective, however determined, alternative methods for achieving pollution reduction are costed and expressed per unit of pollution abated. For example, the International Maritime Consultative Organization (IMCO), in preparation for the 1973 Prevention of Pollution from Ships Convention, had fairly adequate data on marine oil discharges by tankers and projections for future discharges. A study was made of the benefits from reducing tanker discharges, but for many reasons it was quite deficient.[22] Under the circumstances it was agreed that a reduction of oil discharges was desirable, and the question became one of cost effectiveness of various alternatives. These included segregated ballasting, double bottoms on tankers, flexible membranes separating ballast water, and so on. A more tractable problem emerged—estimating the cost per cubic meter of reduced oil discharge under the alternative techniques. The question of whether benefits exceeded costs was avoided, but a misallocation of resources may have resulted.

Cost–benefit analysis can also be supplemented by other analytical techniques. We have described the usefulness of materials balances accounting on an aggregate level to identify waste streams. Closely related are pathways studies and dispersion models for toxic substances that identify the origin, transport, and disposal sites in a spatial context. Water budget accounting, in which both volumes and water quality characteristics are accurately described, can provide information on the quantities and dilution of wastes discharged. Finally, there are many occasions when general valuations of environmental damages can be used, rather than attempting to calculate the monetary damages for each and every project. For example, there have been studies done in the United States that compute the biological productivity of marsh areas and estimate the economic value of undisturbed marsh environments.[23] Valuation studies have also been done for recreational fishing, wilderness experience, and so on. If the circumstances surrounding the projects in question are not markedly different, the values derived from other studies can be substituted in the cost–benefit analysis. An effort could be made to compile an inventory of valuation studies in developing countries to be made available to project analysts.

Project Versus Comprehensive Analysis[24]

The preceding discussion implies that cost–benefit analysis on the project level can be modified to account for environmental externalities and that the process is made easier if pollution standards have been set by a central agency. In fact, in many instances in which pollutants from various sources co-mingle (as is often the case for air pollution), it is virtually impossible to associate specific damages with specific sources. Therefore, separate damage functions for specific projects cannot be constructed, and the partial equilibrium approach of project analysis breaks down. The benefit of pollution abatement in one project depends on arbitrary assumptions regarding emissions from other sources.

The sequence of analysis should be reversed. Ambient air quality standards for the airshed as a whole should be tentatively considered. With information on current emission rates from sources (including industry, autos, residential heating, etc.) and physical dispersion models, the required reduction in aggregate pollutant flows can be estimated. For an economically rational policy, an iterative process would then be followed. First, the least-cost method of achieving the required reduction in pollution flows would be calculated. Different sources would be obliged to abate by unequal percentages in accord with their individual abatement cost functions. This may hit industrial projects more heavily than, say, auto emissions or other sources. The guiding principle would be to equalize marginal abatement costs for each source.[25] Once a least-cost solution is calculated, the aggregate abatement cost would be compared to the economic benefits (including health, materials, vegetation, and amenities), and a rough determination of costs and benefits would indicate whether the tentatively selected ambient standards were too high or too low. Finally, the entire set of calculations would be modified to account for anticipated growth in the region. To do this properly, growth itself, and particularly site selection for polluting industries, becomes a choice variable.

We must conclude that in many cases the project level is too narrow a base for rational environmental policy. Conversely, policies formulated at a higher level must include knowledge of pollution emissions and abatement costs by major individual sources if they are to be efficient. Considering that the profile of environmental consequences of economic development is rough hewn by broad development strategy—transportation systems, land use policy, energy policy, emphasis within the industrial sector, and so on—it becomes evident that an awareness of the environmental consequences of development should exist throughout all levels of government. Modifying project analysis is not enough. The organization, administrative, and educational methods for accomplishing this are of critical importance, but they are outside the scope of this book.

Distributional Considerations

Development project analysis has shown an increasing concern for the distribution of project benefits as well as the level of net benefits. This is a reaction against patterns of economic growth with increasing income inequality, where the lowest income groups are made relatively and sometimes absolutely worse off. It also reflects the need to use development projects for income distributional objectives when more direct mechanisms such as the tax system are unavailable to the government.[26] The distributional consequences of environmental control programs and environmental modifications of development projects should also be analyzed.

Uncontrolled environmental externalities not only reduce the efficiency with which resources are used, but they also affect the distribution of welfare. Waste disposers and consumers of products manufactured by polluting industries secure welfare gains, and "victims" or beneficial users of the resource suffer losses from pollution. The loss may be monetary, for example, crop damage from air pollution, or may be a loss of welfare from directly consumed services, for example, the intangible costs of illness from air pollution. It is not possible to make a general statement regarding whether the welfare transfer is from rich to poor or poor to rich in developing countries. However, just as uncontrolled pollution transfers welfare from one group to another, enforcement of controls on waste disposers and the incorporation of environmental modifications in development projects will also have distributional consequences. Who will gain and who will lose?

One determinant will be the method through which private sector pollution abatement is financed. If developing country governments follow the stated policy of industrial countries, the polluter-pays principle, the costs will be apportioned between the consumers of the products and the factors of production employed in manufacturing the products (labor and capital). The beneficiaries will be the beneficial users of the resource. If the environmental damages in developing countries are mainly to productive resources, as suggested elsewhere in the study, the beneficiaries will be either the owners of these resources or the consumers of the products. In some cases, particularly for environmental controls in the workplace, the costs and benefits can accrue to the same group, the workers. If, in constrast, the government assists the private sector in financing pollution abatement, the cost incidence will depend on the tax structure. In some cases the effect on the distribution of welfare will be easy to spot. Auto emission controls would hit the well-to-do in developing countries and benefit the average urban resident.

Public works projects undertaken in developing countries can have a major effect on the distribution of income and welfare. This is especially true for projects involving the provision of sanitary water supplies and sewage systems, because the full costs of providing the services are not always passed on to users, and differential charges are set for different income groups. The distributional impact of these projects is relatively easy to determine because the services are site and group specific. One either does or does not gain access to clean water or a municipal sewer. Indeed, the question of who gets these services is recognized as the stuff of politics.

ADDITIONALITY

One issue between North and South has been the question of who would select environmental standards for projects financed by development assistance agencies, and who would pay for environmental protection measures incorporated in the projects. A subsidiary issue has arisen concerning the compatability of the assistance agency's overseas operations and its own national environmental legislation. The first, known as the principle of additionality, occasioned considerable debate at the Stockholm Conference. The second involves the obligation of US AID to file environmental impact statements under the National Environmental Protection Act (NEPA).[27]

Early concern for the environment and attempts to involve the developing countries evoked a range of responses from the South: suspicion that environment was a ploy to deny them the fruits of industrialization, indifference based on the view that what the rich have wrought to their environments so must they reap, and guarded optimism that global concern for the environment could revitalize support for development assistance and correct global inequities. Underlyintg each view, however, was a determination that environmental concerns should in no way add to the task of development by diverting resources away from development assistance toward rich country clean-up efforts, by making development projects more expensive, or by adversely affecting trade prospects.

One manifestation of this determination was support for the principle of additionality. Although at no time completely unambiguous, the principle has acquired three different meanings: the narrow interpretation that industrial countries should provide additional funds to cover the environmental protection component of projects they help finance, that industrial countries should provide funds to cover the cost of environmental protection programs undertaken by developing countries, and that development assistance flows should be substantially increased for a massive attack on the environmental attributes of poverty. Complementing the principle of additionality was the principle of compensation—environmental measures undertaken by industrial countries that adversely affect developing country trade should trigger compensatory measures.[28]

The Stockholm Conference Report was not particularly clear on these points. Principle 12 of the Declaration states:

> Resources should be made available to preserve and improve the environment, taking into account the circumstances and particular requirements of developing countries and any costs which may emanate from their incorporating environmental safeguards into

their development planning and the need for making available to them upon their request, additional international technical and financial assistance for this purpose.

Recommendation 108
It being recognized that it is in the interest of mankind that the technologies for protecting and improving the environment be employed universally, *it is recommended* that the Secretary-General be asked to undertake studies, in consultation with Governments and appropriate international agencies, to find means by which environmental technologies may be made available for adoption by developing countries under terms and conditions that encourage their wide distribution without constituting an unacceptable burden to developing countries.

Recommendation 109
It is recommended that the Secretary-General, in collaboration with appropriate international agencies, take steps to ensure that the environmental considerations of an international nature related to the foregoing recommendations be integrated into the review and appraisal of the International Development Strategy for the Second Development Decade in such a way that the flow of international aid to developing countries is not hampered.

With respect to compensation, Recommendations 103b stated:

(b) That where environmental concerns lead to restriction on trade, or to strict environmental standards with negative effects on exports, particularly from developing countries, appropriate measures for compensation should be worked out within the framework of existing contractual and institutional arrangements and any new such arrangements that can be worked out in the future. . . .

Finally, a subsequent UN resolution (3002) recommended:

Respect for the principle that resources for environmental programmes, both within and outside the United Nations system, be additional to the present level and projected growth of resources contemplated in the International Development Strategy, to be made available for the programmes directly related to development assistance.

In short, the exact meaning of additionality was not made clear. The creation of a voluntary Environment Fund to be used by the newly created UN Environmental Programme further confused the issue, because some countries claimed that their fund contribution was in the spirit of additionality.

It is difficult to take these declarations too seriously. There is little hard evidence on the environmental protection costs of development programs. If they turn out to be large, it is unlikely that aid donors would shoulder the burden on the basis of United Nations resolutions. Industrial countries are already in default on more serious aid pledges, including the 1% of GNP target. To add fresh commitments to others not being honored makes little sense.

One can also argue that if the environmental component of development projects is rationally determined, the benefits to the recipient country should justify the incremental costs. There has been a widespread but incorrect impression that environmental protection measures are a diversion of resources away from "productive" uses. We have emphasized that, on the contrary, many protection measures conserve or augment productive capacity. Even if the measures do not increase conventional output, the incremental social benefits should exceed incremental resource costs. Accordingly, the inclusion of these protection measures in development projects should be of net benefit to recipient countries even if no additional funds were provided.[29]

Additionality (narrow definition) would be justified in those instances in which aid donors insisted on environmental standards that went beyond the economic and environmental interests of the developing countries. This is certainly conceivable, since donor countries have considerable leverage, particularly among the smaller and economically weaker countries. Another supporting argument is that developing countries often fail to perceive their true interest in environmental protection for a variety of reasons, and the provision of additional funds for protection measures in development projects assists them in recognizing and acting on their own best interests. Although there may be some merit to this, most industrial countries are new converts to environmental preservation and may also have defective vision.

There is a more compelling reason for assisting developing countries with their environmental protection programs, however, that is based on equity and efficiency arguments, and not on the misleading premise that environmental protection measures divert resources away from socially productive use. The reason is elaborated more fully in Chapter 5, but the essence is stated here. Without question, the industrial countries make disproportionate use of global environmental resources for waste disposal purposes. Even if the assimilative capacity of these resources is not exhausted, the resources provide valuable economic services. If these services are in any sense the "common heritage of mankind," as has been asserted about ocean space, the rental value is currently being appropriated by waste disposers, and it can be argued that a more equitable global arrangement would provide some of the rent to developing countries. In turn, this could finance part of their environmental programs.

More likely, environmental harm is being done to some of these resources, and developing countries must unwillingly accept some of the damages. Although the costs cannot be easily quantified, they support additional resource transfers to finance environmental programs in developing countries. In addition, there are some protection measures undertaken by developing countries that directly improve the well-being of rich countries. One clear example is the preservation of wildlife and wilderness areas. Another might be the preservation of genetic stock. A third is for developing countries to avoid aggravating global problems, such as oil in the marine environment, atmospheric carbon dioxide levels, and fluorocarbons entering the stratosphere. These global problems are mainly caused by industrial countries, and they have a self-interest in preventing additional pollution. The market mechanisms for international negotiations between polluters and damage victims is inadequate. One improvement might be for industrial countries to make "payment" in the form of incremental development assistance to developing countries to avoid additional environmental disruptive activities of a global nature.

US AID AND IBRD EXPERIENCE[30]

No detailed study has been made of AID and IBRD practices is incorporating environmental considerations in their assistance programs. Evaluation becomes complicated because questions of methodology, policy, and procedure are involved. An evaluation should consider problems of method—the redesign of project appraisal to capture externalities and the valuation of damages, damages avoided, and so on. Agency policy is also relevant—the commitment of resources to environmental type projects such as water supply systems and to building an awareness and capacity for environmental management within developing countries. Finally, procedure is important—which programs and projects within the agency require an environmental impact assessment, at what point in the project cycle this should take place, and how the agency should be organized and staffed to deal with environmental matters. The following preliminary observations are based on conversations with officials and a review of certain published material including a limited number of environmental analyses prepared for AID.[31] The International Institute for Environment and Development is just now undertaking a more extensive evaluation, and more information should be forthcoming.

AID faces a troublesome task in addition to the difficulty of performing good environmental cost–benefit analysis. AID lending has changed in composition over the years, away from site-specific physical capital projects such as infrastructure and industrial plant, toward sector loans, commodity import programs, technical advisory services, and training and education programs. The focus is now on the poor majority, and the emphasis is on rural development through agricultural development, education, health, and family planning. This brings the Agency's concerns more directly within a broad definition of "problems of the human environment." However, this makes identification of specific environmental consequences of specific funds very difficult. For example, an agriculture sector loan that channels through a development bank within a developing country may ultimately support activities with identifiable environmental consequences, but AID funds co-mingle with host country funds, and separate identification of the AID component is lost. Moreover, the ultimate use of the funds will not be known until after AID money has been dispersed. Some loans, such as support money for farm cooperatives, may not permit association with specific environmental consequences. As a result of this factor and the earlier AID procedures that required environmental assessment only of capital projects, the Agency has not assembled a body of material that can be examined to answer such questions as the incremental cost of introducing environmental controls into projects or the environmental standards that AID-financed projects should meet.

This is not to say that AID has been unaware of or untouched by concern for the environment. On the contrary, AID environmental concerns have expressed themselves in several ways. One direct expression is the provision of funds for sanitary water and sewage disposal systems, disease control, and family planning. AID has also engaged in training and technical assistance activities. These include short training programs for AID engineers in environmental matters, a joint training program with UNIDO for developing country officials on the environmental aspects of industrialization, and continuing training programs and technical advisory services on integrated pest management. In its recent declaration of policy, AID notes that it is authorized to provide concessional technical assistance to developing countries on environmental matters. It has cosponsored (with the Smithsonian Institution) an extremely useful case study series on tropical reservoirs, urban environment problems, and coastal zone pollution.[32] It is also funding an environmental impact analysis of the $3.5 billion integrated development of the Senegal River Basin. The training and technical assistance role of AID should not be minimized. External financing of development projects is generally small compared to domestic development programs. The ultimate success of efforts to incorporate environmental consequences in project analysis will depend on officials in developing countries perceiving and acting in their own interests. Strengthening their indigenous capabilities in this field is an explicit part of the AID policy.

AID's environmental procedures have responded to a suit brought against it in 1975 by four private environmental groups. The groups maintained that AID has violated the National Environmental Protection Act (NEPA) by failing to provide an environmental impact statement for its pesticide program. The case raised interesting issues—should a distinction be made between environmental effects that are strictly local in the host country or are regional or global? Are "assessments" sufficient or are impact statements that must be open for public comment preferable? Would sensitive negotiations with recipient governments be undermined if impact statements were made public? The case was resolved by court stipulation. AID undertook to prepare a programmatic environmental impact statement on its pest management programs. The rationale is that impacts on the United States or the global environment may be involved. More important, the suit led to a revision of official AID procedures.[33] AID will now undertake an initial screening of all programs and activities (the Initial Environmental Examination). If a significant environmental impact is likely, either an Environmental Assessment or Environmental Impact Statement will be prepared. The impact statement, which generally follows traditional NEPA regulations, will be open for public comment in the United States in draft form. It is reserved for actions that affect the global environmental or areas outside national jurisdiction (e.g., the oceans), or those actions which affect the United States. The benefits, costs, and risks of the project will be considered, as well as the availability of reasonable alternatives. Also, the process of making the assessment is designed to include recipient countries, to strengthen their analytical capabilities.

Although the court action has been resolved, the larger issues remain contentious. The Council on Environmental Quality is still unhappy with AID procedures. Also, AID is not the only government agency engaged in international activities with environmental consequences. The Export Import Bank, the Overseas Private Investment Corporation (OPIC), and the Energy Research and Development Agency (ERDA), to name only three, are also involved. The extent to which NEPA's impact statement provisions apply to the international activities of these and other agencies has not yet been clarified.

One of the most interesting questions with regard to development assistance is the cost of environmental controls relative to the cost of the projects and programs. AID has not compiled this data, but it has made very preliminary estimates of what it will cost to make environmental assessments of projects. Table 4.1 summarizes their estimates. Of a total of 572 AID-financed projects for fiscal 1976, 154 are anticipated to have significant environmental effects. The total cost of assessment is estimated to be $3.18 million, and this represents 0.38% of AID financing for the projects. These figures can be interpreted

Table 4.1 Estimated Costs of Environmental Assessment for AID: Fiscal Year 1976 Projects

	Projects with Significant Environmental Effects				Projects with No Significant Effects	
Region	Number of Projects	AID Financing ($1000)	Environmental Assessment Costs ($1000)	Assessment Costs as Percentage AID Financing	Number of Projects	AID Financing ($1000)
Africa	38	118,814	1145	0.96	113	85,331
East Asia	45	341,913	1006	0.29	57	95,710
Near East and South Asia	31	150,503	628	0.41	33	26,142
Latin America	40	233,257	398	0.17	145	143,443
Technical assistance	0		0		70	78,699
Totals	154	844,487	3177	0.37	418	429,325

Source. AID, "FY76 Environmental Assessment Workloads and Costs" (mimeo).

Table 4.2 IBRD Environmental Review July 1971–December 1973

	Number of Projects Signed and Reviewed	Number of Projects Acted on
Bank/IDA		
Agriculture	104	46
Industry	22	14
Transportation	87	15
Tourism	6	5
Water and sewage	15	15
Power	34	22
Urban projects	7	4
Telecommunications	15	1
Education	38	4
Multipurpose	4	3
Others	44	0
IFC		
Cement	6	4
Chemicals	2	2
Iron and steel	2	2
Mining	3	3
Motor vehicles	4	2
Nonferrous metals	2	1
Petrochemicals	1	1
Pulp and paper	5	4
Textiles and fibers	7	2
Tourism	7	7
Others	19	0
Total	434	159

Source. IBRD, *Environment and Development,* 1975, Table 2.

in two ways. On the face of it they suggest that environmental assessment costs will be quite minor, only necessary for 27% of the projects, and amounting to less than 0.4% of the AID-financed portion of these projects. An alternative interpretation is that the assessments will not be serious in-depth studies in which alternatives are examined and costed.

The World Bank anticipated the concern for environmental consequences of development projects by establishing in 1970 the position of "environmental advisor." The purpose of this advisor is to evaluate all investment projects from the viewpoint of their environmental effects. Because Bank lending continues to be project oriented, some data can be assembled. Table 4.2 reveals that, of a total of 434 projects screened between July 1, 1971, and December 31, 1973, 275 were considered to have no adverse environmental impact, and 159 were found to have potential adverse effects. As might be expected, industrial projects such as cement, chemicals, and pulp and paper, financed through the International Finance Corporation (IFC), had a large percentage requiring environmental review action.

The Bank states that the additional cost attributable to environmental safeguards ranged from 0 to 3% of total project cost.[33] Although this appears to

Table 4.3 IBRD and AID Financing of Environmental Projects

	IBRD Annual Average 1964–1968	IBRD Annual Average 1969–1973	1973	1974	1975	1976
Bank Lending for Water Supply and Sewage (million $)	23.8	117.8	278.8	173.7	145.1	334.6
As percentage of total Bank financing	2.4	4.6	8.2	4.0	2.5	5.0

Project Purpose	AID Annual Average 1955–1960	Annual Average 1961–1965 (millions $)	1966	1967	1968	1969	1970	1971	1972
a. Environmental sanitation	13.3	18.2	11.2	29.9	34.3	0.1	0.3	NA	NA
b. Control of specific disease	12.1	23.0	20.1	33.6	35.4	13.7	6.9	2.6	1.4
c. Malaria eradication			not separately listed					9.1	2.4
d. Urban potable water			not separately listed					9.8	0.7
Total a–d	25.4	41.2	31.3	63.5	69.7	13.8	7.2	21.5	4.5
Total a–d as percentage of health and sanitation	55.2%	68.9%	50.0%	61.9%	42.4%	16.6%	6.3%	14.1%	2.8%
Total a–d as percentage of total projects	4.1%	4.1%	4.1%	5.6%	6.9%	1.8%	0.9%	2.7%	0.5%

Sources. IBRD *Annual Report*, 1975, 1976. *AID Projects, Commitments by Field of Activity 1955–1970* (Washington, D.C.: AID, 1971). *AID Projects FY 1971 and 1972. By Country and Field of Activity* (Washington, D.C.: AID).

be a very modest figure, it should be used with caution. First, it is not clear what definitions were used to cost the environmental controls. Second, we do not know how rigorous were the standards established. The Bank admits that one reason the costs were kept low is that the standards adopted were "appropriate both to their current stage of development and the requirements of the project," and that in the future costs may exceed 3%, because the ecological systems in developing countries will become more severely strained.

To complete the discussion we have assembled in Table 4.3 data on trends in IBRD and AID financing of environmental projects. This is not an exhaustive accounting because of ambiguities in the definition of environmental projects and because records have not been kept on this basis. The table shows that Bank lending for one type of environmental project, water supplies and sewage, rose from an annual average of $23.8 million in 1964–1968 to $278.8 million in 1973, but fell in 1974 and again in 1975. It rose again, however, to $334.6 million in 1976. As a percentage of total Bank project lending, water supply and sewage projects have varied between 2.4 and 8.2%. AID summary records since 1972 do not break down specific environmental type projects as they did previously. However, the table shows that from 1955 through 1972 the total for four types of environmental projects increased from an annual average of $25 million in 1955–1960 to $70 million in 1968 and declined to $4.5 million in 1972. This represents 4.1%, 6.9%, and 0.5% of total project financing in the three periods. These data are not sufficient for strong conclusions, however, because nonproject assistance is not included and because projects listed in other categories (such as land and water resources) may have substantial environmental components.

NOTES

1. M. Taghfarvar and John P. Milton, Eds., *The Careless Technology* (Garden City, N. Y.: Natural History Press, 1972) contains an extensive description of environmental disruptions from development projects.
2. See Raymond F. Dasman, John P. Milton, and Peter H. Freeman, *Ecological Principles for Economic Development* (London: Wiley, 1973); World Bank, *Environmental, Health and Human Ecologic Considerations in Economic Development Projects* (Washington, D.C., 1974); U.S. Agency for International Development, *Environmental Assessment Guidelines Manual* (Washington, D.C., 1974); three volumes by Peter Freeman entitled *The Environmental Impact of a Large Tropical Reservoir, The Environmental Impact of Rapid Urbanization*, and *Coastal Zone Pollution by Oil and Other Contaminants* (Washington, D.C.: Smithsonian Institution, 1974). Ralph Stone, Inc. is currently producing a manual for AID entitled *Decision Makers Guidebook for Industrial Pollution Control in Developing Nations*. See also Bostwick H. Ketchum, *The Water's Edge: Critical Problems of the Coastal Zone* (Cambridge, Mass.: MIT Press, 1972) and The Institute for Ecology, *Evaluation of Research and Applications in the Neotropics* (Hamburg: Springer-Verlag, 1974).
3. See United Nations Industrial Development Organization, *Guidelines for Project Evaluation* (New York: United Nations, 1972); Ian M.D. Little and J.A. Mirrless, *Project Appraisal and Planning for Developing Countries* (London: Heinemann, 1974); Deepak Lal, *Methods of Project Analysis: A Review*, World Bank Occasional Paper No. 16, 1974; Lyn Squire and Herman Van der Tak, *Economic Analysis of Projects* (Baltimore, The Johns Hopkins University Press for the IBRD, 1975). For the theory of public investment decision making, see Robert H. Haveman and Julias Margolis, Eds., *Public Expenditure and Public Analysis* (Chicago: Markham, 1970).
4. J. Price Gittinger, *Economic Analysis of Agricultural Projects* (Baltimore: The Johns Hopkins University Press for the IBRD, 1972).

5. World Bank, *Environment and Development* (Washington, D.C.: 1975) pp. 3 and 4.
6. See Alan V. Kneese and Blair T. Bower, *Managing Water Quality: Economics, Technology, Institutions* (Baltimore: The Johns Hopkins University Press for Resources for the Future, 1968); Charles L. Schultze and Alan V. Kneese, *Pollution, Prices, and Public Policy* (Washington, D.C.: Brookings Institution, 1975); William J. Baumol and W.E. Oates, *The Theory of Environmental Policy* (Englewood Cliffs, N.J.: Prentice-Hall, 1975); Anthony C. Fisher and J.V. Krutilla, *The Economics of Natural Environments: Studies in the Valuation of Commodity and Amenity Resources* (Baltimore: The Johns Hopkins University Press, 1975); Organization for Economic Cooperation and Development, *Environmental Damage Costs* (Paris: OECD, 1975); and Henry M. Peskin and Eugene P. Seskin, Eds., *Cost Benefit Analysis and Water Pollution Policy* (Washington, D.C.: Urban Institute, 1975), David W. Pearce, *Environmental Economics* (London: Longman, 1976).
7. Squire and Van der Tak, *Economic Analysis of Projects*.
8. A fourth category might be projects that augment the assimilative capacity of environmental media for waste disposal. One example is stabilizing or increasing stream flow.
9. Forcing victims to shoulder avoidance costs changes the distributional outcome and may offend a sense of equity.
10. This schema is not comprehensive. For example, loss of genetic material possibly valuable for future research does not fit in neatly.
11. All the estimates are cited by R.E. Wyzga, "A Survey of Environmental Damage Costs," in OECD, *Environmental Damage Costs* (Paris: OECD, 1974) pp. 51–101. Original United States estimates from the U.S. Office of Science and Technology, "Cumulative Regulatory Effects on the Cost of Automotive Transportation (RECAT), Final Report of the Ad Hoc Committee," Feb. 28, 1972. United Kingdom estimate from UK Programmes Analysis Unit, *An Economic and Technical Appraisal of Air Pollution in the United Kingdom* (Chilton, Didcot, Berks, 1971). Italian estimate from Ente Nazionale Idrocarburi, *Economic Costs and Benefits of an Antipollution Project in Italy* prepared for UN Conference on the Human Environment, Stockholm, June 5–16, 1972.
12. A.C. Fisher, *The Evaluation of Benefits from Pollution Abatement* (Washington, D.C.: EPA Office of Planning and Evaluation, 1972) cited by Dennis Tihansky, "A Survey of Empirical Benefit Studies," in Seskin and Peskin, Eds., *Cost Benefit Analysis*, p. 136. Tihansky does an excellent job of critiquing empirical benefit (pollution damage) studies.
13. Council on Environmental Quality, *Environmental Quality, Fourth Annual Report 1973* (Washington, D.C.: GPO, 1973) p. 79. Note, however, that commercial fishing and health effects were not estimated. For a summary of other regional studies see Tihansky, "Empirical Benefit Studies," Tables II and III.
14. Many water-borne diseases are chronic and debilitating but not necessarily fatal.
15. There is inconclusive evidence that the tailings from iron ore processing that have been dumped in large volumes into Lake Superior by the Reserve Mining Company may be contaminating municipal water supplies with carcinogenic substances.
16. Fisher and Krutilla, *Economics of Natural Environments*; V. Kerry Smith, *Technical Change, Relative Prices, and Environmental Resource Evaluation* (Baltimore: The Johns Hopkins University Press, 1974).
17. The change in relative values can be accommodated in the analysis either by permitting amenity benefits forgone to increase over the time period or by reducing the rate at which the future opportunity costs of amenities forgone are discounted.
18. Pigou, *The Economics of Welfare* (London: Macmillan, 1932). For a lucid exposition of the relationships between resource exploitation and efficiency, intertemporal distribution issues, and the discount rate, see Talbot Page, *Conservation and Economic Efficiency* (Baltimore: Johns Hopkins Press for Resources for the Future, 1977).
19. Fisher and Krutilla, *Economics of Natural Environments*, p. 63.
20. Kenneth J. Arrow and Anthony C. Fisher, "Environmental Preservation, Uncertainty, and Irreversibility," *Quarterly Journal of Economics*, **88**, No. 2 (May 1974) p. 312.
21. David Pearce, "The Limits of Cost-Benefit Analysis as a Guide to Environmental Policy," *Kyklos*, **29**, Fasc. 1 (1976) p. 97.
22. International Maritime Consultative Organization, Report of Study No. VI, *The Environmen-*

tal and Financial Consequences of Oil Pollution from Ships (1973) prepared by the Programmes Analysis Unit of the UK Department of Trade and Industry.

23. *New York Times*, Jan 8, 1976, p. 24.
24. Fred H. Abel, "Project by Project Analysis vs. Comprehensive Planning," in Peskin and Seskin, *Cost Benefit Analysis*, p. 333.
25. Differences in enforcement costs should also be considered in the analysis.
26. See Squire and Van der Tak, *Economic Analysis of Projects*.
27. For a clear and thoughtful treatment of additionality, see Scott MacLeod, *Financing Environmental Measures in Developing Countries: The Principle of Additionality*, International Union for the Conservation of Nature and Natural Resources, Environmental Policy and Law Paper No. 6 (Morges, Switzerland, 1974).
28. S. Schneider-Sawiris, *The Concept of Compensation in the Field of Trade and Environment*, International Union for the Conservation of Nature and Natural Resources, Environmental Policy and Law Paper No. 4 (Morges, Switzerland, 1974).
29. Professor M. Weinrobe points out that for projects in the export sector some costs can be passed on through prices to importers.
30. The Inter-American Development Bank has no formal procedures or guidelines for evaluating the environmental impact of projects they finance. Despite IDB President Mena's call for guidelines in his Stockholm Conference address, concern for the environment remains on an ad hoc and unsystematic basis. The organization of American States (OAS) includes an environmental component in their project evaluation training programs. See OAS, *Consideraciones Ambientales en La Formulación y Evaluación de Proyectos* (1975).
31. IBRD, *Annual Reports* and *Environment and Development*; AID, *Environmental Assessment Guidelines Manual* (Washington, D.C. AID, 1974); AID Policy Determination, "Environmental Aspects of Development Assistance" PD-63, August 1975; R. Douglas Bradbury, "Environmental Activities of Development Assistance Agencies," *SAIS Review*, **18**, No. 3 (Summer 1974) p. 14.
32. See note 2 for citation.
33. "AID Environmental Procedures," *Federal Register*, **40**, No. 127 (June 30, 1976).
34. IBRD, *Environment and Development*, p. 11.

APPENDIX AGRICULTURAL PRODUCTIVITY AND FALLOW PERIOD MODEL

The discount rate is important in selecting projects and techniques of production. The following idealized example from agriculture illustrates one way in which the high preference for current consumption in developing countries can lead to a deterioration in the productivity of soils and can undermine long-term yields.[1]

Consider the problem of determining the optimal length of time that land should be left in fallow.[2] Assume that soil quality, measured by yield per acre, y, increases with the length of fallow, F, where F equals the fallow period plus one crop year.

$$y = f(F) \qquad f' > 0 \quad f'' < 0$$
over the interval $F = 1$ to F^*

For $F > F^*$ we assume $f' = 0$, or a maximum biological yield at F^*, with positive but diminishing marginal returns in the interval $F = 1$ to $F = F^*$.

Total yield per acre, Q, will be yield per acre cropped, y, times total number of crops, C, harvested over the period P:

$$Q = yC \qquad \text{where } y = f(F) \text{ and } C = \frac{P}{F}$$

If the farmer wishes to maximize his total yield over the period P without discounting future yields, the optimal length of fallow, $\overline{F}$, is then when

$\frac{dQ}{dF} = 0$, or:

$$f'(F)\frac{P}{F} = \frac{P}{F^2}f(F)$$

$$\overline{F} = \frac{f(F)}{f'(F)}$$

It follows that if y approaches its maximum value at F^* smoothly, then the optimal fallow must be less than the biological maximum F^*, because the marginal gain in yield would be zero, and the marginal loss in terms of crops per period foregone would be positive.

Another interpretation is that the elasticity of the yield function with respect to increase in fallow must be equal to the elasticity of the crop function with respect to fallow at the optimal fallow level,

$$E_{YF} = E_{CF}$$

but E_{CF} is equal to 1 because it is a rectangular hyperbola; therefore, optimal fallow will occur when the elasticity of the yield function is equal to 1, or

$$E_{YF} = f'(F)\frac{F}{y} = 1$$

$$\overline{F} = \frac{f(F)}{f'(F)}$$

If the yield function is such that its elasticity never reaches 1, the problem has a corner solution at the minimum possible fallow period, $F = 1$. Under the assumptions it would be rational to mine the soil in the most rapid manner.[3] In any event, it will be rational to shorten the fallow period below its biological maximum, F^*, and deplete soil quality, even without discounting future yields.

The model is illustrated in Diagram 4A.1. In quadrant 2 the yield function, $y = f(F)$ is illustrated, and in quadrant 4, the number of crops is shown as a function of the fallow period, given the total period under consideration, P. In quadrant 1 the yield function and crop function trace out a trade-off function between number of crops and yield, TT. Specifically, select any fallow period and move clockwise to quadrant 4 to find the number of crops; then move counterclockwise to quadrant 2 to find the yield. TT is then the locus of C and y points corresponding to different levels of fallow, F. Because the total output over the period, Q, is equal to $y \cdot C$, increasing levels of Q can be represented by the curves $\overline{Q}'$, and $\overline{Q}''$. It is then easy to see that $\overline{Q}'$ is the maximum attainable output and is achieved at the point of tangency with the trade-off curve at point e. This implies an optimal fallow period of $\overline{F}$, with the number of crops over the period at $\overline{C}$. Observe that shorter or longer fallow periods result in lower total output. Observe also that the slope of the yield function at the optimal fallow period is equal to the slope of the ray from the origin, implying that the elasticity of the yield curve equals 1.[4]

When the farmer is not indifferent to the time profile of his output but values current output over future, the optimal fallow period is shorter. The higher the

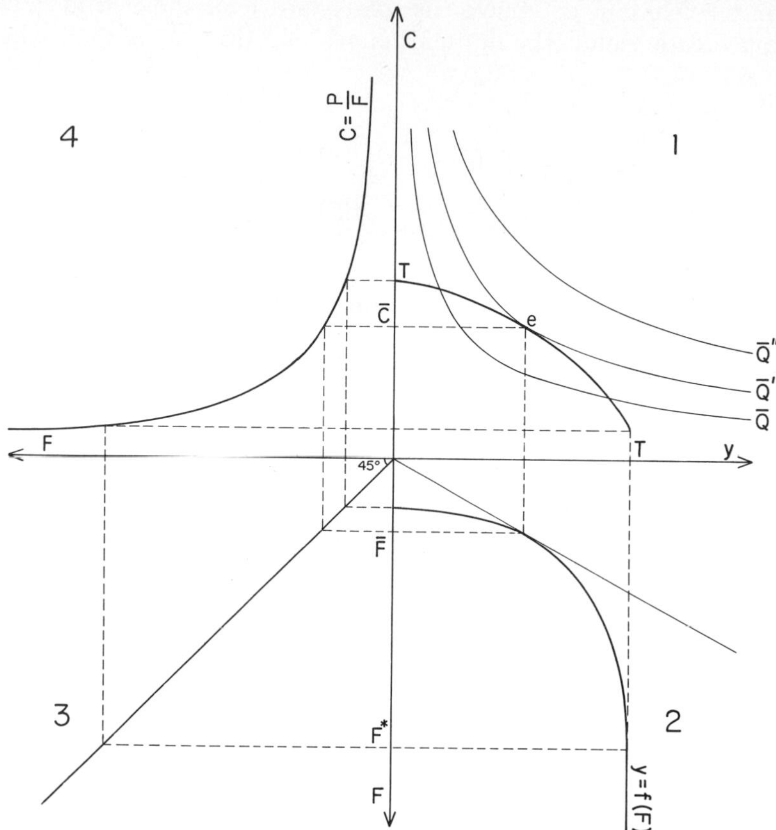

Diagram 4A.1. Optimal fallow model.

discount rate, the shorter the optimal fallow, because a cropping strategy of long fallow, high yields throws more total output toward the end of the time stream where it is heavily discounted, whereas a short fallow, lower yield strategy pushes output closer in time.

To demonstrate this consider the present value of two crop streams with identical undiscounted totals

$$PV_Y = \sum_{i=1}^{n} \frac{Y_i}{r}\left(1 - \left(\frac{1}{1+r}\right)^n\right)$$

$$PV_X = \sum_{i=1}^{m} \frac{X_i}{q}\left(1 - \left(\frac{1}{1+q}\right)^m\right) \quad \text{where } \Sigma Y_i = \Sigma X_i \text{ by assumption}$$

n is the number of crops harvested in the Y stream; m is the number of crops harvested in the X stream. Assume $n>m$; thus Y represents more frequent harvests at lower yields.

The *annual* discount rate applied to each stream must be equal for proper comparison, but because y and x are alternating streams, taking on zero values in fallow years and positive values in crop years, we define r as the discount rate appropriate for the crop cycle y, and q the discount rate corresponding to the crop cycle X. Thus if Y represents a 3-year fallow period plus 1 crop year and the *annual* discount rate is 10%, $(1 + r) = (1.1)^4$. We wish to show that

$$PV_Y > PV_X$$

Define $\alpha = \frac{n}{m}$, $\alpha > 1$. Because $\Sigma x = \Sigma y$; $x_i = x_j$; $y_i = y_j$, we know $x = \alpha y$. We also know that the discount factor applied to the X stream is a multiple of the discount rate applied to the Y stream,

$$(1 + q) = (1 + r)^{\alpha}$$
$$q = (1 + r)^{\alpha} - 1$$

therefore

$$PV_x = \frac{\alpha y}{(1 + r)^{\alpha} - 1}\left(1 - \left(\frac{1}{(1 + r)^{\alpha}}\right)^{\frac{n}{\alpha}}\right) = \frac{\alpha y}{(1 + r)^{\alpha} - 1}\left(1 - \left(\frac{1}{1 + r}\right)^{n}\right)$$

∴ show

$$\frac{y}{r}\left(1 - \left(\frac{1}{1 + r}\right)^{n}\right) > \frac{\alpha y}{(1 + r)^{\alpha} - 1}\left(1 - \left(\frac{1}{1 + r}\right)^{n}\right) \quad \text{for} \quad \alpha > 1, r > 0$$

or

$$\frac{y}{r} > \frac{\alpha y}{(1 + r)^{\alpha} - 1}$$

or

$$(1 + r)^{\alpha} > r\alpha + 1$$

which is true for all $\alpha > 1$, $r > 0$

We therefore conclude that with two cropping patterns yielding identical total output, the shorter fallow, lower yield per crop, lower soil quality pattern yields a larger present value and is preferred to the longer fallow, higher yield pattern whenever future output is discounted.

We can also show that the advantage of the Y stream over the X stream increases as the discount rate increases, implying that the higher the discount rate the shorter the optimal fallow period. To show this the slope of $(1 + r)^{\alpha}$ must exceed the slope of $r\alpha + 1$ or

$$\alpha (1 + r)^{\alpha - 1} > \alpha$$

or

$$(1 + r)^{\alpha - 1} > 1 \qquad \text{for all } \alpha > 1, r > 0$$

Finally, it may be more realistic to assume that for fallow periods less than the biological maximum, the yield diminishes over time as each fallow period fails to restore the previous level of soil fertility. In this case the short fallow pattern throws an even larger proportion of total yield early in the time stream; thus the effect of discounting is reduced. The greater the discount rate, the greater the incentive to mine the soil for immediate output rather than sustained yields.

NOTES

1. We wish to stress that the economics of land conservation has a long history. Earlier analysis included the importance of the interest (discount) rate, the divergence between individual and social welfare, and the economics of soil conservation versus exploitation. See for example Arthur Bunce, *The Economics of Soil Conservation* (Ames, Iowa: Iowa State College Press, 1942).
2. We are aware that land is cropped several times between fallow but have chosen for expositional reasons to treat the several crops as one.
3. The solution might change if fertility can be maintained by the addition of fertilizer, if the price of the crop were expected to rise over time, or if other cropping costs were introduced.
4. A numerical example is useful. Assume an arbitrary yield function, $y = 20\ (F - 1)^{.8}$ over the range $F = 0 - F = 10$, and assume $y = 116$ for all $F > 10$. Assume also a 20-year time period. Then

$$\bar{F} = \frac{f(F)}{f'(F)} = \frac{20(F - 1)^{.8}}{16(F - 1)^{.2}}$$

$$\bar{F} = 1.25(F - 1)$$

$$\bar{F} = 5 \text{ years and output is maximized at the level 242.7}$$

Note that a 2-year fallow period would have total output of 100, and a 10-year fallow period would have a total output of 116.

Chapter 5

TRANSNATIONAL POLLUTION AND INTERNATIONAL COMMON PROPERTY RESOURCES

Pollution does not respect political boundaries. Economic activity conducted within the territory of one state can damage the environment of other states or degrade international common property resources. Transnational (or transfrontier) pollution, then, is a special type of environmental externality in which some damages are transferred from the polluting state and (unwillingly) received by other states. The economic analysis of transnational pollutuion is broadly similar to the analysis of purely domestic externalities. The important questions in both situations involve improving efficiency in the allocation of resources and considering the welfare distributional consequences of both uncorrected externalities and environmental control measures. However, the international context of transnational pollution is sufficiently unique to warrant careful, special cxamination.

Transnational pollution and the degradation of international common property resources is the most direct environmental link between rich and poor countries. We cannot say whether it is the most important. Examples of transnational pollution among countries, rich or poor, are easy to come by. They include pollution of almost all major international bodies of water, acid rains in Northern Europe, and threats to the global atmosphere. But a comprehensive quantitative accounting, including the magnitude of the damage done, is unavailable. Nor is there much experience with international negotiations for establishing environmental controls over transnational pollution. International law in this area is quite new and not definitive. For these reasons, a discussion of the shared use by industrial and developing countries of international common property resources, and of transnational pollution, must be suggestive and not conclusive.

The issues posed by transnational pollution should not be passed over completely. They have become a source of contention between rich and poor countries and therefore affect political relations. Also, there is a presumption that increased global economic activity, increased congestion, and greater access to global commons will create environmental problems where none now exist. Finally, by considering the subject in its extreme form, as an issue between rich and poor countries, some features common to any control system for international common property resources are highlighted. In less dramatic form these features are also present in controlling transnational pollution among industrial countries.

This chapter has three sections. The first considers general principles and difficulties in limiting the abuse of international environmental resources and curtailing transnational pollution. The next section assembles some evidence regarding the disproportionate use by industrial countries of the international commons for waste disposal. The theme is possible environmental exploitation of the South by the North. Finally, because international environmental controls must be negotiated among sovereign states and abstract models of negotiating behavior may be radically different from actual experience, attention should be given to the limited examples of control negotiations that are available. Therefore, the third section considers the ocean environment question as an issue between developed and developing countries within the current Law of the Sea negotiations.

PRINCIPLES[1]

In several respects the negotiation of controls for transnational pollution is closer to private bargaining among individuals to correct an environmental externality than to establishing national environmental controls. If there is no law to the contrary, polluters enjoy implicit rights to environmental media for waste disposal purposes. In so doing, they impose damage costs on beneficial users of the resource. In the private bargaining case the parties are individuals or private groups, and in the international case they are states.

In both the private and international situations, the correction of an environmental externality is brought about through negotiations and bargaining. In neither case is the correction made by a central government with residual environmental authority acting for the general social welfare. Two related conclusions follow. First, in both the private and the international cases a reasonable minimum necessary condition for an individual or state to voluntarily join an agreement to limit pollution is that it made no worse off by so doing. The agreement must be satisfactory to all participants without compulsion. In contrast, national policy can seek national social welfare objectives without being constrained to measures that make each unit better off. The ability to compel compliance and the availability of alternate measures for correcting any undesirable distributional consequences are present at the national level but not in the private and international cases. The second conclusion is that the welfare distributional consequences of controls cannot be separated from the negotiation process in the private and international situations. The right to use environmental media for waste disposal, or for beneficial purposes, is an economically valuable asset. The negotiation of environmental controls is the process of limiting and conferring this right; therefore, changes in the distribution of wealth and welfare are central to the negotiations. Decisions on the efficient allocation of resources for waste disposal and other uses are constrained by welfare considerations. This is in sharp contrast to the establishment of national controls where, in theory, allocative efficiency can be separated from the distributional consequences. The similarities between transnational pollution and private bargaining are noted by Ruff, "If we regard individual nations as sovereign, with power to control their citizens in any way they choose, then the transfrontier pollution problem is no different from an ordinary problem of externalities among a small group of individuals."[2]

Despite these similarities, there are still important differences between private bargains among polluters and victims, and international agreements. The differences rule out uncritical application of theorems derived from one situation to the other situation. In an international context the environment may be only one of several issues negotiated simultaneously. The bargain that is struck may sacrifice environmenal interests for gains in other areas. This has been particularly evident in the Law of the Sea negotiations in which nonenvironmental issues dominate—access to ocean resources such as fisheries and offshore oil, military interests in unimpeded naval passage through straits, freedom of scientific research, and so on.

A second difference is that, in models of private bargaining, one or another legal regime is assumed, and the efficiency with which resources are allocated is then examined. In the one regime rights for waste disposal are awarded to polluters, and damaged parties (victims) negotiate with polluters for abatement. In the other case, rights are awarded to beneficial users, and polluters attempt to "purchase" waste disposal rights. In contrast, international negotiations on common property resources bargain over the legal regime itself, as well as the specific environmental controls. In other words, international negotiations are concerned with awarding environmental rights (a question of the legal regime) and developing specific environmental controls (a question of resource management).

Most important, successful private bargaining between polluters and victims requires a system of payments. If the legal regime awards rights to polluters, victims must be able to "purchase" pollution abatement through bribes to polluters. If rights are awarded to beneficial users, then there must be a network of compensatory payments from polluters to victims. In both cases successful bargaining requires a payment mechanism. This payment mechanism is sometimes available on the domestic level. In the international context, the payment system is not at all well developed, and methods for bribing polluters or making compensatory payments among countries is imperfect.[3] As we shall see, this undermines the prospects for adequate international environmental safeguards.

What are the implications of the differences between private and international negotiations? First, in the domestic context, when private bargaining over environmental externalities fails, because the payment network is not readily available or because the transactions costs (identifying polluters, aggregating the interests of victims, preventing "free riders," and enforcing the agreement) of making the bargain are too high, the government has residual jurisdiction over the resources. It can establish environmental regulations for the improvement in social welfare and can compel compliance. Failure of international negotiations is more serious, since recourse to a supranational authority is not possible. International environmental law may be modestly useful, but the law itself is negotiated and changing rapidly.

Second, the optimism of the powerful Coase Theorem does not carry over to the international situation. This theorem states that under certain restrictive assumptions, including zero transactions costs, the same allocative efficiency result could be obtained regardless of whether property rights were allocated to the polluter or victim. In both cases, bargaining among the two would secure a Pareto optimal use of resources without the need for government intervention.[4] However, the Coase Theorem depends on a well-developed payment network, and the absence of this network among countries suggests that transnational pollution and pollution of international common property resources will not be easily resolved by Coasian negotiations.

The final implication of the differences between private and international negotiations centers on enforcement. In the international context the instruments for enforcing agreements are generally much weaker. Accordingly, the prospects for effective enforcement help determine the particular control instruments chosen.[5] One example of this is the choice of design standards for oil tankers (segregated ballasting) in the Prevention of Pollution from Ships Convention. Although segregated ballasting may not be the least-cost control technique, it requires a minimum of enforcement and sidesteps the touchy issue of international inspection.

Difficulties in negotiating effective controls over transnational pollution are not merely hypothetical considerations. For example, the dominant role of nonenvironmental issues in the Law of the Sea Conference has profoundly affected the draft provisions concerning the environment. It is clear that the efficient use of the ocean environment is not being decided exclusively on its own merits but in conjunction with other parts of the negotiations. More generally, examples of transnational pollution between North and South can be cited. Vessel source petroleum discharges in the San Diego area wash up on the beaches of Baja, Mexico. A Dutch supertanker, the Metula, spilled 18 million gallons of oil within 1 mile of the Chilean coast. The industrial discharge of wastes by the Soviet Union into the Caspian Sea have helped reduce Soviet and Iranian fish catch by 87%. Environmentalists express concern that the continued use of DDT in developing countries for agriculture and public health will offset reduced consumption in industrial countries.[6] In these and in other cases, a serious question is raised about the ability of the international community to establish adequate environmental safeguards. The problem of negotiating international controls in the absence of supranational authorities, with a very imperfect international payment network, must be confronted. It is therefore useful to look more closely at principles for the shared management of international environmentmental resources before turning to specific material on North–South environmental damage flows.[7]

Consider first a situation involving an international resource such as a body of water, to which two countries, North and South, contribute pollution. Assume, however, that all pollution is local and that no environmental damage costs are passed from one country to another. Finally, assume that the damage done by pollution is to amenities and not to the productivity of the resource in producing conventional goods, and that pollution abatement requires real resources (capital and labor) whose cost can be measured in terms of conventional goods forgone.

If, as is widely believed, the income elasticity of the demand for environmental quality is greater than unity, the level of environmental quality and amenities chosen by the richer North will be higher than the level chosen by the poorer South, and the relative price of environemtal amenities as measured by conventional goods forgone will also be higher in the North than in the South. The situation is shown in Diagram 5.1. *TT* represents the transformation function between conventional goods and environmental amenities that both the North and the South confront. It is convex to the origin on the assumption of increasing marginal cost of attaining higher levels of environmental amenities. Preferences for conventional goods and for environmental amenities are represented by indifference curves *N* and S and S′ for North and South, respcctively. S represents a higher level of welfare than S′. The optimal combinations of conventional goods and environmental amenities to maximize welfare is given by point *ON* for the North and point *OS* for the South. The price of environmental amenities relative to conventional goods is the slope of *PN* for North and *PS* for South. The higher price in the North (*PN* > *PS*) follows from the assumptions.

If a single environmental standard for the shared resource based on the optimal level of environmental amenities in the North were imposed on the South, the South would be obliged to move along *TT* from *OS* to the inferior position *ON*, and its welfare would fall from S to S′. In simplified terms, this forms the heart of developing countries' insistent arguments that standards appropriate for rich countries are inappropriate and too costly for them. This argument is the justification for a long series of reservations and saving clauses inserted by developing countries in international conventions and resolutions. It has been used with regard to controls on international common property resources and developing country obligations within their own borders.

The defense of dual standards, lower for developing countries, is correct

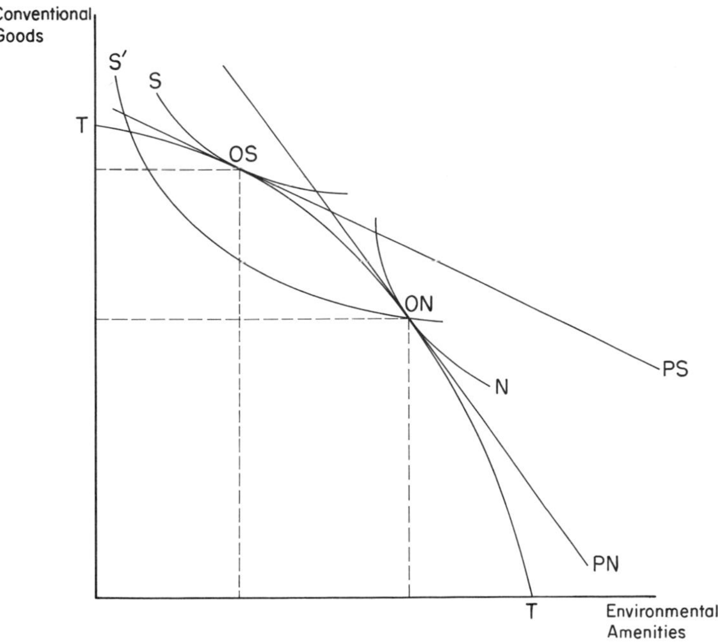

Diagram 5.1. Dual versus uniform environmental standards.

given the restrictive assumptions, but this is a contrived example and fails to consider two important features of environmental deterioration. The first, discussed in Chapters 1 and 3, is that the capacity to produce conventional goods is not independent of the quality of environmental resources. For this reason alone one cannot assert that the optimal level of environmental qualtiy for a jointly shared resource will be higher in the North than the South. The second feature not captured is the external costs passed among countries as they utilize the resource. This second feature is now examined.

Assume two countries, N and S, that pollute a shared body of water and use the resource for beneficial purposes. For ease of exposition, assume that each contributes an identical amount of pollution and the marginal damages from pollution are constant. Assume also for the moment that the pollutant once in the water causes identical damages regardless of whether it comes from North or South. Finally, assume that the marginal cost of abatement is higher in N than S, reflecting, for example, difficulty in finding alternative disposal sites, and that the marginal damage from pollution is at a higher level for S than N.

The situation is depicted in Diagram 5.2. The horizontal axis measures pollution abatement by both; thus at 100% neither country is polluting. Marginal costs of abatement are MC_N for N, MC_S for country S. The assumption of rising marginal costs for abatement is well founded in the literature. The assumed constant marginal damage from pollution implies constant marginal benefits from abatement; MB_N for country N; MB_S for country S. The global marginal costs of abatement, assuming that abatement responsibility is efficiently allocated between N and S, is the horizontal sum of MC_N and MC_S, or MC_{N+S}. Without considering the distributional consequences for N and S, it is clear that only at level Q_0 will the incremental real resource costs of abatement be equal to the incremental damages avoided. North would undertake abatement at the level Q'_N, and South would undertake abatement at the level Q'_S. At

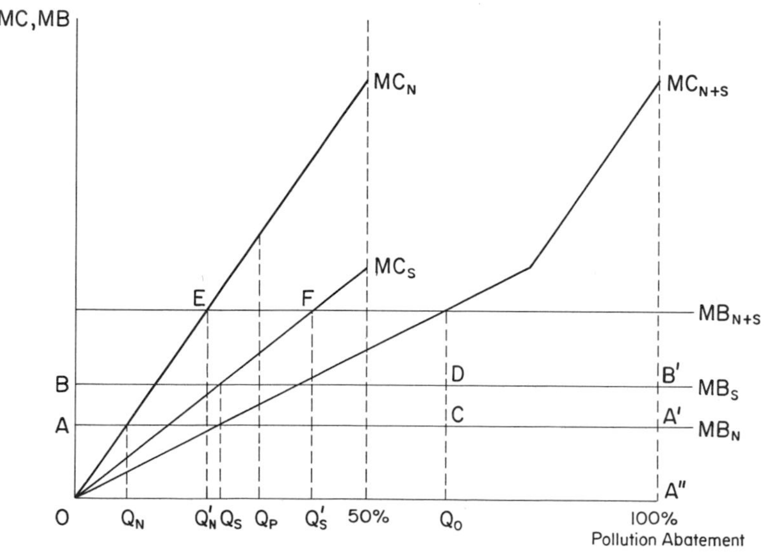

Diagram 5.2. Optimal abatement with shared resources.

this point, resources will be allocated in an optimal fashion from a global perspective. It is important to note, however, that dual criteria for optimality exists; $MC_{N+S} = MB_{N+S}$ *and also* marginal abatement costs from all sources are equalized, $MC_N = MC_S$.

The diagram provides some insight into international negotiations. If no abatement is undertaken by either N or S, S suffers greater total damages than N ($OBB'A'' > OAA'A''$). Whether this is some form of environmental exploitation of S by N is semantic; both contribute equal quantities of pollutants, but S suffers a greater welfare loss. The second point is that unilateral action, taken independently and from a national perspective, can improve welfare for both, but will result in suboptimal abatement from a global perspective. Acting in this fashion, N would equate its marginal costs and benefits ($MC_N = MB_N$) and choose an abatement level Q_N; country S would choose $MC_S = MB_S$, or level Q_S. The sum of the unilateral abatement efforts, $OQ_N + OQ_S$, is less than the optimal OQ_o. This simply illustrates the essential failure of environmental externalities and common property resources—incidental damage to others is not included in decisions to undertake pollution abatement. Note also that there is nothing inherent in this situation that results in a richer country undertaking more abatement than a poorer country in either relative or absolute terms. From a purely local perspective, the optimal levels of Q_N and Q_S are fully determined by the respective abatement cost functions and damage functions. Unless they can be shown to differ systematically between North and South, nothing can be said about richer countries undertaking greater abatement.

What are the prospects that an international agreement between the two countries will select the globally optimum abatement level, Q_o? They are not very good unless there are methods for making compensatory payments between the two. First, note that globally optimal abatement at Q_o will require a greater relative and absolute abatement effort by S than N ($Q'_S > Q'_N$). If the negotiating decision is to require equal abatement, the optimal level Q_o would be reached if each undertakes Q_p, but at Q_p the marginal cost for N exceeds the marginal cost for S, and the allocation of abatement effort is inefficient. Optimal environmental policy for shared resources will generally require disproportionate cost burdens, with countries having relatively low-cost alternatives undertaking greater abatement. This may be resisted on equity grounds, particularly if no compensatory payments can be made.

In this example, if the optimum level were chosen, both countries could be better off than if there were no abatement; therefore, the possibility of optimal abatement is not ruled out. This can be seen by comparing the area under the marginal benefit curves for N and S. Country N received net benefits equal to gross benefits less abatement costs, or $OACQ_o - OEQ'_N$. Net benefits for S are $OBDQ_o - OFQ'_S$. However, it is not always the case that each country is made better off. Consider the following example.

In this case we examine the more realistic situation in which pollution damages are source specific—that is, the pollutants are not homogeneous once they enter the body of water, but each country's pollution damages can be separated into those done to itself and those done by others. It follows that abatement benefit functions must be specific to the country doing the abatement. For example, damages to Italy from a polluted Mediterranean are caused by its own actions and the actions of other littoral states, but a unit increase in its own pollution will not create the same damage to Italy as a unit increase in pollution by others.

Specifically, assume that countries N and S contribute equal amounts of pollution, marginal abatement costs are identical in each country, S is a major beneficial user of the ocean resources and suffers greater relative damages than N from pollution, and the flow of damages from N to S exceeds the flow of damages from S to N because N's pollution is not local, but S's tends to be local. Denote by MC_N and MC_S the marginal costs of abatement for N and S. Denote by MB_{ij} the marginal benefit to the ith country from abatement by the jth country. Thus MB_{NN} is the marginal benefit to N of its own abatement, MB_{NS} is the marginal benefit to N from S's abatement, and so on. The situation is shown in Diagram 5.3.

By assumption, MC_N depicted in the top panel equals MC_S depicted in the bottom panel for all abatement levels. For ease of exposition we assume that all marginal benefits are constant, and that $MB_{NN} = MB_{NS}$ and $MB_{SS} = MB_{SN}$. Additionally, to accord with our assumptions that S is a major beneficial user of

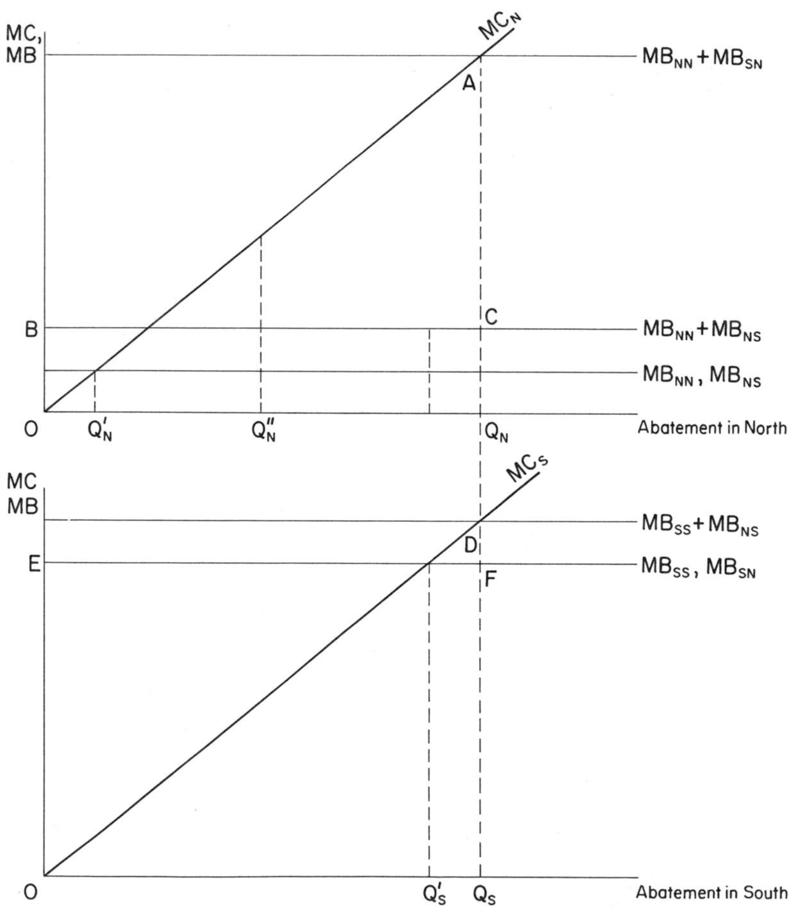

Diagram 5.3. Joint pollution, separable damage functions.

the oceans and that the flow of damages from N to S exceeds the flow of damages from S to N, we make total marginal damages to S, $MB_{SS} + MB_{SN}$, greater than total marginal damages to N, $MB_{NN} + MB_{NS}$, and the flow of damages from N to S, MB_{SN}, greater than the reverse flow, MB_{NS}.

To maximize global welfare, marginal abatement costs in N are equated to total marginal benefits, or $MC_N = MB_{NN} + MB_{SN}$. In country S this optimum is found at $MC_S = MB_{SS} + MB_{NS}$. The globally optimum levels are then Q_N and Q_S, respectively. (The equality of abatement levels results from the assumption of equal marginal costs and the assumed equality of MB_{NN} and MB_{NS}, and MB_{SS} and MB_{SN}.)

Assuming that the only choice is between no abatement and abatement to the optimum levels Q_N and Q_S and that no compensation could be paid, the global optimum would not be achieved. With the reasonable constraint that no country would enter an agreement that makes it worse off, abatement would be suboptimal because at the optimal levels N would be worse off; N would incur a cost of OAQ_N which exceeds its benefits of $OBCQ_N$. In contrast, S would gain because its costs would be ODQ_S, whereas its benefits would be twice the area $OEFQ_S$. Observe also that unilateral abatement, based on a local cost–benefit calculus, would provide some protection to the environment but would be suboptimal from a global perspective. Unilateral action by N in its own self-interest would establish the abatement level Q'_N (where $MC_N = MB_{NN}$). S would choose abatement level Q'_S (where $MC_S = MB_{SS}$).[8]

The conclusions from this theoretical analysis seem quite clear. First, unilateral action by countries based on their narrow cost-benefit calculus will go some distance toward protecting the international resource. The more local the pollution damages (the smaller the external costs passed among countries), the more adequate will be the protection of the resource if countries act in their narrow self-interest. Technical assistance with cost–benefit analysis by industrial countries may, in some cases, encourage developing countries to take protective measures for shared resources that can be shown to be in their self-interest. Local pollution of bays, harbors, estuaries, and coastal zones in developing countries are examples. Second, voluntary agreements among states to limit the pollution of shared resources can encourage each to go beyond their parochially determined abatement levels. Although this may be subject to considerable bargaining, the potential for each being made better off is present. That the ultimate levels of environmental quality chosen may be suboptimal does not mean that the agreements are worthless. Third, in some cases it may be necessary to have some international compensatory system to approach globally optimum abatement levels. Finally if compensation mechanisms are not available, international agreements may be written so that each country is given broad discretion to establish its own standards. This can be seen in the Ocean Dumping Convention. In the extreme, these agreements reduce to a series of unilaterally established standards, and are therefore suboptimal.

One other aspect of the theory of environmental resource management should be mentioned, because it presents special difficulties in an international setting in which no central authority exercises residual rights. The issue is the diversion or shunting of pollutants. The basic problem is common to all environmental resource management. If one form of pollution is strictly controlled, it may simply reappear in another form or at another site. The disposal of sewage sludge is a good example. If burned, it creates atmospheric pollution unless very expensive incineration methods are used. If burning is banned, land disposal may create environmental hazards, including contamination of ground water supplies. If these two options are closed off, ocean disposal of sludge may be practiced, by marine outfalls or ocean dumping.[9] The obvious conclusion is that regulations should be comprehensive about site and disposal media. At a minimum, the prospects for shunting should be considered when regulations are drawn up.

An attempt has been made to do this at the domestic level.[10] Internationally, the problem is more difficult. There is no comprehensive agency charged with managing international resources such as the oceans. The controls that exist are fragmented by the type of pollutant, the method of introduction into the marine environment, and the spatial location. For a number of reasons, mainly attachment to national sovereignty, international controls are more highly developed for ocean-based sources of marine pollution, such as shipping, than for land based sources, such as dirty river discharge. It is possible that strict regulation of one type of pollution may simply divert the pollutants to another disposal site, perhaps more damaging.[11]

ENVIRONMENTAL EXPLOITATION

Developing countries claim that industrial countries make disaproportionate use of the world's resources, especially nonrenewable resources. They also claim (although less frequently) that industrial countries make disproportionate use of the global environment for waste disposal and thereby harm the interests of developing countries. The first assertion can be easily documented for a wide range of raw materials. In Chapter 1 we noted that this is more a reflection of disparities in income than a cause of poverty, and in any event the proper focus is on the price of raw materials entering trade.

The second assertion is of interest here. It cannot be easily documented. If valid, however, it would represent a direct welfare transfer from the poor to the rich, and could reasonably be called environmental exploitation of the South by the North. There are a number of reasons why the assertion is difficult to demonstrate or refute. First, there are major gaps in our knowledge of pollution production rates, the relative contribution of natural and manmade sources (for example, natural oil seeps in the ocean floor), spatial dispersion and dilution, and degradation rates. Second, it appears that for many pollutants the most severe damages, hence the largest environmental costs, are borne by those in the immediate vicinity. Accordingly, as a general proposition, it may be said that most environmental damage costs from industrial country economic activity are borne by the industrial countries themselves. If a particular pollutant is released exclusively in industrial countries and has serious environmental consequences, it does not necessarily follow that developing countries are strongly and adversely affected. Finally, there is a distinction between waste disposal and environmental damages. It has been claimed that environmental media have a capacity to assimilate wastes without causing damage. The damage threshold beyond which wastes become pollutants varies from one waste to another and from one location to another and is subject to controversy.

Still, for some wastes disposed in international common property resources, the issue is not one of environmental damages to developing countries. Rather, the question is, who gets the rent from assimilative capacity?

We have assembled data on four types of global environmental threats—oil in the marine environment, the increase of atmospheric carbon dioxide levels, fluorocarbons released to the atmosphere, and DDT and related pesticides. The purpose is not to build an incontrovertible case for or against exploitation. Rather, the purpose is to investigate in a preliminary manner whether there is substance to the disproportionate use assertion. If so, it would provide a foundation for increased assistance to developing countries in meeting their environmental problems. We are not suggesting direct compensation in the amount of environmental damages inflicted, but rather a justification, founded on more equitable use of the global commons, for supporting environmental programs in developing countries.

Petroleum in the Marine Environment

Acute and chronic pollution of the ocean by oil has a number of adverse effects, some documented and some speculative. The effects range from the potential hazard of eating seafood contaminated by carcinogenic oil compounds to the disamenities of tar lumps on bathing beaches. The long-term effects of low-level chronic oil pollution in the open ocean are generally unknown. It is not our purpose to review oil pollution damage studies but to estimate the relative contribution of industrial and developing countries to marine oil pollution.

Table 5.1 contains estimates, by source, of petroleum hydrocardons introduced into the oceans. The basic data source is work done by the National Academy of Sciences.[12] We modified their work by including two additional features. The first is an attempt to estimate the relative contribution of three groups of countries—industrial, developing, and centrally planned economies—for each method of introduction of oil to the oceans. The techniques are described in the table notes. Second, the table contains a judgment as to whether the oil pollution is primarily local, with damages to the coastal state, or regional or global in nature. This is an imperfect exercise, because it does not account for the proximity of other countries (for example, oil discharged into semienclosed seas such as the Mediterranean) and other factors. Nevertheless, some methods of introduction tend to disperse oil pollution more than others, and a rough judgment can be made.

The table shows the total petroleum discharges to the oceans to be about 5.5 million metric tons per year, excluding natural seepage. Of this, land-based sources account for the majority, 60%, and marine-based sources account for 40%. It is significant that land-based sources are more difficult to bring under international control than marine-based sources, and amounts are determined in part by the incidental effect of national environmental policies. The largest single marine-based source of ocean oil pollution is marine transportation, specifically, normal tanker operations. Contrary to popular opinion, tanker accidents contribute relatively minor volume (less than 4% of all oil reaching the oceans). This does not, of course, measure the relative damages from accidents. The oil spilled or discharged in biologically productive coastal waters is probably most damaging. Dirty river discharge is the largest land-

Table 5.1 World Consumption of Petroleum and Petroleum Hydrocarbons Introduced into the Marine Environment

	World [million metric tons/annum (mta)]	Industrial Countries		Developing Countries		Centrally Planned Economies		Primarily	
		(mta)	(%)	(mta)	(%)	(mta)	(%)	Local	Regional or Global
Consumption of petroleum	2792	1911	68	407	15	474	17		
Marine pollution									
Natural seeps	0.6								x
Marine-based sources									
Offshore production	0.08	0.014	17	0.066	83			x	
Transportation									
Normal tanker operations	1.08	0.842	78	0.216	20	0.022	2		x
Tanker dry-docking and terminal operations	0.253	0.197	78	0.051	20	0.005	2	x	
Bilges and bunkering	0.5	0.380	76	0.095	19	0.025	5		x
Tanker accidents	0.2	0.156	78	0.040	20	0.004	2		x
Nontanker accidents	0.1	0.076	76	0.019	19	0.005	5		x
Land-based sources									
Atmosphere	0.6	0.408	68	0.090	15	0.102	17		x
Coastal refineries	0.2	0.128	64	0.046	23	0.026	13	x	
Other coastal industrial discharges	0.3	0.204	68	0.045	15	0.051	17	x	
Coastal municipal wastes	0.3	0.204	68	0.045	15	0.051	17	x	
Urban runoff	0.3	0.204	68	0.045	15	0.051	17	x	
River discharge	1.6	1.088	68	0.240	15	0.272	17	x	
Totals (excluding seeps)	5.513	3.901	71	0.998	18	0.614	11	2.880	2.633

Notes and Sources. Petroleum consumption data from *International Petroleum Encyclopedia 1975* (Tulsa, 1975).

Estimates for world marine pollution by petroleum hydrocarbons, by source, are taken from National Academy of Science, *Petroleum in the Marine Environment* (1975). A judgment was made as to whether each source produces primarily local (damaging the coastal state) pollution or primarily regional or global pollution. Also, we estimate the relative and absolute contributions to world total by three groups of countries—industrial, developing, and centrally planned economies. The following notes describe NAS estimates and our procedures for classifying between local and regional/global and among country groups.

Natural seeps: Wilson, "Estimates of Annual Input of Petroleum to the Marine Environment," (NAS Background Papers Vol. 1 for *Workshop on Input, Fates, and Effects of Petroleum in the Marine Environment, 1973)* shows that seepage is widely distributed and is therefore considered here as regional or global in nature. A world total was not assigned to country groups because it is not the result of deliberate economic activity.

Offshore Production: The NAS estimate is a combination of small (less than 50 bbls) and large (more than 50 bbls) spills and oily brine discharges. Their estimate generally uses United States discharge data scaled up to global offshore production levels. Except for small spills, they assume foreign operations meet as high pollution standards as the United States. If this is not true, their estimate is understated.

Offshore production is generally close to coastlines and is considered here as local. The total world discharge allocated among country groups on the basis of actual 1974 offshore production rates by country. Data source for offshore production is *International Petroleum Encyclopedia 1975*.

Normal Tanker Operations: Oil discharged from tank washings and oily ballast. The NAS estimate is based on 90% efficiency of load on top (LOT) procedure. It is classified as primarily regional or global on the basis of the spatial pattern of tanker routes and the wide dispersal of oil tar lumps that have been associated with tanker discharge (see NAS Report, Chapter 3). It is allocated among country groups on the basis of their respective shares of world petroleum imports arriving by ocean transport. Data on 1972 imports of crude and refined oil arriving by tanker, by country, is from *UN Statistical Yearbook 1974* (1975). The developing country share includes Caribbean refineries.

Tanker Drydocking and Terminal Operations: Classified as mainly local. This is allocated among country groups on the basis of their respective shares of world petroleum imports that arrive by tanker.

Bilges and Bunkering: This is classified as mainly regional or global because it is vessel source pollution. However, it could be mainly local if most discharge occurred while loading bunker fuel. It is allocated among country groups on the basis of their relative volume of nonpetroleum cargo passing through their ports. Data on cargo tonnage by port is from *UN Statistical Yearbook 1974* (1975). USSR port tonnage is unavailable.

Tanker Accidents: Analysis shows that over 50% of the total oil discharged from tanker accidents occurs more than 50 nautical miles from land, making this source regional or global in scope. See Porricelli and Keith, *Tankers and the U.S. Energy Situation*, 1973. But subsequent Coast Guard data do not support this. See text. This is distributed among country groups on the basis of relative shares of world petroleum imports by tanker.

Table 5.1 (Continued)

Nontanker Accidents: This is considered regional or global, although no firm data are available for location with oil discharge amounts. It is allocated among country groups on the basis of their relative volume of the nonpetroleum cargo passing through their ports.

Atmospheric Fallout: The NAS estimate is quite speculative. The total world petroleum hydrocarbons entering the atmosphere are estimated to be 68 million metric tons. The 0.6 mta figure used by the NAS assumes that the great bulk of hydrocarbons (64 mta) are converted to other substances in the atmosphere, and the majority of remaining hydrocarbons are returned to land. The MIT SCEP study in 1970 estimated this source of marine pollution to be 15 times as large, or 9 mta. See Study of Critical Environmental Problems (SCEP), *Man's Impact on the Global Environment* (Cambridge, Mass.: MIT Press, 1970). The effect is, of course, classified as regional or global. The world total is allocated among country groups on the basis of relative shares of total world consumption of petroleum.

Coastal Refineries: The NAS study apparently made no adjustment for less rigorous environmental standards in developing countries and may underestimate actual discharge. The world total is allocated among country groups on the basis of their respective shares of the total world refining capacity. Capacity data is from *International Petroleum Encyclopedia*, as of January 1, 1975.

Other Coastal Industrial Discharges, Coastal Municipal Wastes, Urban Runoff, River Runoff: Each of these is considered to be primarily local. The technique used by the NAS to arrive at global discharge levels for these four sources was to make estimates for the United States and scale up to global levels on the basis of United States to world petroleum consumption ratio. Here we reverse this, allocating world totals to country groups on the basis of their relative shares of world consumption of petroleum.

based source. There is much question about atmospheric fallout; an earlier estimate was 9 million metric tons per year.

Without taking the classification too seriously, it appears that local pollution is somewhat greater than regional or global pollution, particularly of the high seas. The major source of regional or global pollution is normal tanker operation. This occurs from on-route washing of cargo tanks and using cargo tanks for sea water ballast. The second major source is the assumed regional or global distribution of atmospheric fallout. Although the distinction between local and global ocean oil pollution is not precise, it is important. To the extent that discharge is local, external costs passed on to other countries are less.

With regard to the distribution of pollution activities among country groups, Table 5.1 supports the assertion that industrial countries make disproportionate use of the oceans for waste disposal. The totals show that industrial countries contribute 71% of oil discharged to the marine environment, developing countries 18%, and centrally planned economies 11%.[13] These are speculative estimates. The contributions of 71%, 18%, and 11% compare with oil consumption percentages of 68%, 15%, and 17%, respectively.[14] The low share of pollution by centrally planned economies relative to their consumption of petroleum is because they do not engage extensively in ocean shipping of petroleum.

Although the data indicate that industrial countries make disaproportionate use of the marine environment for disposal of petroleum wastes, they do not show the extent of external costs passed on to developing countries, or even if there is a welfare transfer from poor to rich on this account. To do this would require investigation of the types of damages associated with marine oil pollution, including their economic costs and the distribution of costs among countries.[15] Much of this is unknown.

Some data are available concerning oil spills from tanker accidents and generally confirm the view that oil spill pollution is widespread and affects developing countries. In an analysis of 1416 tanker casualties, of which 269 resulted in oil pollution, Keith and Porricelli found that 56% of the total outflow occurred more than 50 nautical miles from land. Ninety percent of high seas accident outflow was caused by the structural failure of tankers.[16] A partial description of the spatial location, frequency, and outflow from polluting tanker accidents is presented in Table 5.2. Although it is not complete, it suggests that oil spills are widely distributed and may affect developed and developing countries alike. In a more recent analysis for 1973–1975, the Office of Marine Environmental Protection of the Coast Guard estimates that 75% of oil spilled from tankers occurs in harbor and port areas.

Increases in Atmospheric Carbon Dioxide

Increased levels of carbon dioxide in the atmosphere and the relative contributions to the increase by industrial and developing countries are of special interest for a number of reasons.[17] First, CO_2 is not a pollutant in the traditional sense. It does not directly damage human health, vegetation, materials, or aesthetic values.[18] Rather, increased atmospheric CO_2 can affect the global climate, including temperature and weather patterns.

Table 5.2 Location, Frequency, and Size of Tanker Spills

Area	Number of Polluting Incidents	Total Oil Outflow (long tons)
Northwest Atlantic	35	93 049
Northeast Atlantic	78	86 969
Northwest Pacific	27	26 848
Mediterrean Sea	17	17 400
East Indian Ocean (including Arabian Gulf)	11	54 163
Subtotal	168	278 429
Other areas		152 291
Total		430 720

Source. V. Keith and D. Porricelli, "An Analysis of Oil Outflows due to Tanker Accidents," in Environmental Protection Agency, U.S. Coast Guard, American Petroleum Institute, *Proceedings of Joint Conference on Prevention and Control of Oil Spills, 1973.*

Second, the issue of atmospheric concentrations of CO_2 is of truly global significance. Unlike many polluting activities in which externality damages are passed on in part to other countries or to international resources such as the oceans while much of the damage remains local, climate changes resulting from increased CO_2 levels would be neither local nor regional, but global. We show that increases in atmospheric CO_2 levels are mainly the result of fossil fuel used for energy, and industrial countries are mainly responsible. Accordingly, if there is a change in global climate, the consequences will not be borne exclusively by the countries most responsible; they will be shared throughout the global community.

Third, atmospheric CO_2 appears to be the most important source of a global climate change attributable to man's activities. Schneider and Dennett conclude that it is still unclear whether aerosols from fossil fuel combustion have a globally significant direct effect on the earth's radiation (and hence temperature). They do conclude, however, that CO_2 accumulation over the next several decades can cause climate alterations far in excess of the potential thermal effects of energy use. More specifically, the temperature effects of CO_2 may be 10 or more times greater than the global thermal effects from energy use.[19]

Fourth, the CO_2 problem illustrates the class of environmental disturbances characterized by great uncertainty, potentially catastrophic consequences, and very high damage avoidance costs. These points are now elaborated.

Carbon dioxide is a trace gas in the atmosphere, with current concentrations of about 330 parts per million (ppm) or 0.033%. It is important in regulating global temperature. Increased CO_2 levels will intercept larger amounts of infrared radiation emitted from the earth. This will retard the surface cooling rate and produce a "greenhouse" effect, with an increase in global temperatures and an alteration of weather patterns.

There are two areas of scientific uncertainty. The first is the final disposition of CO_2 released by fossil fuel combustion between three sinks: the oceans, the atmosphere, and through photosynthesis to the biomass. The usual assumption is that about 50% of CO_2 released by fossil fuel consumption remains in the atmosphere, with the balance entering the oceans and to a lesser extent the biomass.[20] The major uncertainty is the relative importance of the oceans versus the biomass. The fact that 50% enters the atmosphere has been confirmed by comparing time series of CO_2 released and measured increases in atmospheric CO_2 levels.

The more important uncertainty concerns the impact of increased atmospheric CO_2 on temperature. Schneider has reviewed the literature on surface temperature response to a doubling of atmospheric CO_2 levels to 600 ppm. He concludes that, given the present atmospheric moldeling technique, the best estimate for global temperature increases from doubling atmospheric CO_2 is between 1.5 and 3°C, and that the effect could be several times greater at the polar regions. This range includes the estimate of 2.9°C recently made by Manabe and Wetherald. Broecker notes that the relation between temperature change and CO_2 levels is not linear, but temperature increases as the logarithm of atmospheric CO_2. Accordingly, if a doubling of CO_2 levels leads to a 2.4°C increase in temperature, a 10% increase in CO_2 will raise the temperature by 0.32°C.

What is the relationship between fossil fuel consumption and atmospheric CO_2 levels, and what is the importance of the resulting increase in temperature? The actual level of atmospheric CO_2 has been measured since 1958 at the Mauna Loa (Hawaii) station. It has increased from 315.5 ppm in 1958 to 331.2 ppm in 1975, an increase of 0.9 ppm per year.[21] When studied together with fossil fuel consumption data for this period, the increase is consistent with the assumption of 50% CO_2 retention in the atmosphere.

Pushing the analysis backwards, Broecker estimates the preindustrial CO_2 level to be 293 ppm. Thus the current level of 331 ppm is about 13% higher than in the preindustrial period and is attributable to fossil fuel energy use, mostly in the last three decades. Projecting forward and assuming a 3% year energy growth post 1972, he finds that the atmospheric level will reach 403 ppm by the year 2010. This is an increase of 38% over preindustrial levels and 22% over current levels. Clearly, man's energy use can have a very substantial effect on the atmospheric levels of a gas that is critically involved in maintaining global temperatures.

Assuming that global temperatures increase by 0.3°C for each 10% increase in CO_2 levels, the current (1975) increase in average global temperature attributable to fossil fuels would be about 0.35°C; by the year 2010 it would be 1.1°C. Again, the temperature increase would not be evenly dispersed, but could be several times as great in the polar regions.[22] The economic effects of a change in global temperature of this magnitude (and consequent changes in weather patterns) are unknown. It is not certain whether on balance a warming of 1°C would create net benefits or net costs, nor is the distribution of benefits and costs among countries known. One very rough estimate is that a 1°C decrease in mean annual temperature would have a net cost of $8.5 billion on an annual basis, or $170 billion on a present value basis (5% discount rate).[23] We cannot assume that a warming of 1°C will have net benefits, particularly if the stability of the polar ice fields is threatened. In any event, 1°C changes are large relative to naturally occurring cyclical changes.

A deliberate effort to curtail fossil fuel energy use to moderate temperature change would have enormous economic costs and international distributional consequences. As discussed in Chapter 2, absolute and per capita commercial energy use in rich and poor countries is highly unequal, with per capita use in North America 67 times as great as Africa and 24 times as great as Asia. This suggests two conclusions. First, taking into account population growth and projected increases in industrial countries, an attempt to close the absolute energy gap between North and South use of fossil fuels would surely have a profound impact global temperatures.[24] Second, the disproportionate energy use suggests a disproportionate contribution to atmospheric CO_2 level by industrial countries. We now attempt to estimate this.

The method involves assembling data by region on the types and quantities of fuels consumed.[25] Next, the average carbon content of each fuel is estimated, and the fraction of this carbon that is converted to CO_2 immediately on combustion is calculated. Adjustments are made for nonenergy uses of fuels (asphalt, petrochemical feed-stocks, etc.), and the subsequent conversion of unburned fuel products to CO_2 are added in. Finally, the carbon content of natural gas flared should be added in. The results show the relative contribution of each group of countries to atmospheric CO_2

The procedure involves several difficulties. Both Keeling and Rotty have estimated global CO_2 emissions using world *production* data, but they did not attempt to build up CO_2 emission by region of consumption, since their main interest was an accurate measure of global emissions. Data on production are more reliable than data on consumption. Keeling and Rotty also encountered difficulties in determining average carbon content by fuel. Another problem is that fossil fuel consumption is not the only source of man-induced atmospheric CO_2. The kilning of limestone for the purpose of manufacturing portland cement is another source, estimated by Keeling to be 2% of fossil fuel release of CO_2.

Another source of atmospheric CO_2 is the use of nonfossil fuels for energy—wood, grass, straw, cattle and camel dung, and so on. These may be quite significant for total CO_2 emission, even though they are excluded from official United Nations energy statistics.[26] For example, Chapter 2 pointed out that in 1967 perhaps 4% of global energy came from noncommercial fuels, and in India noncommercial fuels may provide 48% of the total energy consumption. Finally, the incineration of solid wastes, especially in industrial countries, and the widespread practice of agricultural burning, especially slash and burn agriculture as practiced extensively in developing countries, are additional sources of atmospheric CO_2. For example, Grigg cites United Nations estimates that in the 1950s, 33 million square kilometers were used for shifting cultivation, with most presumably subject to slash and burn. This is an area more than twice the size of the world's cropland.[27] The burning of the world's vegetation for fuel or for clearing land presents conceptual as well as data problems. The release of CO_2 from burning is not a net addition to atmospheric CO_2. Some CO_2 would have been released through normal decomposition. Also, the world's vegetation acts as a natural sink for atmospheric CO^2, and reductions in surface vegetation reduce the assimilative capacity of the sink, throwing a greater burden on the atmosphere.

Recognizing these limitations, we assemble in Table 5.3 and Table 5.4 the relative contributions to atmospheric CO_2 of industrial, developing, and cen-

Table 5.3 Global CO_2 Emissions for 1973 by Country Group and by Type of Fossil Fuel or Other Source

	Country Groups			
Emission Source	Developed	Developing	Centrally Planned Economies	World
Coal				
Consumption[a] (million metric tons, mmt)	1025.1	123.8	1003.3	2152.2
Carbon fraction[b]	0.70	0.70	0.70	0.70
Fraction of carbon oxidized to CO_2[c]	0.99	0.99	0.99	0.99
Total carbon in coal converted to CO_2 (Mmt)[d]	710.4	85.8	695.3	1491.5
Lignite				
Consumption (mmt of coal equivilent)[a,e]	81.9	3.2	247.7	332.8
Carbon fraction[f]	0.63	0.63	0.63	0.63
Fraction of carbon oxidized to Co_2[c]	0.99	0.99	0.99	0.99
Total carbon in lignite converted to CO_2 (mmt)[d]	51.1	2.0	154.5	207.6
Total carbon in solid fuel converted to CO_2 (mmt)	761.5	87.8	849.8	1699.1
Liquid fuels				
Consumption[g] (mmt)	1720	309	416	2444
Carbon fraction[h]	0.84	0.84	0.84	0.84
Fraction of carbon oxidized[i] to CO_2	0.975	0.975	0.975	0.975
Total carbon in liquid fuels converted to CO_2 (mmt)[d]	1408.7	253.1	340.7	2001.6
Natural gas marketed				
Consumption ($m^3 \times 10^9$)[j]	836.4	87.1	291.3	1214.8
Carbon content (g/cm^2)[h]	540	540	540	540
Fraction of carbon oxidized to CO_2[h]	0.97	0.97	0.97	0.97
Carbon in marketed natural gas converted to CO_2 (mmt)[k]	438.1	45.6	152.6	636.3
Natural gas flared				
Amount[l] ($m^3 \times 10^9$)	13.9	143.1	12.9	169.9
Carbon content (g/cm^2)[h]	540	540	540	540
Fraction of carbon oxidized to CO_2[h]	1.0	1.0	1.0	1.0
Carbon in flared gas converted to CO_2 (mmt)[k]	7.5	77.3	7.0	91.7
Cement				
Production (mmt)[m]	370.1	114.9	154.0	639.0
Carbon fraction[n]	0.137	0.137	0.137	0.137
Carbon converted to CO_2 from cement production (mmt)	50.7	15.7	21.1	87.5

[a] Consumption data for 1973 by region from *U.N. World Energy Supplies 1970–1973* (1975). Their data are for solid fuels combined (coal and coal equivalent of lignite). We apportion solid fuel consumption between coal and lignite on the basis of relative

Table 5.3 (Continued)

production of each in the three regions. Production data on coal and lignite, by country, from *World Energy Supplies*. We do not follow Rotty in adjusting low-grade coal from the USSR and reallocating it to lignite, because we are interested in the sum of CO_2 emissions from solid fuel.

[b] Carbon fraction, by weight, of coal from Rotty, his Table 1. Note that Keeling was able to use a single carbon fraction for solid fuels (0.683) on the basis of a constant global coal/lignite production ratio. We cannot, because the coal/lignite ratio varies among regions.

[c] The adjustment used by Rotty and Keeling for incompletely burned fuel and nonenergy usages.

[d] Multiply consumption (by weight) by the carbon fraction and the fraction of carbon oxidized to CO_2. This gives the weight of carbon released to the atmosphere. To convert to tons of carbon dioxide, multiply by 3.664 (Keeling).

[e] Tons of lignite have been converted to BTU equivalent tonage of coal.

[f] Carbon fraction, by weight, of coal equivalent of lignite. From Rotty.

[g] Consumption of liquid fuels by region from *World Energy Supplies*. Converted from United Nations million metric tons of coal equivalent back to million metric tons of liquid fuel by dividing by 1.47 (United Nations conversion factor).

[h] From Keeling.

[i] From Keeling. These are net of losses in combustion, as particulates and hydrocarbons that are *not* subsequent oxidized. Our data refer to liquid fuels used as energy and therefore do not include CO_2 emissions that ultimately may result from nonfuel use of fossil fuels, that is, ultimate oxidation of petroleum used for asphalt and petrochemicals.

[j] United Nations consumption data in millions metric tons coal equivalent. Converted to billions of cubic meters at 1000 cm = 1.332 metric tons coal equivalent.

[k] Volume times carbon content per unit volume times fraction oxidized.

[l] Data on amount of flared gas by region from Rotty for 1971.

[m] Production data by country group from *UN Statistical Yearbook 1974* (1975).

[n] From Rotty.

trally planned economies. The general procedure follows Keeling and Rotty. Because the carbon fraction varies among fuels, consumption data is broken down by country groups for the following emission sources: solid fuels (coal and lignite), crude petroleum, natural gas marketed, natural gas flared, and cement production. The data are presented on a flow basis for 1973, the latest year for which comprehensive material is available. Therefore, the estimates are for flow emissions, not cumulated stock contributions.

Table 5.4, which summarizes the calculations, shows total worldwide CO_2 emissions as 4516 million metric tons. Of this amount, about 38% is accounted for by solid fuels (mainly coal), 44% by liquid fuels (petroleum products), 14% by marketed natural gas, 2% by flared gas, and 2% by the kilning of limestone for cement production. With regard to relative contributions, the industrial countries account for 59% (mainly petroleum and products), the developing countries less than 11%, and the centrally planned economies 30%. The developing countries contributed a disproportionate share to flared gas emissions mainly because of their remote production locations, which makes marketing uneconomic, but the amount is quite minor—less than 2% of world total. In summary, the evidence supports the contention that industrial countries contribute a disproportionate share of atmospheric CO_2 emissions.

Table 5.4 CO_2 Emissions by Region and Emission Source: 1973 Summary

Source	Developed Countries	Developing Countries	Centrally Planned Economies	World Totals
	Quantities (million metric tons carbon converted to CO_2)			
Solid fuels	761.5	87.8	849.8	1699.1
Coal	(710.4)	(85.8)	(695.3)	(1491.5)
Lignite	(51.1)	(2.0)	(154.5)	(207.6)
Liquid fuels	1408.7	253.1	340.7	2001.6
Natural gas marketed	438.1	45.6	152.6	636.3
Natural gas flared	7.5	77.3	7.0	91.7
Cement production	50.7	15.7	21.1	87.5
Total (all sources)	2666.4	479.5	1371.2	4516.2
	Percentage World Totals			
Solid fuels	16.9	1.9	18.8	37.6
Coal	(15.7)	(1.9)	(15.4)	(33.0)
Lignite	(1.1)	(0.0)	(3.4)	(4.6)
Liquid fuels	31.2	5.6	7.5	44.3
Natural gas marketed	9.7	1.0	3.4	14.1
Natural gas flared	0.2	1.7	0.1	2.0
Cement production	1.1	0.3	0.5	1.9
Total (all sources)	59.0	10.6	30.4	100.0

Fluorocarbons[28]

Current scientific information suggests that man-made fluorocarbon gases released in the lower atmosphere diffuse slowly up to the stratosphere where they are decomposed by ultraviolet radiation from the sun (biologically active ultraviolet radiation, or UV-B) and release free chlorine atoms. The free chlorine atoms, through catalytic chain reactions, react with ozone, a gas whose molecules have three oxygen atoms, and reduce the ozone concentration in the stratosphere.

The extent of ozone depletion is unknown and has been subject to great controversy. In the spring of 1976, studies conducted by F.S. Rowland, J.E. Spencer, and M.J. Molina suggested that earlier theoretical depletion rates may have been too high, because some chlorine is diverted to the formation of chlorine nitrate and is therefore unavailable for ozone depletion. The very recent report by the National Academy of Sciences concluded that "the effect of chlorine nitrate formation is to decrease the projected ozone reductions by about a factor of 1.85 compared to the values calculated for the CMF's (chlorofluoromethanes) without this reaction."[29] Nevertheless, even accounting for diversion to chlorine nitrate, projected ozone depletion remains a very serious problem.

Ozone is a shield against ultraviolet radiation; reduced ozone concentrations permit increased UV-B to penetrate to the earth's surface. Increased exposure to UV-B causes skin cancer and premature skin aging. There is some speculation, as yet inconclusive, that decreased ozone and increased UV-B may cause chromosome mutations, plant mutations, stunting of plant growth, increased weathering of certain materials, and may inhibit photosynthesis of phytoplankton, disrupting aquatic life in coastal regions.

Perhaps more serious, fluorocarbons released to the atmosphere may effect global climate. One direct effect would be that the accumulation of these inert gases at all levels of the atmosphere may increase absorption and emission of infrared radiation and trap thermal emissions from the earth's surface. This would warm the lower layers of the atmosphere and act in the same direction as increases in atmospheric CO_2. Indirectly, ozone destruction could alter the temperature/altitude profile of the stratosphere and therefore effect the climate at the earth's surface. This process is poorly understood, and even the direction of the effect toward warming or cooling is unknown.[30]

The theory of ozone depletion by fluorocarbons has not been conclusively demonstrated by empirical measurements. One measurement difficulty is that there is a natural variation in ozone concentrations. Daily fluctuations at midlatitudes can be 5-10% and up to 25% between seasons. There are also natural variations at different latitudes. For this reason, "a 5% to 10% decrease in ozone persisting and measured for several years, would be needed before a change could be attributed to man's activities with any statistical reliability."[31] Another reason the theory cannot be empirically demonstrated is the long time delay between the release and ultimate accumulation in the stratosphere. Thus the growth of the fluorocarbon industry is too recent for significant effects to have occurred.

There is somewhat less controversy concerning the direct health effects of decreased ozone protection and increased exposure to UV-B. Increased levels of UV-B increase the incidence of non-melanoma skin cancer (which is rarely fatal but quite common). It may also increase the incidence of the more rare but fatal melanoma type cancer, but the evidence is less conclusive.[32] According to the Federal Task Force on Inadvertant Modification of the Stratosphere (IMOS), a 1% reduction in ozone concentration will lead to a 1.4 – 2.5% (2% median) increase in UV-B radiation. A 1% increase in UV-B radiation will lead to a 0.5 – 2% increase in non-melanoma skin cancer after a long latency period. Therefore, at midlatitudes a 1% reduction in ozone can lead to a 0.7–5% increase in nonmelanoma cancer, with a best estimate of 2%. With current new cases in the United States at 300,000 per year, this implies an increase of 2100 to 15,000 new cases per year, with a medium estimate of 6000, for the United States[33] However, the the IMOS skin cancer estimates were conservative and quite controversial.

To place this in perspective, the IMOS estimated (before the most recent findings) that fluorocarbons released to date and reaching the stratosphere may already have reduced ozone concentrations by 0.5–1% and possibly 2%. When fluorocarbons *already released* reach the stratosphere, the ozone layer will be depleted by 1.3–3%. Note also that the relationship between ozone depletion and increased UV-B radiation is not linear. For larger reductions in ozone, the increase in UV-B radiation is disproportionately larger.[34] Finally, to underline the seriousness of the problem, it should also be noted that the stability of the ozone layer may also be threatened by the atmospheric testing of nuclear weapons, stratospheric flights of supersonic transports (SSTs), and other chemical compounds, including the widely used carbon tetrachloride and N_2O from nitrogen fertilizers.

Time lags play a critical role in recognizing, confronting, and resolving the danger posed by fluorocarbons. There are five important lags: the time between commercial introduction and when fluorocarbons were recognized as a threat to the environment, the time before there is widespread action curtailing their use, the lag between time emitted and accumulation in the stratosphere (transport lag), the time it will take for the ozone layer to recover from depletion, and the time between exposure to UV-B and the development of cancer (estimated to be 15–40 years).

Fluorocarbons were first used in the early 1930s as refrigerants and after World War II as propellants for aerosols. It was not until 1974, more than 30 years after their introduction, that they were recognized as an environmental threat to the atmosphere. Even this might have gone unnoticed had it not been for intense concern for the ozone layer arising from prospective SST flights. The lag between recognition of the problem and curtailment is not yet known. The United States government moved swiftly to set up a study group (IMOS) whose report was filed in June 1975. Earlier work on the SST atmospheric problem laid a useful foundation. Additionally, the National Academy of Science conducted an intensive study of the hazards, and released a report in September 1976. The OECD's Environment Committee met on the issue and developed global use data. Restrictions have not yet been established, however, and both the Food and Drug Administration and the Consumer Products Safety Commission have rejected petitions by several states and environmental organizations for restrictions on F-11 and F-12. Presumably they were awaiting the NAS study, since the FDA finally proposed labeling requirements in November, 1976. As might be expected, the fluorocarbon industry is emphasizing the uncertainty of the studies conducted to date, the importance of the industry in terms of jobs, and the need for more evidence and deliberation before establishing restrictions.

The delay between recognition and restriction may also be a consequence of fragmented responsibility. Within the United States, the authority for regulating fluorocarbons has been split between the Consumer Products Safety Commission (CPSC), the Environmental Protection Agency (EPA), and the Food and Drug Administration (FDA). The CPSC regulates consumer products generally, but is specifically prohibited from regulating motor vehicles and equipment, insecticides and fungicides, and food, drugs, and cosmetics. Accordingly, it could apparently regulate only fluorocarbons used as refrigerants in home refrigerators and air conditioners and fluorocarbons used as aerosol propellants in household items such as window cleaners and spray paint. The EPA could not regulate fluorocarbons under the Clean Air Act. Its responsibility for fluorocarbons appears to be insecticides, fungicides, and rodenticides using fluorocarbon aerosol propellants. The FDA had jurisdictional authority over fluorocarbon aerosol propellants used for cosmetics, drugs, and foods. Automobile air conditioners that use F-11 or F-12 and industrial uses fell between the cracks and could not be regulated under existing statutes. The passage of the Toxic Substances Control Act in October 1976 may improve the regulatory mechanism.

The other lags involve diffusion to the stratosphere and ultimate recovery of the ozone layer. These lags are especially interesting because of the long times involved and the fact that, regardless of what action is taken today, the environmental danger will continue to grow over the next decade. Ultimate reduction in ozone concentration will depend, of course, on future emission rates, but even accepting a single emissions scenario, predictions of ozone depletion change both up and down as new studies are made. The IMOS estimated that ozone reduction to date from past fluorocarbon emissions may be 0.5–1%, and if no new emissions took place, ozone decrease might be between 1.3 and 3% after a time lag of 10 or more years.

The most recent National Academy of Sciences report concluded that, "it appears that their [F-11 and F-12] continued release at the 1973 production rates would cause the ozone to decrease steadily until a probable reduction of about 6 to 7.5 percent is reached with an uncertainty range of at least 2 to 20 percent, using what are believed to be roughly 95 percent confident limits. The time required for the reduction to attain half of this steady state value (3 to 3.75 percent) would be 40 to 50 years."[35] They also concluded that a resumption of the 10% growth rate that had prevailed until 1975 would lead to a 10% reduction in ozone in 23–28 years. Finally, they estimated that a sharp cut-off in the release of fluorocarbons would reduce the ozone depletion, but the perturbation of the ozone layer would continue to grow for 10 years, and another 50 years would be needed for recovery of the ozone layer.

Fluorocarbon Production and Use.[36] There are three major types of fluorocarbons with overlapping end uses—F-11, F-12, and F22. F-11 and F-12 are considered a threat to the ozone layer, whereas F-22 is considered less harmful because of a much shorter atmospheric residence time. However, F-11 and F-12 account for 92% of the cumulative production of the three types and 83% of all fluorocarbons produced in 1974. The growth rate of F-11 and F-12 production has been about 10% in recent years, but it declined by 15% in 1975. It is unknown how much of the decline is attributable to the recession and how much to consumers' awareness of environmental dangers. Total production of F-11 and F-12 since its first manufacture is estimated to be 8.527 million metric tons.[37]

The major end use for F-11 (75%) is as a propellant for aerosol products, with hair sprays and deodorants being the major products. About 15% of F-11 is used as a blowing agent in the production of foamed plastics. F-12 is used as both a propellant and a refrigerant, and the dominant use of F-22 is as a refrigerant. Taking F-11 and F-12 together, aerosol propellant use accounts for 49% of total use in the United States and 55% of total use world wide, whereas refrigerant use accounts for 28% in the United States and 29% worldwide.[38]

Comprehensive data on production and consumption by region are not available, but some incomplete estimates have been made. In 1960 world production of F-11 and F-12 was 171 thousand metric tons, and the United States share was 70%. By 1973, world production had increased to 809 thousand metric tons, but the United States share fell to 43%. In 1975, 45 firms in 23 countries manufactured raw fluorocarbon. Of the 23 countries identified, seven are developing countries (including China), four are in Eastern Europe, and 12 are Western industrial countries.[39] Countries and firms that purchase raw fluorocarbons and manufacture products therefrom are not included.

The best production estimates by region were made by E.I. du Pont de Nemours and Co., who developed and held the patent for fluorocarbons for many years. Table 5.5 is an adaptation of these estimates. Of total 1974 world

Table 5.5 Estimated Production of F-11 and F-12 Fluorocarbons, by Region, 1974

Region	Quantity (metric tons)	Percentage of World Total
World	870 123	100
Western industrial countries	750 333	86.2
Developing countries[a]	13 790	1.6
Eastern Europe and USSR	106 000	12.2

Source. Based on estimates provided by E.I. du Pont de Nemours and Co. and cited in United States and Canada, Report to the Environmental Committee of the Organization for Economic Cooperation and Development, *Fluorocarbons: An Assessment of Worldwide Production, Use and Governmental Issues* (unpublished, Paris, November 1975).

[a] Includes People's Republic of China.

production of F-11 and F-12, 86% took place in Western industrial countries, 12% in Eastern Europe and the USSR, and less than 2% in developing countries. However, production data by region are not identical with regional consumption and emission patterns. Differences can arise from international trade in raw fluorocarbons or products such as aerosol containers and refrigerant units. Moreover, the build-up of inventories and, more important, the delayed emission to the atmosphere in closed cycle refrigerant units also splits production and emission patterns. Without a collection system, however, the low boiling point and low water solubility suggest that, ultimately, almost all fluorocarbons will find their way into the atmosphere.

The most comprehensive estimates of fluorocarbon *emissions* by region were made by A.D. Little and are summarized in Table 5.6. These data are for aerosol and refrigerant use only, but this is about 89% of all fluorocarbon emissions.

Table 5.6 Estimated World Emissions of Fluorocarbons, by Region, 1973

	Aerosol Propellant Emissions		Refrigerant Emissions		Total Aerosol and Refrigerant Emissions	
Region	Quantity (1000 metric tons)	Percentage of Total	Quantity (1000 metric tons)	Percentage of Total	Quantity (1000 metric tons)	Percentage of Total
United States	232	48	96	47	328	47
Europe	170	34	81	39	251	36
Other	86	18	30	14	116	17
Total	488	100	207	100	695	100

Source. U.S. Environmental Protection Agency, Office of Air Quality Planning and Standards, prepared for the EPA by Arthur D. Little, Inc., *Preliminary Economic Impact Assessment of Possible Regulatory Action to Control Atmospheric Emissions of Selected Halocarbons* (Research Triangle Park, N.C.: EPA, 1975) Tables III-6 and III-7.

The data apparently also include F-22, which is not as great a threat to ozone. Of the total world emissions of 695,000 metric tons, aerosol propellants account for 70% and refrigerants 30%. The United States accounted for 47% of total emissions and Europe for 36%. If emissions from Canada, Japan, and Eastern Europe and the USSR were subtracted from the "Other" category on the basis of production, developing countries might release between 3 and 5% of total world emissions. The relative contribution of developing countries to world emissions of 3–5% is given some confirmation by United States export data. United States exports of raw fluorocarbon account for 4% of production. Of this amount, about 60% is destined for developing countries. Accordingly, if other producers follow a similar export pattern and if both trade in products that contain fluorocarbon and production within developing countries is considered, a 4–6% contribution by developing countries appears reasonable.

We conclude that the relative contributions to atmospheric emissions of fluorocarbons on a flow basis may be about 83% for Western industrial countries, 12% for centrally planned economies (excluding China), and 5% for developing countries.

DDT and Other Chlorinated Hydrocarbons[40]

The final global pollutant to consider is DDT and related pesticides. Pesticides can be grouped in several ways. One is by use—insecticides, herbicides, fungicides, fumigants, and so on. A second grouping is by composition—inorganic compounds based on minerals such as copper, lead, and mercury, organic compounds of chlorinated hydrocarbons, and organic compounds of phosphate and carbonate. The distinction between chlorinated hydrocarbon and organic phosphate pesticides is generally on the basis of persistence and toxicity. Chlorinated hydrocarbon insecticides are more persistent (degrade less rapidly) but are less directly toxic to man than organic phosphate insecticides. DDT and related compounds (e.g., aldrin/dieldrin) are persistent chlorinated hydrocarbon pesticides. They are the major focus of this section.

DDT and related compounds appear to be serious pollutants of global significance. They are produced in volume, are toxic to a wide spectrum of organisms, are persistent, and exhibit biomagnification, or concentration as they pass up the food chain. Moreover, they apparently can be transported long distances and are globally (if unevenly) dispersed. They are not frivolous products, but serve important functions in agricultural, public health, and in other uses. Accordingly, restrictions on their use cannot be undertaken lightly.

The extent of the global problem remains speculative. For example, Harvey concludes on the basis of sampling in the North Atlantic that "DDT is not as persistent as once believed and is confined fairly closely (in the ocean) to the point of its introduction," and cites EPA studies that show that the half-life of DDT in naturally illuminated seawater is only about 10 days.[41] Also, it may be that another chlorinated hydrocarbon, polychlorinated biphenyls (PCBs), is more toxic and persistent and presents graver threats, despite the much smaller volume produced. PCBs are not pesticides, but they are widely used in industry for such diverse products as electrical transformers, hydraulic fluids, additives in sealants, and flame proofers.

Another difficulty is establishing the global significance of DDT and related pesticides is inadequate spatial accounting and diffusion models. Pesticides are used in diverse ways for disease control purposes and agriculture. A comprehensive pathways study that accounts for the physical movement of, say, pesticides sprayed on the interior of buildings for malaria control and also insect control in temperate zone agricultural crops is not available. Moreover, the damage done by pesticides that reach the marine environment is subject to controversy. We know that pesticides can be transported long distances through aerial drift during application, vaporization into the atmosphere, and surface water runoff, but quantitative accounting for movement has yet to be accomplished. Indeed, good global data on the spatial pattern of consumption are not available.[42]

Another reason that a comprehensive pathways accounting is difficult to compile is the persistence of these pesticides. DDT introduced to the soil may be immobile until erosion transports it to water courses. During that time it may partially degrade into harmless substances. Therefore, transport models must have a time dimension that includes both physical movement and degradation rates. A final reason for the difficulty in accounting is biomagnification, that is, the pesticides concentrate as they move up the food chain. Biomagnification can be dramatic. For example, one study showed chlorinated hydrocarbons in parts per million (ppm) as follows:[43]

Lake bottom sediment	0.0085 ppm
Small invertebrates	0.41
Fish	3.0–8.0
Herring gulls	3177.

However, the magnification makes a useful final accounting difficult.

Biomagnification is part of a more subtle question. What exactly is meant by a global pollution threat? Fish are not only caught in international waters but are traded internationally. If DDT levels in fish are sufficient to contribute to accumulation in human tissue and if these fish are marketed internationally, is the problem international even if the pesticide did not directly enter international waters or the territory of another country? Less direct and on the same point, is the problem of reduction of species and genetic stocks occasioned by pesticide use. It might be shown that the loss of genetic material or species was entirely internal to one country because of its pesticide usage patterns, but the loss of that stock and these species represents a reduction in ecological "capital" available to all mankind. The issue cuts two ways. Industrial countries have already depleted global ecological capital, and developing countries may be moving along the same path.

It is not our purpose to describe in detail the environmental consequences of pesticide use. Rather, we review the fragmentary evidence to see if a disproportionate disposal pattern can be supported. Global production, trade, and use data by country for either pesticides, organic pesticides, or chlorinated hydrocarbon pesticides are not available. Indeed, aggregate world production data are unavailable. The SCEP, in its earlier study, estimated that global production of DDT was 100 million kg/yr, and the production of the related Aldrin-toxaphene group was also 100 million kg/yr. This was apparently based on United States production data with an assumption that world production was 1.5 times United States production.[44] According to an EPA report based on Tariff Commission data, United States production of Aldrin-toxaphene fell from 54.5 million kg in 1967 to 52.7 million kg in 1971, but reached 64.4 million kg in 1972 and was at that level in 1974. United States production of DDT fell from 46.9 million kg in 1967 to 26.9 million kg in 1970 and was down to 20.4 million kg in 1972.[45] The decline in United States DDT production is attributable to the 1972 EPA prohibition for almost all domestic uses. Accordingly, nearly all DDT produced in the United States is exported. The USDA's *The Pesticide Review 1975*, reports that United States DDT exports in 1974 were 25.6 million kg, about the same average of the previous 5 years.[46] Exports of the Aldrin-toxaphene group were at about 29 million kg in 1973–1974 but were down to less than 10 million kg in 1975. It is unknown if this is the start of a trend or a reflection of the global 1975 recession.

Obviously, production data, even if they were complete, would not indicate the spatial pattern of pesticide uses. International trade in pesticide is large and therefore splits the spatial production and consumption patterns. Instead of production data, we use two incomplete indicators—trade data for pesticides as compiled by the OECD and consumption data compiled by the FAO. Partly because the data do not appear exactly as we would wish and partly because of recent pesticide restrictions in industrial countries, we look at trends as well as current amounts.

Although the United States may be the dominant world producer, it does not dominate international trade in pesticides. In fact, the United States accounts for only about 17% of total OECD exports of insecticide, fungicides, and disinfectants.[47] Therefore, it is necessary to look at the export destination pattern for the entire OECD rather than just the United States. Unfortunately, by using OECD data it is no longer possible to break down chlorinated hydrocarbons from the general group of pesticides.

Table 5.7 displays the growth in world trade in pesticides from 1965–1966 to 1973. The total volume of exports grew from 270,000 metric tons in the earlier period to 605,000 metric tons in 1973, the latest year for which data are available. Although the developing countries increased their imports from 136,000 to 269,000 tons over the period, their market share fell from 50 to 44%.

Table 5.7 OECD Exports of Insecticides, Fungicides, and Disinfectants, Selected Years 1965–1973

	Average 1965–1966		Average 1970–1971		1973	
Destination	Q[a]	Total (%)	Q[a]	Total (%)	Q[a]	Total (%)
Developed countries	94	35	250	52	300	50
Sino-Soviet bloc countries	40	15	37	8	36	6
Developing countries	136	50	192	40	269	44
Total world	270	100	481	100	605	100

Source. OECD *Trade by Commodities, Series C*, various issues.

[a] Quantities in 1000 metric tons.

The table should not be interpreted as indicating the pattern of consumption, because the substantial production for domestic use in industrial countries and, to a lesser extent, in developing countries is not included. Also, volume data are apparently an amalgation of trade in active ingredients and formulated weight. If the production for domestic use were also included, it appears that industrial countries have in the past and continue to consume larger quantities of these pesticides. The material is too aggregated to draw the same conclusion for chlorinated hydrocarbons.

Thc FAO has compiled consumption data by country for various types of pesticides. The data are for agricultural use only and do not include pesticides used for public health and other purposes. Unfortunately, because of incomplete coverage and because some quantity figures are for the weight of active ingredients whereas others are for the formulated weight (including dilutent), aggregation into regional totals can be misleading. The coverage for DDT, however, appears somewhat better. Table 5.8 shows the agricultural consumption of DDT for the periods 1961–1965, 1966–1968, and 1973 for those developed and developing countries for which data are available. According to these figures, world consumption of DDT declined from 45.3 million kg in the 1961–1965 period to 23.6 million kg in 1973. All the decline is accounted for by the reduced use of DDT in developed countries, whose proportion of the total fell from 72 to 51%. In developing countries absolute amounts rose slightly, but their relative share increased sharply from 23 to 45%. Again, these are only suggestive numbers based on incomplete coverage and different definitions.

Table 5.8 Trends in Consumption of DDT in Agriculture

	1961–1965 Average		1966–1968 Average		1973	
	Quantity (100 kg)	Total (%)	Quantity (100 kg)	Total (%)	Quantity (100 kg)	Total (%)
Developed countries	327 385	72	232 165	55	119 560	51
Developing countries[a]	102 593	23	118 834	28	106 984	45
Total available world[b]	453 023		418 538		235 724	

Source. FAO *Production Yearbook*, various issues.

[a] Includes Israel.

[b] Includes Eastern European Countries not shown separately.

Obviously, the industrial countries have not given up all pesticides, but an examination of FAO data does not permit any conclusions. Table 5.9 displays the relative consumption for agriculture of several other chlorinated hydrocarbon pesticides for 1965 and 1973. The exclusion of many important countries, both industrial and developing, limits the use of the data. For example, one could show from FAO sources that developing countries use about 89% of all reported toxaphene (5.2 million kg), but we know from other sources that United States agricultural usage is estimated to be 22.4 million kg.[48]

Table 5.9 Agricultural Use of Selected Pesticides

Year and Pesticide	Percentage of Total Reported Consumption[a]	
	Developed	Developing[b]
1965		
Benzene hexachloride (BHC)	48 (inc. U.S.)	51
Aldrin	67 (exc. U.S.)	28
Dieldrin	67 (exc. U.S.)	31
Chlordane	23 (exc. U.S.)	77
Toxaphane	1 (exc. U.S.)	97
1973		
BHC	22 (exc. U.S.)	77
Lindane	22 (exc. U.S.)	9
Aldrin	96 (inc. U.S.)	4

Source. FAO *Production Yearbook,* various issues.

[a] Total reported consumption includes Eastern European countries.

[b] Includes Israel.

In summary, there appears to be an increase in the relative use of DDT in developing countries over time. However, developed countries have contributed larger amounts to DDT contamination in the past. Additionally, developed countries probably consume larger quantities of both persistent and degradable pesticides than developing countries.

DDT has also been widely used for public health purposes by industrial and developing countries. Its principal use was for vector control for malaria, yellow fever, filariasis, and viral encephalitis. Partly because of insect resistance and partly because alternatives have become available, its main public health use is now malaria control. At its peak, global malaria control use of DDT was perhaps 60,000 metric tons and is now 35,000 metric tons, estimated by WHO to be 15–20% of total DDT produced. Galley estimated that because of the method of application (mainly spraying interior walls of dwellings) only one-thirteenth of global DDT contamination is contributed by malaria control. If this is reasonably correct, the public health use of DDT would be a relatively minor contributor to global DDT pollution.[49] It is interesting that United States exports of DDT for malaria control abroad have declined from 19 million kg in 1967 to 3.6 million kg in 1974. The 3.6 million kg is only 14% of United States DDT exports in that year. Thus the public health use of United States DDT exports appears small relative to agricultural use.[50]

An earlier study done for the World Health Organization suggests that there might be substantial costs in switching from DDT to biodegradable insecticides for malaria control. Rafatjah estimated that the cost of material for annual preventative spraying per million persons protected is $72 thousand with DDT, $371 thousand for Malathion, and $1376 thousand for Propoxur. Including the cost of applications, the figures are $205 thousand for DDT, $637 thousand for Malathion, and $1762 thousand for Propoxur.[51]

ENVIRONMENT IN THE LAW OF THE SEA NEGOTIATIONS

There are few instances in which industrial and developing countries directly negotiate over international environmental issues. One such occasion is the current UN Conference on the Law of the Sea (UNCLOS), and an examination of these negotiations is instructive. Two questions are of central importance: Has the marine environment become an arena for serious dispute between North and South? Is UNCLOS moving toward adequate protection of the marine environment?

To understand environmental issues within UNCLOS, several features of the negotiations should be kept in mind.[52] First, the negotiations have been drawn out, disorderly, complicated and are incomplete. The process began with Ambassador Pardo's 1967 speech to the UN General Assembly urging that the resources of the seabed and ocean floor beyond territorial waters be declared "the common heritage of mankind." In 1970, the UN General Assembly passed a resolution proclaiming that the seabed and its resources beyond national jurisdiction were indeed the common heritage of mankind. The Seabed Committee was enlarged and charged with the responsibility of preparing for a comprehensive law of the sea conference. The first organizational session of UNCLOS met in 1973 (Geneva), and substantive sessions were held in 1974 (Caracas) and 1975 (Geneva). The fourth and fifth sessions were held in New York in 1976. It cannot be assumed that a comprehensive, detailed, and widely accepted treaty will emerge. Part of the difficulty rests with the sheer size of the Conference—141 states and 25 agenda items. Part of the difficulty arises from sharp substantive differences among states and blocs of states.

The multiplicity of issues being simultaneously negotiated is the second feature to bear in mind. The full spectrum of ocean questions is up for discussion, from the breadth of the territorial sea to the freedom of scientific research and from fisheries conservation to regimes for mining manganese nodules on the deep seabed floor. The negotiations touch on one or more vital interests of states. Powerful domestic groups are also involved—military security, hard mineral and offshore oil interests, fisheries groups, commercial navigation, and so on. In these circumstances environmental issues are not often decided on their own merit but incidental to the resolution of other areas accorded higher priority.

It also follows from the multiplicity of issues that simple bloc alignments such as East versus West or North versus South are inadequate for analysis. Countries are grouped along several dimensions: coastal, shelf-locked, and land-locked states; naval powers with global security interests versus regional and small powers; countries with large commercial transport or fishing fleets versus others; mineral exporting states versus importers and those with the technological capability of mining deep seabed minerals, and so on. These cross-cutting cleavages imply that states with common interests in one issue may be directly opposed on other issues. Indeed, there are sometimes major splits among and within domestic interest groups as well, for example, between coastal and distant water fishing interests. The developing countries have maintained considerable unity within the negotiations, a greater unity than would have appeared rational based on the narrow economic interests of individual countries. Still, there are major differences within the Third World with regard to the extent of their access to continental shelves, their position as hard mineral buyers or sellers, their interest in maritime commerce, and so on. As the negotiations progress, the degree of unity slips.[53]

The third feature of the UNCLOS negotiations that should be kept in mind is that they are only one part of a broader process of modifying the historic regime governing the oceans. The earlier regime was characterized by the traditional freedoms of the seas, including the freedom of navigation and the right of capture to fish stocks in the broad area of the oceans beyond narrow territorial waters. The process of asserting coastal state rights to ocean space began with the Truman Proclamation of 1945. At the time, the United States unilaterally laid claim to offshore oil in the continental shelf beyond our three-mile territorial waters. The process of coastal state expansion accelerated with a profusion of coastal state claims, mainly by Latin American countries, to fisheries resources within zones ranging up to 200 miles. The current direction within UNCLOS is toward official international acceptance of economic zones of 200 miles, within which coastal states will have rights to economic resources.

The departures from the historic freedoms of the sea have come about not only through the extension of coastal state control, but also through negotiated restrictions on high seas activities. One purpose has been to limit abuse of the oceans and improve maritime safety. Two of the potentially most important environmental agreements are the 1972 Ocean Dumping Convention, and the 1973 Prevention of Pollution from Ships Convention. Both are voluntary commitments undertaken by states that limit their "right" to pollute the marine environment. The 1972 dumping convention came into force in 1975, and currently 25 states have ratified or acceded to the Convention. Thirteen are developing countries. The 1973 Convention, which has important provisions for limiting oil tanker pollution, is not in force. No country has ratified it, and only three—Jordan, Kenya, and Tunisia—have acceded to it. There have also been a large number of agreements related to conservation of ocean fisheries, but they have not had spectacular success.

The primary motive for replacing the traditional laissez faire regime is the appropriation of the increased wealth of the oceans by coastal states. A subsidiary objective is the improvement of the efficiency with which ocean resources are allocated. Under the old common property system, free access led to its traditional abuses, notably overfishing and depletion of fish stocks, in addition to excessive use of ocean space for waste disposal purposes. In some instances the wealth appropriation motive is clearly dominant. Offshore oil is a good example. In other instances restrictions on activities in ocean space are for the purpose of improving resource allocation (or curbing abuses); the two marine environmental conventions provide examples. In some cases, however, it is not possible to disentangle the wealth appropriation motive from the resource allocation or conservation motive, and this is true for coastal state claims to broad fisheries zones.

The developing countries have been deeply involved in the process of modifying the legal regime of the oceans. They have felt, with considerable justification, that the old regime was formulated by and in the interests of the industrial countries at a time at which many countries in the South were not even independent. Also the prospect for commercial exploitation of manganese nodules from the deep seabed floor provides a potentially important new source of revenues for development. It gives considerable support to the assertion that the resources of the seabed are the common heritage of mankind.[54]

This process of carving up ocean space and awarding it to coastal states has profound implications for the marine environment. Broad reaches of the oceans, including the most biologically productive coastal zones, are being brought within the jurisdiction of coastal states. Thirty-six to forty percent of the world's oceans would fall into 200 mile zones. The United States would have jurisdiction over about 22 million square miles of ocean. On one hand, it can be argued that by removing these areas from their status as international common property resources and placing them under national jurisdiction, the first step toward rational environmental management is being taken. Since coastal states bear the major burden of near-shore environmental damages, they should be given the authority to control activities that might cause environmental harm. However, the opposite argument is compelling. Industrial countries have a rather dismal record of conserving their environmental patrimony. Developing countries burdened by poverty and bent on industrialization may do little better. Removing large areas of ocean space from international status and awarding them to coastal states is risky unless international controls provide a base for national responsibility. Even so, jurisdiction over ocean space will not be a clear-cut all or nothing affair. The process of dividing up the oceans is also accompanied by an "unbundling" of rights. There is an attempt being made to separate out rights by function. The most notable of these is to grant coastal states the right to economic resources within a broad zone, while maintaining the traditional free rights for commercial navigation within this zone and within straits that may be overlapped by expanded (12 mile) territorial seas. The "right" to control pollution arising from commercial vessels within the economic zone is a particularly contentious issue within UNCLOS. It divides coastal states interested in protecting themselves against pollution and major maritime states with an interest in unimpeded navigation. In summary, jurisdiction over ocean space is divided three ways—by function or economic activity (fishing, navigation, offshore minerals), by distance from shore (territorial waters, economic zone, high seas), and vertically (seabed floor, water column, surface, and superadjacent air space). Since pollution can be generated in any one of these divisions, and can be physically transported through these divisions, the task of negotiating reasonable environmental controls is enormously complex.

Within the complicated web of UNCLOS, developing countries generally pursue two basic environmental interests. The first is the right to protect their coastlines from environmental insult, mainly resulting from vessel source pollution. The second is the avoidance, when possible, of international environmental standards that would restrict their rights to establish their own abatement standards. These two objectives are now examined. Although vessel source pollution of the oceans is quantitatively less important than land-based sources, it has been controversial in the negotiations, whereas the control of land-based sources has been neglected. The control of vessel source pollution involves both setting standards and enforcing them. Standards may be for vessel design and equipment, operating procedures, or discharge limits. Enforcement can be by coastal, flag, or port state. The dilemma is to have a system in which coastal states can protect themselves from vessel pollution and at the same time prevent them from conducting arbitrary harassment of commercial marine transport. In general, maritime states favor standard setting authority by international organizations such as The International Maritime Consultative Organization (IMCO), with flag state enforcement. In contrast, developing coastal states and some industrial countries such as Canada have argued for coastal state standard-setting authority and enforcement rights within territorial waters and the proposed 200 mile economic zone. The developing countries position is more insistent, however, with regard to enforcement rights, because some aspire to increase their commercial fleets. In that regard, they are concerned about vesting coastal states with too much standard-setting authority.[55]

The concern of coastal and strait states, including developing countries, for protecting themselves against vessel source pollution may not be simply higher environmental ethics on their part. The broader objective of these states is to secure the economic resources within their coastal zone.[56] Environmental jurisdiction in this region is part of a larger jurisdictional package they seek. As such, extension of their environmental rights is in harmony with and supportive of their claims to the economic resources of the area. In fact, developing countries have not shown much evidence of a strong commitment to clean oceans (nor have many industrial countries). Rather, developing countries have worked toward their second environmental objective—preserving their right to set lower standards.

The economic rationality of dual standards, less restrictive for developing countries, was examined earlier. Here we note that developing countries habitually attempt to insert a statement in conventions and agreements to the effect that abatement measures should reflect the economic capabilities of the countries—a code word for dual standards. For example, Article 3 of the Geneva Single Negotiating Text reads:

> States have the sovereign right to exploit their natural resources pursuant to their environmental policies and they shall, in accordance with their duty to protect and preserve the marine environment, taking into account their economic needs and their programmes for economic development. . . .

Although this was dropped in the revised negotiating text, other examples are found there:

> States . . . shall endeavor to establish global and regional rules, standards and recommended practices and procedures to prevent, reduce and control pollution from land based sources, taking into account characteristic regional features, the economic capacity of developing countries and their need for economic development. (Committee III Text, Article 17, para. 4)

In short, they do not wish to be burdened by rigorous standards that they feel are only appropriate for rich countries.

Apart from the clash between developing countries and maritime states over vessel source pollution and the preoccupation of the developing countries in avoiding burdensome environmental standards, how has the environment fared within UNCLOS? First, it should be recognized that the negotiations are mainly concerned with jurisdictional rather than resource management questions. Consequently, UNCLOS may provide the legal regime within which marine pollution is to be regulated, but it will not provide a detailed management program. Jurisdictional changes may make resource management more or less difficult, but they will not determine the specific abatement levels or instruments to be used.

Second, neither developed nor developing countries have given the environment high priority in the negotiations, despite the contentious nature of vessel source pollution. This can be seen most clearly in the relative lack of attention given to important land-based sources of marine pollution and in the failure to press for a comprehensive international marine environment protection agency, with broad powers over most pollution sources. It was apparently accepted early that there was no hope for agreement on controlling land-based sources, despite their enormous importance to the quality of the marine environment.[57] Also, there was never any serious discussion of an international agency with standard-setting and enforcement authority for marine environment control, despite the ecological unity of ocean space and sound economic arguments for a comprehensive environmental program for the oceans.[58] This inattention and disinclination to view the oceans as an ecological unity is shared by most participants.

More specifically, the text as it now stands contains a general obligation to protect the marine environment, calls for regional and global cooperation, and advocates technical assistance to developing countries for marine pollution control.[59] The last point contains no specific obligations or implementing mechanisms. There follows a series of provisions dealing with marine pollution by source: land-based sources, seabed exploitation under national jurisdiction (i.e., offshore oil production), deep seabed mining, ocean dumping, vessel source pollution, and atmosphere. There are subtle differences among these provisions, but the general format is to have states endeavor to establish international standards and regulations by source, and for states to establish national regulations in light of the international standards. There are two weaknesses in this approach. First, in most instances international standards have not been formulated, and unless and until they are, there is no floor provided for national standards. Even when international rules exist (for example, ocean dumping), the international rules leave very wide discretion to national governments. Second, the drafting requires national laws to "be no less effective than international rules," which is weaker than a requirement for equal stringency. In sum, developing countries and others who do not wish to be burdened by international pollution standards have little to fear from the draft text of the treaty.[60]

Another disturbing feature of the text is the ambiguity of environmental controls on deep seabed mining. The Conference is proposing the establishment of an "International Seabed Authority" to control the exploitation of seabed manganese nodules. The Authority has both a development mandate and an obligation to prevent pollution and contamination. This may pose a conflict of interests. Moreover, there is a question as to whether the Authority would have control over just the seabed and ocean floor, or in addition, the superadjacent water column and surface activities. It is not known whether manganese nodules will be processed at sea or transported to land. If they are processed at sea, it will be the processing that poses the greater environmental threat. If the control of the Authority does not extend to surface activities, the most serious potentially polluting activity will have escaped regulation by the Authority.

The final point is that developing countries have largely refrained from using UNCLOS as a forum for attacking the industrialized countries on the issues of disproportionate waste disposal and environmental despoliation of the oceans. They have not pointed to environmental mismanagement by industrial countries, although examples would have been easy to cite, nor have they requested compensation for any alleged damages done to them or insisted that the industrial countries cease polluting the global commons. Rather, they have attempted to protect themselves against the most visible threat—oil tanker spills—and to reserve the right to take less stringent environmental control measures.

CONCLUSIONS

This Chapter has analyzed certain difficulties in controlling transnational pollution from a theoretical perspective. The theoretical material was supplemented by examining four pollutants of alleged global significance and by examining environmental issues within a major international negotiation, the UN Law of the Sea Conference. What conclusions emerge?

First, it appears that transnational pollution problems can be usefully analyzed by using the environmental externality/market failure framework and by moving up from the level of externalities among individuals to the level of externalities among countries. This framework and its major conclusion, that a system of bribes or compensation payments is necessary for efficient environmental controls, is most relevant for problems wherein the environmental damages and abatement costs are visible and amenable to quantification.

It can be shown that the failure to develop an international payment network has already affected the form and content of international environmental controls. For example, the Ocean Dumping Convention, which has been ratified, delegated most responsibility for specific controls to the members, thereby escaping the dilemma of imposing controls on members that are in the global interest but not in the narrower interests of a particular member. In contrast, the Prevention of Pollution from Ships Convention requires members to undertake very specific and costly abatement measures that may go beyond the narrow interests of a particular state. It is significant that this convention has not been ratified by any major maritime state. Finally, the absence of an international payment network is in part responsible for the failure of the Law of the Sea Conference to take up control of land-based sources of marine pollution in a serious manner.

Elevating externality theory to the analysis of transnational pollution explains only part of the story. Alternative approaches are needed, especially for global problems and those subject to great scientific uncertainty. For the fluorocarbon issue, the dominant features are the total innocence that characterized its use for decades and the rapidity with which the international scientific and bureaucratic communities have responded. It is still too early to judge whether effective controls will be established. It would not be fair to say that there has been deliberate exploitative use of the global environment by one group of countries because they knew that some of the damages were external to themselves. This suggests it is useful to distinguish between inadvertant and deliberate transnational pollution. It also suggests that for the inadvertant category of pollution problems, predictive and preventative work is perhaps more critical than difficulties in establishing international controls.

A second conclusion is that transnational pollution problems are not really dominated by a North-South split. It appears that the industrial North contributes a disproportionate share of certain global wastes, but the second part of the North-South exploitative proposition—that this results in a net welfare transfer from South to North—cannot yet be conclusively demonstrated. Also, welfare transfers among industrial countries are likely to be at least as important as those between rich and poor countries. Recognizing this uncertainty, all that can be said is that the major burden for reducing global waste release must be borne by the industrial countries. More generally, it is our belief that global environmental problems should not be mainly viewed as a cause or consequence of international disparities in income; therefore, they should be a minor aspect of North-South disputes.

Although in general the developing country contributions to global environmental problems is small relative to industrial countries, there are aspects of the global problems that require the cooperation of developing countries for effective solutions. This certainly is the case for DDT and other persistent pesticides. The enforcement of oil discharge controls on developing country tanker fleets is another example. Obviously, a successful Law of the Sea Conference requires the support of many developing countries. If the preservation of wildlife and wilderness areas located in developing countries is truly an interest of the industrial countries, better cooperation in this area is also essential.[61] The need for developing country cooperation and the disproportionate waste loads placed on global commons by the industrial countries suggest that a generous flow of assistance from North to South for environmental protection would be desirable.

NOTES

1. For an introduction to the literature on transnational pollution, see Organization for Economic Cooperation and Development, *Problems of Transfrontier Pollution* (Paris: OECD, 1974); OECD, *Economics of Transfrontier Pollution* (Paris: OECD, 1976); and Part III of Ingo Walter, Ed., *Studies in International Environmental Economics* (New York: Wiley-Interscience, 1976). See also OECD, "Recommendations of the Council on Principles Concerning Transfrontier Pollution," Paris, November 21, 1974.
2. Larry E. Ruff, "The Economics of Transnational Pollution," in OECD, *Economics of Transfrontier Pollution*, p. 8.
3. As explained in Chapter 1, the failure to develop an international market for expressing preferences in monetary form is also a problem with regard to wildlife and wilderness areas located in developing countries.
4. For a statement of the Theorem and extensions, see R. H. Coase, "The Problem of Social Costs," J. Dales, "Land, Water, and Ownership," and G. Calabresi, "Transactions Cost, Resource Allocation and Liability Rules," all reprinted in Robert Dorfman and Nancy Dorfman, Eds., *Economics of the Environment* (New York: Norton, 1972).
5. Paul Burrows, Charles K. Rowley, and David Owen, "Operational Dumping and Pollution of the Sea by Oil: An Evaluation of Preventative Measures," *Journal of Environmental Economics and Management*, **1**, No. 3 (November 1974) p. 202.

6. The Metula was bound for a Chilean port. It was a major disaster, spoiling 40 miles of coastline and doing extensive damage to fisheries. See *Washington Post,* February 14, 1975. The Caspian fish catch data exclude herring, which were not caught in the earlier period. Sturgeon catch is down 83%. Overfishing may also be implicated. See A. G. Kasymov, "Industry and Productivity of the Caspian Sea," *Marine Pollution Bulletin,* **1,** No. 7 (July 1970).
7. These ideas are developed more fully in Charles S. Pearson, "International Externalities: The Ocean Environment," in Ingo Walter, *Studies in International Environmental Economics.*
8. If we allow for intermediate abatement levels between zero and the global optimum, the negotiations and outcome become more complicated. For example, if N were certain that S would move to its parochial optimum of Q'_S, equating MC_S with MB_{SS}, then N would move to its parochial optimum at Q'_N (where $MC_N = MB_{NN}$), but would have no incentive to go further. Alternatively, S might "demand" that N move to a higher level, say, Q''_N in exchange for abatement at Q'_S. This would be feasible, because both countries would be better off, but it is not a necessary outcome. Game theory analysis appears appropriate.
9. For example, sewage sludge is dumped in the New York Bight by metropolitan New York and New Jersey, and Philadelphia dumps sludge 40 miles east of Ocean City, Maryland. Upgrading of sewage treatment and the lack of appropriate land disposal sites are said to be the reasons for ocean disposal. Council on Environmental Quality, *Environmental Quality, Seventh Annual Report* (Washington, D.C.; GPO, 1976) p. 278.
10. For example, in the development of effluent guidelines for water discharge, the Environmental Protection Agency attempts to identify significant air or solid waste pollution problems that might arise from controlling effluents. Also, the 1973 United States ocean dumping legislation requires the EPA to consider the financial and environmental impact of using alternative disposal methods.
11. Two possible examples come to mind. The requirement that tankers be fitted with slop tanks to retain oily wastes from cargo tank cleaning will only be effective if adequate on-shore receiving stations are established. Also, if stringent controls are ultimately placed on refining manganese nodules at sea, some refining activity may be shifted to less regulated, but more damaging coastal sites. See Robert E. Osgood et al., *Toward A National Ocean Policy 1976 and Beyond,* report prepared for National Science Foundation (Washington, D.C.: GPO, 1976).
12. Ocean Affairs Board, Commission on Natural Resources, National Research Council, *Petroleum in the Marine Environment* (Washington, D.C.: National Academy of Sciences, 1975) Table 1.5.
13. Pollution from refineries and offshore production in developing countries is allocated to them even though the oil may be destined for industrial country markets. The justification is that these activities are nominally under the control of the country in which they are located. However, oil discharged from tankers has been allocated to the importing country, not the tanker flag state.
14. Not surprisingly, since some pollution categories were allocated on the basis of consumption.
15. For a summary description of the biological effects, see National Academy of Sciences, *Petroleum in the Marine Environment.* For an attempt to measure the economic cost of oil pollution, see International Maritime Consultative Organization (IMCO) Report of Study No. VI, *The Environmental and Financial Consequences of Oil Pollution from Ships,* prepared by the Programmes Analysis Unit of the UK Department of Trade and Industry, 1973.
16. See V. Keith and D. Porricelli, "An Analysis of Oil Outflows due to Tanker Accidents," in EPA, Coast Guard, American Petroleum Institute, *Proceedings of Joint Conference on Prevention and Control of Oil Spills 1973.* A more recent and comprehensive study by Card, Ponce, and Snider supports this. See "Tanker Accidents and Resulting Outflows 1969–1973," in EPA, Coast Guard, American Petroleum Institute, *Proceedings of Joint Conference on Prevention and Control of Oil Spills* 1975.
17. For earlier surveys of the problem, see Study of Critical Environmental Problems (SCEP), *Man's Impact on the Global Environment* (Cambridge, Mass.: MIT Press, 1970) and William H. Matthews, Frederick E. Smith, and Edward Goldberg, Eds., *Man's Impact on Terrestrial and Oceanic Ecosystems* (Cambridge: MIT Press, 1971). Concerning the effects of CO_2 on climate, see Syukuro Manabe and Richard T. Wetherald, "The Effects of Doubling the CO_2 on

the Climate of a General Circulation Model," *Journal of the Atmospheric Sciences,* **32,** No. 1 (January 1975) p. 3; Wallace Broecker, "Are We on the Brink of a Pronounced Global Warming?" *Science,* **189,** No. 4201 (August 8, 1975) p. 460; Stephen H. Schneider, "On the Carbon Dioxide-Climate Confusion," *Journal of the Atmospheric Sciences,* **32,** (November 1975) p. 2060. Concerning the climate impact of both CO_2 and waste heat from energy production, see Stephen H. Schneider and Roger D. Dennett, "Climatic Barriers to Long Term Energy Growth," *Ambio,* **4,** No. 2 (1975) p. 65. For the effect of increased CO_2 on terrestrial vegetation, see Daniel B. Botkin, "Natural Eco-Systems and the Industrial Production of Carbon Dioxide," Appendix to Section III, National Academy of Sciences Committee on Mineral Resources and The Environment Report, *Mineral Resources and the Environment* (Washington, D.C.: NAS, 1975).

18. Indeed, increased CO_2 levels can stimulate vegetation growth. See Bodkin, "Natural Eco-systems."
19. Schneider and Dennett discuss regional "heat islands" that can disturb the natural regional climate. Broecker states that CO_2 is the only man-induced source of climate change that can be conclusively demonstrated to be globally significant.
20. SCEP, Broecker.
21. Data supplied by National Oceanic and Atmospheric Administration based on work by Keeling. Note that the year to year increases are not constant.
22. Broecker argues that the CO^2 -induced increase in temperature over the past 30 years has been more than offset by a natural cooling and that the natural cycle will soon reverse and reinforce the CO_2 effect.
23. Ralph C. d'Arge, "Transfrontier Pollution—Some Issues on Regulation," in Ingo Walter, Ed., *Studies in International Environmental Economics,* p. 271.
24. Schneider and Dennett discuss the adverse impact of curtailing energy growth on developing countries.
25. This procedure draws heavily on the work by Keeling and Rotty. See Charles D. Keeling, "Industrial Production of Carbon Dioxide from Fossil Fuels and Limestone," *Tellus,* **25,** No. 2 (1973) p. 174 and Ralph M. Rotty, "Commentary on and Extension of Calculative Procedure for CO_2 Production," *Tellus,* **20,** No. 5 (1975) p. 508.
26. UN Statistical Papers, Series J No. 17, *World Energy Supplies,* 1974. Some countries such as Brazil rely on wood charcoal for iron and steel production.
27. David B. Grigg, *Agricultural Systems of the World: An Evolutionary Approach* (Cambridge: Cambridge University Press, 1974) p. 60.
28. The two fluorocarbon compounds most seriously implicated in ozone reduction are fluorocarbon 11 ($CFCL_3$) and fluorocarbon 12 (CF_3CL_2). They are sometimes referred to as F-11 and F-12.
29. Panel on Atmospheric Chemistry, Committee on Impacts of Stratospheric Change, Assembly of Mathematical and Physical Sciences of the National Research Council, *Halocarbons: Environmental Effects of Chlorofluoromethane Release* (Washington D.C.: National Academy of Sciences, September 1976) p. 8–23. The original paper describing the fluorocarbon threat was M. J. Molina and F. S. Rowland, "Stratospheric Sink for Chlorofluoromethanes—Chlorine Atom-Catalyzed Destruction of Ozone," *Nature,* **249** (1974) p. 810. For descriptions of the stratospheric effects and the effects of reduced ozone, see Interdepartmental Committee for Atmospheric Sciences, Federal Council for Science and Technology, *The Possible Impacts of Fluorocarbons and Halocarbons on Ozone* (Washington, D.C.: GPO, 1975); Interagency Task Force on Inadvertant Modification of the Stratosphere (IMOS) Federal Council for Science and Technology and Council on Environmental Quality, *Fluorocarbons and the Environment* (Washington, D. C., June 1975); National Academy of Sciences, Climatic Impact Committee, *Environmental Impact of Stratospheric Flight: Biological and Climate Effects of Aircraft Emissions in the Stratosphere* (Washington, D.C.: National Academy of Sciences, 1975); and U. S. Department of Transportation, Climatic Impact Assessment Program (CIAP), *The Effects of Stratospheric Pollution by Aircraft* (Washington, D.C., 1974). The most recent comprehensive reports were done for the National Academy of Sciences; these are *Halocarbons: Environmental Effects of Chlorofluoromethane Release,* cited above, and Panel on Atmospheric Chemistry, Committee on Impacts of Stratospheric Change, Assembly of Mathematical and

Physical Sciences of the National Research Council, *Halocarbons: Effects on Stratospheric Ozone* (Washington, D. C.: National Academy of Sciences, September 1976).

30. See *Halocarbons: Environmental Effects of Chlorofluoromethane Release,* p. 61.
31. United States and Canada, Report to the Environment Committee of the Organization for Economic Cooperation and Development, *Fluorocarbons: An Assessment of Worldwide Production, Use and Environmental Issues* (Paris, unpublished, November 1975) p. 8.
32. The mortality rate for non-melanoma cancer is less than 1%. The rate for melanoma cancer is over 40%.
33. One method for estimating the relationship between UV-B and skin cancer is to relate skin cancer incidence and UV-B exposure that varies according to latitude. The relation shows a doubling of non-melanoma cancer for every 8–11° decrease in latitude. Light-skinned persons are more likely to develop skin cancer.
34. The Natural Resources Defense Council and the Environmental Defense Fund, in a petition to restrict the use of fluorocarbon in cosmetics, drugs, and food, estimated 60–200,000 additional cases of cancer from a 10% loss of ozone and 4000–12,000 additional deaths per year.
35. *Halocarbons: Environmental Effects of Chlorofluoromethane Release,* pp. 1–4.
36. For production and consumption data see IMOS, *Fluorocarbons and the Environment;* U. S. Environmental Protection Agency, Office of Air Quality Planning and Standards, prepared by the EPA by Arthur D. Little, Inc., *Preliminary Economic Impact Assessment of Possible Regulatory Action to Control Atmospheric Emissions of Selected Halocarbons* (Research Triangle Park, N.C.: EPA, 1975); U.S. Department of Commerce, Bureau of Domestic Commerce Staff Study, *Economic Significance of Fluorocarbons* (Washington, D.C., 1975); U.S. and Canadian Report to the OECD, *Fluorocarbons: Production, Use, and Environmental Issues.* Probably the most accurate data on worldwide production since 1931 was collected in a survey of 20 companies by the Manufacturing Chemists Association in 1975 and 1976. See report by Alexander Grant and Company to the Manufacturing Chemists Association, "Environmental Analysis of Fluorocarbons F-11, F-12, and F-22" (mimeo, 1976).
37. Manufacturing Chemists Association, "Analysis of Fluorocarbons" and U.S. Canadian Report to the OECD, *Fluorocarbon Production, Use, and Environmental Issues.*
38. See National Academy of Sciences, *Halocarbons: Environmental Effects,* Tables 3 and 4, pp. 3–12, for a summary of consumption by end use.
39. U.S. Canadian Report to the OECD, *Fluorocarbon Production, Use, and Environmental Issues.*
40. The literature on pesticides is large. For a detailed earlier survey see U.S. HEW, *Report of the Secretary's Commission on Pesticides and Their Relationship to Environmental Health* (Washington, D. C.: GPO, 1969). See also Midwest Institute prepared for Council on Environmental Quality and Environmental Protection Agency, *Production, Distribution, Use and Environmental Impact Potential of Selected Pesticides* (Washington, D.C.: EPA, 1974). For material on DDT in the marine environment, see SCEP, *Man's Impact on the Global Environment* and Matthews, *Man's Impact on Terrestrial and Oceanic Ecosystems,* cited earlier. For a view that deemphasizes the problem, see Rita Gray Beatty, *The DDT Myth: Triumph of Amateurs* (New York: John Day, 1973).
41. George R. Harvey, "DDT and PCB in the Atlantic," *Oceanus,* **18,** No. 1 (Fall 1974) p. 18.
42. SCEP estimates that 25% of all DDT produced has reached the oceans. The major route appears to be through the atmosphere. See Mathews et al., *Man's Impact on Ecosystems.*
43. J. J. Hickey, J. A. Keith, and F. B. Coon, "An Explanation of Pesticides in a Lake Michigan Estuary," cited in Council on Environmental Quality, *Integrated Pest Management* (Washington, D.C.: GPO, 1972).
44. Matthews et al., *Man's Impact on Ecosystems,* p. 279.
45. CEQ, EPA, *Production, Distribution, Use and Environmental Impact Potential of Selected Pesticides.*
46. U.S. Department of Agriculture, *The Pesticide Review 1975* (Washington, D.C.: USDA, 1976) p. 21.
47. Standard International Trade Classification (SITC) number 5992.
48. CEQ, EPA, *Production, Distribution and Use of Selected Pesticides,* Table 1. United States

production of all synthetic organic pesticides rose from 1965 to 1968, declined in 1969 and 1970 and has continued to rise through 1974. See USDA, *The Pesticide Review 1975*, Table 1.

49. R. A. E. Galley, "The Contribution of Pesticide Used in Public Health to the Pollution of the Environment," World Health Organization (WHO) Document: WHO/VBC/71.326, 1971–1972.

50. USDA, *The Pesticide Review 1975*.

51. H. A. Rafatjah, "Operational and Financial Implications of Replacing DDT in the Malaria Eradication Programme," World Health Organization, *Mondaile de la Santé*, 72.768 (1972).

52. For an analysis of United States interests in the oceans, see Robert E. Osgood, Ann L. Hollick, Charles S. Pearson, and James C. Orr, *Toward a National Ocean Policy: 1976 and Beyond*, prepared for the National Science Foundation (Washington, D.C.: GPO, 1976). As of this writing, the most important Conference document is the "Revised Single Negotiating Text" that emerged from the Spring 1976 session.

53. See Roger D. Hansen, "The North South Split and the Law of the Sea Debate" and Terry Leitzell, "Commentary," in *Perspectives on Ocean Policy* prepared for National Science Foundation by Johns Hopkins School of Advanced International Studies, Ocean Policy Project (Washington, D.C.: GPO, 1974). It was not until the fourth (New York) session that the "geographically disadvantaged" states (land-locked and shelf-locked) became an active and cohesive group.

54. Technological advance is the major force that has made the old legal regime obsolete. Technology has increased the wealth to be gained (e.g., offshore oil exploitation) and increased the allocative inefficiencies of free access (e.g., overfishing).

55. Richard A. Frank, "Testimony before the National Ocean Policy Study of the Committee on Commerce of the U.S. Senate," June 3 and 4, 1975.

56. Another objective is institutional control over seabed manganese nodule mining.

57. Frank notes, "It has been generally assumed that the Law of the Sea Treaty would treat the land-based pollution problem in vague terms, and that assumption has turned out to be true." *Testimony*, p. 63.

58. A draft treaty submitted by Malta in 1971 that would have reversed the laissez faire approach to the high seas and limited unfettered sovereignty within areas of national jurisdiction was not vigorously pursued.

59. For a more detailed analysis, see Robert J. McManus, "LOS: Present Status of Environmental Issues," Environmental Protection Agency memo, June 3, 1976.

60. According to Frank, developing countries, led by Brazil and India, beat back an attempt to have a stronger international control over nonvessel activities within the economic zone. Frank, *Testimony*, p. 64.

61. Note that to some extent industrial countries can impose controls on developing countries. A ban on fluorocarbon production within the OECD countries would cut back (perhaps temporarily) use in developing countries. If the major maritime states insist on tankers constructed with segregated ballast tanks, it is unlikely that traditional tankers will be built to serve minor markets in developing countries.

Chapter 6

AGRICULTURE AND ENVIRONMENT IN DEVELOPING COUNTRIES

OUTLINING THE PROBLEM

The world's population has faced a continuing struggle between food needs and food production. Agriculture has evolved over the millenia in response to increased population and new technologies; demographic changes have followed the expansion of grain cultivation from their areas of origin; societies have prospered and declined with the productivity of their agriculture. In the West, the Industrial Revolution was propelled by an earlier revolution in agriculture that introduced scientific farming techniques. Improvements in agricultural productivity released a vast workforce for industry first in Western Europe and later in North America. Simultaneously, the growing scarcity of agricultural labor stimulated the use of technology and capital. For 200 years agriculture in the West has been driven by capitalization, mechanization, and applied research.

Fears of widespread famine have never been absent in many regions and persist to the present day. The global record of the first half of this century is impressive, and since midcentury production growth has accelerated. However, population growth, primarily in the developing countries, has almost matched production increases. When total output is converted to per capita amounts, the record in developing countries is not reassuring. Moreover, regions are not equally self-sufficient in food. Although there is no reason why every region should attain food self-sufficiency, trends in the pattern of food deficits are disturbing. Food deficits as measured by reliance on imports are appearing in many developing countries that are least able to afford sustained food imports. At the same time, the number of countries that enjoy substantial food surpluses and serve as export centers has been reduced, and they are almost all rich countries. Looking forward, population growth over the next 35 years is inescapable and will be dramatic. The current world population of about 4 billion may double to 8 billion. Developing countries that already account for over 70% of the total will find that their populations will more than double in the period. Population growth means greater food needs, and if incomes are rising, still greater amounts will be demanded.

To increase food production, it is necessary to maintain and improve the productivity of agricultural resources, but in attempting to increase food output, the productivity of agricultural resources themselves can be undermined. Hence the fundamental problem: how to secure additional food needed to feed larger populations without threatening the very basis of food production systems. Developing countries have no choice but to take agricultural environmental problems seriously if they wish to feed their growing populations.

The problem should be viewed from two perspectives. Agriculture is a deliberate modification of the natural environment. Change in that environment is inevitable, but the natural environment also shapes and constrains the practices of agriculture and helps determine yields. Therefore, this chapter addresses two issues: the likely environmental consequences of increased cereal production in developing countries and the environmental constraints that may limit production growth. Although the issues are complex and the data are scarce, a start can be made.

Before undertaking the main work of the chapter, it is useful to note some characteristics of environmental problems in agriculture that set it apart from industry. As implied previously, environmental problems in agriculture are more likely to affect output directly and strongly than those in the industrial sector. Environmental damage from agriculture is often to the resource base itself, especially soils. In contrast, environmental damage from industrial production is more apt to be external to the industrial sector and affects human health, amenities, or even productivity in agriculture through crop damage from air pollution.

Another distinction between industry and agriculture is that environmental controls must shift in emphasis from pollution abatement to avoiding destructive practices. Although examples of pollution are frequent in agriculture (e.g., fertilizer runoff), the problem is corrected by altering agricultural practices rather than attempting to collect and treat pollutants. For many other environmental problems in agriculture (such as erosion), the concept of pollution abatement or waste treatment loses meaning. Correction must come about by improved cultivation practices. This means an entirely different set of issues in devising environmental control policies for agriculture than for industrial pollution. Specifically, in the developing world it means taking measures that will guide or alter the production practices of literally hundreds of millions of cultivators. The role for economic instruments—incentives and disincentives—may be larger or smaller, but it will certainly be different from industrial pollution control.

A further difference is found in the type of economic analysis that is most appropriate. The basic and powerful economic interpretation of industrial pollution rests on the theory of externalities and the common property resource nature of environmental media. Neither of these must be abandoned when the discussion shifts to agriculture. Downstream sedimentation from upstream agriculture is a classic environmental externality, but in many instances agricultural production damages the soil itself, and the theory of externalities appears to lose some explanatory force. To put the question differently, why do farmers practice destructive farming, threatening the longer term productivity of the soil?[1] Part of the answer may be ignorance, but there are more satisfying answers that reveal the close link between property rights and the maintenance of soil quality.

The example of overgrazing pasture lands owned in common is well known and fits within the externality and collective goods theory. It is in no one's self-interest, acting alone, to limit the number of his animals grazing the commons. To do so would be to reduce his share of grazing services without appreciable effect on the quality of the pasture. However, if all herdsmen act in this manner, the number of animals exceeds the maximum sustainable yield of the grazing land, the land deteriorates, and all are made worse off. This is an example of mutual external diseconomies. Industry tends to exhibit more unidirectional externalities. Another land tenure failure that is widely recognized arises when tillers do not own their own land but are on short-term tenancy. In this situation they have inadequate incentive to invest in soil conservation and nutrient maintenance measures. Indeed, if they are free to move on, they will have an incentive for short-term gain at the expense of long-term soil quality. Mining the soil is profitable for the cultivator if he does not exercise ownership and can or must move to other land.

Finally, there is the abuse of new lands. If land were truly a free good in abundant supply, a government policy of unlimited access and no requirements for maintaining soil quality might be rational. But to qualify as being economically abundant—that is, a true free good—not only must the current return to land be zero, but also the present value of future returns must be zero to justify a policy permitting soil deterioration. There are two ways in which the policy toward new lands can easily go astray. The first is that the existence of large tracts of currently uncultivated land leads governments to believe that it is abundant, or a free good. The future value of the land is given little or no weight, and the settlement of new lands is uncritically encouraged. The second misconception is that cultivation will invariably increase the value of land. The misconception results from incorrectly attributing the value of capital improvements (clearing, fencing, access, etc.) to the fertility of the land itself. It is probably common that the total value of land including capital improvements increases over time while the quality of the soil deteriorates. Accordingly, the cultivation of new lands is viewed as beneficial, but little thought is given to the cost of decreases in natural fertility. In other words, there may be confusion between land as a renewable resource that is capable of continuing production and land as a nonrenewable resource that can be mined out. Connected with this is the overdiscounting of future production by slash-and-burn farmers discussed in Chapter 4.

Recall also the failures of the capital markets to provide farmers on the margin of subsistence with funds for conservation and improvement in land productivity. A strong preference for current over future consumption by small and poor farmers and expensive or unavailable funds for investment in continued soil quality contribute to destructive farming practives.

The remainder of the chapter is divided into four sections. The first establishes the need for increased food production in developing countries and indicates the possible food deficit range. The next section describes the importance of cereal grains in meeting food needs. In the following section both the environmental stress from increased cereal production and the environmental limits to production are examined. It is necessary to approach this from four directions: the implications of the use of agricultural inputs, erosion, variations among tropical regions and the consequences of different methods of cultivation. Where possible, the discussion follows the descriptive structure of Chapter 2. The final section considers the environmental implications of some new production techniques.

POPULATION GROWTH AND FOOD NEEDS

The major turning points in the struggle for food have been the acceleration of population growth in developing countries and the introduction of new, high-yield, cereal varieties (HYV). As examined in Chapter 2, birth rates in developing countries remained stable from the 1930s to the 1960s at about 40–45 per thousand, but death rates fell from 29–34 to 16 per thousand over the period.[2] The decline in death rates in developed countries was less pronounced, from 15 to 9 per thousand. The resulting growth of population in the South absorbed much of the gain in food production. By the mid 1960s, fears of impending disaster were being voiced.

The 1960s were also the years in which many high-yield varieties of wheat, and later maize and rice, were developed and introduced. The improved varieties were quickly adopted in many developing countries, especially in South Asia. Planting these varieties and using controlled applications of irrigation water, fertilizers, and pesticides, per capita grain production rose in many developing countries. Talk of scarcity was muted, and predictions of food self-sufficiency were made.

Table 6.1 displays the broad trends. Since 1956, the production of food has increased more rapidly in developing than developed countries, moving from an index of 81 to 131, compared to a movement from 85 to 128 for developed countries. However, when placed on a per capita basis, the improvement almost evaporates. The per capita index for developing countries rose from 96 in 1956 to a peak of 104 in 1970 and had fallen to 99 by 1972–74. In contrast, per capita production in developed countries had risen from 93 to 115 over the same period.

The long-term trends in world grain trade, displayed in Table 6.2, are also striking. In the prewar period, six of the seven regions were net grain exporters, and only Western Europe was a net importer. Latin America, Africa, and Asia were net exporters of 12 million tons. By 1976 it is estimated that only two regions will be exporters: North America and Australia/New Zealand. The countries of Asia, Africa, and Latin America are expected to import a total of 60 million tons, a major shift from their earlier export status.

Some argue that the slowdown in per capita food production growth since the late 1960s is not temporary and the result of cyclical adverse weather or an increase in oil and hence input prices. They argue that the slowdown is evidence of a more enduring problem conveniently termed the "limits to growth" syndrome. In this view the world's resources of land, water, and the inputs for energy-intensive, Iowa-style agriculture are nearing exhaustion.

Even though population growth is expected to slow over the next 30 years, absolute increases will be large according to United Nations projections.[3] What is the consequence for cereal demand in developing countries? Projected grain production and food deficit estimates are available from the USDA, the International Food Production Research Institute (IFPRI), and the United Nation's

Table 6.1 Trends in Cereals Production (1961–1965 = 100)

				Production Per Capita		
	World	Developing Countries	Developed Countries[a]	World	Developing Countries	Developed Countries
1956	84	81	85	96	96	93
1957	84	83	85	94	96	92
1958	89	87	91	98	98	97
1959	91	89	92	98	98	97
1960	94	91	95	100	98	99
1961	95	95	95	99	100	97
1962	98	97	98	100	99	99
1963	100	101	99	100	101	99
1964	103	103	104	100	99	102
1965	104	104	104	100	99	102
1966	108	106	110	102	98	106
1967	112	110	113	104	100	108
1968	116	114	117	106	101	111
1969	117	119	116	104	102	109
1970	120	124	118	105	104	110
1971	125	126	124	107	103	114
1972	123	124	123	104	99	113
1973	130	129	126	108	99	114
1974	132	131	128	107	99	115

Source. FAO Production Yearbook, various issues.

[a] Excludes centrally planned economies.

Food and Agriculture Organization. The USDA 1974 report on world food prospects done for the UN Food Conference projected that aggregate world production would keep pace with demand through 1985,[4] but for developing countries the picture is not favorable. Their production was projected to increase by 2.3–3.3% per year, but population growth of 2.3% and increased per capita food demand would lead to a net annual cereal grain deficit ranging from 23 to 73 million metric tons in 1985.[5]

Recent projections by IFPRI for grain production and demand to 1985/1986, based on 1960–1974 trends, also show large food deficits, particularly for the lowest-income developing countries who were already grain importers in 1975.[6] According to their study, the gross grain deficit for non-Communist developing countries could exceed 95 million tons by 1985, which is more than twice the grain deficit for 1975/1976, a bad crop year, and three times the deficit for a normal year such as 1969/1970. The net developing country grain deficit (which is adjusted downward by grain exports of Pakistan, Thailand, Argentina, and Brazil) amounts to 65.5 million tons under the low demand growth scenario. Table 6.3 displays the projections for individual countries and regions. Note that major grain deficits are expected in India, Bangladesh, and Indonesia in Asia, and Egypt and Nigeria in Africa. The high- and medium-

Table 6.2 The Changing Pattern of World Grain Trade: Net Exports by Region and Year (millions metric ton)

Region	1934–1938	1948–1952	1960	1966	1970	1973	1976[a]
North America	+5[b]	+23	+39	+59	+56	+91	+94
Latin America	+9	+1	0	+5	+4	−3	−3
Western Europe	−24	−22	−25	−27	−30	−19	−17
Eastern Europe and USSR	+5		0	−4	0	−27	−27
Africa	+1	0	−2	−7	−5	−5	−10
Asia	+2	−6	−17	−34	−37	−43	−47
Australia and New Zealand	+3	+3	+6	+8	+12	+6	+8

Source. Based on U.S. Department of Agriculture data and estimates by Lester Brown, Worldwatch Institute.

[a] Preliminary, fiscal year.

[b] Plus sign indicates net exports; minus sign, net imports.

Table 6.3 Cereal Production and Cereal Deficit Projections by 1985/1986 for Selected Countries and Regions

Region and Country	Population Growth/pa 1974/1985	Cereal Production Growth/pa 1960/1974	Grain Deficit (Surplus) (Million metric tons) 1974/1975	1985/1986[a]
Total LDC[b] (net)	2.71	2.50	33.4	65.5
Total Asia LDC	2.61	2.42	15.1	36.8
Total North Africa	2.93	2.18	12.0	21.4
Total sub-Sahara LDC	2.88	1.54	2.1	13.7
Total Latin America	2.79	3.48	4.2	(6.4)
India	2.46	2.59	6.7	14.2
Bangladesh	2.88	1.21	2.3	5.3
Pakistan	3.26	5.47	0.3	(3.9)
Indonesia	2.56	2.74	1.2	6.7
Philippines	3.17	3.63	0.8	1.5
Thailand	3.20	3.71	(3.2)	(5.6)
Egypt	2.31	2.54	3.5	3.6
Middle East OPEC	3.28	2.00	4.8	10.7
Nigeria	2.99	−0.09	0.3	7.6
Mexico	3.41	4.32	3.6	0.8
Argentina	1.21	3.28	(7.8)	(16.1)
Brazil	2.82	3.94	1.5	(3.4)
Venezuela	2.93	3.20	1.5	2.1

Source. International Food Production Research Institute, Research Report #1, *Meeting Food Needs in the Developing World,* February 1976.

[a] "Low growth of demand" scenario.

[b] LDC, less developed countries.

income developing countries are expected to increase their share of the food deficit, and this is related to their increased ability and willingness to pay for food. The unequal distribution of grain deficits among countries has implications for agricultural environmental stress.

It is not our purpose to substantiate or reconcile these gap estimates. Indeed, none of the studies purports to make estimates of actual food needs. Instead, they are projections based on the extrapolation of certain initial conditions and trends. They do, however, demonstrate in a general sense the need for increased food production. The undermining of food systems through environmental abuses could make these increases difficult if not impossible. If grain deficits by 1985 or 2000 are to be held to manageable size, the question cannot be whether to intensify production in the developing world, but rather how this intensification can be done. Production must be stepped up and sustained over the long term, and environmental management will play a critical role.

There are two ways to increase agricultural output: increase output per unit of land and/or increase land under cultivation. It is tempting to analyze the environmental implications of additional output by distinguishing between the problems of intensified agriculture and the extension of agriculture. The first requires greater inputs per unit land, and the second requires farming new lands. The distinction suggests typical types of environmental stress. One can visualize the consequences of using ever greater quantities of fertilizer and pesticides on a given plot of land, and one can visualize erosion and soil destruction resulting from bringing virgin land, unsuited for tillage, under the plough. On reflection, however, we do not find a distinction between extensive and intensive expansion a useful approach for classifying environmental problems. One reason is that many environmental problems are not really distinctive to just one type of expansion. For example, pesticides are used on both new acreage and to increase yields on existing cropland. Also, in developing countries it is the change in agricultural practices—for example, from shifting cultivation to continuous cropping or from natural to chemical fertilizers—that is of greatest interest, and the distinction between extensive and intensive expansion is not well suited to analyzing changes in cultivation practices.

This is not to say that the potential for expanding agricultural acreage is unimportant. On the contrary, the choice between intensive and extensive expansion is of considerable importance. Also, as shown in Chapter 2, the percentage of arable land currently cultivated in each region varies enormously. These data are summarized in Table 6.4. For developing regions the percentage of arable land permanently cultivated ranges from a low of 11% for South America to 83% for more densely populated Asia. Obviously, some regions have greater choice than others between intensive versus extensive expansion. Still, as a method for classifying environmental issues, we do not find it a useful distinction.

The balance of the chapter focuses on cereals production. Environmental stress arising from the production of other food crops and agricultural raw materials is not discussed in detail, nor have we examined damages arising from livestock production (mainly overgrazing) and the implications for agriculture of deforestation. It is our contention that the issue of the environment and increased food production in the developing countries has often confused cereal production with other aspects of agricultural development (such as the

Table 6.4 Percentage of Arable Land that is Cultivated, 1965

Region	Percentage
Africa	22
Asia	83
Australia	2
North America	51
South America	11
USSR	64
Europe	88

Source. The World Food Problem, vol. II, 1967. See also Table 2.18.

production of other food crops, nonfood crops and livestock, as well as soil degradation arising from nonagricultural removal of ground cover). All we attempt here is an analysis of the potential environmental implications of increased cereal production. Although all these aspects of agriculture are directly and strongly linked, they are sufficiently large and complex to require separate studies. In focusing on cereal production, we emphasize a neglected aspect—the spatial distribution of crops and the special climate characteristics of the regions in which they are grown.

SIGNIFICANCE OF CEREAL GRAINS

Cereals (Graminaea) are the world's most important crop. Almost 70% of the total harvested acreage is devoted to their production. They are highly nutritious and compact, and they travel and store easily. Considering their importance, there are surprisingly few members of the species. Oats and barley are the major grains of the temperate North, and wheat and barley are grown in the warmer temperate regions of Northern Europe, Russia, Canada, and Northern United States. In southern temperate and tropic climates, maize (corn), sorgum-millet, and rice are the major varieties cultivated.

Table 6.5 displays the basic pattern of world crop acreage. Worldwide, cereals account for almost 70% of arable and permanent cropland excluding land in fallow. For developing country regions, cropped acreage devoted to cereals is highest in the Middle East (77%) and lowest in Africa (51%), which relies more heavily on root and tuber crops and pulses. Three cereals are of central importance: wheat, maize (corn), and rice. Globally they account for 65% of all cereal acreage, and in developing countries, 70%. In Africa, these three represent 43% of cereal acreage, with maize dominant; in Latin America 85% with maize again dominant; in the Middle East 66% with wheat dominant; and in Asia 74% with rice dominant. Pulses are nutritionally important, but they account for a much smaller percentage of crop area. Root crops and tubers can be important to individual countries (e.g., Brazil and Nigeria), but on a global scale they are much less significant than cereals. Coffee, tea, cocoa, cotton, and other crops that often use higher levels of pesticides and fertilizers account for a small percentage of world crop acreage (4%). In some locations they become much more significant. Obviously, crop acreage cannot measure

Table 6.5 Acreage by Crop and Region, 1974

	World	CPE[b]	Developed	Developing	Africa	Latin America	Middle East	Asia Excluding China
Total arable land and land under permanent crops (1000 km²)	1473	437	396	666	186	128	80	272
Of which								
Fallow land[a]	416	41	184	193	80	38	33	39
Cultivated land	1057	396	212	473	106	90	47	233
Ratio of cultivated to fallow	2.6	9.1	1.1	2.5	1.3	2.4	1.4	5.9
Percentage of cultivated in various crops								
Total cereals	69	74	74	64	51	56	77	70
Wheat	21	26	31	13	6	10	44	11
Rice	13	10	2	20	4	7	3	35
Maize (corn)	11	6	19	12	11	31	4	6
Other cereals	24	32	22	19	30	8	26	18
Roots and tubers	5	8	2	5	14	5	2	2
Pulses	6	4	2	10	10	8	3	11
Soybeans	4	4	10	1	1	6	1	1
Coffee, cocoa, tea	1	1	1	3	7	7	1	1
Cotton	3	2	2	4	3	5	6	4
Sugar (beet and cane)	2	2	2	2	1	7	1	2

Source. Adapted from 1974 FAO *Production Yearbook.*

[a] There are definitional difficulties in designating land as arable land left in fallow versus permanent meadows and pastures. The significance of these figures for fallow may vary from region to region depending on the evaluation of the land out of production. The difference between fallow and permanent pasture may simply be the length of time of the fallow period.

[b] Centrally Planned Economies.

economic importance, nor does it directly measure contribution of food supplies.

Tables 6.6 through 6.9 show production and yields for total cereals, and for wheat, rice, and maize for major regions. In addition, Maps 6.1–6.3 illustrate the spatial pattern of the production of wheat, rice, and maize. The tables confirm the striking difference in yields per acre between the North and South.

Wheat is the major food for 35% of the world's population. The USSR is the world's largest producer. Wheat originated in the Near East and is widely cultivated in the semi-arid region, from the Mediterranean to India. Wheat is adapted to both intensive machine and fertilizer production and to extensive, low-input production methods. It has been hybridized to produce seeds with very specific attributes; high-yield varieties have made wheat an important crop in many developing countries, but it is not readily adapted to the very warm tropics.

Developed countries account for 39% of the world wheat production, developing countries 20%, and the USSR 31%. Yields vary widely, with Africa lowest at 0.7 tons/ha and Western Europe highest at 3.1 tons/ha. Wheat grows best in a cool temperate climate or, if properly irrigated, a subtropical climate. In the United States only 5.5% of wheat acreage is irrigated, but this produces almost twice the yields and provides 9% of United States wheat production.[7]

Rice is the principal crop for over 60% of mankind. The major producing countries are China, Japan, Indonesia, Thailand, India, Pakistan, and Bangladesh. Rice is basically a tropical crop, and is normally grown either in "paddies" (man-made ponds that are emptied and worked as necessary) or in

Table 6.6 World Cereal Production and Yields, 1974

	Production		Yields	
Region	Million Metric Tons	Percentage of World Total	Metric Tons per Hectare	Yield Index (Average World Yield = 100)
World Total	1334	100	1.8	100
Developed	442	33	2.8	154
North America	236	18	2.7	149
Western Europe	159	12	3.4	187
Oceania	17	1	1.4	76
Other	30	2	2.7	149
Developing	387	29	1.3	70
Africa	44	3	0.8	44
Latin America	77	6	1.5	85
Middle East	45	3	1.3	69
Far East	221	16	1.4	75
Centrally Planned Economies	505	38	1.9	102
Asian CPE	241	18	1.9	105
European CPE	263	20	1.8	98

Source. 1974 FAO Production Yearbook.

Table 6.7 World Wheat Production and Yields, 1974

Region	Production		Yields	
	Million Metric Tons	Percentage of World Total	Metric Tons per Hectare	Yield Index (Average World Yield = 100)
World Total	360.2	100	1.6	100
Developed	139.2	39	2.14	134
North America	63.0	17	1.99	124
Western Europe	62.6	17	3.11	194
Oceania	11.5	3	1.38	86
Other	2.1	1	1.39	87
Developing	71.9	20	1.18	74
Africa	4.6	1	0.71	44
Latin America	12.9	4	1.59	99
Middle East	24.1	7	1.07	67
Far East	30.3	8	1.26	79
Centrally Planned Economies	149.1	41	1.52	95
Asian CPE	37.4	10	1.27	79
European CPE	111.7	31	1.63	102

Source. *1974 FAO Production Yearbook.*

Table 6.8 World Rice Production and Yields, 1974

Region	Production		Yield	
	Million Metric Tons	Percentage of World Total	Metric Tons per Hectare	Yield Index (Average World Yield = 100)
World Total	323.2	100	2.40	100
Developed	23.2	7	5.58	233
North America	5.2	2	4.98	208
Western Europe	1.7	1	5.26	219
Oceania	0.4	<1	6.10	254
Other	15.9	5	5.84	243
Developing	174.9	54	1.87	78
Africa	5.2	2	1.30	55
Latin America	11.8	4	1.94	81
Middle East	4.8	1	3.62	151
Far East	153.1	47	1.87	78
Centrally Planned Economies	125.1	39	3.19	133
Asian CPE	122.9	38	3.18	132
European CPE	2.1	1	3.69	154

Source. *1974 FAO Production Yearbook.*

Table 6.9 World Maize Production, 1973

	Production		Yield	
Region	Million Metric Tons	Percentage of World Total	Metric Tons per Hectare	Yield Index (Average World Yield = 100)
World Total	310.4	100	2.78	100
Developed	179.5	58	4.95	178
North America	146.2	47	5.72	205
Western Europe	28.8	9	4.38	158
Oceania	0.2	1	3.20	115
Other	4.2	1	1.04	37
Developing	68.1	22	1.26	45
Africa	11.0	4	0.94	34
Latin America	37.5	12	1.46	52
Middle East	4.5	1	2.36	85
Far East	15.2	5	1.04	37
Centrally Planned Economies	62.6	20	2.97	107
Asian CPE	32.5	10	2.75	100
European CPE	30.2	10	3.20	115

Source. *1974 FAO Production Yearbook.*

fields. The latter, "upland" rice, produces only 5% of the world's rice crop but accounts for almost 10% of the world's acreage planted to rice. Paddy rice is normally labor intensive, but the heavy use of machines and fertilizers in the United States (accounting for only 1% of the world's rice crop) gives yields three to six times the normal tropical yield.

Over 85% of world rice production and 88% of rice acreage is in Asian developing countries, including China. Rice is readily adapted to intensive cultivation, given proper irrigation and either capital or labor. The great yield differentials found for rice (setting world yields equal to an index of 100, Japan is 243 and Africa is 55) are due to these input availabilities and to the variation in rice species.

Maize is a New World cereal that is readily adapted to tropical climates. More than 44% is produced in the United States, with much of that going for cattle and hog feed. The major direct maize-consuming countries are in the developing world, particularly Latin America. In Indonesia and much of Asia, maize is grown on land unsuited for rice and is generally less preferred than rice. Maize is still an important crop in Southeast Asia, accounting for 25% of the region's acreage and 15% of its production. It is second only to rice in Thailand, Indonesia, and the Philippines.[8]

Maize, like wheat, is grown in various regions throughout the world but prefers warm to hot climates. The midwest United States has an acceptable climate and adequate rain for one crop. In many developing countries, there is good potential for year-round production if proper inputs are available. Almost 50% of the world's maize crop area is found in the tropical developing

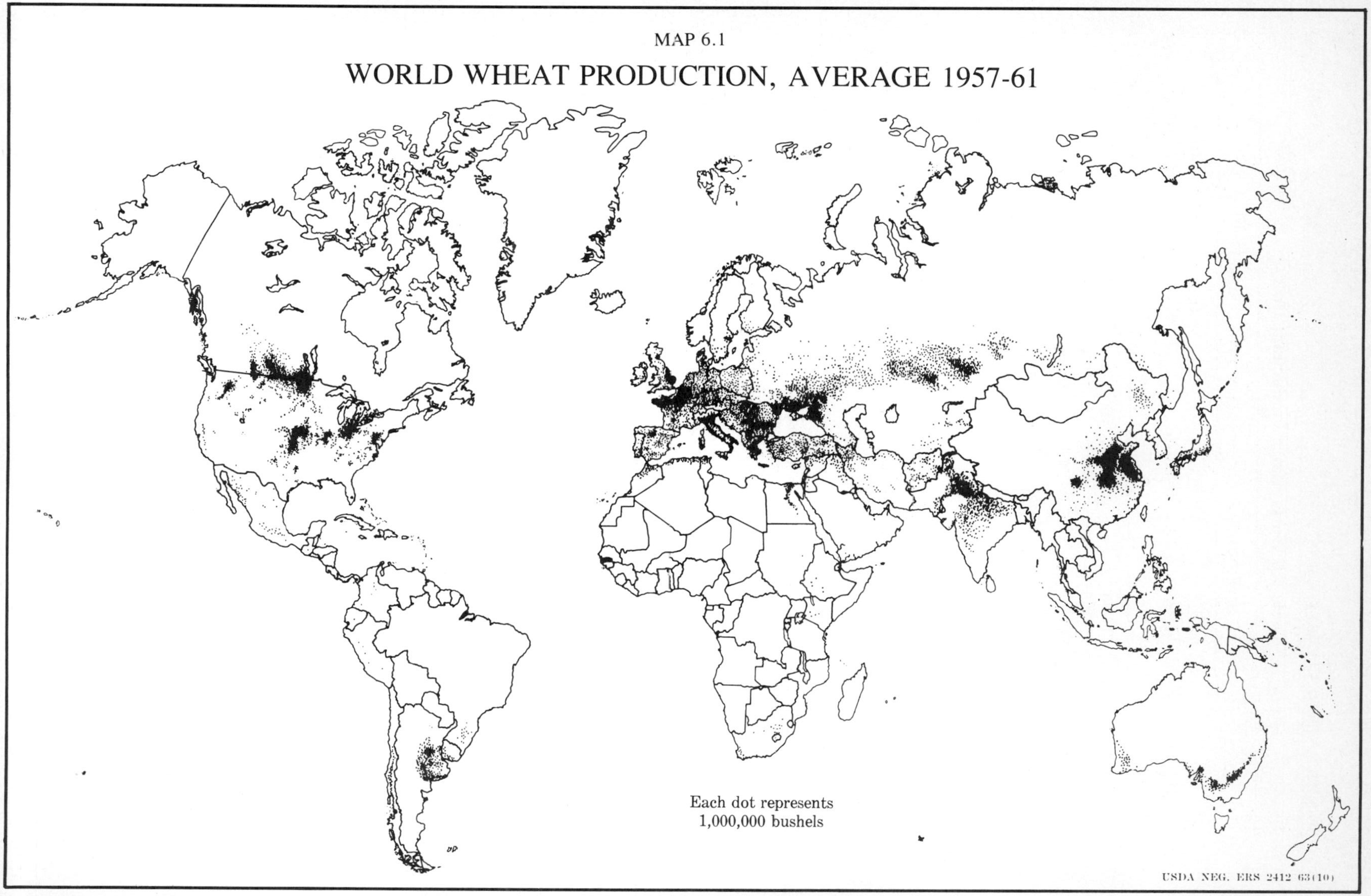

Map 6.1. World wheat production.

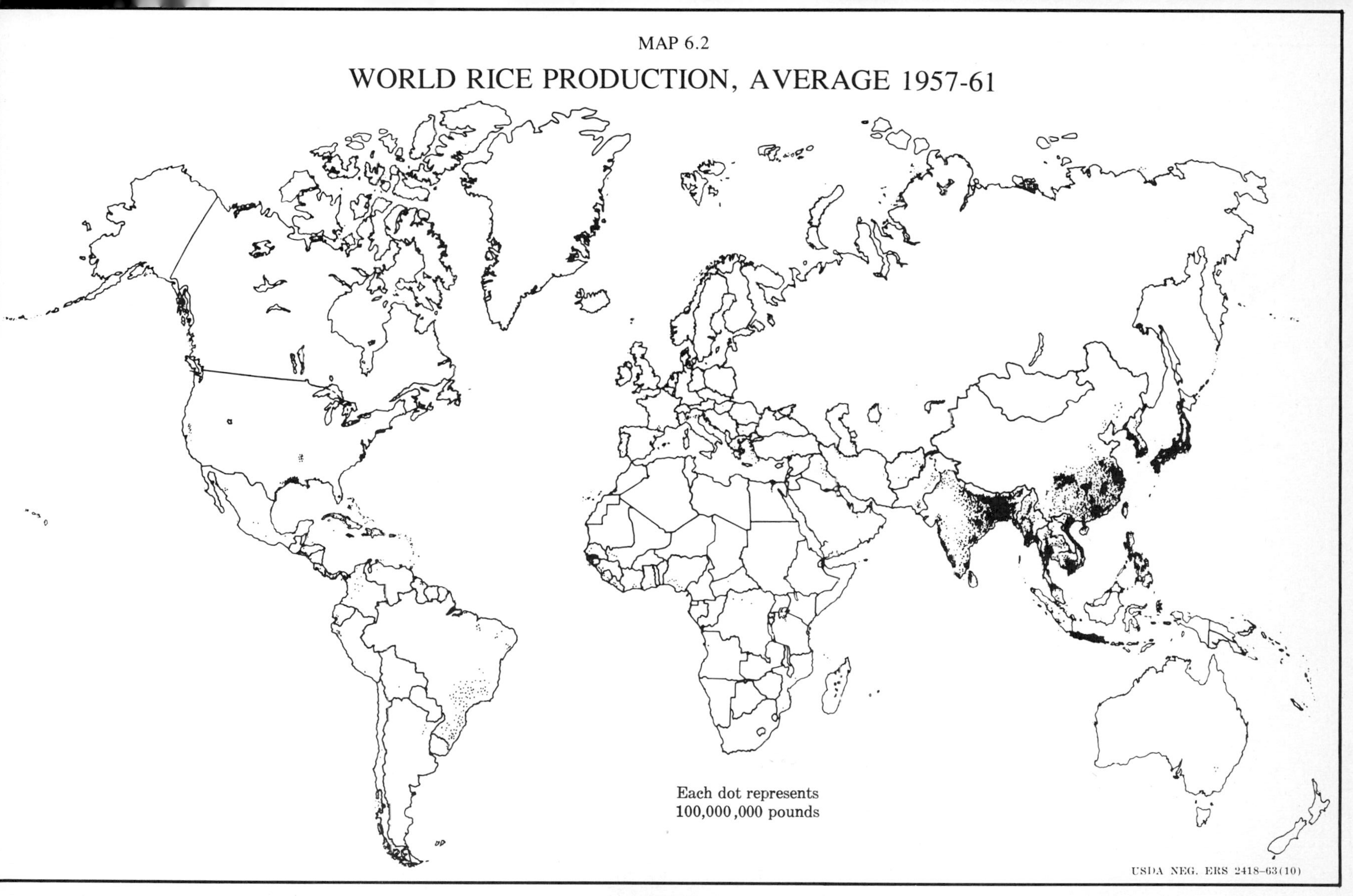

Map 6.2. World rice production.

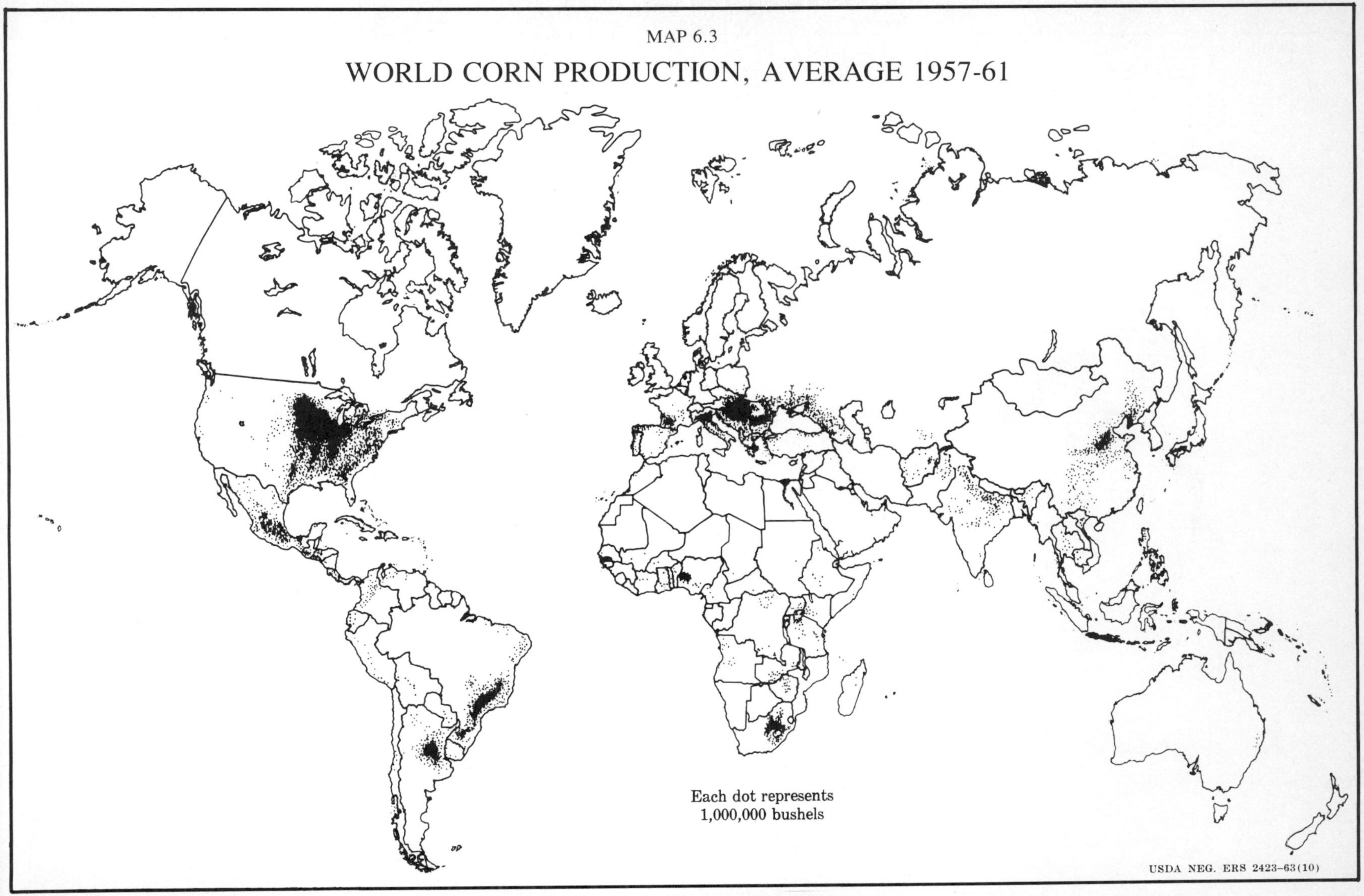

Map 6.3. World corn production.

countries, with another 10% in China, whereas only 31% is found in developed countries. However, because of tremendous yield differentials, developing countries including China account for only 32% of production.

ENVIRONMENTAL STRESS AND LIMITS

There is no simple satisfactory approach to the interrelationships between expanded agricultural production and the environment. Neither the intensive versus extensive distinction nor any other single perspective is adequate for capturing the different aspects of the relationships. Accordingly, we chose four ways to view the issues: the use of agricultural inputs, erosion, variations among tropical regions, and methods of cultivation. Although this complicates the exposition, it respects the great diversity of agriculture in the developing world.

Agricultural Inputs

Fertilizer. Natural levels of soil fertility under continuous cultivation are seldom maintained. Nutrients are usually added; the most important are nitrogen, phosphate, and potassium. The amount of fertilizer used per unit of land surface depends on the crop grown, the method of cultivation, and the quality of the soil. Ultimately, however, it is an economic decision and depends on the incremental cost compared to the incremental revenue from increased yields. By and large, it is uneconomic to use fertilizer as abundantly on grain crops as on certain other crops such as palm, cotton, or tobacco.

It is important to have some notion of fertilizer use by crop when environmental implications are considered, because fertilizer runoff problems are concentrated in regions of heavy use, and therefore crop patterns determine in part the spatial pattern of runoff problems. Tables 6.10 and 6.11 display some data on fertilizer use in the United States. Application rates for soybeans are low, particularly for nitrogen, because it is a legume and fixes nitrogen in the soil.[9] Additions of nitrogen do little to expand yield. Application rates for

Table 6.10 Nitrogen Fertilizer Application Rates in the United States, 1968, 1974, and 1980

	Kilograms per Hectare		
Crop	1968	1974[a]	1980[b]
Corn	105	122	152
Wheat	22	36	52
Cotton	64	61	64
Soybeans	3	3	4

Source. United States Department of Agriculture, Economic Research Service, *United States and World Fertilizer Outlook, 1974 and 1980,* May 1974.

[a] Estimated.

[b] Projected.

Table 6.11 United States Agricultural Use of Fertilizer 1969

Crop	Hectares Fertilized (1000)	Percentage of Total Crop Fertilized	Average Application Rate (kg/ha)	Percentage of Total Fertilizer Use
Cropland, pasture	4,127	15	377	6.6
Field corn	19,239	81	446	36.4
Sorghum	3,930	64	243	4.0
Wheat	9,787	55	174	7.2
Oats	3,063	46	198	2.6
Rice	859	100	438	1.6
Peanuts	456	82	513	1.0
Soybeans	3,997	26	248	4.2
Cotton	3,475	78	401	5.9
Sugarbeets	592	100	555	1.4
Irish potatoes	504	99	1,204	2.6
Tobacco	316	99	2,205	2.9
Hay	3,204	16	332	4.5
Vegetables	1,181	89	930	4.7
Orchards	1,420	87	859	5.2
Nurseries	84	73	1,090	0.4
Total United States	62,815	41	375	100.0

Source. U.S. Department of Commerce, 1969 *Census of Agriculture*, vol. II, ch. IV, Equipment, Labor Expenditures, Chemicals.

wheat in the United States are also relatively low. Corn is the greatest cereal user of fertilizer, accounting for 36% of all fertilizer used in the United States. The application rate, however, is far less than for certain specialty crops. Overall, the United States used about 20 million metric tons for harvested crops in 1974; the growth rate over the past 10 years is about 6.8% per year.

There are diminishing marginal physical returns to fertilizer use as conventionally measured by a response curve. This has led some observers to conclude that both fertilizer use and yields per acre are beginning to level off in industrial countries. In contrast, developing countries are further down their response curves and have greater scope for increased consumption. Brown states "Since they currently use very little or no fertilizer, most farmers in the developing countries are still near the low end of the fertilizer response curve, with the largest and cheapest yield gains still in the future. Farmers in the agriculturally advanced nations of Western Europe, Japan, and the United States, in contrast, are far up on the curve, with crop yields relatively unresponsive to additional chemical fertilizer."[10] In fact, the actual picture is far more complicated. The planting of HYVs, as well as the use of irrigation, may alter the curve by raising it and changing its slope. For example, in one test the yield response to nitrogen was more than doubled by irrigation.[11]

Fertilizer use in developing countries is clearly connected with the particular crops grown and the introduction of high-yield varieties of grains.[12] We cannot expect that use by crop will follow the same relative pattern, only at lower levels, as it does in the United States in part because the relative prices of crops are not identical internationally; therefore, an economic pattern of fertilizer consumption in one country may be uneconomic in another. Also the relative prices of other inputs, including land, vary and the most economic bundle of inputs will also vary.

It is clear that the widespread use of HYVs and the increasing demand for food will stimulate fertilizer consumption in developing countries. What are the environmental consequences? It would appear that, apart from some cases of overfertilizing in which yields are actually depressed, the major consequence of fertilizer use is runoff water pollution and the resulting eutrophication of lakes, streams, and ponds.[13] Only a part of chemical fertilizers applied to land is actually taken up by plants. The remainder can be transported through surface or underground runoff and find its way into water courses. (It can also simply stay in the soil.) There the nutrients stimulate the production of algae and other plant life and in the process consume dissolved oxygen. Apart from the visual objections to algae blooms, the reduction in oxygen impairs the ability of the water to support other commercially valuable life forms. It also stimulates aquatic weed growth that interferes with fishing, may clog intake facilities, accelerates siltation of reservoirs and irrigation channels, reduces the quality of water for personal use, and decreases recreational values. The process of eutrophication or premature aging of lakes, is complex and the literature quite large.[14] It does appear that tropical lakes and streams, particularly shallow ones with long flushing times, are sensitive to eutrophication.

How serious is this, and what is the contribution of grain production in the tropics to this process? We do not know, although individual instances of pollution by fertilizer runoff in developing countries can be cited. Certainly one can anticipate localized problems in high population density regions that have high per acre application rates. Also, the nature of the soils and hydrological systems and the variability of rainfall and stream flow are determinants. In any event, the alternatives to greater fertilizer use in intensive agriculture in developing countries should be kept in mind. If fertilizer substitutes for other more destructive methods of increasing food output, there may still be a net benefit.

Chemical fertilizers are not the only source of soil nutrients. More efficient use of other sources—manure, leguminous crops that fix nitrogen from the air, and natural soil fertility—can reduce the expense of chemical fertilization and moderate environmental damages. Organic fertilizers are widely used, but there remains considerable potential for expansion. One study estimated that total production in developing countries of organic material capable of being used as fertilizer (plant, animal, and human wastes) was almost eight times the actual consumption of inorganic fertilizers.[15] Problems of increased use include farmer acceptance, collection and transport costs, and the use of dung for fuel, especially with the sharp increases in the cost of fuelwood and kerosene.

Besides manure and "green manure" (a crop especially grown and then left to rot on the field), legumes in a multiple cropping scheme can effectively increase the nutrient level of the soil, since their roots have the ability to biologically "fix" nitrogen from the air.[16] Legumes grown in rotation not only may allow continuous cultivation (with adequate water), but also help to keep a continuous ground cover, cutting down on erosion. The inclusion of legumes into cropping systems, both to protect against erosion and to add nutrients, is far from systematized in most regions, even where such practices exist. Scientific expansion of cropping systems including legumes holds great promise for increasing yields in LDCs without the extensive use of chemical fertilizers. As with manures, however, legumes must be supplemented to obtain significant yield increases. At present, one of the stumbling blocks in the intensive development of a legume-grain crop system is the legumes' resistance to chemical fertilizer inputs, limiting their yield.

Natural soil fertility is another source of nutrients. If renewed through natural ground cover (or fallow), the natural soil can be utilized continually. It is incorrect, however, to assume that nutrient runoff is only associated with chemical fertilizers. There is some evidence that well-fertilized nutrient-poor soils under certain circumstances may produce less nutrient runoff than very fertile, unfertilized soils. Also, eutrophication of ground water is not always explained by chemical inputs. The Agricultural Research Service of the USDA reports studies in which fertile soil underlying the reservoirs of farm ponds may be the sole source of eutrophication without any fertilizer being present.[17]

Pesticides. Insecticides are being applied increasingly to control various pests and diseases that plague agriculture. Herbicides are also used to limit or eradicate weed growth that competes with crop plants for nutrients. These chemical inputs are extremely important to modern agriculture and are already widely used in developing countries. It appears inevitable that their use will increase as food needs continue to increase, yet there is great ambivalence toward them. One view connects pesticides with agricultural plenty and another view with serious and pervasive environmental deterioration.

The full implications of pesticide use are hard to determine, in part because the amount of pesticides used on different crops is not uniform. Another reason is that there are large numbers of herbicides and insecticides, and their characteristics, including persistence and toxicity, vary. Also, the use of pesticides can be associated with changes in the technique of production, and this will have environmental implications. For example, herbicides may replace traditional slash and burn agriculture for weed control, or pesticides may encourage a monoculture system. Much of the evidence against the use of pesticides in the developing world has been extrapolated from individual studies, more often than not based on cotton rather than grain production, and also based on misuse of pesticides in the 1950s and 1960s rather than what is probably more normal use. Cereals usually require and can economically support smaller quantities of these chemicals than cotton and other nonfood crops. Although nonfood crops are a vital part of tropical agriculture, one should not attribute environmental problems of pesticide use to grain production if the major cause is use on other crops.[18]

Before discussing the environmental consequences of expanded pesticide consumption, use patterns should be examined. The United States, although obviously not illustrative of LDC agriculture, clearly demonstrates the spatial and crop distribution of pesticides. Insecticide use in United States agriculture increased by about 2.6% per year from 1966 to 1971, whereas herbicide use increased by 14.6%. The tonnage of herbicides used in agriculture now exceeds insecticides. Table 6.12 displays insecticide and herbicide use by crop and application rates. Corn is the major crop for which herbicides are used, with

79% of acreage treated and an average application rate of 1.94 kg/ha. Soybeans are next in terms of quantity, but the percentage of acreage treated (68%) and the application rate (1.38 kg/ha) are less than the percentage of acreage treated for rice (95%) and the application rate for rice (5.17 kg/ha). Cotton also has a higher percentage acreage treatment (82%) and application rate (2.91 kg/ha). Wheat has both lower area treatment (41%) and application rate (0.59 kg/ha).

Insecticides are extensively used in citrus (88% acreage) and vegetable crops (56%), with application rates of 3.29 and 4.97 kg/ha, respectively. Cotton

Table 6.12 Total Insecticides and Herbicides Used in the United States in 1971

Crops	Chemical	Quantity (1000 kg)	Area (1000 ha)	Percentage of Total Area	Kilograms per Hectare
Corn	Insecticide	11,581	10,489	(35)	1.10
	Herbicide	45,858	23,676	(79)	1.94
Wheat	Insecticide	776	1,524	(7)	0.51
	Herbicide	5,262	8,928	(41)	0.59
Rice	Insecticide	429	258	(35)	1.66
	Herbicide	3,629	702	(95)	5.17
Soybeans	Insecticide	2,550	1,407	(8)	1.81
	Herbicide	16,556	11,963	(68)	1.38
Cotton	Insecticide	33,274	3,050	(61)	10.91
	Herbicide	8,890	4,100	(82)	2.91
Other vegetables	Insecticide	3,750	755	(56)	4.97
	Herbicide	NA	540	(40)	NA
Citrus	Insecticide	1,383	420	(88)	3.29
	Herbicide	NA	119	(22)	NA

Selected Crops as Percentage of Total (Not Including Pasture)

	Acreage	Herbicide Use	Insecticide Use
Corn	20	45	11
Wheat	15	9	1
Rice	1	4	1
Soybeans	12	16	2
Cotton	3	9	33
Other vegetables	1	1	4
Citrus	1	1	1
Other	48	16	48

Source. U.S. Department of Agriculture, "Farmer's Use of Pesticides in 1971: Quantities," USDA Economic Research Service, Agricultural Economic Report #252 (Washington, DC: GPO, July 1974).

clearly dominates insecticide use in aggregate and in application rates (10.91 kg/ha). Although not shown on the table, tobacco is also a heavy user of insecticides, with 77% of acreage treated and application rates of 6.19 kg/ha. Peanuts are also high at 87% and 4.2 kg/ha. The use of insecticides for rice in the United States is modest at 1.66 kg/ha.

The differences among crops in pesticide use suggest that the crop mix in specific developing countries is one determinant of whether pesticides present major environmental problems. In addition, it suggests that the effects of pesticides may be concentrated or localized within countries according to the crop acreage pattern. Figures for pesticide use by crop in developing countries generally are not available, but Table 6.13 shows that the same trend toward herbicide use is evident in many developing countries. The increase is most noticeable in those areas in which HYVs are being introduced. We can also assume that cotton produced in developing countries is a major end use for pesticides.

Some limited information on pesticide use in India is shown in Tables 6.14 and 6.15. There appear to be substantial differences among crops as to the proportion of crop area to which pesticides are applied, as well as the pesticide expenditures per crop.

Table 6.13 Pesticide Use in Selected Developing Countries, 1971–1977

Region	Number of Countries	Total 1971 (1000 metric tons)	P.A. Growth 1971–1973 (%)	Total 1975 (1000 metric tons)	P.A. Growth 1975–1977 (%)
Latin America	10				
Herbicide		4.9	21	7.1	9
Insecticide		30.0	18	61.1	10
Fungicide		14.1	21	38.0	3
Total		49.0	21	106.8	5
Asia and Oceania	15				
Herbicide		4.1	35	6.2	17
Insecticide		28.7	36	54.0	12
Fungicide		10.1	31	20.3	10
Total		42.9	35	80.5	12
Africa	13				
Herbicide		0.4	108	2.6	76
Insecticide		14.4	−11	11.3	11
Fungicide		0.6	9	0.7	41
Total		15.4	− 6	14.6	27
All countries	38				
Herbicide		9.4	32	16.5	25
Insecticide		73.1	21	126.4	9
Fungicide		24.8	25	59.0	5
Total		107.3	23	201.9	9

Source. FAO, *Pesticide Requirements in Developing Countries*, AGP:PEST/PH/75/B44, April 1975.

Table 6.14 Pesticide Use by Sample of Farmers in Andra Pradesh, India, 1969–1970

Crop	Percentage of Total Area	Percentage of Each Crop Area Receiving Pesticides	Per Hectare Expenditure on Pesticides[a] (rs)
Paddy (rice)	31	47	27.4
Wheat	1	NA	NA
Sorghum	8	4	12.4
Millet	14	30	29.6
Pulses	7	20	68.7
Tobacco (Virginia)	10	98	79.6
Tobacco (native)	4	90	18.5
Chillies	4	90	366.7
Cotton	2	36	219.2
Groundnut	3	20	37.1
Sugar cane	1	NA	NA
Fodder crops	9	NA	24.7
Other	6	NA	NA

Source. From a sample of farmers in Gunter District, Andra Pradesh, 1969–1970, *Pesticides Market Studies*, vol. VI (New Delhi, India, Pesticide Association of India, 1971).

[a] Note that expenditure should not be viewed as an exact equivalent to quantity, since a different range of pesticides (with different prices) may be used for any one crop. The per hectare expenditure figures, however, are useful as a general approximation of the intensity of pesticide use.

The importance of pesticides to agricultural production is illustrated by an FAO study of herbicide use and food production. According to that study, 11% of world food production is lost to weeds. The percentage of losses were estimated to be 5%, 10%, and 25% in most developed regions, intermediate regions, and least developed countries, respectively. Taking into account food production in each region, this implies that 18% of the loss occurred in most developed countries, 38% in intermediate countries, and 44% in least developed countries (who could least afford the food loss). More extensive use of herbicides could, according to the FAO, reduce global food loss from 11% to 5–6% by 1985, with most of the improvement in the least developed countries. The ambivalence toward increased herbicide use, however, is clear from the conclusion: "It is with some reluctance that one suggests increased use of herbicides as one does not wish to see dependence on herbicide being built up as has happened in the developed world . . . if food supplies are to be substantially increased however, herbicides are almost unavoidable and could make considerable contribution to increases in yield, particularly of maize, which (a) is very sensitive to weeds, (b) is grown under the high rainfall conditions making weeding difficult, and (c) can be very safely treated with a number of available herbicides."[19]

For our purposes we can classify the environmental damages associated with increased pesticide use into three groups: those effects that may directly or indirectly limit food production itself, those effects that may cause economic

Table 6.15 Pesticide and Fertilizer Use, Sample of Farmers in Bihar, India 1968/1969–1969/1970

Crop	Percentage of Total Crop Area	Percentage of Individual Crop Area Receiving Pesticide		Pesticide Expenditure Per Hectare[a] (rs)		Fertilizer Expenditure Per Hectare[a] (rs)	
		1968/1969	1969/1970	1968/1969	1969/1970	1968/1969	1969/1970
Food crop	90	25.3	29.0	NA	NA	NA	NA
Paddy	43	29.5	44.6	7.2	22.0	50.2	76.4
Wheat	23	43.8	29.0	6.2	21.3	110.0	120.3
Maize	3	5.6	11.0	5.9	3.2	25.7	12.6
Pulses	21	1.9	NA	NA	NA	NA	NA
Other	4	NA	NA	NA	NA	NA	NA
Cash crops	6	7.1	20.1	NA	NA	NA	NA
Potato	3	4.7	0.9	68.2	48.2	146.5	152.7
Sugar cane	1	53.7	48.1	NA	NA	72.6	65.2
Other cash crop	2	18.2	58.6	52.1	57.8	28.9	24.0
Total	100	24.7	28.6	10.1	23.0	53.6	75.6

Source. *Pesticide Market Studies*, volume XI, Shahabod District, Bilhar State, (Resurvey) (New Delhi, India, Pesticides Association of India, 1971).

[a] Expenditure per hectare of arable land.

NA, not available.

damages outside of agriculture, and occupational health problems that occur during application. Turning to the first group, the most direct and perhaps important effect of increased pesticide use is the development of pesticide-resistant insects. There are two costs associated with the appearance of resistant insects—the pest populations can multiply beyond their initial levels, decreasing rather than increasing yields, and farmers can be forced into more frequent and expensive sprayings with yet more toxic chemicals. This is not a hypothetical consequence. There is evidence that the number of resistant insect pests in agriculture has increased. A similar loss of efficiency for DDT against malaria mosquitoes has occurred.[20] Closely related to this perverse effect is the decline in the populations of nontarget parasites and predators as pesticides initially reduce the target pest. When the resistant insect appears, natural controls are absent, and its population expands beyond previous limits.[21] Also, when herbicides are used to control certain weeds, the area may be invaded by other vegetation with even more undesirable characteristics and further worsen the prospects for eradication. Weed populations may return at even greater rates after the herbicide effect wears down.[22] Thus a vicious circle can be started. In an effort to improve yields and meet increased food demands, pesticides may unwittingly create conditions that worsen rather than improve yields.

There are other ways in which increased pesticide use incidentally limits rather than increases food production. Under a multiple cropping system, herbicides used during a previous crop may retain their toxic qualities and damage subsequent crops.[23] This problem may become more prevalent in the tropics that are suited for multiple cropping, where weed growth is luxuriant, and where manual weed removal may decline over time. Also, pesticide runoff has been shown in some cases to produce fish kills in adjacent waters. This may be a particularly sensitive problem in Southeast Asia where insecticides are applied to paddy rice and the inundated fields and fish ponds are used for raising fish for food and income.[24] Direct application of pesticides to water bodies (e.g., herbicides for aquatic weed control and insecticides for disease vector control) is another source of fish kills.

It is possible to trace more complex interactions between increased pesticide use and agricultural productivity, but the exposition is less satisfactory. For example, one can argue that the availability of pesticides permits and encourages major changes in production techniques, for example, monoculture and multiple cropping. Although both of these can have positive effects on productivity, both can cause new types of environmental stress. The traditional position has been that monoculture increases the problem of pest control because large areas are devoted exclusively to the cultivation of one crop. However, a recent National Academy of Sciences report is cautious on this point. It observes that some insect diseases and weeds flourish more in monoculture than in mixed cropping systems, but the reverse is true for others. The report concludes, "we believe the need for pesticides per unit of land area is increased in narrow-based cropping systems. There are, however, tradeoffs in terms of higher yields per unit of land area and lessened environmental impact because of reduced land area."[25] However, these less direct interactions involving changes in production techniques are not always undesirable. For example, the techniques of minimum tillage require the use of herbicides for weed control, but in this situation the availability of herbicides permits a technique to be used that reduces erosion, directly maintaining soil fertility and reducing pesticide runoff into adjacent waters.

Apart from the effects of pesticide use on agricultural productivity, there are two other sources of concern. The first is the effect of pesticide residues on human health, and the second is poisoning during application. There is great uncertainty about the long-term effects of pesticide build-up in human tissue. Synergistic effects among pesticides or between pesticides and other chemical substances are unknown. In a 1973 report on environment and agriculture the National Academy of Sciences cited a series of studies on pesticide build-up in man, and concluded that "it has not been established (given the potential for pesticide concentration within human tissue) however, that these chemicals pose any threat to health."[26] With regard to residual build-up in human tissue, it is the persistent pesticides (chlorinated hydrocarbon) that pose the greater danger.

Biomagnification through the food chain is another pathway to humans. Pesticide residue in grains is seldom a problem, but residues in fruits and vegetables can be. The importance of fish as a protein source in many developing countries and the extensive use of fishponds and fish raising in irrigation waters in intensively farmed areas in South and Southeast Asia suggests that pesticide contamination of food sources may become an increasingly serious problem. One interesting study showed exceptionally high levels of DDT residues in humans in Pakistan and India. The study, sponsored by US AID, gave the following measurements of DDT in human tissue.[27]

	Parts per Million DDT, 1973
Karachi, Pakistan	25.0
India	25.1
Germany	2.3
Hungary	12.4
France	5.2
United Kingdom	2.6
Holland	2.0
Italy	10.1
United States	9.5
Canada	3.8

The suggested explanation for the high levels in India and Pakistan was the incidental spraying of vegetable crops and in-house use of DDT for malaria control. Although the study found that only 5–10% of the total crop area in Pakistan is treated, localized and inappropriate use of DDT for fruits and vegetables may be serious problems. Guen-Soen Lim cites an FAO study that showed that 20% of market vegetables in Thailand were contaminated with excessive residues. It is hard to imagine that small cultivators, without much training or traditions of insecticide use, are very exact and conservative in using pesticides on fruits and vegetables, nor can one imagine a sophisticated and effective government inspection and monitoring system as these products are domestically marketed.

The problem of occupational poisoning in pesticide application has been exacerbated as countries have moved away from persistent pesticides to those that are more easily degradable but much more lethal. FAO data show accidental poisoning by the short-lived but lethal organophosphates to have increased in Thailand from 29 in 1970 to 125 in 1972.[28] The United States and other industrial countries have yet to solve the problem of harm to agricultural workers from the application of pesticides and from field worker poisoning. One can only assume that the problem will be more difficult in developing countries with casual and untrained laborers, less experience with pesticides, no agricultural labor unions, and perhaps indifferent government attitudes. Effective and comprehensive controls in pesticide application and subsequent reentry of workers to the fields could presumably keep occupational damages to a minimum, but we do not believe these controls are likely.

The environmentalists' answer to ever increasing pesticide use is usually termed "integrated pest control,"[29] or the appropriate combinations of a variety of natural enemies of the target pests, including the use of virus and bacteria pathogens, crop manipulation (interplanting, crop rotation), physical and mechanical means (flooding, burning, barriers, and light traps), and genetic controls (including sterile mating and disease-resistant breeding). Pesticide use is also a part of integrated pest control, but it is to be used selectively against specific pests at their most vulnerable stage. A.W.A. Brown states the matter clearly when he says an insecticide should be "used as a stiletto rather than a scythe. Ideally, it should be employed to punch a particular hole in the food-chain which, if it cannot be filled in by other species in the neighboring elements of the biota, at least should be done at such a time of season that it does not seriously disturb the biota."[30]

Irrigation. The provision of adequate water is often the key factor in increasing grain yields in developing countries. Expenditures on irrigation systems have absorbed a large share of domestic and multilateral development financing. Irrigation is critical to the success of the new high-yield grain varieties.

From an environmental perspective, irrigation systems can be the "victim" of environmentally disruptive practices and the cause of soil problems and pesticide runoff. The victim status is the result of erosion and consequent siltation of irrigation reservoirs and canals. Less directly, watershed deforestation that is associated with erosion will also increase the rapidity of water runoff, increasing the need for irrigation to provide controlled water supplies to crops. The evidence for erosion and siltation resulting from deforestation was reviewed in Chapter 2 and has been vividly described by Eckholm. Because our chief concern here is the direct environmental implications of increased grain production rather than the effects of deforestation on food output, our observations are restricted to the second subject, irrigation as a cause of soil problems and contamination of runoff water. Also, because irrigation problems are often region specific, some of the discussion is deferred to the later section on arid regions.

Surface irrigation water contains salts. As it is applied to crop lands, evaporation and transpiration by plants remove the water and salt deposits are left. If allowed to build up, salt deposits reduce the fertility of soils and decrease yields.[31] Eventually salt-sensitive crops can no longer be grown, and more salt tolerant but less valuable crops are sown. In extreme cases, all commercial cropping must cease. To sustain output on irrigated land, it is necessary to flush salts downward into the soil or to remove them by saline water drainage. They may be flushed downward or leached from the surface by sufficient application of water, but this can create another problem. Continued high water input will start to raise the water table in areas of poor underground drainage. As the water table approaches the surface, the soil becomes waterlogged, and crop root structures are damaged by lack of oxygen or saline subsurface water. Water tables do not have to actually reach the surface for damage, since water can move to the surface through capillary action and, following evaporation, deposit a surface salt film. The problem is less serious in regions with good underground drainage characteristics or those in which periodic flooding can leach salt into runoff waters.

In the United States, grain crops are not generally irrigated. The major exceptions are rice in the South and corn in the drier regions of the Great Plains. In the semi-arid tropics, however, irrigation of grain crops is critical. Rice, too, is sometimes irrigated, but the paddy system is apparently successful in flushing out excess salts. The extent to which soil loss through salination and water logging is a constraint on grain production in developing countries is discussed later.

The general uncertainty about the relation between irrigation and pesticide runoff is evident from studies of pesticide use in the San Joaquin Valley in California, where irrigation is extensive and pesticide use is heavy (22 kg/ha):

1. "While crop irrigation does give rise to pesticide runoff in some cases, a previous report that agricultural runoff is the greatest source of pesticides reaching California waters was *not* confirmed for the San Joaquin Valley."
2. "Subsurface drainage appears to be a much less likely route of pesticide transport than surface runoff . . . (and) direct application of pesticides to water is considered to be one of the major pathways of pesticides in the aquatic environment. . . ."
3. Herbicides are generally less toxic to aquatic fauna than are "insecticides" (although the use of herbicides in paddy may create problems similar to those in point 2).
4. In conclusion, "the limited evidence available indicates that the agricultural use of pesticides in the San Joaquin Valley would seem to have no significant adverse effects upon the aquatic environment."[32]

Erosion and Nutrient Loss

Erosion and the leaching of nutrients is related to the topography and climate of a region and its agricultural practices. It is therefore difficult to generalize. Certainly critical variables are the intensity of rainfall, the slope of the land, and the type of soil. In addition, irrigation can cause erosion, although terracing and other water control techniques associated with irrigation should generally act to retard erosion. The density of ground cover and the amount of time the soil is left unprotected are also important.

In considering the impact of expanded grain production on erosion, it would appear that the gravest danger is extending tillage to soils unsuited for cropping. These are often of two types—mountainous slopes subject to intense tropical rains and rangelands and savannas where tillage breaks up natural ground cover and exposes the soil to both water and particularly wind erosion. Unlike fertility loss, which can be offset by the use of organic and inorganic fertilizer, erosion of top soil lacks cyclical renewability. Once topsoil is removed, very little can be done to restore productivity. It is therefore important that proper caution be exercised in cultivating new "marginal" lands. (Also, by limiting erosion there may be some reduction in the transport of pesticides that are found in the soils.) Unfortunately, the ability of governments to ensure that marginal cultivators on marginal lands, on the fringes of agricultural systems, exercise this caution is open to serious question. Indeed, internal migrations by the land hungry and control of their tillage practices already escapes effective government control in many countries.

The amount of soil lost through wind and water erosion cannot be accurately stated. One estimate suggests that "to date" about 2000 million ha have been lost globally. This is more than the present world arable land. The annual estimate is 6–7 million ha/yr.[33] Such estimates, however, have little meaning. Even in the United States the amount lost is uncertain. Wadliegh estimates that erosion by wind displaces each year 30 million tons of soil and water erosion 4 billion tons.[34] Four billion tons equals 5 tons per acre annual loss in the United States, with most occurring on cropped lands. The National Academy of Sciences estimates that water erosion is severe on 179 million acres of cropland and significant on another 50 million acres. However, some erosion is a normal occurrence, and the very concept of excessive erosion is difficult to define. Soil removal is not necessarily identical with soil loss.[35] Pimentel et al.[36] recently reviewed the significance of erosion in the United States, pointing out the tradeoff between erosion and yields over the past 50 years. Some of their evidence on erosion seems to us to be outdated, although there are some points that need emphasis. It is quite true that erosion loses both fertility and top soil, and there is considerable documentation on the loss of productivity of corn and other cereals.[37] Beyond what we mention in this section, however, we feel that insufficient evidence exists to compute properly the amount of topsoil "lost" for the United States as a whole that is directly caused by certain forms of agriculture.

If topographical conditions were respected and soil conservation methods followed, intensified cereal production need not produce unacceptable erosion either in the United States or in the developing countries. Basic soil conservation techniques are well known. They include terracing, contour plowing, the planting of wind breaks, and sufficient ground cover to protect soils. In addition, the planting of small grain rather than row crops, crop rotation, the addition of mulch and green manure, minimum tillage, and the avoidance of clean tillage can all reduce soil loss.[38] As noted earlier, there is, however, a tradeoff between minimal tillage and pesticide use. Minimal tillage requires herbicide treatment for weed control, whereas tillage increases the potential for erosion but helps control weeds and may kill dormant insects in temperate zones. On balance, it appears that techniques for erosion control are adequate and that the major requirement for protecting food systems in developing countries is the acceptance of these practices, and the management of activity such as overgrazing and excessive firewood collection.

Variations Among Tropical Regions

The developing world faces the need to expand food output. However, the developing world is not homogeneous. As described in Chapter 2, some regions are densely populated and others sparsely settled. Some have most of their arable land under cultivation, and others have large expanses of virgin territory. Rainfall is often at the extremes, both in annual average and in seasonal concentrations. Crop patterns vary. Therefore, it seems useful to examine the question of environment and food output regionally, as well as from other perspectives. The divisions follow the climate regions described in Chapter 2.

Desert and Semi-Arid Regions of the Tropics and Subtropics. Overgrazing, excessive removal of burnable material, and irrigation-caused soil deterioration are the main current and prospective environmental problems of the arid regions. Although the Near East is not the only arid region, it is useful as an important example. Only 5% of its land is arable, and 36% of the arable land is irrigated. The irrigated land, however, produces over 70% of total crop value. Yield differences between irrigated and rainfed crops are striking: 240% for wheat, 375% for coarse grains, and 167% for pulses.[39] Seed cotton is an important crop on 17% of irrigated land. This is interesting because of the heavy pesticide use, whose connection with irrigation is noted in a previous section.

Total irrigated area is projected to increase to 56% of arable land by 1985 if regional food needs are to be met.[40] Increased oil income will permit some countries of the region to construct expensive irrigation systems. Persumably, it will also permit the installation of works to limit salination and waterlogging.[41]

The environmental record of arid lands to date is not reassuring. Much of the region has been affected in the last two decades by increasingly saline water. In West Pakistan, 58% of arable land was irrigated in 1962. The Indus area, which contains 95% of the arable land in the region, has major soil problems. Even back in 1954, 24% was considered poorly drained, 24% had saline patches, and another 10% was predominately saline.[42] Moderate salination, although not necessarily causing immediate land abandonment, can seriously limit yields. Iraq and West Pakistan, for example, both severely affected by saline conditions in the 1950s and early 1960s, had rice yields of about 16% and wheat yields approximately 33% of Egypt's. Much of this difference has been attributed to the severe salinity problems in these two countries relative to that of Egypt. Even in Egypt, where annual flooding helps leach salts, nearly 60% of its cultivated area was estimated to be moderately to severely affected by salinity and water logging.[43]

The use of tubewells that pump water from the water table, thus reducing its level and leaching out the salt build-up, has enabled vast areas of the arid regions in the developing world to be reclaimed. This technique was used in India and Pakistan in the late 1960s after tests by Revelle and others proved successful.[44] It is still uncertain whether this progress can be continued and expanded enough to satisfy the rapidly growing population in these regions. Note that the arid regions of the Indian subcontinent have some irrigation potential; such potential is almost nonexistent in the vast Sahelian region of Africa except for the Nile valley. However, the Sahel does not support a large population, as is the case with the northern Indian Gangetic plain.

Fertilizer and pesticide contamination may not be serious problems for increasing cereal production in arid regions, if only because it is unlikely that they will be heavily used for economic reasons, although more will be required as HYVs gain ground in these areas; the utilization of irrigation with the HYVs would then pose some danger. Environmental problems are more directly related to population pressures, livestock grazing, and the use of pesticides and fertilizers on cash crops, particularly cotton, than to cereal production. To increase yields *as well as* decrease environmental damage, certain farming techniques may prove helpful.

The development of a rotational mixed farming system for the semi-arid wheat regions of North America has not only reduced erosion but has also produced cattle forage. The leguminous crops cultivated in sequence with wheat have helped to restore the nitrogen content of the soil. This is beneficial in two respects. Not only does the nitrogen increase wheat yields, but "a soil with a high nitrogen content generally has a better water-holding capacity than one with a low nitrogen status."[45] Arid regions in the LDCs may also benefit from mixed farming *if* enough water is available.

Tropical Wet and Dry. Tropical wet and dry (savanna) regions are lightly populated but have localized areas of heavy density. Although grains are a key crop in arid regions, they are not as important in savanna areas. Other food crops are often of greater importance, but have not yet been successfully interbred for increased yields. Irrigation is not extensively practiced.

At present, soil conservation techniques are not being rapidly adopted. Soil problems appear to be caused by misuse and indifference to the consequences of erosion and fertility loss and to the stress of localized population centers. The very existence of unexploited land may encourage neglect. Latin American savannas are not intensively used, but in areas in which agricultural land is developed, erosion problems are often severe. Regions farmed by migrants rather than established residents are exploited for short-term rather than long-term sustained yields, even when fallow land methods are used. As analyzed in Chapter 4, there are economic pressures to shorten fallow. Sustained production will perhaps require greater capital, a more appropriate crop mix that does not quickly exhaust soils, and the planting of crops and shade trees.[46]

Because of low population densities at the present time, food self-sufficiency does not appear unrealistic if sensible policies are followed. The use of manure and other traditional fertilizers can be important in areas of heavy grazing, such as parts of Africa. Better use of these nutrients could increase yields in the short run and would sustain long-term yields through improved soil structure, reduced erosion, and reduced nutrient leaching.[47] Cash crops and livestock production are important agricultural sectors. The transfer of temperate zone grain production may not be successful without modification; heavy ploughing can aggravate erosion and accelerate the loss of soil nutrients, forcing increasingly large application of fertilizers. The careful use of irrigation and rotational cropping will also help to improve and sustain yields.

Tropical Rainy. There are many environmental problems that limit conventional farming in the rainy tropics.[48] The humus content of the soils is not seriously deficient, but there is an extremely rapid turnover from decomposing nutrients back into growing plants. Although this explains the luxuriant growth, it may pose serious problems for conventional agricultural production, particularly for grains. Ploughing and clearing land without some kind of protecting cover from palms or legumes will seriously expose the soil, which is inherently vulnerable to the elements. Also, cereal plants simply do not return nutrients back into the soils as efficiently as other crops, but effectively transfer most of the nutrients upward into the harvested crop. "The fertility (of humid forest soils) is in fact tied up with the forest system, disappearing if the forest is replaced by more widely spaced, shallow-rooted and short-cycle crops, which expose the soil to weathering."[49]

Traditional tropical agriculture has survived under these circumstances by adopting a rather complex shifting, fallow-land culture. To maintain soil fertility, a fallow system is often adhered to, allowing the jungle to return and reattain a delicate nutrient balance. This system of agriculture, allowing 2–5 years of cropping followed by 5–30 years of fallow, is ecologically sound in the sense that fertility is renewed, but the tropical rain forest is still drastically changed. The forest under slash and burn shifting cultivation will indeed reproduce itself, but the complete process takes up to 250 years. Before this, a secondary forest of lower trees and grasses will rapidly take hold. "Much of the humid tropics is now covered by secondary forests, and extensive areas of primary rain forest occur only in the Amazon basin, parts of the Congo, and in the remote parts of Southeast Asia."[50]

Even without pressure to decrease the fallow period, the removal of the primary forest results in extremely low yields. Research and new technology are desperately needed to raise this agriculture above the subsistence level. Pesticides may be extremely important, both in limiting plant loss and in increasing the habitable (and therefore cultivatable) area by eradicating health hazards. The danger from insecticides is misuse and localized overuse. Herbicides may also play an important role if properly controlled. "A number of authorities consider that weed control problems are a major factor limiting agricultural output in the tropics, especially in the high rainfall areas . . . shifting cultivation is sometimes as much a concession to weeds as to declining soil fertility. Chemical weed killers are being used quite extensively in a number of tropical countries, but without benefit of analytical data showing conditions under which such measures are economic."[51]

The removal of weed cover is important in grain production, but experience in the rainy tropics would indicate that some form of rotational cropping, to limit the time the soil is unprotected, may be the most beneficial method of dealing with weeds. Insecticides and herbicides, if used in conjunction with some form of multiple-crop, rotational farming, perhaps with cash crops providing cover, may play an important role in the humid tropics. "The tropical environment, which favors the fast luxuriant growth of crops and vegetation, also favors weeds which compete for moisture and nutrients, and the parasitic fungi, insects, spider mites, eelworms, and virus diseases which make for serious reductions in crops."[52] It is probable, however, that chemical inputs will generally be limited to nongrain crops and that cereals production will have a limited environmental effect unless extensive clearing is also practiced.

The potential for erosion in the rainy tropics is not completely understood, and there is still considerable difference of opinion as to the seriousness of erosion in the rain forests.[52] It is clear, however, that erosion control and protection of soils from sun and leaching in the rainy tropics is critical to support agriculture and may be more so than in temperate regions.

The most controversial environmental result of "modern" agriculture is the supposed reduction of the environment into a monoculture. Many individual examples portraying pollution and soil exhaustion relate to the rainy tropics. Milton stated that the "simplification of tropical ecosystems, such as necessarily accompanies agriculture or pastoralism as well as intensive forest culture, must always tend to upset the balance developed in the mature biotic community. Where only one or a few species of plants are encouraged to grow in place of the diversity of the natural forest, an environment is created that is highly favorable to the rapid increases of their predators or parasites."[54]

It is extremely doubtful that true monocultures can or should ever be successfully grown in the humid tropics. Rather, some form of rotational and mixed cropping with limited demand for added nutrients will have to be developed to increase yields and limit soil destruction. Often, chemical fertilizers are simply too expensive in large amounts (except, again, for nongrain crops); manure is not available in quantity; at present, successful methods of legume rotations, or green manuring, have not been fully developed.

Tropical Humid. In some areas in the humid regions, waterlogging and saline conditions (Pakistan and India in particular) can pose serious constraints. Unlike the arid regions, water is often sufficient for crops in terms of yearly rainfall, but the distinct division between dry and wet periods, coupled with the extremely wet monsoon seasons,[55] produces both environmental and agricultural management problems. The solution of the latter by means of a large-scale reservoir and irrigation system may aggravate the former. Land management techniques for paddy production are centuries old and in general environmentally sound. Environmental problems can occur as increased population growth either forces the utilization of otherwise marginal land (particularly in hill country) or an intensification of yields per hectare by increasing inputs of fertilizer and pesticides.

Wetland rice production is the most productive of all food systems in the developing world and is far and away the most productive in the humid monsoon region. Shifting upland cultivation, on the other hand, is of lesser importance. "In India, Southeast Asia and Southern China, about 50 million people depend upon shifting cultivation. They grow crops each year on between 10 million and 18 million hectares out of a total area of from 100 million to 110 million hectares of crops and fallow. In contrast, in the same area, some 675 million live by permanent agriculture, using between 220 million and 230 million hectares of cropland. Shifting cultivation is characteristically found in upland areas, whilst the dominant farming system in the low-lands is wet rice cultivation."[56]

Traditional methods (other than paddy) of food production in these regions, often utilizing potentially destructive shifting cultivation, are the true environmental menaces to the monsoon regions. Together with nonfood crop production and forestry, vast tracts of virgin rain forest are being irrevocably altered by shifting cultivation. The production of nonfood crops in the monsoon regions has also led to a series of classic over-use pollution situations[57] in which the intensive use of chemicals on monocrop structure has worsened yields in the long-run and increased pests.

In many respects, the humid regions are the most important in the tropical world in part because of the massive populations they are called on to support. For the foreseeable future, it will be the monsoon regions that will be most in need of increased food output. Environmentally, there are fewer constraints on agricultural production in the monsoon lands than in the other segments of the tropical developing world, yet these areas are being crippled by population growth. (See pp. 326–330 for more on rice production.)

In summing up the environmental limits to monsoon agriculture (which definitionally includes parts of our wet and dry region), Grigg states: "The problems of monsoon Asia, and of India in particular, differ substantially from the three ecological regions discussed earlier . . . the higher population density precludes any substantial expansion of cultivated area, and the large annual additions to the population nullify much of the increased output. But in India (7.5% of the world's population) it is not ecological problems that are the prime obstacles to agricultural progress. It is true that the variability and timing of the monsoons is an all-pervading influence on agricultural life. But the irrigated area is large; the main problem is effective utilization. Whilst ecological difficulties must not be ignored, they do not provide such obstacles as they do in the arid, wet-dry or rainy tropics."[58] Still, we note that abuses of traditional agriculture in upland areas and soil loss in watersheds are serious environmental problems that can affect monsoon agriculture.

Methods of Cultivation

Developing countries exhibit the full range of cultivation systems. Two systems of special interest are shifting cultivation and wetland rice production.

Shifting Cultivation. It is estimated that over 30% of the world's arable soil is farmed under some variant of shifting cultivation.[59] Shifting cultivation uses natural fallow, a method that varies considerably depending on population density, soil fertility, types of crops at hand, and cultural traditions. Beyond the common denominator of fallow, however, the term has some ambiguities. The expression usually connotes temporary occupancy, but, for example, in the Philippines the word "Kaingin" means shifting agriculture and is used for the cutting and burning of forests for temporary use or for permanent agricultural development. In other countries the term is more strictly limited to temporary agriculture.[60]

The motives for fallow in shifting agriculture can also vary. One dominant reason is to replenish soil nutrients and restore soil fertility. Another reason can be that the fallow cycle is effective as a weed control mechanism for farmers who can neither afford chemicals nor keep up with continuous manual weeding. Cook notes that "once taken by weeds the land must be allowed to grow up to bushes so that it can be cleared again by fire, or at much greater expense by hand labor."[61] In many temperate semi-arid regions the total moisture storage capacity of the soil exceeds normal rainfall. Therefore, fallow periods can be used to build up soil moisture and increase yields. In semi-arid tropics, however, the seasonal rainfall can exceed soil storage capacity. Unless the land has good cover, extreme soil loss can result.[62]

Shifting cultivation is very seldom composed of a monoculture, but is usually a rotating system of cereal, pulses, and possibly nonfood crops. Cereals are usually the main crop, but this is variable. Many cereals are not noted for their high yields as much as their hardiness (millet, for example); thus many exist in extensive, low-yield agriculture.[63] Very little ploughing is used with shifting cultivation in the humid tropics because of root problems and equipment costs.[64] This will protect the soil during farming if fallow is allowed but produces extremely low yields. Maize yields in West Africa, for instance, are usually around 100 kg/ha, whereas the potential for these crops in the same area with the same frequency of cultivation is over 8000 kg/ha.[65] To achieve high yields, fertilizer, pesticides, and proper management of both soil and water through terracing, green manuring, and so on, are needed.

Shifting cultivation under modest population pressure is often environmentally satisfactory, but rapid population growth can force farmers to extend cultivation to fragile soils or to shorten the fallow period. The latter process, in the best of circumstances, is the first step in the transition to continuous farming with sustained yields. To accomplish it successfully, it is often necessary to apply additional fertilizers to offset declines in natural soil fertility and to take other soil conservation measures. Too often, however, the fallow period is shortened without any change in farming practices. The result is reduced soil fertility and reduced yields. In extreme cases the land is prematurely abandoned after being stripped of nutrients.

Erosion occurs when hill land is cleared under shifting cultivation and fallow periods are not sufficient to adequately cover and renew the soil. Many authors have noted with alarm the occurrence of shifting cultivation on a slope of 70–80% in the tropics, particularly in Latin America.[66] In temperate zones a slope of 20% is considered dangerously prone to erosion. However, shifting cultivation with proper fallow may be less destructive than permanent cropping on steep lands. Some tropical soils also have higher water infiltration rates than temperate soils, and this minimizes runoff. Steeper land on porous soils in Latin American tropics cannot be directly compared to similar gradients in temperate areas. For example, in Costa Rica, Ives found that the soil structure dominated vegetation in the control of runoff.[67]

Closely related to the extension of shifting agriculture to fragile lands is the problem of migrants who bring with them cultivation practices that are inappropriate to their new surroundings. The example of the Peruvian highlands is instructive. Here the Andean population, moving away from the eroded mountain regions, are settling the lower humid tropics. Watters states that the effects of this migration "are most unfortunate in the initial years of occupation, and are associated especially with the production of annual crops, such as maize, rice and beans . . . the consequence of this type of settlement is usually some early success with large harvests obtained from virgin soils, followed by later crop failures which, coupled with land tenure problems and insecurity, leads to further migration . . ."[68] In the Philippines and Indonesia, access to remote hill regions by increased commercial lumbering has produced an uncontrolled migration of lowland cultivators who use inappropriate farming techniques.

Methods to minimize soil damage from shifting cultivation depend on the features of the region, including population density. Obviously, land ownership patterns can be improved. A combination of nonfood and food crops in a modified shifting cultivation may be the best answer for the humid tropics. For areas of high population density, the transition to continuous cropping is necessary.

In savanna areas the development of continuous agriculture from shifting cultivation is not as dependent on soil protection methods, since the soil is not usually favorable to perennial cropping without expensive inputs. "The cost of mechanization, construction of proper erosion control measure, and adequate chemical inputs is larger for savannas than for the forested areas under a modified shifting cultivation, and the costs are often greater than the value of the food crops produced . . . The transition from shifting cultivation to continuous management in these areas will necessarily be slow, and it will be best achieved by introduction of improved varieties and fertilizers and pesticides into the existing system, rather than by any attempt to replace it by larger scale mechanized agriculture."[69]

Research is continuing to find methods to give the small farmer a practical substitute for traditional shifting cultivation. For example, in a recent report on the International Institute of Tropical Agriculture (IITA), it was mentioned that their work has demonstrated that "using herbicides (and no tillage), water receptivity of the soil can be greatly improved and erosion controlled."[70] Moreover, Greenland of the IITA suggests that continuous cultivation based on intercropping of both grain and legume crops, minimum or zero tillage, mulch, and little capital requirements can be successfully developed for the shifting cultivator in the rainy tropics, which would both increase yields and lower erosion rates. The erosion and yield results from experiments in conventional versus zero tillage and single versus intercropping are shown in Table 6.16. Clearly, zero tillage and intercropping can have positive yield and soil conservation results.

Rice Cultivation. Rice, because of its enormous importance and special production characteristics, deserves separate comment. In fact, there are two distinct methods for rice cultivation—paddy (either irrigated or rainfed) and upland. Paddy rice is suited for tropical monsoon and alluvial regions. It is grown in enclosed areas that are regularly flooded during the growing season. Up to three crops per year are possible, but this is uncommon. As practiced in South and Southeast Asia, it is a labor-intensive activity, and grain yields per year per acre can be higher than for any other grain crop. In addition, irrigation networks used to supply the rice paddies and store water can be used for freshwater fish production, a form of simultaneous multiple cropping. A common fish is tilapia, and pesticide damage to fisheries is said to be of great concern in Bangladesh, Burma, Indonesia, Malaysia, and Thailand.[70] In contrast to paddy rice production, upland rice is grown in a more conventional fashion without the flooding of the fields. Upland rice may rely on slash and

Table 6.16 Soil and Water Loss with Alternative Tillage Systems

	Grain Yield[a] (kg/ha)	
	Conventionally Plowed	Zero Tilled
Single-cropped cow pea	1185.0	1649.0
Intercropped cow pea plus corn	2370.0	3750.0
	Erosion[b]	
Soil loss (ton/ha) on 10% slope	4.4	0.1
Runoff (mm) on 10% slope	52.4	20.3

Source. D.J. Greenland, "Bringing the Green Revolution to the Shifting Cultivator," *Science*, November 28, 1975.

[a] Plowed and ridged for "conventional plowed." From Greenland, Table 2 (included 90 kg/ha of fertilizer).

[b] Conventional plowed defined simply as "plowed." Based on maize production. From Greenland, Table 1.

burn techniques for field preparation, and, unlike paddy rice which is continually cropped, upland rice is usually in a fallow system or a form of shifting cultivation. Accordingly, the environmental constraints and consequences of paddy and upland rice production are quite different.

Interestingly, only 33% of the rice crop area in South and Southeast Asia is irrigated, although this produces 48% of the harvested crop. As shown in Table 6.17, rainfed paddy rice accounts for the largest crop area (57%) but a smaller fraction of the total crop (47%). Upland rice in Asia accounts for 10% of the crop area but only 5% of production. Yields on upland rice are generally much lower than rainfed or irrigated paddy production, in part because research on rice hybrids has been mainly devoted to irrigated paddy rice. The concentration of hybrid research on irrigated paddy rice accounts for the apparent slower growth of rice production in developing countries compared to wheat and maize production.

Worldwide, the relative reliance on upland versus paddy rice varies sharply, and this helps to explain major differences in yields. Available data for upland versus paddy rice is contained in Table 6.18. An index of rice yields per hectare, with United States 1969–1973 yields serving as a base of 100, is displayed in Table 6.19. The contrasts are strong. For example, in Brazil 14% of arable land is in rice, and upland rice is 77% of the total. Yields in Brazil are only 28% of United States yields. Yields in Korea, which has almost no upland rice, exceed those of the United States. As seen from Table 6.18, upland rice production is of great importance in Latin America and Africa. Although upland rice is not as important in Asia, some countries such as Bangladesh, the Philippines, and Indonesia, have considerable production. These countries also have increasing population pressures; thus the potential for destructive practices associated with upland rice production exists.

What are the environmental implications of each type of production? By and large, traditional paddy production is an ecologically stable and sustainable system. Erosion does not present a serious problem, because terracing and

Table 6.17 Estimated Rice Crop Area by Specified Land Type in South and Southeast Asia

	Percentage of Crop Area		Percentage of Total Rice Production	
Land Type	Mid-1960s	Early 1970s	Mid-1960s	Early 1970s
1. Irrigated				
Single cropped	10	14	15	24
Double cropped	10	19	25	24
Total irrigated	20	33	40	48
2. Rainfed[a]				
Deep water	10	10	8	7
Other	50	47	42	40
Total rainfed	60	57	50	47
3. Upland	20	10	10	5
Total	100	100	100	100

Source. S.K. de Dalta and W.P. Abilay, "Varietal Adaptation to Water Conditions in Rainfed Rice Under Different Land Management Systems," IRRI, 1974; R.W. Cummings, Jr., *Food Crops in the Low-Income Countries: The State of Present and Expected Agricultural Research and Technology*, Rockefeller Foundation Working Paper, May 1976.

[a] Some of the differential between rice yields among countries can be explained by the slow progress made in producing HYVs for these rices. "Deep water rice" must be either resistant to high flood levels or have sufficiently long stalks. Although relatively unimportant regionally, rice is grown extensively under deep water conditions in Bangladesh, Thailand, and other delta, monsoon countries. "Other rainfed" regions either have adequate rainfall so as not to require irrigation or may experience water shortage difficulties and have not been irrigated because of economic, climatic, or policy reasons.

bunding entraps water and reduces sediment runoff. Whatever environmental stress is present and projected appears to be related to the increased use of fertilizer and pesticide inputs and perhaps to the spread of disease in irrigation systems and flooded fields. On this latter point, cultivation requires the farmer to wade out into the paddies, and diseases such as schistosomiasis can be transmitted.[71] The use of increased quantities of fertilizers and pesticides can cause problems. As noted, pesticide contamination can adversely affect fish production. Limited amounts of fertilizer may be beneficial to aquaculture, but not in excess. Also, as noted, pesticide residues in the soil can affect the growth of the subsequent crop. Grist observes that sustained paddy culture with chemical fertilizers can create problems, even though rice yields may be maintained at a high level almost indefinitely by the use of artificial fertilizers without the addition of organic matter. This use of inorganic fertilizer sometimes has unfortunate side effects. It is reported to be a factor in the creation of worn-out and low productive areas in Japan and to cause an increase of blast and other rice diseases. It is probable that the most satisfactory course to follow is to combine fertilizer application with green manuring.[72]

Where upland rice is grown in significant amounts, as in Africa and Latin America, particularly with slash and burn agriculture, erosion may be a very serious problem. No comprehensive estimate of the erosion problem stemming from slash and burn rice production exists. De Datta states that upland rice yields are limited by many of the same factors that limit rainfed paddy rice, but to a more critical degree. Traditional upland rice poses more environmental problems (erosion, nutrient loss, etc.) than traditional paddy rice production. Although input quantities similar to those added to HYV paddy rice might cause severe pollution problems, moderate inputs, as well as a more systematic approach to seed selection and ground cover techniques, could increase yields without serious increased erosion or nutrient loss. It is dangerous to generalize about rice production, but it does seem that traditional upland rice production, without yield increases through HYV use or inputs, would be rather costly from an ecological standpoint as population pressures mount.

Three factors affecting upland rice are

1. Input Requirements. Upland rice is less responsive to fertilizer than paddy rice. At the same time, however, upland rice may suffer more from nutrient deficiencies than paddy rice. The reason is that, with the irrigated production and flooding, some nitrogen is directly fixed by algae in the water.
2. Weeds. In general, weeds are a more critical problem in upland than lowland rice, since the flooding of paddy rice helps to control them. Although herbicides are sometimes heavily used on paddy rice, particularly when multiple cropped, under single crop conditions it is the upland, lower-yielding rice that requires greater weed control.
3. Diseases. Some diseases such as rice blast are more common in upland rice.[73]

One-half of all rainfed rice is single cropped in Southeast Asia because of rainfall variability. Normally, the farmers must wait until there is sufficient water to soften the paddy enough to plow the soil and control the weed population. By the time the rice seedlings are transplanted, the slower growing varieties reach maturity near or beyond the fall off of the monsoon rains. The International Rice Research Institute has developed a method whereby the rainfed rice farmer can grow two crops per year, yielding almost 10 tons/ha/yr.[74] To accomplish this, early-maturing rice is seeded directly in the early part of the monsoon, with the weeds controlled through the uses of herbicides. This leaves time after harvesting to plant a second, transplanted, early-maturing crop before the rains end. This technique, together with increased water collection systems through reservoirs or water tanks, could grow at least two crops per year. If all single-cropped irrigated rice could then be double-cropped in Southeast Asia, "effective" rice acreage would be increased about 20%. This scheme depends on the increased use of herbicides as well as some fertilizer. Whether the levels of herbicides per hectare needed for this purpose would create environmental problems, particularly where crops other than rice are also grown, is unknown at the moment, although herbicide pollution problems certainly deserve increased attention, especially under paddy conditions.

Table 6.18 Patterns of Rice Production, 1960s

	Total Rice Area (1000 ha)	Rice Area as Percentage of Total Arable Land	Upland Rice Acreage as Percentage of Total Rice Acreage
Latin America			
Brazil	4,858	14	77
Colombia	275	5	65
Guyana	138	32	55
Mexico	167	1	25
Panama	130	24	95
Ecuador	105	3	63
Peru	50	2	21
Central America	140	NA	90
Venezuela	139	3	80
Africa			
Sierra Leone	320	9	60
Guinea	280	6	60
Nigeria	160	1	62
Ivory Coast	290	3	89
Mali	190	2	
Liberia	280	16	100
Senegal	90	2	
Ghana	42	2	76
Gambia	28	8	10
Upper Volta	45	1	11
Togo	29	1	96
Niger	13	1	
Dahomey	2	NA	90
Mauritania	1	NA	

NEW PRODUCTION METHODS IN THE TROPICS

How adaptable are "modern" Iowa-style techniques to this strange world of small farms, tropical jungles, deserts, and growing populations? Irrigation and the addition of nutrients have been practiced in many of the regions for millennia, with the history of multiple cropping going back more than 3000 years. Some have argued that energy-intensive agriculture as now practiced in the West is not only outrageously expensive, but is also inherently pollutive even in temperate areas and may be actually counterproductive in the tropics. Is this actually the case, or are there ways to adapt the techniques responsible for the high yields obtained in the West to the special environmental, social, and economic circumstances of the developing world? This section highlights some of the key environment problems of "green revolution" technology and suggests some elements of modern agriculture that can help produce an environmentally sound, sustainable agriculture capable of raising yields above the present near-subsistence levels.

Table 6.18 (Continued)

	Total Rice Area (1000 ha)	Rice Area as Percentage of Total Arable Land	Upland Rice Acreage as Percentage of Total Rice Acreage
Asia			
South Asia		25	NA
Bangladesh	10,200	82	23
India	3,600	23	NA
Nepal	20	61	9
Pakistan		8	NA
Sri Lanka	671	31	2
Southeast Asia		43	NA
Burma		45	NA
Indonesia	7,348	45	21
Khmer Republic		80	NA
Laos		70	NA
Malaysia	448	20	5
Philippines	3,175	35	20
Thailand	6,697	59	NA
South Vietnam	2,296	86	3
East Asia		56	NA
Japan	3,281	53	4
South Korea	1,236	52	1
Taiwan	787	90	1
Mainland China	29,597	30	NA

Source. International Rice Research Institute, *Major Research in Upland Rice* (Los Baños, Philippines: IRRI, 1975) pp. 2–11.

Multiple Cropping

In areas subject to high and increasing population densities, additional production must come from an increase in yields, not expanded acreage. The relevant measure is not output per acre of crop harvested, but output per acre per year. Obviously, increasing the number of crops grown per year increases total output, as does improving yields per acre of crop sown. Some regions in the developing world have been able to greatly increase production by taking advantage of the long tropical growing season and the availability of labor. In Hong Kong, one of the most successful intensive agricultural areas in the world, over 80% of the farmers produced four crops a year per hectare in 1965, with 45% producing over nine intermixed crops.[75]

There is a distinct difference between this high-yield continuous cropping and the rotational cropping often practiced with shifting cultivation in the savanna, semi-arid, and humid tropics. In Asia, the extreme population pressure calls for intensive use of what land is available; in other regions a less

Table 6.19 Index of Rice Yields (U.S. 1969–1973 Average of 50.5 qu/ha = 100) Countries Producing More than One Million Metric Tons in 1975

	1969–1971	1974	1975[a]	Percentage of World Production
United States	100	98	101	2
EEC[b]	95	102	100	<1
USSR	73	76	79	1
Brazil	26	26	28	2
Colombia	70	86	88	<1
Egypt	104	91	101	1
Malagasy R.	38	33	33	1
Bangladesh	33	34	33	1
CPR	66	70	70	35
China, R.	85	85	86	1
India	33	31	35	19
Indonesia	48	53	55	7
Iran	73	69	74	<1
Japan	108	112	118	5
Khmer R.	29	26	30	<1
North Korea	86	99	105	1
South Korea	93	102	105	2
Malaysia	56	60	61	1
Nepal	39	36	36	1
Pakistan	45	43	44	1
Philippines	32	32	34	2
Sri Lanka	42	47	42	1
Thailand	37	35	35	4
North Vietnam	38	36	38	1
South Vietnam	45	47	49	2
World	47	48	49	100

Source. Department of Agriculture, *Rice Situation*, March 1976.

[a] Preliminary.

[b] European Economic Community.

intensive rotational system of different crops helps to maintain the limited fertility. Labor plays a key role, since large populations encourage intensive agriculture, and abundant labor makes intensive farming possible. Capital may replace labor as yields climb. This is so for Japan, where high-yield varieties are used in quantity. The relation between agricultural land density and multiple cropping (which is *not* limited to rice) can be seen in Table 6.20.

The FAO evaluates the potential for multiple cropping as follows:

> Thus, although the potential seems to be considerable, and possibly holds out the best long-term guarantee both for a sustained increase in food supply and for the improvement of the diet, it is still a long way from realization. We believe that multiple-cropping is unlikely to assume major significance outside certain Asian and Near East countries such as UAR before 1980, but that if the pioneering work now being undertaken in these countries could be studied and adapted . . . it could become a major contributory factor to growth after that year in all developing regions where ecological

Table 6.20 Multiple Cropping and Population Density (1970)

	Estimated Agricultural Land Per Capita (ha)	Cropping Index[a]
Egypt	0.2	166
South Korea	0.2	152
Taiwan	0.2	184
North Vietnam	0.3	147
China	0.3	140–147
Indonesia	0.4	126
India	0.8	114
Burma	1.5	115

Source. Dana Dalrymple, *Survey of Multiple Cropping in Developing Countries,* USDA ERS, October 1971.

[a] Cropping Index is derived by dividing total land area planted in 1 year (including land multiple cropped) by the amount of land physically available, that is, 100 means all land cropped just once per year.

conditions are suitable. Multiple-cropping could be of particular significance in obtaining a high financial rate of return from new investments in irrigation projects in Latin America and Africa south of Sahara, even though pressures on land would not render its general adoption as urgent as in Asia, the Near East or Northwest Africa.[76]

Increased production per acre puts additional stress on the land, requiring an increased amount of nutrients to halt the depletion of the soil that is almost constantly cultivated. Land under multiple cropping may become susceptible to erosion as well as fertilizer and pesticide pollution. If too much production is demanded or if soil is not inherently suitable for intensive use, yields may decrease. Pesticides requirements under a sequence of monocrops may have a perverse affect on production. "Continuous cropping with susceptible varieties of rice increases the likelihood of large-scale buildup of insect populations and disease organisms. Recent outbreaks of . . . viruses in the Philippines have been attributed to large-scale introduction of double-cropping with rice."[77]

The extent to which ecological considerations limit multiple cropping is unknown.[78] Green manures, minimum tillage, mulching, and other advanced soil and nutrient conservation techniques assist in expanding multiple crop production. The provision of irrigation is often necessary for production, and multiple cropping can provide economic justification for the irrigation expenditures. Although perhaps making soil more vulnerable to environmental abuse (and placing sustained production in jeopardy), multiple cropping can relieve the pressure on and environmental damage to marginal agricultural land.

High-Yield Varieties of Cereals (HYVs)

HYVs are hybrid strains of certain grains, developed to produce large yields in a particular environment. Normally, they require closely regulated and rather large amounts of fertilizer, pesticides, and irrigation water. The fertilizer is used by the plant more for grain production, not vegetative growth of the stems. Hence the semidwarf and dwarf characteristics. Wheat, corn, and rice are the important HYVs. Researchers are now attempting to find hybrids of other foods, particularly roots and leguminous crops.

The extent of HYV of wheat and rice are summarized in Table 6.21. Two-thirds of HYV wheat in developing countries is grown on irrigated land, mainly in India and Pakistan. Although water supplies are important for increased yield, the HYV wheat tends to be superior to local varieties even under drought.[79]

The "green revolution," or the introduction of HYV wheats into the Indian subcontinent in the mid-1960s, raised environmental criticisms. The essential

Table 6.21 Rice and Wheat High-Yield Varieties (HYVs)

	1969/1970		1974/1975	
	Hectares in HYV Wheat (thousand)	Percentage of Total Hectares in HYV Wheat	Hectares in HYV Wheat (thousand)	Percentage of Total Hectares in HYV Wheat
Asia				
Bangladesh	9.0	7.6	30.0	23.4
India	5,000.0	30.1	11,780.0	61.7
Iran	40.0	0.9	290.0	6.7
Pakistan	2,630.0	43.0	3,600.0	62.5
Turkey	620.0	7.6	650.0	8.0
Africa				
Algeria	5.0	2.2	600.0	27.9
Morocco	50.0	2.5	300.0	16.7
Tunisia	50.0	7.1	50.0	5.5
	Hectares in HYV Rice	Percentage of Total Hectares in HYV Rice	Hectares in HYV Rice	Percentage of Total Hectares in HYV Rice
Asia				
Bangladesh	260.0	2.6	1,440.0	14.9
Burma	140.0	2.9	330.0	6.4
India	4,250.0	11.3	11,050.0	29.9
Indonesia	830.0	10.4	3,440.0	40.3
South Korea			3,070.0	25.5
Pakistan	500.0	29.9	630.0	40.3
Philippines	1,350.0	43.5	2,180.0	64.0
Sri Lanka	26.0	3.9	350.0	52.8
Thailand	3.0		450.0	5.5

Source. D. Dalrymple, *Development and Spread of High Yielding Varieties*, USDA, ed., August 1976.

point involves susceptibility of grains to disease, the forced reliance on pesticides, and perhaps a dangerous simplification of the ecological balance that accompanies monoculture. There may be some truth to this. The temperate areas have much larger monoculture areas and therefore could be seriously hurt by disease, but the tropics are a more hospitable home for pests. There is also a real threat that new varieties are genetically vulnerable. The Irish Potato Blight, the Bengali rice disease of 1942, and the United States Southern Corn Blight of 1970 can be cited as occasions on which a disease struck a particular strain of each crop. Since in each instance there were relatively few strains within the crop area, the disease was able to affect a large portion of the total crop. Genetic vulnerability means simply that a very few genetic varieties are dominant in a region; hence any disease attacking that strain can spread without being stopped by resistant strains. By removing many traditional, low-yielding species in favor of a few high-yielding varieties and planting large single-crop fields to use machinery and chemical inputs more efficiently, the "green revolution" may have increased the potential for genetically related blights.[80]

The argument should be taken only so far. A broad lineage base for the new varieties can be developed to avoid the type of pest infestations that have plagued both wheat and temperate corn.[81] Also, high-yield varieties are not simply developed to give the highest yield, but rather to produce successfully in a particular environment with a certain constellation of pests, soils, and water supply. There is increasing interest in developing wheat that produces only moderate yields but is disease and drought resistant. There does not seem to be any overwhelming environmental weakness in the future use of HYV wheat.

Concerning rice, it is often noted that the Japanese, Chinese, and Taiwanese have very high rice yields, whereas other areas of Asia have extremely low yields. What causes the difference? One reason is the critical need for water in rice production, up to three times that needed by wheat. In Japan, water is more uniformly available than in the other areas, particularly India and Indonesia, where there are large fluctuations of river flows. There are differences in labor productivity, capital inputs, and fertilizer and pesticide use. The most critical difference, however, is in rice type.[82] Of the two varieties of rice in the world, the Japonica rices of the temperate regions are short stemmed and hence react very well to added fertilizer. Unfortunately, they were not very useful in the tropics because of their need for precise water, susceptibility to disease and excess heat, and unappetizing consistency for the peoples of the monsoon regions. Although the Indica variety of South and Southeast Asia is adapted to tropical monsoon climates with poor soil, it is not very receptive to increased fertilizer. The International Rice Research Institute and others have attempted to develop hybrids featuring the best elements of both types.

Although rice hybrids have existed for many centuries, IR-8 was the first modern success to blend the Japonica and Indica strains. To some extent, strains are now modestly resistant to most problems plaguing tropical rice (including irregular water and a variety of pests) and to bring higher yields than traditional Indica varieties. Disease-resistant grains have been particularly favored in research because of the planting expense and relative ineffectiveness of pesticides in the tropical environment. This trend will probably continue.

There may be some threat of genetic vulnerability with rice, as with wheat, as a great number of indigenous varieties are replaced by a relatively small number of hybrids. Also, some pests have thrived in the HYVs' fertilizer-enriched environment, although the newer varieties have some resistance to this. "Other things being equal," concluded the National Academy of Sciences in their 1972 Report, "the danger of serious crop losses from the attacks of main diseases and insects is greater today than in the past. However, the improved cultural practices have reduced the vulnerability of the crop to organisms . . . that are associated with nutritional or physiological disorders."[83]

Minimal Tillage

Minimal tillage is an agricultural technique particularly suited to areas that experience erosion problems. Yields are not necessarily increased over conventional ploughing, but production tends to be cheaper because fewer tools and labor are required. Water is conserved, and there is less concern about erosion. Whether it is well suited for tropical agriculture is open to question. It is not unlike slash and burn cultivation in the sense that the latter often does not deep plough but leaves roots and sound ground cover in the planting area.

Minimal tillage has been very successful in Japanese rice production, but it has not spread rapidly to tropical Asia. One reason is that it is labor saving, both in field preparation and subsequent weed control. Consequently, areas of abundant or surplus labor have less incentive for adopting it. It may be capital saving in aggregate, since the increased use of herbicides is substituted for ploughing equipment (including draft animals). The weed control aspect appears critical. Ploughing and cultivation are important as weed control in both dry farming and paddy production. When minimal tillage is practical, there seems no escape from herbicide use if output per acre is to be maintained.[84]

Set against the obstacles to adoption in tropic agriculture are the advantages of reduced erosion, better water retention, some reduction in tools needed, and a shortened cultivation time. The environmental tradeoff then seems to be a reduction of erosion at the expense of increased herbicide use. Herbicides are generally not water soluble, and would remain in the soil or be transported by water runoff.[85] As observed elsewhere, there is uncertainty about potential damages.[86] In any event, herbicides are not the persistent pesticides of the DDT class. Also, minimal tillage should reduce water runoff from agricultural land, and this would limit the transport of the herbicides themselves, as well as the transport of insecticides and fertilizers.

In the United States minimal tillage has grown quite rapidly, with minimal tilled acreage expanding from 3.8 million acres in 1963 to 32.6 million acres in 1974. According to another classification, it was estimated that by 1974, 6.3% of total acreage in the United States, or 48.5 million acres, was either zero tilled or minimum tilled.[87]

The USDA makes an interesting comment on both the potential for erosion reduction and the difference between government and farmers' motivations in encouraging minimal tillage. It is fortunate that the social objective of soil conservation is supported by the farmers' financial incentive of reducing labor and equipment costs.

Available estimates and data suggest occurrence of a potential decrease in the national soil erosion problem with continued reduction in tillage. More soil erosion reduction could be accomplished through change in tillage systems during the next 30 years than has been accomplished in about 40 years . . . the principal reason for farmer adoption of soil-conserving tillage systems will be prospects for financial gains or legal restraints on land uses or production practices, not a farmer desire for conservation, per se. However, prospects for conservation has been a principal motivation underlying research, development and education that has laid the foundation for the projected reductions in tillage.[88]

To accomplish this, the United States farmer must use significantly larger quantities of herbicides and insecticides to combat weed and insect pests normally controlled by tilling. To produce the projected gains in minimum tillage by the year 2000, an additional 2 pounds per acre (1 pound insecticide, 1 pound herbicide) would be needed. The projected total pesticide use by year 2000 of 300 million pounds would be at least 50% higher than projections based on conventional tillage. This increase would occur primarily on acreage sown to the "selected" grain crops. Grains and soybeans would account for a higher proportion of total pesticide use.

CONCLUSIONS

Before 1776, the upper reaches of the Potomac River and the valleys beyond were covered with lush wheatfields, and the call of this fertile land aided the westward migration of farmers from Pennsylvania and the already decaying tidewater regions in which tobacco yields had quickly dropped. The demand for wheat soon had adverse effects, however, because the monoculture of the grain robbed the soil of its fertility. Yields in Loudoun County and its environs began to plummet, causing another migration westward in search of virgin territory. This destruction of the soil fertility was decried by many, including Washington and Jefferson, who knew something was inherently wrong with a single crop. It was not until 1786, however, when an enterprising Loudoun resident, John Binns, began to experiment with a 3-year rotation consisting of clover fertilized with lime, which fed cattle, which in turn fertilized the soil and made it ready for another crop of wheat. This system was successful, and yields climbed steadily. The region's westward expansion was momentarily halted as farmers returned to the "rehabilitated" acreage. This situation improved so much, in fact, that until the Civil War, over one-half of the wheat produced in the United States came from the Virginia and Maryland Piedmont region.[89]

The lesson here is that environmental factors are vitally important to sustainable agriculture. Adverse conditions such as steep slopes, poor fertility, or misuse of water can only be ignored for a limited time. In the past, these environmental factors have provided the impetus for migrations and the rise and fall of civilizations. With time, however, it became apparent that the environment could be carefully managed. In regions such as Asia, where populations could not easily move into virgin, easily tillable land, it was best to learn how to produce sustained yields as well as high yields.

Much is now known about soil structures and fertility, erosion, water use, and so on. There is some awareness, not yet enough, of the fragility of food systems. There is a limit to every agricultural system beyond which production cannot go without causing environmental degradation and ultimately reduction of yields. In this sense, agriculture *is* different from industry, whose wastes cause external damages. In agriculture, environmental deterioration is mostly internal and is indexed by productivity losses.

There are elements of stability in all agricultural systems; traditional shifting cultivation with slash and burn, localized intensive irrigated grain production in semi-arid regions, intensive paddy rice cultivation, modern Iowa-style farming. Each can persist over long periods of time without unacceptable damage if precautions appropriate to the region and farming system are followed. Environmental stress appears, however, when these precautions are neglected and when short-term production is pressed too far. In developing countries, this pressure is inescapable as populations grow and food needs multiply.

The developing world faces a singular set of environmental problems different in complexity and intensity from those faced by Western agriculture. The general solution, however, is common to both—the development of an environmentally and ecologically appropriate agriculture that is capable of producing sustained high yields. We do not feel on balance that the "environment" is a necessary obstacle to agricultural modernization. On the contrary, even more critical problems would occur if the more traditional agricultural practices were left untouched, but obligated to provide ever-increasing food. One could then envision a series of increasing misfortunes as fallow times were cut, steeper slopes farmed, grazing land tilled and washed away, cover removed, and nutrients leached.

A transition must be made. The high yields and durability of intensive agriculture in some areas, especially the rice-producing areas of Southeast Asia, and some temperate climate farming give promise that this can be accomplished. However, temperate-zone farming will not be duplicated in the tropics. What we have come to know as capital intensive agriculture, or Iowa-style farming, is not the final result of high-technology agriculture. Rather, it evolved in a special matrix—temperate climate with good seasonal rainfall, economic characteristics of labor scarcity and energy abundance, and an exceptionally effective research and extension system funded in large measure by progressive government policy. It is difficult to believe that different systems cannot be developed under different constraints with different opportunities. Obviously, however, time is quickly running out.

To be successful, change must take into account the physical, demographic, social, and economic characteristics peculiar to each region. Much work must be done to ensure that environmentally sound production techniques are also economic and financially attractive to small cultivators, for it is the small farmer who dominates in the developing world. The vast numbers of small farmers and the limited administrative capacity in most developing countries means that farming practices—soil conservation, crop selection, and caution in the use of pesticides—cannot be compelled by ministries of agriculture and environment. Rather, the transition must be managed through incentives and self-interest. For the farmer, this means seeing the prospect of more income or lower cost. Fortunately, there is a common interest in maintaining and improving productivity.

Finally, the measures must go beyond the topics taken up in this chapter, which have concentrated on grain production. The environmental consequences of animal husbandry and the production of agricultural raw materials are at issue. Food production is also tied to integrated river basin developments, rural public health programs, and large-scale land development projects. The environmental aspects of these projects as they affect agricultural productivity should be considered. One important issue is forest use policies—commercial wood products and the use of firewood and charcoal. Agricultural systems are interrelated, and nonfood production activities are a major factor in determining whether food output can keep pace with population and food needs over the rest of the century and beyond.

NOTES

1. "Destructive soil practice" is an ambiguous term. In the developed countries declines in natural soil fertility are often offset by the additions of fertilizers. Arthur Bunce, *The Economics of Soil Conservation* (Ames, Iowa: Iowa State Colleges Press, 1942). Bunce makes an economic distinction between the loss of fertility and the loss of top soil, with the latter representing an irreparable loss of rent.
2. See Table 2.12 in Chapter 2.
3. See Table 2.13. The range between United Nations projections can be substantial. By 2000, the world population under the "median" variant would number around 6.25 billion. The "high" variant gives 384 million more and the "low" variant 415 million less. See "World Population Prospects—1970 to 2000, as Assessed in 1973," Population Division, Department of Economic and Social Affairs, United Nations Secretariat ESA/P/W, 3/10/1975, p. 53.
4. Demand and hence food deficits are estimated on the basis of population growth and income growth. They are not, therefore, determined exclusively on the basis of nutritional needs.
5. United States Department of Agriculture, *World Food Situation and Prospects to 1985*, Economic Research Service, Paper No. 98, October 1974.
6. International Food Production Research Institute, *Meeting Food Needs in the Developing World*, Research Report No. 1, February 1976.
7. Kenneth B. Porter, "The Future of Irrigated Wheat in the United States," in *Proceedings of the 9th National Conference on Wheat Utilization Research*, United States Department of Agriculture, ARS-NG-40, February 1976.
8. United States Department of Agriculture, *Foreign Agriculture*, April 19, 1976.
9. See A. S. Whitney, "Nitrogen Fixation by Tropical Agricultural Legumes," 1975 and R. W. Hardy, Ed., *Dinitrogen Fixation* (New York: Wiley, 1976).
10. Lester Brown and Erik Eckholm, *By Bread Alone* (New York: Praeger, 1974) p. 118.
11. United States Department of Agriculture, *Crop Responses to Fertilizer in the United States* (Washington: GPO, 1968) p. 5. This is not to say that increases in yield are still easy to achieve. See the National Academy of Sciences report, *Agricultural Production Efficiency* (Washington: GPO, 1975).
12. See Chapter 2, Tables 2.23 and A2.8 for fertilizer consumption data in developing countries.
13. In the United States some municipal water supplies have been contaminated by phosphate, and the major source is said to have been detergents. See J. Verduin, "Significance of Phosphorous in Water Supplies," and C. A. Black, "Behavior of Soil and Fertilizer Phosphorous in Relation to Water Pollution," in G. Smith and T. L. Willrich, Eds., *Agricultural Practices and Water Quality* (Ames, Iowa: University of Iowa Press, 1971). See also Marvin C.

Goldberg, "Sources of Nitrogen in Water Supplies," in *Role of Agriculture in Clean Water* (Ames, Iowa: Iowa State University, 1971); George E. Smith, "Pollution—How Much of a Problem Comes from Fertilizers," Thirty-Third Annual Forum, National Farm Institute, Des Moines, Iowa, February 1971; E. Smith, "Contribution of Fertilizers to Water Pollution," Second Compendium of Animal Waste Management, Paper No. 7, (Columbia, Missouri: University of Missouri Water Resources Research Center, June 1969); M. Owens, "Nutrient Balances in Rivers," *Journal of the Society for Water Treatment and Examination*, vol. 19, Part I (1970), pp. 239–252. On all issues of agricultural runoff, see U. S. Department of Agriculture, *Agricultural Runoff: A Bibliography*, NTIS No. PB-207-514, January 1972.

One study by Hotes placed the contribution of agricultural land to total nitrogen wastes entering United States water bodies at between 29 and 67%. See Frederick Hotes and Erman Pearson, "Effects of Irrigation on Water Quality," given at the conference on "Arid Land in Developing Countries: Environmental Problems and Effects," Academy of Scientific Research and Technology, Cairo, Egypt, 1975. There is also a theory, with some supportive evidence, that the conversion of nitrogen from fertilizer to N_2O could affect the ozone layer. On this point, see the various papers given during the American Geophysical Union's Symposium on "The Terrestrial Nitrogen Cycle and Possible Environmental Effects," 1976 Annual Meeting, Washington, D. C., April 1976.

14. See Organization for Economic and Cultural Development, *Scientific Fundamentals of the Eutrophication of Lakes and Flowing Waters, with Particular Reference to Nitrogen and Phosphorus as Factors in Eutrophication* (Paris, 1971); D. E. Armstrong, "Effects of Agricultural Pollution on Eutrophication," in *Agricultural Practices and Water Quality* (Ames, Iowa: Iowa State University, 1970); J. Verduin, "Eutrophication and Agriculture in the U. S.," in *Agriculture and the Quality of Our Environment*, (Washington: American Association for the Advancement of Science, 1967); R. Fish, "The Value of Recent Research to Measure Eutrophication and to Indicate Possible Causes," *Journal of Hydrology* (New Zealand), **8**, No. 2 (1969) pp. 77–85.

15. See S. P. Dhua, "Need for Organo-Mineral Fertilizer in Tropical Agriculture," *The Ecologist*, June 1975, and M. S. Swaminathan, "Organic Manures and Integrated Approaches to Plant Nutrition," paper given to Technical Advisory Committee, Consultative Group on International Agricultural Research, 8th Meeting, July 1974.

16. See Hardy, *Dinitrogen Fixation*. There is recent evidence that not only algae in rice paddies fix nitrogen, but also that it is becoming possible to inoculate some grasses, such as millet, with nitrogen-fixing bacteria, possibly leading the way to bacteria inoculation of other cereal grasses. See R. W. F. Hardy and V. D. Havelka, "Nitrogen Fixation Research: A Key to World Food?" *Science*, **188**, May 9, 1975; R. L. Smith et al., "Nitrogen Fixation in Grasses Inoculated with Spirillum lipoferum," *Science*, **193**, No. 4257 (September 1976); and J. J. Child, "New Developments in Nitrogen Fixation Research," *BioScience*, **26**, No. 10 (October 1976) pp. 614–615.

17. United States Department of Agriculture, Agricultural Research Service, *Agricultural Research*, October 1975.

18. Discussion such as found in Brown and Eckholm, *By Bread Alone*, tend to confuse legitimate reports concerning severe ecological problems related to pesticides use on cotton, with use of pesticides on grain crops, the main source of food in the developing world. Some high-yield grains have encountered serious disease and pest problems, but often these have been caused by the shrinkage of the crop's genetic pool as well as the development of pesticide-resistant insects and diseases. Although these insect and disease outbreaks have often been serious, such as in the Philippines with the rice-eating brown leaf hopper, the problems have had more to do with the type of seed than with the consequences of pesticide use. See p. 333 of this chapter.

19. United Nations Food and Agriculture Organization, "Weed Control Problems Causing Major Reductions in World Food Supplies," AGP:PEST/PH/75, B33, April 1975.

20. Raymond Dasman, John Milton, and Peter S. Freeman, *Ecological Principles for Economic Development* (New York: Wiley, 1972).

21. Dasman et al., *Ecological Principles*, p. 151.

22. As mentioned elsewhere in Chapter 2, herbicides pose fewer direct environmental problems than other pesticides, although there have been some disturbing reports connecting the

interaction of certain herbicides and insecticides with the production of dioxin (see Dasman, p. 164) and various nitrosomines, reputed to be carcinogenic (see report to American Chemical Society 1976 Annual Meeting, mentioned in the *Washington Post,* September 3, 1976).

23. See Dasman et al., pp. 164–165.
24. See L. Tikok, "Toxicity of Insecticides Used for Asiatic Rice Control to Tropical Fish in Rice Paddies," in M. Taghi Farvar and John P. Milton, Eds., *Careless Technology* (Garden City, New York: Natural History Press, 1972); references cited in Guan-Seon Lim, "Integrated Pest Control in the Developing Countries of Asia," in *Environment and Development,* collected papers of SCOPE/UNEP Symposium (Indianapolis, Indiana: SCOPE, 1974); Dasman et al., p. 195; and P. A. Frank, R. L. Timmons, and R. J. Demint, "Herbicide Residues in Agricultural Water from Control of Aquatic and Bank Weeds," in *Agricultural Practices and Water Quality.*
25. National Academy of Sciences, *Contemporary Pest Control Practices and Prospects,* vol. I, (Washington: GPO, 1975).
26. National Research Council, National Academy of Sciences, *Productive Agriculture and a Quality Environment* (Washington: GPO, August 1974) p. 51.
27. "Analysis of Pesticide Use in Pakistan, A Multidisciplinary Study Team Report," University of California at Berkeley for USAID, 1974.
28. Guan-Seon Lim, "Integrated Pest Control in Asia," p. 53.
29. See Lim, "Integrated Pest Control in Asia," for a clear concise discussion of integrated pest control. Also, see US Council on Environmental Quality, *Integrated Pest Control* (Washington: GPO, 1972).
30 A. W. A. Brown cited in Murray Bookchin, *Our Synthetic Environment,* revised ed. (New York: Harper & Row, 1974) p. 97.
31. See R. C. Reeve and M. Fineman, "Salt Problems in Relation to Irrigation" and W. H. Durun, L. V. Wilcox, "Quality of Irrigation Water," p. 109, in R. M. Hagen et al., Eds., *Irrigation of Agricultural Lands* (New York: American Society of Agronomy, 1967).
32. Hotes and Pearson, "Effects of Irrigation on Water Quality."
33. UNESCO, *Nature and Resources,* July 1975. For more on erosion and agriculture, see Chapter 2, pp. 72–76, as well as M. Amemiya, "Land and Water Management for Minimizing Sediment," in *Agricultural Practices and Water Quality;* L. M. Glymph and H. C. Storey, "Sediment—Its Consequences and Control," in *Agriculture and the Quality of the Environment;* and S. J. Mech and D. P. Smith, "Water Erosion Under Irrigation" and Mech and Woodruff, "Wind Erosion on Irrigated Lands," in *Irrigation of Agricultural Lands.*
34. Cecil Wadliegh, *Wastes in Relation to Agriculture and Forestry,* USDA miscellaneous publication No. 1065, 1968.
35. National Academy of Sciences, *Productive Agriculture and a Quality Environment,* 1975, p. 249. Although it is possible to estimate the amount of soil removed from one place, it is more difficult to discover the origin of any given amount of sediment. One can estimate soil removal per acre for certain kinds of soils with certain slopes, but it becomes almost impossible to estimate regional rates. Text information came from many sources, including R. Dideriksen of the United States Soil Conservation Service. See the USDA publication, "Predicting Rainfall-Erosion Losses from Cropland East of the Rocky Mountains," USDA-ARS publication No. 282 (Washington: GPO, 1965) for an introduction to the methods for estimating specific rates of soil movements. See also "Estimation of Soil Loss," in Indian Council of Agricultural Research, *Soil and Water Conservation Research—1956–1971* (New Delhi, 1975) pp. 311–334.
36. David Pimentel et al., "Land Degradation: Effects on Food and Energy Resources," *Science,* **194,** No. 4261 (October 8, 1976) pp. 149–155.
37. See R. D. Barre, "Effect of Erosion on Crop Yields," 1949, citation number 68 of Pimentel, "Land Degradation: Effects on Food and Energy Resources." On the removal of nutrients caused by erosion, see P. N. Bhatt et al., "Influence of Cropping Pattern and Land Use on Plant Nutrient Losses in Doon Valley," proceedings of the *International Symposium on Soil Fertility Evaluation,* vol. 1 (New Delhi, 1971) pp. 541–547.
38. See for example NAS, "Productive Agriculture and a Quality Environment," pp. 250–252 and L. M. Glymph and H. C. Storey, "Sediment—Its Consequences and Control," p. 205.

39. M. El Gabaly, "The Problems and Effects of Irrigation in the Near East Region," given at the Arid Lands Irrigation in Developing Countries, Environmental Problems and Effects Conference, Academy of Scientific Research and Technology, Cairo, Egypt, 1975, pp. 239–240.
40. *Ibid.*, p. 239.
41. The efficiency of irrigation in the Near East is also affected by calcareous or sandy soil. See El Gabaly, "The Problems and Effects of Irrigation," pp. 240–243.
42. FAO, *Indicative World Food Plan,* vol. II, 1975, as well as Eckholm, *Losing Ground,* pp. 119–123. See also A. A. Michel, "Impacts of Modern Irrigation Technology in the Indus and Helmond Basins in S. W. Asia," in *The Careless Technology.*
43. El Gabaly, "The Problems and Effects of Irrigation."
44. United Nations Food and Agriculture Organization, *Drainage of Saline Soils* (Rome: FAO, 1973).
45. David Grigg, *Agricultural Systems of the World: An Evolutionary Approach* (Cambridge: Cambridge University Press, 1974).
46. See p. 343 for more on fallow, as well as D. J. Greeland, "Shifting Cultivation vs. Systems for Continuous Production in Arable Lands in the Tropics," Nigeria, International Institute of Tropical Agriculture, 1974.
47. See NAS, Productive *Agriculture and a Quality Environment,* pp. 249–251, for comparative data on cropping systems and their effect on erosion rates.
48. This region, perhaps the most lush and mysterious of all the tropics, also possesses tremendous potential: year-round rain allowing for continuous cropping. Unfortunately, this promise of unrealized bounty on one hand, with prophesies of severe ecological stress on the other, have exposed the humid tropics to far more than their share of interest on the part of developed country environmentalists. See Eckholm, *Losing Ground,* pp. 136–152.
49. Dasman et al., *Ecological Principles for Economic Development.*
50. Paul W. Richards, "The Tropical Rain Forest," in *The Scientific American,* December 1973.
51. Grigg, *The Harsh Lands: A Study in Agricultural Development,* Focal Problems in Geography Series (London: St. Martins, 1970).
52. A. Kamarck, *Climate and Development* (Washington: International Bank for Reconstruction and Development, 1973) p. 21.
53. See H. M. Southworth and B. F. Johnston, *Agricultural Development and Economic Growth* (Cornell: Cornell University Press, 1967) p. 211. This is in part because of the continued misunderstanding and lack of information on the essential forces of erosion in the humid tropics. See M. F. Thomas, *Tropical Geomorphology: A Study of Weathering and Land Form Development in Warm Climates* (New York: Wiley, 1974) for a more detailed and somewhat complex discussion, as well as Sanchez and Buol, "Soils of the Tropics and the World Food Crisis," *Science,* **188,** No. 4188 (May 9, 1975).
54. Dasman et al., *Ecological Principles for Economic Development,* p. 62.
55. The tropical humid region (see Map 2.2) by definition has only 0–2.5 dry months per year. Not all tropical humid regions have "monsoons," however. Monsoons are a meteorological phenomena found in many parts of the world, but they are most important to South and Southeast Asia. The word monsoon commonly refers to wind systems of a continental scale that seasonally reverse themselves, bringing abrupt changes of rainfall.
56. Grigg, *Agricultural Systems of the World: An Evolutionary Approach* (Cambridge: Cambridge University Press, 1975) p. 63.
57. See for example *The Careless Technology,* pp. 373–489.
58. Grigg, *The Harsh Lands,* p. 278. India's drier western regions probably suffer more erosional stress than the eastern tropical humid regions, particularly with continued deforestation. This, coupled with erosion in the Himalayan foothills, probably will increase the sediment load of many of the Indian rivers and, it is claimed, has already led to more frequent and severe flooding. Both factors affect the environmental conditions of humid tropic, monsoon India, regardless of its intrinsic stability. See Eckholm's interesting discussion of the importance of the relatively minor mountain regions of Asia in *Losing Ground,* pp. 74–100.
59. David Greenland, "Shifting Cultivation vs. Systems for Continuous Production in Arable Lands in the Tropics" (Nigeria: International Institute for Tropical Agriculture, 1974) p. 1.

60. Florencio Tamesis, "Problems of Shifting Agriculture in Asian Area," 5th World Forestry Conference Proceedings, 1965. See also Grigg, *Agricultural Systems of the World* pp. 59–74.

61. R. F. Watters, *Shifting Cultivation in Latin America*, FAO (Rome: United Nations Food and Agriculture Organization, 1971) p. 37.

62. J. Kampan, "Water Conservation Practices and Their Potential for Stabilizing Crop Production in the Semi-Arid Tropics," paper by the Institute for Crop Research in the Semi-Arid Tropics (ICRISAT) for FAO, December 1974.

    Kampan suggests two reasons for fallowing in the tropics. In the dryer regions, it is used as a risk evasion measure, since the monsoon rains are too unpredictable to be reliable. In the wetter tropics, fallowing is used mainly because of the lack of an alternative technology. "Poor drainage difficulties in cultivation and weed control as well as inadequate crop technology result in a choice for the post-monsoon season as the main crop season. The land is repeatedly ploughed to eliminate weeds and to enhance infiltration. The result of this system is relative stability at a low general level of production. In both systems a substantial part of the mean rainfall is lost due to the increased runoff and evaporation losses under fallow conditions."

63. For the range of cereals, see Janick et al., *Plant Science* (New York: H. Freeman, 1974) and J. R. Harlow "The Plants and Animals that Nourish Man," and R. S. Loomis, "Agricultural Systems," *Scientific American*, September 1974, and Grigg, *Agricultural Systems of the World*, 1974.

64. Greenland, "Shifting Cultivation," p. 7. See also G. Wrigley, *Tropical Agricultural* (New York: Praeger, 1969) and C. C. Webster and P. N. Wilson, *Agriculture in the Tropics* (New York: Humanities Press, 1966).

65. United States Government, *The World Food Problem*, vol. II (Washington: GPO, 1967).

66. Watters, *Shifting Cultivation in Latin America* and Eckholm, *Losing Ground*.

67. Ives, referred to in Watters, *Shifting Cultivation in Latin America*, p. 35.

68. Watters, pp. 207–239.

69. Greenland, IITA, "Shifting Cultivation vs. Systems for Continuous Cultivation," 1974.

70. IITA, Idaban, Nigeria.

71. F. E. McJunkin, *Water, Engineers, Development, and Disease in the Tropics*, U.S. AID, July 1975, pp. 82–84.

72. D. H. Grist, "Rice," *World Crops* (1969) p. 17. For an excellent analysis of the evolution of paddy rice cultivation in Asia, see Grigg, *Agricultural Systems of the World*, 1974, pp. 75–111, in particular pp. 109–111. He concludes that much of the variation in yield can be attributed to farming practices, which in turn are often related to the rate and direction of population growth.

73. International Rice Research Institute (IRRI), *Major Research in Upland Rice* (Los Baños, Philippines: IRR, 1975) pp. 46–71.

74. IRRI *Reporter*, May 1975. See also IRRI, *Research Highlights for 1975*.

75. United Nations Food and Agriculture Organization, *Indicative World Food Plan*, vol. I (Rome, 1971) p. 132.

76. *Ibid.*, pp. 132–133.

77. NAS, *Vulnerability of Major Crops*, p. 187.

78. See Dana Dalrymple, *Multiplecropping, Survey of Multiple Cropping in the Developing Countries*, USDA/AID, FAER 91 (Washington: GPO, 1971) pp. 103–104. Dalrymple felt that ecological factors would limit the growth of multiple cropping as predicted by the FAO's Indicative Plan and the US World Food Problem report of 1967.

79. Dana Dalrymple, *Development and Spread of High Yield Varieties*, USDA 5th ed. (Washington: GPO, 1976). See the Indian Government's 5th Five-Year Plan for an interesting discussion of this. Not all the new varieties, particularly rices, outperform their native relatives, but in general some yield increases occur.

80. See National Academy of Sciences National Research Council, *Genetic Vulnerability of Major Crops* (Washington: NAS, 1972). There have been numerous articles pinpointing the elimination of variation as one of the Green Revolution's key flaws. Particularly for wheat, the problem has been more serious in the wheat-growing temperate regions because of the extent

of production by the 1970s and the almost universal use of hybridized sced (although not always the short-stalked hybrids of Mexico). Grigg, in an excellent section on extensive wheat production in North America, discusses the inadequacy of the term "monoculture," in *The Agricultural Systems of the World,* p. 258. See Dalrymple, *Development and Spread of High-Yield Varieties* for an interesting discussion of the spread of these new varieties.

81. NAS, *Genetic Vulnerability of Major Crops,* 1972. See also, *CIMMYT Review 1976,* pp. 47–48, as well as "Multilines: Safety in Numbers," *CIMMYT Today,* No. 4 (1976) for discussions of genetic variation of tropical wheat.
82. See Dalrymple, *Development and Spread of High-Yield Varieties,* 1974, pp. 8, 15–19.
83. National Academy of Sciences, *Genetic Vulnerability of Major Crops,* p. 187.
84. US Department of Agriculture, *Minimum Tillage: Preliminary Technology Assessment* (Washington: GPO, 1975). See also L. E. Gard, "No-Till Crop Production Proving a Most Promising Conservation Measure," *Outlook on Agriculture,* U. K., **7** (1973); J. A. Brown and R. A. Quentrill, "Role of Minimum Tillage in Rice in Asia with Particular Reference to Japan," *Outlook on Agriculture,* (1973); D. Gibbon, J. Harvey, and K. Hubbard, "A Minimum Tillage System for Botswana," *World Crops* (September/October, 1974) pp. 229–234; and S. P. Mittall et al., "Minimum tillage studies under rainfed conditions," 1974 *Annual Report,* Central Soil and Water Conservation Research and Training Institute, Dehra Dun, India, pp. 104–105.
85. USDA, *Minimum Tillage: Preliminary Technology Assessment,* 1974, p. 85.
86. See Chapter 6, pp. 310.
87. USDA, *Minimum Tillage: Preliminary Technology Assessment.*
88. *Ibid.,* p. 83.
89. Frederick Gutheim, *The Potomac,* Rivers of America Series, 2nd ed. (New York: Holt, Rinehart and Winston, 1974) pp. 167–194.
90. Grigg notes that, although agricultural development both fueled and was fueled by industrial development in the developed West during the nineteenth Century, since 1920 no similar movement has occurred in the developing countries; thus developing countries increased production "by the wider adaption of farming practices; but there was no fundamental break with the past." *Agricultural Systems of the World,* p. 56. The Green Revolution notwithstanding, this still is true for most of the developing world today.

Chapter 7

OBSERVATIONS AND CONCLUSIONS

The two central themes of this study are the links between environmental quality and economic development and the environmental relations between the developed and developing countries. The first theme considers environmental deterioration as a possible consequence of and constraint on economic growth in developing countries. The second theme considers the direct environmental contact between North and South through the joint use of shared international resources and the indirect contact through international trade, investment, and development assistance flows.

To accomplish the purposes of the study, it was necessary to construct an analytical framework for identifying and grouping issues, to advance the relevant theory, and to survey, compile, and interpret a large amount of empirical material. More specifically, Chapter 2 presents a global descriptive environmental geography that is fully original with regard to both the compilation of environmental data and the manner in which it is presented and interpreted. Chapter 3 pursues the question of whether environmental assimilative capacity is a useful extension of the international trade theory of comparative advantage. The chapter also contains a comprehensive empirical evaluation of the trade and investment dimension of North–South environmental relations. Chapter 4 provides a synthesis between the literature on environmental resource management and project evaluation methodology. Chapter 5 develops the theory of transfrontier pollution and supplements the theory by examining the relative contributions of North and South to global pollution threats and by analyzing environment within the Law of the Sea negotiations. Finally, in Chapter 6 we return to the interrelationship between environment and economic development in a case study of agriculture, especially cereal grain production.

What observations and conclusions emerge? One conclusion that stands out is that the traditional tools of economic analysis, suitably used, are of great help in understanding the issues and suggesting appropriate policies. The body of theory concerned with externalities has been profitably employed throughout the study, from evaluating border adjustments to offset international differences in abatement costs, to explaining current failures to control transnational pollution, and from analyzing the downstream effects of deforestation to speculating on the trade effects of increased resource recovery. In similar fashion, the great principle of cost–benefit analysis, that an activity should be undertaken up to the point at which the marginal benefits are equal to the marginal costs, is fundamental to the establishment of rational environmental policy. As described in Chapter 4, there is much work to be done in valuing environmental damages (abatement benefits), especially those that are indirect, subtle, and cumulative, but the marginal principle provides a benchmark for policy evaluation.

We have shown that in many respects the nature of environmental problems *does* differ between poor and rich countries. Although the indices of the physical environment developed in Chapter 2 were inadequate for an empirical extension of comparative advantage theory to include assimilative capacity, they indicate major differences among countries and regions with regard to the level and variability of rainfall, riverflow per unit land surface, river flow variability, population density per unit land surface, and other measures. All these differences do not, however, correspond to a North–South division. Interestingly, there is no evidence that developing countries as a group have a relatively large endowment of assimilative capacity. Indeed, the evidence points the other way. Furthermore, there are obviously major differences between the North and the South with respect to the level and structure of economic activity and therefore major differences in pollution loads and waste compositions. This is most obvious with regard to per capita or per unit land surface energy use, but it is also present for other waste-generating activities. We do not wish to overemphasize this difference, because industrial production and consumption are apt to be highly concentrated within developing countries, and they will increasingly confront pollution problems typical of industrial countries.

There are other differences. For instance, poverty and headlong urbanization give a special urgency to the problems of sanitary water supplies and sewage disposal systems in developing countries, whereas the basic infrastructure for water and sewers is in place in the industrial countries. With regard to agriculture, we argue that an attempt to expand yields to meet multiplying food needs cannot be accomplished without a change in certain traditional production techniques. In the developing world there is a real threat that efforts to meet increasing food needs will lead to great environmental damage—excessive shortening of fallow period, nutrient exhaustion, cultivation of fragile soils, and erosion—and that the long-term productivity of soils will be undermined. Extreme poverty can easily lead to long-term disruptive practices. Agriculture in developed countries is not immune to environmental damages, but the nature of the problem shifts. Acute poverty of the farmer is not a basic cause for destructive practices.

Also, major differences in income levels between the North and South mean that different types of environmental damages will have different weights in the two regions. Specifically, the higher incomes in the North imply that amenity damages are given relatively greater weight, whereas conservation of the productivity of resources provides the main justification for environmental protection measures in developing countries. Two conclusions follow: First, environmental concerns are not merely in the domain of the rich, but are essential for sustained economic development in poor countries. Second, environmental standards should conform to a local calculus of costs and benefits, not to a single uniform global calculus.

There are, then, major differences, but we do not believe that a simple expansion of the definitional scope of environmental problems to embrace all the attributes of poverty is useful. That is, the assertion that there are two types of environmental problems—the "effluents of affluence" and the "pollution of poverty"—is misleading. The characteristics of poverty are not environmental problems as such; they are simply the characteristics of poverty and can only be overcome by economic growth. To lump environmental concerns in developing countries under the umbrella term of poverty or to define all aspects of poverty as environmental diverts attention from the real and pressing issues of preserving the productivity of environmental resources and minimizing the adverse environmental consequences of growth.

Is there a fundamental harmony between sound economic development policy and sound environmental policy? At the most general level the answer must be yes. Development policy that recognizes and accounts for the productive contributions of environmental resources and environmental policy that seeks to maximize the direct and indirect welfare contributions of environmental services is consistent and mutually supportive. Conversely, the lack of economic development undermines a willingness and ability to undertake environmental preservation, and in some cases makes environmental problems more acute. Also, the lack of an environment policy can frustrate economic development potential. But this conclusion lies in a rarified level of generality. Developing countries are confronted daily with specific development/environment choices for which there are no easy answers. What are the appropriate workplace standards when controls are expensive and labor is cheap? Should natural stands of timber be exploited now with later reliance on plantation forests? Are wildlife parks affordable when arable land is scarce and densely populated? If DDT is cheap and reliable and biological pest controls expensive or untried, what should be the pesticide policy? How clean is clean enough for industrial waste discharges in societies in which sewers are simply open gutters? Bland assurances that sound environment policy is sound development policy conceal much more than they reveal.

There must be a synthesis between environmental policy and development policy within developing countries. At the most basic level, environmental considerations should enter into project analysis, and special attention should be given to the difficulties of enforcement. Environmental concerns must also enter at all levels of the planning process, especially when strategic development decisions are taken concerning transportation systems, regional development, agriculture and forestry, and patterns of industrialization. Development assistance agencies can make a variety of contributions. They can fund environmental-type projects. They can insist that projects they fund meet appropriate environmental standards. They can provide considerable technical expertise in areas such as damage valuation, pollution abatement techniques, and waste flow modeling. Perhaps most important, they can support the establishment of effective environmental protection agencies within developing countries.

What about environmental relations between the North and the South? Is there indeed a harmony of interests based on a global ecological unity? We believe that to assert a harmony based on a global ecological unity is a little pious and a little naive. Except for a few (serious) global pollution threats, most environmental damages appear to be local or regional. For the global threats, the evidence in Chapter 5 indicates that industrial countries are the major contributors. It would be disingenuous to suggest that rich and poor share equally the task of clean-up. For the more mundane types of local pollution, control policies should reflect local needs. All countries do not and should not share equally the desire for environmental purity.

At the same time, the study does not provide evidence that environmental concerns should be a cause of fundamental and pervasive conflict between rich and poor countries. It cannot be shown that the environmental behavior and policies of industrial countries are a principal cause of poverty in the South or that the economic growth prospects of poor countries are being eroded by the environmental policies of the rich. Nor can it be shown that accelerated development of the South would pose intolerable burdens on the global environment. Developing countries were correct in reacting with caution to the enthusiasm of Stockholm, but a detailed look at the issues provides no grounds for the extreme distrust that was present earlier.

Especially in the trade policy area, the actions of the industrial countries—adoption of the polluter-pays principle, renouncing border adjustments, and minimizing the use of environmental product standards as trade barriers—serve the interests of the developing countries. It is true that the incorporation of environmental controls in product cost will alter the patterns of international trade, and developing countries will feel other trade effects, some positive and some negative, but the evidence developed in Chapter 3 suggests that the effects will generally be quite small.

Even though the environment need not be the source of deep and abiding conflict between developed and developing countries, there are contentious issues and issues requiring cooperative solutions. The contentious issues include the environmental practices of multinational firms, especially hazardous industries and firms engaged in extractive activities, and the use by industrial countries of shared resources, regional and global, for waste disposal. We do not believe this last issue is primarily a North–South conflict, although disproportionate use was shown in Chapter 5. Rather, transnational pollution results from inadvertent actions and a general failure among nations to negotiate effective controls.

Finally, the areas that require cooperative solutions include the preservation of wildlife and wilderness areas, some transnational pollution threats including persistent pesticide and oil tanker pollution, and improvement in the environmental effectiveness of development assistance agencies. Most important, sustaining, transforming, and improving the productivity of agriculture is environmentally critical and requires the joint efforts of developed and developing countries.

SELECTED READINGS

Brown, Lester and Erik Eckholm, *By Bread Alone* (New York: Praeger, 1974).

Castro, Jauo Augusto de Araujo, "Environment and Development: The Case of the Less Developed Countries," *International Organization*, **26**, No. 2 (Spring 1972).

Council on Environmental Quality, *Environmental Quality*, Annual Reports.

Cummings, Ralph, Jr., "Food Crops in the Low Income Countries: The State of Present and Expected Agricultural Research and Technology," Rockefeller Foundation Working Paper, May 1976.

Dasman, Raymond, John Milton, and Peter Freeman, *Ecological Principles for Economic Development* (London: Wiley, 1973).

Dorfman, Robert and Nancy Dorfman, Eds., *Economics of the Environment* (London: Wiley, 1973).

Eckholm, Erik, *Losing Ground: Environmental Stress and World Food Prospects* (New York: Norton, 1976).

Freeman, Peter, Ed., *The Environmental Impact of a Large Tropical Reservoir* (Washington, D.C.: Smithsonian Institution, 1974).

———*The Environmental Impact of Rapid Urbanization* (Washington, D.C.: The Smithsonian Institution, 1974).

———*Coastal Zone Pollution by Oil and Other Contaminants* (Washington, D.C.: The Smithsonian Institution, 1974).

Grigg, David, *The Harsh Lands: A Study of Agricultural Development* (London: St. Martins Press, 1970).

———*Agricultural Systems of the World: An Evolutionary Approach* (Cambridge: Cambridge University Press, 1975).

International Bank for Reconstruction and Development, *Environmental Health and Human Ecologic Considerations in Economic Development Projects* (Washington, D.C.: IBRD, 1974).

———*Environment and Development* (Washington, D.C.: IBRD, 1975).

Matthews, William, Frederick Smith, and Edward Goldberg, Eds., *Man's Impact on Terrestrial and Oceanic Ecosystems* (Cambridge: MIT Press, 1971).

Organization for Economic Cooperation and Development, *Economics of Transfrontier Pollution* (Paris: OECD, 1976).

———*Problems in Transfrontier Pollution* (Paris: OECD, 1974).

———*Problems of Environmental Economics* (Paris: OECD, 1972).

———*Environmental Damage Costs* (Paris: OECD, 1975).

Pereira, H. C., *Land Use and Water Resources in Temperate and Tropical Climates* (Cambridge: Cambridge University Press, 1973).

Pearson, Charles, "Implications for the Trade and Investment of Developing Countries of United States Environmental Controls," UNCTAD (New York: United Nations, 1976).

SCOPE, *Environment and Development* (Indianapolis, Indiana: SCOPE/UNEP, 1974).

Study of Critical Environmental Problems (SCEP), *Man's Impact on the Global Environment* (Cambridge, Mass.: MIT Press, 1976).

Taghfarvar, M. and John Milton, Eds., *The Careless Technology* (Garden City, New York: Natural History Press, 1972).

The Cocoyoc Declaration, adopted by participants in the UNEP/UNCTAD Symposium, Cocoyoc, Mexico, 1974.

United Nations World Food Conference, *The World Food Problem*, Item 9 of Provisional Agenda, E/CONF 65/4, August 1974.

United Nations Conference on the Human Environment, *Declaration and Action Plan*, Stockholm, 1972.

United States Government, Department of the Interior, *Agricultural Runoff: A Bibliography*, NTIS (Washington, D.C.: GPO, 1972).

United States Government, Agency for International Development, *Environmental Assessment Guidelines Manual* (Washington, D.C.: AID, 1974).

Walter, Ingo, *International Economics of Pollution* (London: Macmillan, 1975).

———Ed., *Studies in International Environmental Economics* (New York: Wiley-Interscience, 1976).

INDEX